Samuel A Hoke

Introduction to Computer Data Processing

at N D computer

Nelson Smith

283-2811

June 25, 1978.

6:15 at N D.

a location
starts soccer.
alternate weeks

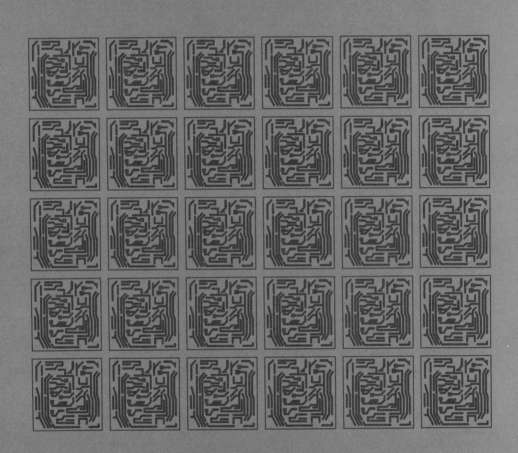

Introduction to Computer Data Processing Second Edition

Wilson T. Price

Merritt College
Oakland, California

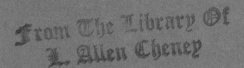 The Dryden Press   Hinsdale, Illinois

Library of Congress Catalog Card Number: 77-187112

ISBN: 0-03-089844-7

PRINTED IN THE UNITED STATES OF AMERICA

7 8 9 0 1   032   9 8 7 6 5 4 3 2 1

To my daughter Diana

Preface

To say that the computer has had a broad and significant impact on our lives would be the understatement of the year. Indeed, high-speed computational devices have been a primary factor in rapidly changing techniques used in many areas. For instance, with the computational and information manipulation capabilities of the computer, the office clerk sees many of the office procedures significantly changed, the accountant must adjust to dramatically changing accounting techniques, the business manager must learn to use highly sophisticated market forecasting tools, the engineer must become reoriented to a whole new set of ground rules in problem solving, and most importantly, the average individual must adjust to the manner in which computers affect his or her life. As a result, it seems important that every college student gain a basic knowledge of how this powerful tool affects our lives in so many ways and of how it can be made to serve our needs best.

As a vehicle for presenting these fundamental concepts, the first edition of this book made extensive use of a hypothetical college using the case study approach. In general, the reaction of users to this approach proved very positive. Generally speaking, students relate much more easily to concepts and principles presented via example rather than in sterile, definition-type form. On the other hand, the biggest single criticism related to the extent to which the example was used. Many instructors felt that they were forced to use the grade reporting case study to a greater extent than they desired, since it was used as a unifying theme throughout the book.

Needless to say, every effort has been made in this second edition to include and expand upon the strong points of the first edition and to eliminate or replace those portions which were weak or have become outdated. In this vein, the technique of presenting concepts via example applications, as well as the case study approach, has been expanded. For instance, the reader is given a first insight to the many sides of the "computers in our lives" through an automated college class scheduling system (Chapter 1). Then a down-to-earth wholesale hardware customer billing system is detailed to provide an insight to basic data processing concepts such as field, record, file, file processing, batch processing, unit record concepts, and so on. Other applications utilized in the book include the following:

- Grade reporting and summarizing to illustrate the basic concepts of a computer and a program of instructions.
- An automated library circulation system to illustrate online processing.
- A payroll system to illustrate computer batch processing principles using magnetic tape.
- A simplified database system to give an insight to just what a database actually is and what is meant by database management.
- A case study of the evolution of computer and data processing needs of a small business to illustrate the many-sided nature of data processing management.

The basic organization of this book differs from most introductory texts (including the first edition of this one) in that the chapters on programming languages are more toward the middle of the book rather than the end. In fact, the evolution of the computer, its logical structure and components, input and output techniques and devices, and computer data coding methods are covered in Chapters 4–6. With this foundation, Chapter 7 quickly moves to program and algorithm preparation, and to flowcharting. Each of the Chapters 8–11 involves an introduction to a programming language: machine language, Basic, Fortran, and Cobol, in that order. Users of the first edition will note that the two chapters on IBM 360/370 assembly language have been replaced with chapters on machine language and Basic. The inclusion of Basic needs no explanation. On the other hand, a machine language presentation using a hypothetical computer, as is done in Chapter 8, usually draws criticism. While it is true that hypothetical machines do not exist except in the pages of a textbook, if properly utilized they provide a valuable tool which can much more easily illustrate the *basic* principles of the stored program computer than any real machine. Furthermore, programs can be run on a real computer using the simulator program included in Appendix III. The more sophisticated and advanced concepts, such as magnetic tape and disk and associated applications, operating systems, and data processing management, follow the programming chapters. It is felt that many of these topics become much more meaningful after a brief exposure to programming language.

To facilitate the learning process, each chapter includes a number of exercises within the chapter with the answers given at the end of the chapter. In general, it is intended that each exercise be completed and checked before proceeding with the following pages. Experience has shown that this serves an excellent subject reinforcement purpose to the student. Furthermore, each chapter is followed by a collection of objective questions, thus combining some of the features of a study guide with the conventional text. Each of the programming chapters also includes a small selection of programming problems which are consistent with concepts presented in the chapter. Additional questions, exercises, and programming problems will be found in the Study Guide which accompanies this book.

ACKNOWLEDGMENTS

The first recognition must go to my students who have in so many ways contributed, directly and indirectly, to the concept of the first edition and to this revision. Needless to say, the comments and suggestions of many colleagues were invaluable. I am indebted to a Texas women's rights group for detailing the extent to which the first edition reflected a discriminatory stereotyping of women in positions of lesser responsibility and authority. These unfair references were totally unconscious; however, every conscious effort has been made to avoid any such repetition in this edition.

In addition to the many who contributed to the first edition, the following have contributed their expertise to this second edition through responding to detailed questionnaires, forwarding written suggestions, careful and enlightening reviews, and by direct discussion: Richard Bidleman, College of Alameda; Stanley J. Birkin, University of South Florida; Irwin Kruger, University of Miama; Melchiore LaSala, Queensboro Community College; F. Hollis Latimer, Tarrant County Community College; William N. Ledbetter, Auburn University; Bennett Lewis, San Bernardino Valley College; Gerry E. Manning, San Francisco State University; Jeffrey H. Moore, Stanford University; Jack Olson, College of Alameda; Jesse Peckenham, Merritt College; Frank M. Rand, New York City Community College; Richard W. Reynolds, Orange Coast College; John Stubbe, Mount San Antonio College. To these and others who participated, I extend my sincerest thanks.

W.T.P.

Contents

Decimal.
Binary.
Octal
Hexadecimal

TANK McNAMARA

by Jeff Millar & Bill Hinds

Chapter 1

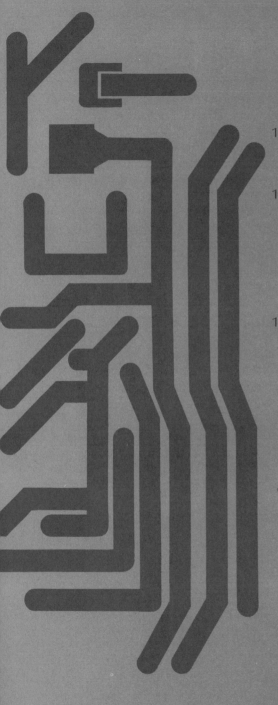

A Microcosm of
Our Computerized Society

1.1
AUTOMATED
CLASS
SCHEDULING

PLANS FOR A NEW SYSTEM COMPUTERS!! COMPUTERS!! COMPUTERS!! We are being overrun by computers. They tell the farmer when to plant. They tell the doctor when to operate. They tell the clerk our account is overdrawn. The poor guy down the street—they threatened to remove his telephone and take legal action but he has never even had a telephone. Those crazy machines seem to be in every phase of our life. Are they a threat or a blessing to us? The answer to that is not as simple as it might appear. Most everyone has read many articles on valuable uses of the computer; but then there are also stories of abuse.

To gain an insight, let us consider various ways in which computers are used in a college environment—in many respects, a microcosm of our computerized society.

Sandon University is one of several institutions of higher education in the state. Their computer center is a source of considerable pride, and heavy emphasis is placed on maximizing computer services to all areas of the University—administrative as well as education. The large data processing department is continually developing new applications for the computer and improving existing ones.

The process of making up the class schedule and of enrolling students into the classes has just become completely automated. For an overall idea of what this means, consider the following article from the school newspaper, the *Observer,* dated May 2.

COMPUTERIZED ENROLLMENT PROCEDURE FOR FALL SEMESTER

By Ace Hall

Beginning next September, students of Sandon University will no longer go through the drawn-out hassle of class enrollment characteristic of previous years. Long lines to pick up enrollment materials, longer lines to get into the gym to enroll in classes, snail's-pace lines to sign up for each course, frantic rearranging of class schedules when the courses you want have been closed: all of these were nightmares of the past. At least, that is what this reporter was told by Mrs. Anna Wong, the registrar here at Sandon. "Never happen," you say. Well, read on, fellow students; better days are ahead.

Here is how it will work. On May 15 a master list of all courses to be offered during the Fall semester will be published. This will *not* be a class schedule which includes the time, instructor and room number as in the past. It will only tell you which courses will be offered and whether they will be scheduled in the morning or afternoon (or both). From this list you make up a list of courses you would like to take. In addition, you list substitute courses you would accept in the event your first choices are not available. If you have a part-time job and cannot attend class at certain times, be sure to put that down. (Detailed instructions for making up your schedule are included on page two of today's *Observer,* read them carefully.)

If you need any help, see your counselor; if you don't need help, go in anyway to get your program approved and then it will be sent to the magic land of data processing. Then have a pleasant summer because on September 8 your class schedule will be ready.

All of this will be accomplished through the wonders of our new electronic computer.

In a nutshell, all of our course requests (including those gathered during the summer) will be fed into the computer together with the master list of courses to be offered. After a lot of arguing between the administration and the computer, the official class schedule and a class schedule for each student will be printed by the computer.

This is all very simple for you and me, but believe me, a lot goes on behind the scenes—thanks to the computer. The administration has great expectations for this new system. If it works as planned, we can all rejoice.

Let's hope.

Most of us have encountered a description of this type illuminating all the great things that are scheduled to happen once the new computerized system is installed. In some cases, we have been delighted with the improved results and in others, completely frustrated by a thousand problems that commonly arise. In this case, the automation of a clumsy, inefficient system sounds like a step in the right direction.

REACTIONS TO A NEW SYSTEM   Is the new system going to be a success or just a big bust? Or something in between? Well, let us follow up on this matter and consider the following article from the school newspaper, dated September 12.

COMPUTERIZED ENROLLMENT SUCCESS—BUT THERE WERE PROBLEMS

By Ace Hall

The much-heralded computerized enrollment system seems to have been a qualified success. During an overnight run, the machine printed out the final course schedule for the college and a class schedule for each of the 8000 Sandon students. Although everything appeared to work reasonably well, a lot of people are still pulling their hair and cursing the entire operation. To gain an insight into some of the successes and failures of the computer, your man on the spot interviewed a number of students and staff members and their remarks follow.

Diana Zermatt, sophomore, political science: "I really can't complain, the computer gave me everything I requested although I'm not very happy about the time schedule. Some of my friends were really mad about the alternate courses the computer gave them."

Jock Wilson, sophomore, physical education (defensive tackle on the Sandon football team): "Man, I *really* dig that computer. It scheduled me for a *woman's* physical fitness class with 35—count them— 35 pretty little chicks. But the first day of class, some clown from the registrar's office came by and changed my schedule. Oh well, it was fun while it lasted."

Annette Charles, freshman, sociology: "This is my first semester here at Sandon and, quite frankly, I am very disturbed with this computerized scheduling. I am a human being and all this computer stuff just reduces me to another number and treats me as if I were a sack of potatoes in the grocery store or a book in the library. The next thing I know, those computers will be spying on me—like in the book *1984*. It scares me. Oh, by the way, it gave me the courses I wanted."

Irwin B. Miller, sophomore, data processing: "Hey pal, what do you expect me to say? Data processing is my major. It's a good system, sure beats all of those long lines. Of course, there were some foul-ups, but that's to be expected the first time around. My schedule is not the greatest, but I doubt I could have done better by the old method."

Dr. Elaine Leader, Faculty Senate President: "I think I can speak for the entire faculty when I say we do not feel deprived without our two-day stint in the gym for enrollment. Overall, the system appears to have been a success. We had several complaints from the faculty concerning the schedules of individual faculty and a few pet courses which were eliminated due to very light enrollment. A couple of the professors had valid complaints about their schedules. The remainder of the gripes simply did not hold water."

Marvin Marvelous, Dean of Instruction: "You would never believe the frantic two days we had; at times we felt that the whole thing was crazy. But I must admit, it was all worth it. For the first time ever, we have been able to adjust the course offerings to fit student needs best. With preliminary runs from the computer, we were able to close down lightly requested courses and open new sections of those with un-

usually heavy demand. Now we can truly respond to student needs."

Doreen File, Office of Instruction clerk: "I think the whole thing is just awful. Last week everybody was running around like a bunch of nuts—no one knew what was going on. The old way was a lot easier. Besides, if this thing ever works the way they say it will, a lot of people are going to be put out of work."

D. P. Williams, manager, data processing: "The system was a tremendous success—never before has the class enrollment been so well balanced. Of course, we had our bugs, but that's to be expected the first time around. The case of 135 students being scheduled for a conference session limited to 15 was the result of a last-minute change we made to the computer program. Don't you believe the case of the football player in the woman's physical ed class being an error; he simply figured out how to outsmart the computer. It won't happen again, though."

Well, there you have it, faithful readers. Like it or not, computerized enrollment is here to stay.

Yes, there we have it, a kind of situation which is repeated again and again in a multitude of areas of our normal lives—conversion from a system with which we are familiar to a more highly automated one with which we are not familiar. The problems and fears expressed are common; we hear them almost every day. Let us consider each of them.

Negative responses
1. Alternate courses assigned were unacceptable.
2. Undesirable schedules for some faculty.
3. Too much confusion.
4. The computer was "outsmarted."

Positive responses
1. Provided adequate schedules.
2. Eliminated long lines normally associated with enrollment.
3. Freed faculty from two-day enrollment period.
4. Provided great flexibility in scheduling classes the best way to meet student demand.

5. Errors made in scheduling by the computer.
6. Will put people out of work.
7. Assignment by computer is too impersonal.

5. Yielded a well-balanced enrollment.

Everyone seems to gripe about the computer in this day and age. The basis for the majority of complaints from the average citizen who must "coexist" with the machine relates to the above negative responses (6) and (7): *will put people out of work* and *too impersonal*. In many instances, automated procedures provide us far better services than we could otherwise obtain, but fear of the unknown (i.e., the workings of the computer) manifests itself in these two areas: concern about impersonal service with a resultant loss of identity and fear of being replaced by the computer.

New computerized systems commonly receive a great deal of criticism, much of which is based on emotions with few actual facts to justify the complaints. (On the other hand, there *have* been many colossal failures.) Let us make a brief comparison of the old and the new systems at Sandon to gain some insight into what the computer can do.

THE OLD AND THE NEW SYSTEMS   Under the old procedure, preparation of the class schedule and class enrollment was a time-consuming task abhorred by all; it involved the following steps (refer to Figure 1.1):

1. Department chairpersons met with their departments and prepared a list of courses to be offered.
2. The chairpersons prepared a class schedule including hours and days, room assignment, and instructor assignment for each course. This was a tedious, error-prone job.
3. Upon receiving tentative class schedules from department chairpersons, the Office of Instruction correlated all of the classes, resolving room and time conflicts among courses.
4. Student enrollment in classes involved a two-day enrollment period in the university gymnasium during which students stood in various lines to sign up for desired classes, and instructors staffed the various enrolling stations.
5. As enrollment progressed, the department chairpersons and the Office of Instruction monitored class enrollment with the intent to open new sections where an unusually heavy demand justified it and, correspondingly, to close underenrolled courses.

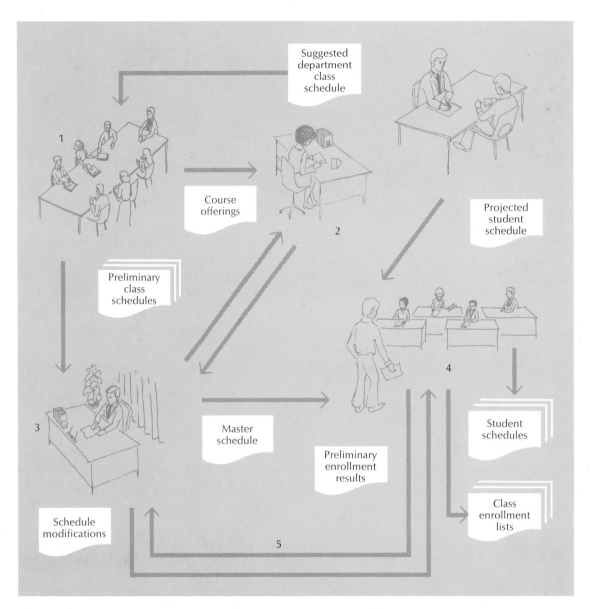

Fig. 1.1 Class
enrollment—old method.

Now, let us see what is involved under the new computerized system (refer to Figure 1.2).

1. Department chairpersons, coordinating with the Office of Instruction and working with their departments, prepared a list of courses.
2. From this list, each student submitted a list of courses desired for the coming semester. This request form allowed the student to fix a priority

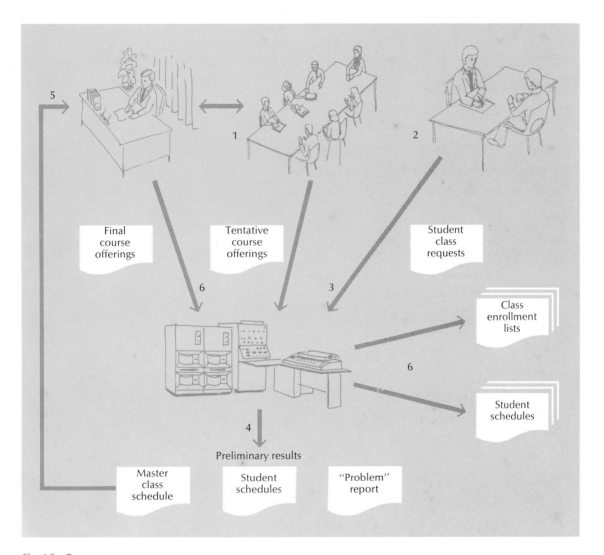

Fig. 1.2 Computerized class enrollment.

level for each course (for example, first choice, second choice, and so on), request a particular instructor for a course, and request free time during particular hours of the day due to employment or other needs.

3. The students' requests together with the tentative course offerings were submitted to the computer.

4. A computer run was made yielding the following preliminary reports: (a) a detailed master class schedule, (b) the class schedule for each student, and (c) a report on various conflicts, including tallies of the number of students not assigned their high priority classes.

5. The Office of Instruction, working with departments through department chairpersons, made necessary adjustments to resolve inequities and complaints of the faculty.
6. The data was submitted to the computer and rerun producing the final class and student schedules.

Before considering the pros and cons of the old and the new systems, we must remind ourselves that the primary objective of any instruction of higher learning is:

To provide a comprehensive offering of courses to best serve the needs and requests of the students within the limitations of available funds.

Usually the demands on an educational system are greater than the resources to support those demands. Thus, it is imperative to use the available resources in the most efficient possible manner. This involves careful balancing and scheduling of courses to maximize the number of courses fully enrolled and minimize the number marginally enrolled (with the usual exception of special programs). In this light, let us consider the advantages of the new system over the old one.

Old
1. Course offerings are determined by department personnel.

New
1. Course offerings are determined by department personnel.
1a. Course offerings are modified by student needs.

2. Master class schedule is determined by department chairpersons working with Office of Instruction. This involves some degree of "educated guesswork" based on prior experience with considerable interplay between faculty, department chairpersons, and the Office of Instruction. Unfortunately, some degree of the faculty's desires for themselves adversely affects the schedule decisions.

2. The list of course offerings, of available faculty, and of college facilities together with student requests are submitted to the computer. The computer, by virtue of its great speed, makes thousands of comparisons and adjustments to generate a master schedule which yields the fewest conflicts while satisfying the majority's needs.

3. Students enroll in classes by progressing from one line to another. Early enrollment students get their courses. Others, upon finding desired courses full, must check out alternate courses (via long lines), often to find them also full. Communication between the students and the school concerning other courses still open and those newly opened is poor.

3. The student schedules are a result of the computer run in which the master schedule was determined. The computer optimizes each student's schedule by making literally thousands of comparisons.

1.2
ANALYSIS OF COMPLAINTS

Once again let us consider the complaints lodged against the new computer system.

"ALTERNATE COURSES ASSIGNED SOME STUDENTS WERE UNACCEPTABLE"

In any system there will always be inequities; one purpose of an organized society is to minimize these. By allowing the students to designate first priority, second priority, and so on, virtually all students were assigned their high priority requests. Through its tremendous speed the computer was able to give every student the same opportunity in the most equitable way. Also, the students were able to specify their own alternate courses. However, in any system some degree of unfairness will result which requires the insight and judgment of a human being to correct. It is all too often that we hear, "Sorry, the computer did it that way; there is nothing I can do." It is as if the computer is purposely trying to cause us problems. Remember, the computer can only do what people tell it to do.

Courtesy Field Newspaper Syndicate.

"UNDESIRABLE SCHEDULES FOR SOME FACULTY"   The purpose of the university is to serve the students, not the faculty. In some instances, the efficiency of the computer will encroach on personal domains (domains that are not always in the best interest of the institution). On the other hand, each instructor is entitled to a reasonable and fair teaching schedule. Again, actual inequities for the most part are handled manually.

The following verse seems appropriate; it appears to say everything necessary about this particular complaint.

*The Information System**

"An information system," said the president, J. B.
"Is what this company sorely needs, or so it seems to me:
An automated, integrated system that embraces
All the proper people, in all the proper places,

.
.
.

Yet when the system went on line, there was no great hurrah,
For it soon became apparent that it had one fatal flaw:
Though the system functioned perfectly, it couldn't quite atone
For the information it revealed—which was better left unknown.

"TOO MUCH CONFUSION"   Whenever any type of new system involving people is brought into play, there will be a certain amount of confusion. This confusion can be considered in two general categories: (a) genuine confusion resulting from something new and (b) "self-generated" confusion resulting from reluctant individuals who are opposed to any type of change. Both types of confusion are lessened, the latter with considerable difficulty in some cases, by education.

> . . . "a system may fail to achieve company goals even though it is technically and economically feasible if company personnel are not sold on it and do not want to make it work." In too many cases, however, company personnel have not been convinced of the merits of the changes taking place and no attempt has been made to counter this attitude. Why not? One reason is that executives and data processing specialists have frequently become so preoccupied with systems problems of a technical nature that they have ignored the human factors involved in the transition. In short, the emphasis has too often been placed on work rather than on workers.†

---

*Marilyn Driscoll, from *The Arthur Young Journal*, Winter 1968, copyright 1968 by Arthur Young & Company.

†From *Computers and Management in a Changing Society*, 2nd Ed. Copyright 1974, McGraw-Hill. Used with permission of McGraw-Hill Book Company.

"THE COMPUTER WAS OUTSMARTED"   This is a way of life in the computer industry. No matter how much care is taken to insure the integrity of a computer system, someone will always figure out how to get around the safeguards. With each episode, however, computer personnel learn something new and refine the safety of their system. The general notion of protecting files of private data in large shared computers is an important area on which literally millions of dollars have been spent.

COMPUTER BANDIT TOLD TO MAKE GOOD PHONE COMPANY THEFT

By Marvin Smalheiser

LOS ANGELES. A "computer bandit" who later became a security consultant has been ordered to start paying back the Pacific Telephone Company for equipment he stole from it.

:
:

Jerry Neal Schneider, 23, who is now a consultant to firms seeking to protect themselves from theft by computer, was arrested in February 1972 and charged with stealing equipment that was later resold by his firm.

Investigators said Schneider broke the code to the telephone company's computerized ordering system and used a Touch-Tone phone to place large orders.

The orders were delivered to docking areas throughout Los Angeles County between midnight and 2 a.m. Schneider was able to pick up the equipment before telephone company employees reported for work.

Copyright by Computerworld, Newton, Mass. 02160. December 11, 1974.

"ERRORS MADE IN SCHEDULING BY THE COMPUTER"   The computer rarely makes errors that are undetected by internal circuitry designed to perform checking functions. However, people who program the computer commonly make errors in planning and writing programs. For instance, a programmer might accidentally add withholding tax to gross pay rather than subtracting it. This type of error is commonly located by testing the program (discussed extensively in Chapter 7). However, testing all aspects and possibilities of large and complex programs is a huge job, and most such programs contain some errors ("bugs") when they are put into use. For instance, occasionally we will read in the newspaper about the welfare recipient who received the January welfare check made out for $1,000,000. Such errors are normally corrected as they occur and are detected once the system is in operation. In some very large and complex systems, errors relating to infrequently occurring conditions may not be observed for several months of operation.

"WILL PUT PEOPLE OUT OF WORK"   Now we get down to a very fundamental complaint, one responsible for much employee unrest in all walks of life when a computer is installed to take over many chores previously done manually. Let us consider the computer's impact on the time devoted at Sandon to various aspects of the class scheduling and enrollment processes.

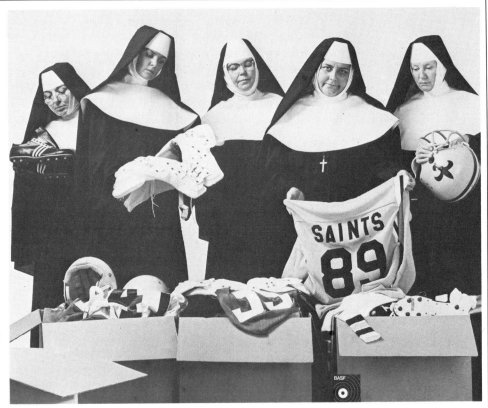
Courtesy BASF Systems.

Personnel	Hours Spent		
	Old System	New System	Reduction
Dean of instruction	60	30	30
Department chairpersons (20)	350	80	270
Faculty (180)	720	240	480
Clerical	840	340	500

The savings in time to the dean of instruction, department chairpersons, and faculty represented time during which they were performing functions basically clerical in nature. This time was rechanneled far more efficiently into counseling students and performing professional functions which better utilized the talents and abilities of those involved. During the enrollment period, many of the other college clerical operations slowed to a snail's pace due to the heavy workload. With the computerized system, clerical help was assigned to more creative functions.

In general, this freezing of time allowing for more creative and professional functions to be performed is a significant result of the introduction of automation. Also, the computer has a tendency to create more new jobs than those it eliminates. Furthermore, the jobs eliminated are commonly those with high boredom and drudgery factors.

> The reigning economic myth is that automation causes unemployment. It has only a slight element of truth—just enough to make the proposition plausible. Automation causes displacement. A few become unemployed because of it. However, it does not create unemployment in the sense that a larger number are unemployed than would have been if no automation had occurred. . . .Many persons point to a specific person unemployed as a result of automation. What they fail to do is point to the unemployed who found jobs because of automation or to those who would have joined the jobless if new technology had not appeared.*

"ASSIGNMENT BY COMPUTER IS TOO IMPERSONAL" Here we have the second very fundamental complaint. We are all individuals, and we value our individuality highly. Yet the computer simply reduces us to a number and treats us like a "sack of potatoes." However, it is important to recognize that the directions to the computer are written by people like you and me. The computer does not think; it merely follows directions—at a very high rate of speed. (For example, it would take a modern computer less than one millionth of a second to add two numbers such as 2,587,369 and 4,625,743. Try it and time yourself.) In the case of the Sandon system, students were allowed to state their individual priorities, list alternate courses, specify particular instructors, request that certain hours not be scheduled, and so on. In a fraction of a second the computer can make far more checks and comparisons to optimize programs than would be possible by manual methods.

Very many of the services that we have come to expect as a part of our lives would not be possible without the computer. Yet in many ways we still fear the computer and its influence on our lives—perhaps in a great part due to the fear of what we do not understand. The primary purpose of this book to provide that basic understanding of the computer, what it cannot do for us, what it can do for us, and how it is programmed to serve our needs.

It is a paradox that, due to student and faculty resistance to the fully computerized class scheduling system (relating mainly to the "impersonal" aspect), the Sandon administration is seriously considering a less effective partially computerized system for future use.

---

*Yale Brozen, "Putting Economics and Automation in Perspective," *Automation,* April 1964.

From *Wall Street Journal,* courtesy Eli Stein.

1.3
COMPUTERS IN
OUR SOCIETY—
TODAY AND
TOMORROW

The Sandon University example illustrates a variety of experiences each of us has had in our daily lives in dealing, directly or indirectly, with computers "in the background." The extent to which the computer has become an integral part of our lives is overwhelming and, in some cases, perhaps a bit frightening. When we consider that the computer as we know it is approximately 30 years of age, we are truly astonished to find that it ranks with energy, transportation, and communication as one of the major determinants of progress. It is interesting to note that before electronic computers became available, the solving of many types of problems was quite impractical. However, early computers were first used for applications formerly considered too expensive or impractical. This in turn generated new needs, leading to new problem-solving techniques in science and business that required even more powerful machines. It is a seemingly never-ending situation. The computer allows for futher refined techniques, which in turn require better and more efficient computers. In this rapidly evolving field, the computer professional must indeed "run" to keep up with progress. As a further introduction to the influence of the modern computer on our lives, let us consider some additional applications—present and future.

THE CANDIDATE

Reprinted with permission of *Creative Computing.* Copyright © 1976 by Creative Computing, P.O. Box 789-M, Morristown, NJ 07960.

COMPUTERS IN MEDICINE   The hospital, like any business, finds itself involved with normal data processing functions, such as employee payroll, billing of patients, and other general bookkeeping functions. Like most businesses, most hospitals use computers for these operations. However, these applications are relatively standard in the business world and do not represent anything unique to medicine. However, there are a number of areas where the computer has had a significant impact in medicine; additionally, there are many other areas into which the computer is just beginning to make inroads.

Physical Examination Data.   The Kaiser Permanente Health Services (centered in Oakland, California) has been one of the pioneers in developing an automated and computerized physical examination system. By very extensively streamlining the procedures, the staff can perform complete examinations, including such tests as audiometer, glaucoma, lung capacity, electrocardiogram, and a multitude of physical measurements, at low cost. The standard procedure is to perform the examination yearly with all the results stored in a computer. With each new examination, results are compared with those of preceding years. Dangerous trends or signficant changes can be identified for the doctor, who can then prescribe further tests or corrective actions for ailments that might otherwise have gone undetected. Much research is currently being carried out to attempt to identify trends that generally lead to particular types of medical problems (such as heart disease). Through studies such as these, it should be possible someday for physicians to prescribe for serious health problems long before they manifest themselves in their common damaging symptoms.

Hospital Information Systems.   Computers can be found performing a wide variety of functions other than bookkeeping in most modern hospitals. However, broad hospital information systems are more the exception than the rule. Although the computer and its associated capabilities are well entrenched in most industries, broad computerization of the health care field has been relatively slow in coming. However, several factors are bringing pressure to bear for expanded use of computers. For one thing, well over 50 percent of a typical hospital budget is set aside for personnel costs (excluding physicians' fees). With soaring medical costs, this is a significant factor. For another, acute shortages of trained technicians and nurses exist in many areas. It simply does not make good sense for skilled personnel to devote excessive time to shuffling papers when they could dedicate that time to laboratory work or to the patients. This is especially true when much of the paperwork could be done far more efficiently by the computer. Fortunately, much effort is currently being directed to using the computer in all areas of medicine. (For instance, specialized professional organizations such as SCM—Society for Computerized Medicine—have emerged in the past few years.)

A good example of what can be done in hospitals is the system used at the Canyon General Hospital in Anaheim, California. This hospital is somewhat unique: because it is new, computerized facilities were designed into it rather than being added on. Hospital staff members were hired with the clear understanding that they would be working with an automated system. Some of the functions performed by the system* include: maintaining patients' charts, handling the ordering of supplies and services, scheduling the use of operating rooms and other facilities, and keeping track of accumulated charges. The complete computer system includes ten minicomputers in a central location; distributed throughout the hospital are 60 typewriter-like terminals with video screens and 20 printers all connected directly to the computer.

As an indication of how such a system works, let us consider a typical patient being admitted for surgery.

1. The doctor provides basic information concerning the patient and his/her admission. This is entered into the system by a clerk for storage in the computer. At that time, the admission date is recorded and various facilities are scheduled.
2. Upon admission, the patient provides further information which is entered into the system. At that time, special printing devices print necessary identification labels and various departments are notified via terminal that the patient has arrived.
3. Special menus, medications, required lab tests, and so on, which are required before and after surgery, are entered into the system from the physician. These orders are automatically distributed to the appropriate departments.
4. Data normally kept by manual means during the patient's stay is entered into the computer system.
5. At any time, physicians can instantly obtain accurate and up-to-date information about any of their patients merely by depressing the proper keys on one of the terminals.

---

*These descriptions were adapted from *Datamation*, September, 1975.

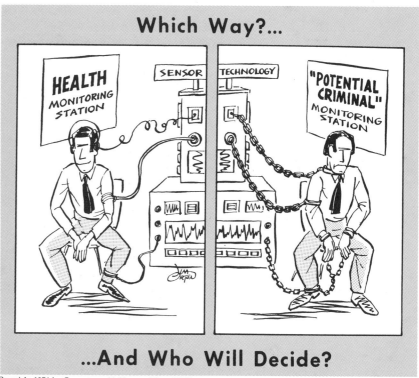

There is no doubt that hospitals of the future will make increasingly greater use of the computer to slow their spiralling costs and improve medical care. Many people in medicine feel that this is absolutely essential to avoid the further intrusion of government in medicine.

Diagnosis by Computer. Doctors at the Tufts University–New England Medical Center are using the computer on an experimental basis to diagnose complex kidney ailments. Experiments involving 18 "difficult-to-diagnose" kidney cases indicated that the system shows great promise. In 14 of the 18 cases, the computer and the physicians agreed on the proposed tests and treatment. In the other four cases, the recommendation of the computer was considered by the physicians to be a "reasonable" alternative. Of course, we might wonder, "Why use a computer if it simply agrees with the doctor?" The answer relates to the time and effort required of the physician in making determinations for highly complex cases. The computer can perform the evaluation in seconds, thereby becoming a tremendous asset to the physician. Furthermore, as such computer diagnosis systems are further developed, they can take into account far more factors than would otherwise be practical, thus providing the physician with more data from which to make the final decision.

On the other hand, physicians working with this system see broad use of computer diagnosis and decision making as five to ten years away. The problem relates to "good old common sense." A physician can use years of experience and accumulated knowledge together with judgment. The computer sorely lacks these qualities. For instance, consider the following observation of one of the participating physicians in this project.

> . . . If a patient with a kidney failure has also been hit by a truck, a computer might come up with ridiculous answers unless it is equipped to sort out the injury sustained by the truck injury from the problems caused by the failing kidney.*

Time and experience will see vast improvements in medical diagnosis and decision making by computers.

DATA BANKS AND PRIVACY   What is a data bank? The answer lies in the words themselves: loosely speaking, a large, organized collection of information. Operation of the automated student scheduling system described early in this chapter was based on a data bank which included extensive student information as well as data on the available courses to be offered. Each of the medical applications in the preceding section is based on data banks relating to extensive (and in some cases very private) information about each patient. Many of the conveniences and, in fact, some of the inconveniences which we experience today are the result of both large and small data banks. In 1972 a rather dramatic example of the value of a computerized data bank was described in the *San Francisco Chronicle*. The story involved the ten-year-old daughter of a migrant family who attended local schools wherever her parents worked in the crop harvests. While attending school in Utah, she received a routine tuberculosis test. Laboratory results indicated that she had a severe case of tuberculosis requiring immediate treatment. Upon checking at the school and the migrant camp, officials learned that the family had moved and no one knew where. Fortunately for this young girl, the U.S. Office of Education maintains a computerized Migrant Student Record Transfer System in Little Rock, Arkansas, where information on every migrant child in the United States is maintained. Without this system, locating her would have been virtually impossible. However, through use of this system, she was located in five hours. It seems that an urgent message was sent to Little Rock at noon. By 1:00 p.m., messages were dispatched to 137 terminals located throughout the country triggering a nationwide search of migrant worker camps. By 5:00 p.m., a message was received that she had been located in a migrant labor camp near

---

*Copyright by Computerworld, Newton, Mass. 02160. April 3, 1974.

Sacramento, California. She was given treatment the same day the search was begun.

Although this system is designed to provide continuous school records for migrant children as they move from location to location, it also proved itself in a potential life or death emergency. Numerous data banks exist with important information on each of us, ranging from census data to school records to credit information. Much of this information is highly useful and can be used for studies in urban planning and ecological management. In fact, with more sophisticated computers and computer techniques, the concept of a "national data bank" containing details of the life story of every American has been advanced.

Such a system already exists in Sweden where each person is assigned a ten-digit identification number (somewhat analogous to our Social Security number as it is coming to be used). All records such as employment, marriage, medical, and so on are stored in central data banks by means of this identification number. We might ask if the thought of all this data is offensive. The head of Sweden's vital statistics agency remarked:

> . . . In Sweden there is no opposition to a system we find natural and efficient. How else can you keep such an effective check on voting and tax collecting, for example, or on school and conscription obligations? It's a tool that helps us implement democracy, whereas, I can't see anything at all democratic in the American way of doing things* . . .

Is a national data bank the right thing for the United States? We might even ask that same question of the myriad existing data banks over which we have little control. Clearly, the concentration of data about individuals stored in computerized data banks provides great potential for misuse. Such files, if not rigidly controlled, jeopardize the basic rights of every individual. If standards of record keeping are not carefully drawn and followed, and if individuals are not informed of the files and allowed to inspect their own, then the danger of misuse is very real. (Recent disclosures of secret surveillance files maintained by various government agencies have shown how private citizens can be wrongly harassed with the aid of such files.)

Sweden, the country with the national data bank, has recognized these problems and in 1974 instituted a national data act consisting of 25 sections, including the following:

1. A central agency defined for regulation of data banks.
2. Restrictions on access to information stored in a data bank.

---

*Reprinted with special permission from *Infosystems* magazine, June 1971 issue, Hitchcock Publishing Company, Wheaton, IL 60187, all rights reserved.

3. Provisions for individuals to obtain a copy of information on themselves.
4. Provisions for an individual to have incorrect data corrected.
5. A means for ensuring that files in the data banks are secure (ensure an individual's privacy).
6. Penalties and legal responsibility for the misuse of data and legal recourse for the offended individual.

The importance of privacy and the rights of individuals with regard to data banks has not been completely ignored in this country. In 1970 Congress passed the Fair Credit Reporting Act which, among other things, gave individuals the right of access to information on them in credit company files. However, it is generally recognized that this law was written by lawmakers with minimal technical assistance, and it proved relatively ineffective.

In December, 1974 the Privacy Act of 1974 was passed by Congress and signed by President Ford. Many feel that it contains some weaknesses, ambiguities, and unnecessary features but must still be considered adequate as a first real attempt at such legislation. One serious shortcoming of the law is that it refers *only* to governmental data bases while specifically exempting law enforcement agencies. Furthermore, private data bases such as those maintained by credit bureaus were deleted from the bill due to pressures from private business. (The rationale went that no bill was better than a poor bill.) One of the important features of the bill provided for the establishment of the Privacy Protection Study Commission, which will make extensive studies of the privacy issue and recommend appropriate legislation to Congress.

It is clearly time for a comprehensive law regulating data banks and protecting individual privacy (composed free from typical American politics). The significant step forward taken by Sweden to protect its citizens from the dangers of computerization should be carefully considered by our elected officials.

Exercise

1.1 Two points commonly made about the computer are as follows: Some argue that standardization brought about by the computer can clearly result in economies and increased efficiency, but it can also lead to unwanted conformity and depersonalization. Others argue that standardization and the computer can lead to a more humane and personalized society which will reduce the need for conformity. Do these arguments necessarily represent opposite viewpoints? Give your opinion of the reasoning behind each of the arguments.

Chapter

2

Basic Concepts of Data Processing

If the average person were asked, "What is data processing?" the reply would very likely include the word *computer*. This common misconception is very misleading and grossly incorrect. Actually, the phrase "data processing" is best defined by its very words, that is, the *processing* of *data* or of *information*. (*Information processing* is a term that is sometimes used in place of data processing.) However, rather than presenting a sterile set of definitions, this chapter provides a common example of data processing application: processing customer charge accounts. As we shall see, this simple bookkeeping example illustrates many of the fundamental principles of data processing.

INTRODUCTION TO COA   Conglomerate Operations Amalgamated (COA)* is a hardware wholesale company that buys certain hardware items from manufacturers and sells them to retail hardware stores. The firm was founded in 1932 and for most of its existence was family owned and operated. Due to the relatively small size of the company, all record processing was done by manual methods (that is, no automatic machines were used). However, the founder of COA, having spent much of his life in the accounting field, was careful to set up modern and efficient bookkeeping procedures. These represented several record-keeping systems within the company, one of them being the *customer accounting system* that we shall study. Briefly, this system involves maintaining customer account records for purchases and payments as follows:

- As each purchase was made, the charges and other information were recorded.
- As each payment was received, a receipt was prepared and recorded.
- At the end of the month, each customer account was brought up to date by adding new charges and subtracting payments.
- When the account records were updated, a bill was prepared and mailed to each customer.

A broad simplification of this overall processing, illustrated in Figure 2.1, gives us an insight into the system. Basic to the system are the following data components:

1. *Customer Master Records*, which compose the *Customer Master File*.
2. *Sales Order Records*, which compose the *Monthly Sales File*.
3. *Payment Received Records*, which compose the *Monthly Payment File*.

---

*The concept of Conglomerate Operations Amalgamated (COA) was evolved at College of Alameda, Alameda, California by Mr. Jack Olson and is used as an example in this text with his permission.

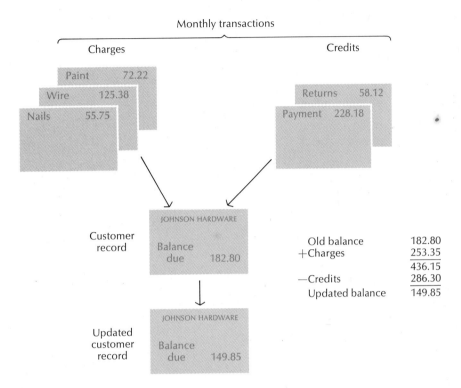

Fig. 2.1   Updating a customer account.

The Sales Order Record and Payment Received Record are commonly referred to as *transaction records;* each transaction record contains data on one sale or payment. The operation of bringing the accounts up to date at the end of each month is called the *account updating procedure.*

THE CUSTOMER MASTER RECORD AND FILE   For each customer of COA, a *Customer Master Record* is maintained. The master record, shown in Figure 2.2, includes the company name, address, and other general data as well as a monthly summary of transactions for that company. A master record is prepared for each new customer desiring an account with COA. At the end of each month this record is updated by entering the summary of monthly transactions (described in a later section of this chapter).

All of the Customer Master Records are stored in a file cabinet in alphabetic order. This file, called the *Customer Master File,* is also illustrated in Figure 2.2. Note that the Customer Master File is simply a collection of all Customer Master Records arranged in a useful and logical order. The file does *not* contribute any additional information above and beyond that contained in the individual records.

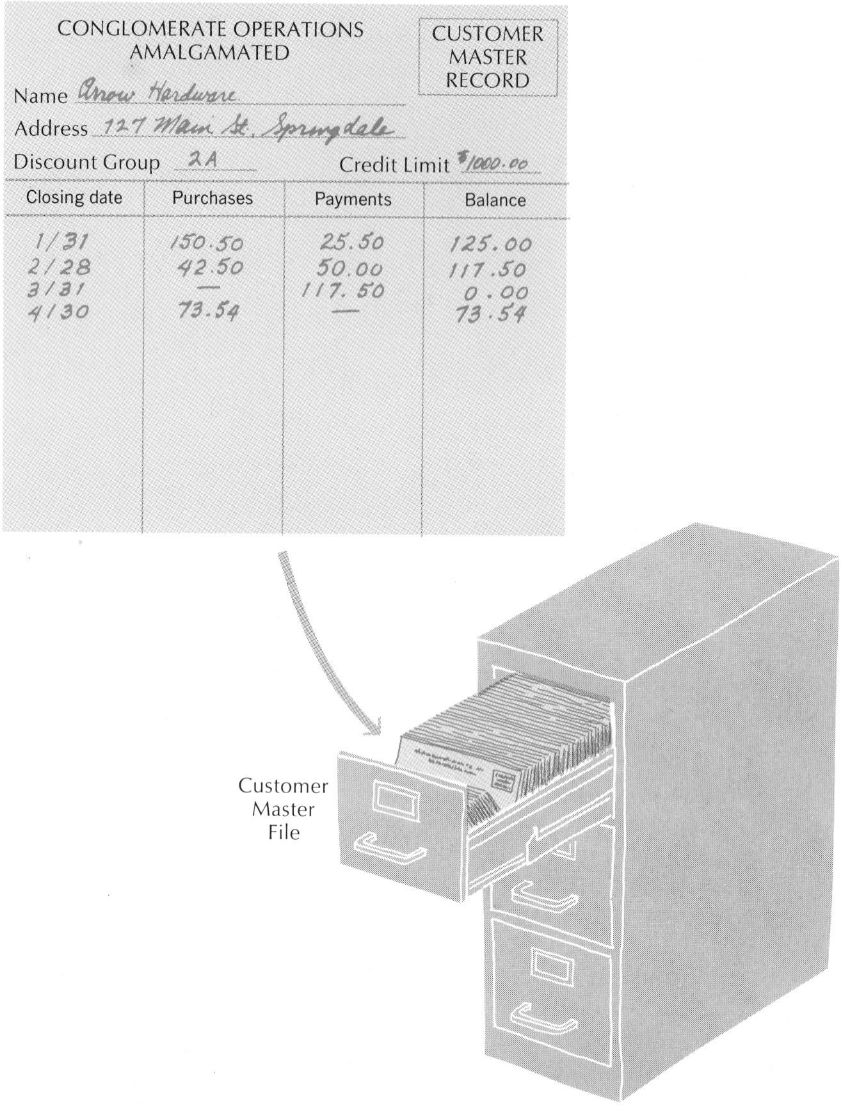

CONGLOMERATE OPERATIONS AMALGAMATED			CUSTOMER MASTER RECORD

Name *Arrow Hardware*

Address *127 Main St. Springdale*

Discount Group *2A*   Credit Limit *$1000.00*

Closing date	Purchases	Payments	Balance
1/31	150.50	25.50	125.00
2/28	42.50	50.00	117.50
3/31	—	117.50	0.00
4/30	73.54	—	73.54

Customer Master File

Fig. 2.2 The Customer Master Record and File.

DATA INPUT   As suggested by the representation of Figure 2.1, two types of customer account data come into the accounting department: sales orders from salespeople and payments from customers. Each sales order is prepared on a standard *Sales Order Form* and transmitted to an accounting clerk where it is copied onto a summary report called the *Daily Sales Listing*. The Sales Order Form is then placed in a file drawer labeled *Monthly Sales File*, where it remains until the end of the month. At the end of the day, the Daily Sales Listing is summarized and given to the president of COA so that she can scan the sales activity for the day. The overall process and the Sales Order Form are illustrated in Figure 2.3.

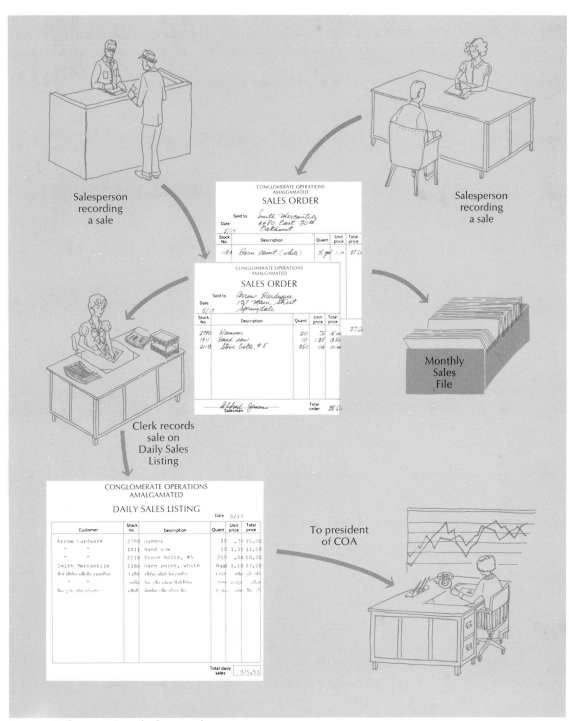

Fig. 2.3 Daily processing of sales records.

The other data received by the accounting department consists of the customer payments. As each payment is received, a clerk fills out a Payment Received Form and places the money in the cash register, where it remains until the end of the day, when it is taken to the bank. One copy of each Payment Received Record is given to the customer; the other is placed in a file drawer labeled *Monthly Payment File,* where it remains until the end of the month. This process and the Payment Received Form are illustrated in Figure 2.4.

Exercise

2.1 What is the difference between the Payment Received Record and the Monthly Sales File?

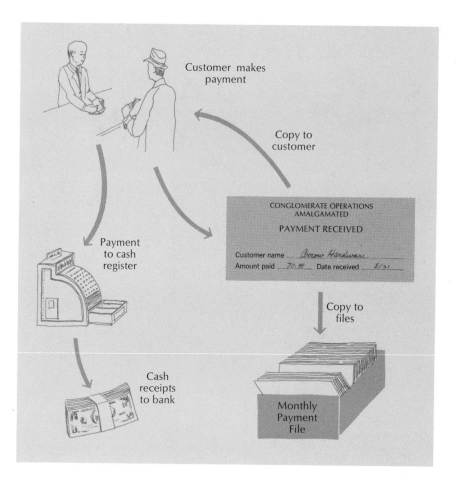

Fig. 2.4 The Payment Received Form.

ACCOUNT UPDATING PROCEDURE   At the end of the month, each customer account is updated using the data stored in the Monthly Payment File, the Monthly Sales File, and the Customer Master File. At this time, a customer *Statement of Account* is prepared (see Figure 2.5) and mailed to the customer. We can see that master data from the Master File is *merged* with transaction data from the Payment and Sales Files to update the account and prepare the Statement of Account. The updated Master Record is also shown in Figure 2.5.

The steps involved in updating the Customer Master Record are as follows:

1. The Monthly Payment File is arranged in an alphabetic sequence. Thus, all payment records for each customer are grouped together as shown in the accompanying illustration.

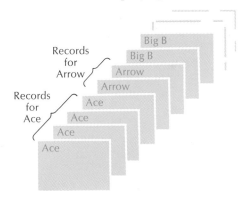

2. The Monthly Sales File is also arranged in an alphabetic sequence yielding the same grouping as the Payment File.
3. Using the data for each customer from the corresponding Payment and Sales Records, the accounts are updated. Since all three files are in alphabetic sequence, the first record in the Master File and the first group in the Sales File (assuming that payments and sales had taken place) are for the first customer. In the illustration of this process in Figure 2.6 (see page 33), the reader will note that Aztec Hardware has no Sales Records in the Sales File. Apparently they made no purchases during the current month.
4. Concurrently, a statement of account is prepared (refer to Figure 2.5).

Exercise

2.2 What is the reason for arranging the Payment and Sales Files in alphabetic sequence before performing the updating operation?

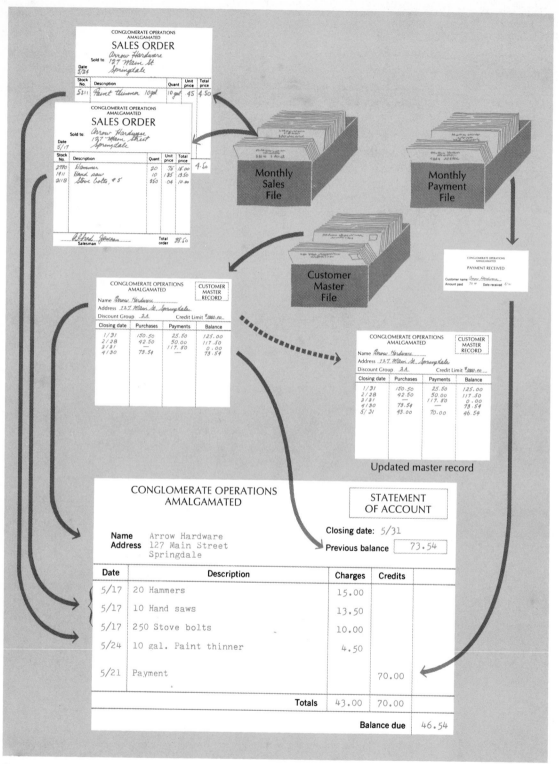

Fig. 2.5 The account updating procedure.

T3

**2.2
DATA
PROCESSING
ASPECTS OF
THE CASE STUDY**

BASIC TERMINOLOGY Before proceeding further with this case study, let us pause and review the data processing concepts introduced by this example. At the outset we considered the customer accounting system. The function of this system is to

- maintain a record of customer purchases and payments
- prepare management reports summarizing sales
- periodically update customer accounts
- prepare customer billings

In general, the term *system* may be defined as

> **SYSTEM** The method or means by which an organization or individual accomplishes a task or set of tasks required by the organization.

A person employed in data processing continually encounters systems. For example, all employees are quite concerned about their periodic pay check, which is one of the end results of a *payroll* system. At first consideration, calculating take-home pay might appear to be a simple job, but it often involves one of the more complex systems in the operation of the average company (a sample payroll system is discussed in Chapter 12). This complexity is usually caused by the many intricate deductions which are withheld either at the employee's request or as required by the government. The actual printing of the check is a very small part of the operation. The reader will note that a payroll system can be manual for a very small company, or it can be highly automated for a large corporation.

Fig. 2.6 Matching Transaction Records with the corresponding Master Record.

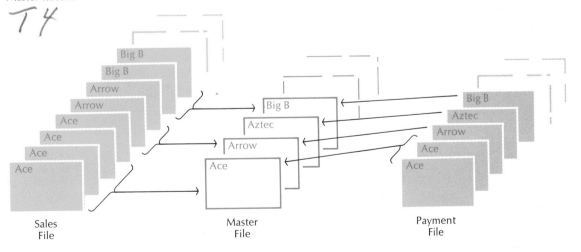

Sales File   Master File   Payment File

Fundamental to COA's customer accounting system is the *data base*,* that is, the basic set of information around which processing revolves. For COA this is, of course, the Customer Master File consisting of the customer records. In a real-life situation, these records would contain far more information on the customer than is shown in the simplified example. From the data base, a broad set of reports can be prepared, such as accounts which are past due, sales patterns of various customers, and so on. Obviously, the broader the data base (that is, the more information contained in the customer record), the more versatile and useful it is to the management and employees of COA.

The terms *file* and *record* are often confusing to the beginning data processing student. As we have seen, the Customer Master Record is a set of information describing a customer account. In general, a record is defined as

RECORD   A group of related facts or *fields* of information treated as a unit.

Thus, the master record consists of the customer name *field*, the address *field*, and so on. The payroll record for the employees of a business firm would contain all fields relating to them for payroll processing, such as name, Social Security number, pay rate, and so on. Similarly, each transaction record in the COA system includes data on one particular transaction, which may be a purchase or a payment. As we have seen, the collection of master records form the master file, the payment records form the payment file, and so on. In general, we can think of a file as

FILE   The organized collection of all the records of a given type.

Thus we see the following relationships:

A COLLECTION OF RELATED **FIELDS** forms A **RECORD**
A COLLECTION OF **RECORDS** forms A **FILE**

The data base for our accounting system is the Customer Master File; the system itself consists of a basic procedure through which the end objective, that of maintaining customer records and preparing required reports, is achieved. This procedure illustrates the basic principles of data processing (whether manual or automated), namely, the *gathering, processing, storing,* and *transmitting* of information.

DATA COLLECTION AND RECORDING   As the name implies, data collection is the gathering of the original information to be entered into the system. In

---

*The term *data base* is defined and used in a much more comprehensive sense in Chapter 12.

the COA system, this occurred each time a salesperson wrote out a sales order or a payment receipt. Needless to say, as each record is written, it is then checked to verify that all entries are correct. In each case, the original information is recorded on a *source document* and then entered into the system.

SORTING   A number of processing operations are performed on the data within this sytem. Prior to performing the account updating, the records in each Payment and Sales File are arranged in alphabetic sequence. In data processing, this is commonly called *sorting*, which simply means to place data in some type of order. This may be alphabetic, as is the case in this system, or it could be numeric based on customer number (not used in this simple illustration). In numerical sorting, records can be sorted into an ascending sequence in which the smallest number would be first, with progressively larger numbers following; for example, 25, 33, 59, 82, 128 is an ascending sequence. Occasionally a descending sequence, which is just the opposite, is used; for example, 128, 82, 59, 33, 25 is a descending sequence.

MERGING   The operation of bringing two or more sets of data together for processing purposes is illustrated in Figures 2.1 and 2.6, in which the transaction record information is combined with the master record to update the master record. This process is commonly referred to as *merging*.

CALCULATING AND SUMMARIZING   At the end of each month it is necessary to perform mathematical operations in order to bring each customer's record up to date. This involves calculating total charges and total credits as illustrated in Figure 2.5 for Arrow Hardware. In referring to the Statement of Account, we see that the information is recorded in two forms, that is, the *detailed* information, which includes the item descriptions, dates, and so on, and the monthly *summaries*, which are results of the calculations. As we can see, the updated Customer Master Record includes only the monthly summaries.

REPORT GENERATION   The information retained in the master file (or any other data file, for that matter) is of little value if it cannot be retrieved. In the example, Statement of Account reports are prepared from the data files at the end of each month. Note that this report contains detailed information in the form of the items purchased and the payments received. The preparation of other reports would be a simple matter; for example, the clerk might be instructed to prepare a report consisting of the customer names and their account balances for all customers whose balances exceed their credit limit.

MASTER-DETAIL PROCESSING This process of bringing together two or more files (or *merging*, in a broad sense of the word) to perform updating is commonly referred to as *master-detail processing* (or *master-transaction* processing) and is the most common type of task encountered in business data processing. In this example, the Customer Master File is the *master file* and the Monthly Sales File and Monthly Payment File are the *detail files*. Information recorded on detail records is used to update the corresponding master record and produce an updated master record and a billing statement. The sequence of operations is then (1) sort the detail file(s) and the master file (if it is not already in proper sequence), (2) get the next set of detail records and their corresponding master record, (3) update the master, and (4) repeat steps 2 and 3 until the processing is complete. In Figure 2.7, this procedure is illustrated graphically in an abbreviated form of a so-called *system flowchart*. Through use of this flowchart, various operations in the account updating function are clearly illustrated. Adjacent to each box illustrating an operation to be carried out is a number; these correspond to the numbered descriptions

Fig. 2.7 A flow-chart of the account updating procedure.

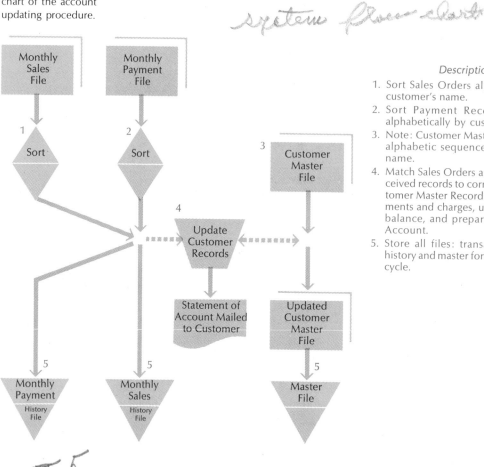

Description

1. Sort Sales Orders alphabetically by customer's name.
2. Sort Payment Received Records alphabetically by customer's name.
3. Note: Customer Master File stored in alphabetic sequence by customer's name.
4. Match Sales Orders and Payment Received records to corresponding Customer Master Records. Total the payments and charges, update customer balance, and prepare Statement of Account.
5. Store all files: transaction files for history and master for next processing cycle.

to the right of the flowchart. The use of systems flowcharts is a valuable tool in studying or changing an existing system and in designing a new one.

SUMMARY   This simple illustration of a customer account processing system illustrates many of the basic principles of data processing. It is significant that, through this example, we see the meaning of the term "data processing," and that no machines or computers are necessarily involved. As we shall see, the use of machines will significantly increase the capacity for performing these basic data processing functions.

Exercises

Prev,5 X

2.3   What is the difference between a record and a data base?

2.4   Define, either by description or by examples, the following terms: field, record, file, data base, system, merge, and summarize.

2.3

THE PUNCHED CARD AND CARD PROCESSING MACHINES

Some data processing applications are well suited to manual methods and, in fact, are relatively poorly suited to automated machines and/or computers. On the other hand, most of the services that we have come to expect would be quite impossible without automated data processing techniques. Like most businesses, COA reached a point in their evolution as a company where it was felt that the time had come for conversion to a unit record system using automatic punched card equipment.

Every now and then an article appears in a newspaper or magazine about someone who became so frustrated with their automated data processing equipment that they sent it back. The following is typical of what we might read.

MAN FIGHTS BACK

Alfred Finis, the owner of Everyday Supermarket, is a happy man today after 18 months of frustration. For it was 18 months ago that a "slick salesman" sold him on the idea of converting his manual recordkeeping system to an automated punched card system. "Timely reports, reduced bookkeeping costs, more efficient operation and all that hogwash was sold to me," said Finis. He further explained, "We never did get timely reports, and I had to put on two more people. Besides, the summaries were usually wrong and the machine just seemed to shred cards and eat them everytime we turned our backs. I am convinced it hated me; if so, then the feeling was mutual."

Yesterday the machine was sent back and the manual system was reinstalled. Today Mr. Finis is a happy man.

THE PUNCHED CARD   The punched card used by COA for their automated system (and still commonly used today) is frequently referred to as the IBM card. It contains 80 punching positions into which data can be recorded. The coding system used for the card is capable of representing any letter of the alphabet, the digits 0–9, and certain special characters (for instance, the comma and the period). One or more punches in a single punching position represents a character. The card is often called the *unit record*, because information is restricted to the 80 columns (or characters) and the card is read by processing machines as a complete unit of information. (Details of the code are described in Chapter 3.)

In the average data processing installation, the punched card serves a variety of uses. Thinking of it in terms of the COA system (where sales information was formerly stored on the Sales Order Record in handwritten or typed form), we should anticipate that a punched card could be used to *store* this data. Second, the card is still commonly used as an *input medium*, which enters data into the processing machines, and sometimes as an *output medium* for recording results of the machines' computations. In other words, the punched card provides a capability for man to communicate with the machine. These and other capabilities are described more extensively in Chapter 3.

With the conversion by COA to the unit record system for customer account processing, three standard punched card forms were incorporated into the system: the Current Charge card, the Current Credit card and the Master-Balance card (these are described and illustrated in the next section). Before exploring how these were incorporated into the system, let us consider the basic card processing machines.

UNIT RECORD EQUIPMENT   A unit record installation includes a variety of machines, each capable of performing one or more of the basic functions of data recording (punching), sorting, selecting, merging, summarizing, or reproducing. However, the important principles relate to the overall concepts rather than to the actual machines on which the work is performed. The unit record machines commonly encountered in a unit record installation are:

1. *Card punch*—to punch information into cards.
2. *Verifier*—to insure that the punching operation was accurate.
3. *Sorter*—to arrange cards in a required sequence.
4. *Collator*—to merge two data files into a single deck of cards.
5. *Reproducing punch*—to copy data from one deck of cards into another.
6. *Interpreter*—to print information on a card from the holes punched in the card.
7. *Accounting machine*—to prepare reports from data punched in cards.

The machines and their features are summarized in Figure 2.8.

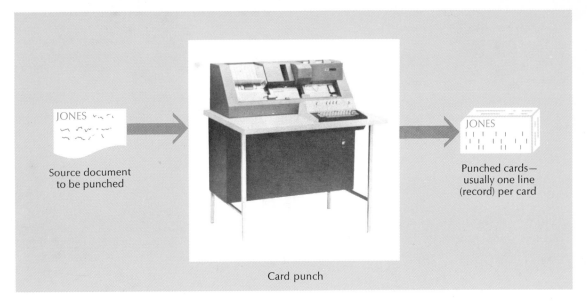

Card punch

Used to record source information (commonly in handwritten or typed form) into machine-readable punched cards. The operator keys the data into a machine through a keyboard which is very similar to that of an ordinary typewriter. The appropriate hole combinations are automatically punched for each character entered, and that character may optionally be printed along the top edge of the card directly over the punching position. By means of a special program unit, certain functions such as automatically skipping fields, duplicating from the preceding card, and shifting between numeric and alphabetic punching can be accomplished.

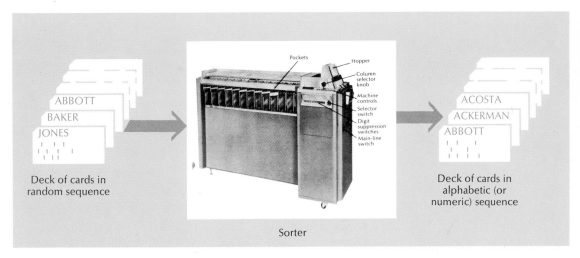

Sorter

By repeatedly passing the cards through the sorter, a deck of cards can be arranged in a numeric sequence or an alphabetic sequence. *Numeric sorting* requires that the cards be passed through the sorter once for each position of the field on which sorting is being done. For instance, sorting on the 5-digit student number would require five passes. *Alphabetic sorting* requires two passes for each position of the sorting field. For instance, sorting on a 20-position name field would require 40 passes. Through operating methods, the sorter can also be used to arrange cards in particular grouping arrangements. It can also be used to select particular types of cards from a deck: for example, the cards for all foreign students (based on a one-digit code). Common sorter speeds range from 750 to 2000 cards per minute.

Fig. 2.8   Unit record machines. (Photos courtesy IBM Corporation)

Reproducing punch

Since cards are subject to wear, the reproducing punch can be used to make a duplicate of a deck of cards; all or only part of the data punched in each card can be duplicated into the same or other card columns of the new card. This machine can also be used to punch information from selected columns of one card into corresponding blank columns of all cards which follow (termed *gang punching*).

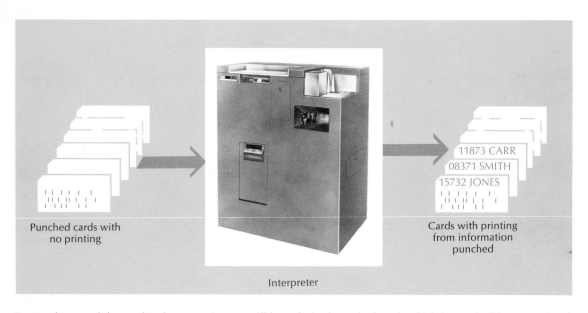

Interpreter

Frequently, one of the results of a processing run will be a deck of punched cards which is punched but not printed. The interpreter will read a card and print on that card all or part of that which is punched. The interpreting may or may not be printed above the positions in which it is punched depending upon the programming of the machine. With some interpreters, the printing can be located on any one of 25 interpreting lines from the top of the card to the bottom.

Fig. 2.8   *(Cont.)*

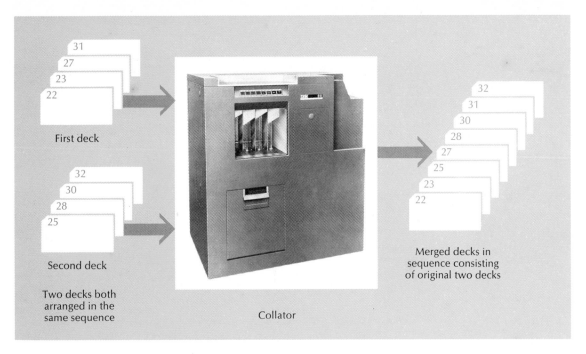

First deck

Second deck

Two decks both
arranged in the
same sequence

Collator

Merged decks in
sequence consisting
of original two decks

The bringing together of two or more files (*merging*) for processing is one of the most common functions in business data processing. The collator is a complex filing machine capable of reading two files concurrently. However, to process files on the collator, they first must be sequenced using the sorter. If a file has been broken into two subfiles for processing, these subfiles (sorted) may be combined (merged) to form the original file still in the sorted sequence. Cards from two different files, for instance Master and Detail, can be combined (*match-merged*) to form a file in which each Master is followed by its corresponding Details (Figure 2.12). The collator can also check to insure that cards are in their proper sequence and can separate particular types of cards from a deck without destroying the sequence.

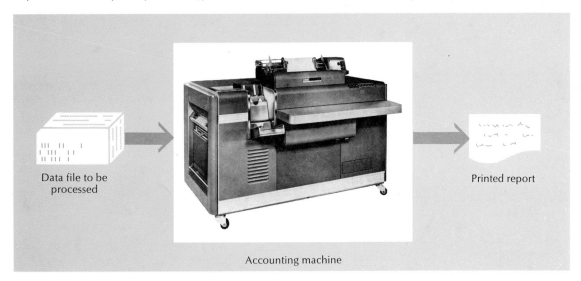

Data file to be
processed

Printed report

Accounting machine

Generation of reports (output for "human consumption") is done by the accounting, or tabulating, machine. This machine is capable of reading a card and printing all or part of the information from the card. At the same time, the data read from cards may be added, subtracted, and compared as programmed by the operator. The basic functions performed by this machine are: *detailed printing,* where one line is printed for each card; *group printing,* where one line is printed for each group of cards; *summarizing,* or *accumulating,* numeric quantities; and *summary punching.*

Fig. 2.8   (*Cont.*)

Exercises

2.5 Match the list of card processing machines with the functions to be performed; note that a given machine might be required for more than one of the functions and that a given function might require more than one of the machines.

1. card punch   2. sorter
3. verifier   4. collator
5. interpreter   6. accounting machine
7. reproducing punch

5 a. Print the name and student identification number on the top of a card from data already punched in the card.

1,3 b. Punch a set of test scores from handwritten data and check to insure its accuracy.

2,4 c. The accumulated Transaction Records are to be merged with the Master-Balance File.

1 d. One card in a deck has been damaged slightly and must be reproduced.

2 and 4 e. The Master-Balance cards for all customers with a code of 3 in card column 1 are to be selected from the Master-Balance File.

7 f. A deck of cards is to be duplicated and stored for safekeeping.

2 g. The Current Charge cards are to be arranged in numeric sequence.

6 h. The updated Customer Balance is to be calculated and a Statement of Account printed.

2.4
BASIC PRINCIPLES
OF A UNIT
RECORD SYSTEM

ESSENTIALS OF THE SYSTEM With the decision to install unit record equipment, all aspects of the COA data processing system were carefully analyzed. In planning the new customer billing system, many modifications and adjustments to the overall data gathering and processing network were incorporated. These included significant changes to the internal accounting system used by the company. However, many of the overall features of the customer billing system (as described in preceding sections of this chapter) were used to form the basis for the new system. The three basic components from the manual system are expanded to the following five for our consideration of the unit record system:

1. Sales order form.
2. Current Charge cards, which compose the Current Charge File.
3. Credit receipt.
4. Current Credit cards, which compose the Current Credit File.
5. Customer Master-Balance cards, which compose the Customer Master-Balance File.

As we can see, the system involved three different punched card forms; we shall see in the following sections how each of these is included as a component of the system.

SALES TRANSACTION RECORDS As in the manual system, when each order is taken, it is manually recorded on a Sales Order Form. At the end of the day, these forms are transmitted to the data processing department where each entry (line item) is keypunched into a Current Charge card. These documents and their correspondence are illustrated in Figure 2.9. Note that each line from the order form is punched into one card. In this case three Current Charge cards result, since there are three line entries on the order form. Upon completion of the punching, each of the cards is placed in the Current Charge File

Fig. 2.9 The Sales Order Form and the Current Charge card.

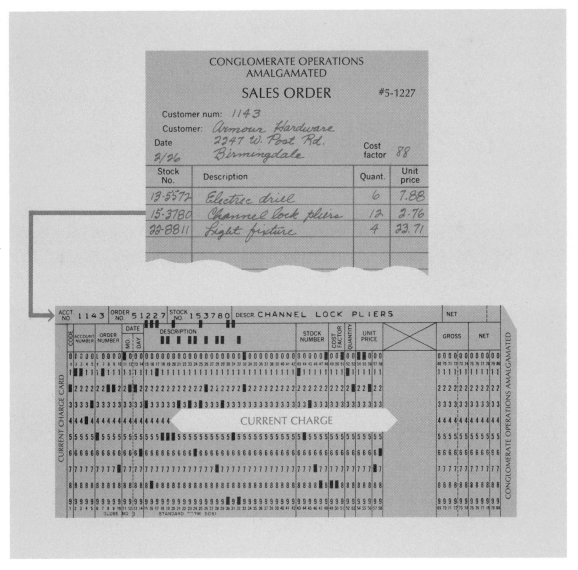

for later processing. Note that the values for *Quantity* and *Unit Price* are entered into the card from the sales order. The total price will be calculated during the machine processing cycle.

CREDIT TRANSACTION RECORDS For each credit (payment, refund, or account adjustment) a *credit receipt* is prepared. At the end of the day, these receipts are also transmitted to the data processing department where the data from each receipt is punched into a Current Credit card. These documents and their correspondence are illustrated in Figure 2.10. Each of the cards is

Fig. 2.10 The Credit Receipt Form and the Current Credit card.

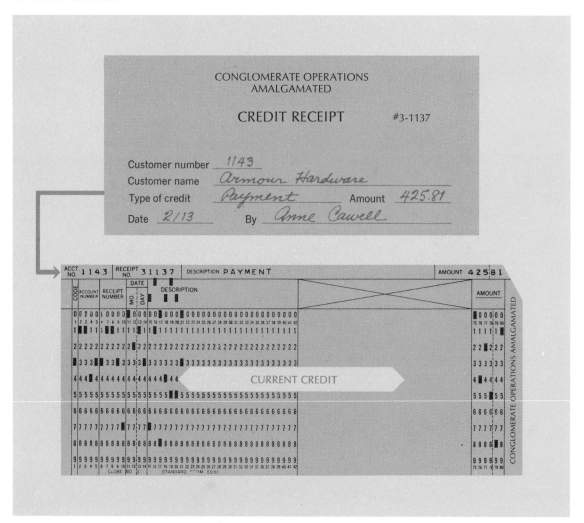

then placed in the Current Credit File for later processing. Thus, the combination of the Current Charge File and the Current Credit File formed the transaction file for the processing cycle.

Exercise

Pg 35

2.6 How many cards will be punched from each Credit Receipt Form? How many from each Sales Order Form? *one or more depending on ...*

MASTER-BALANCE CARD   For billing purposes, the Master-Balance card shown in Figure 2.11 serves the purpose of the Customer Master Record used in the manual system. Note that the Master-Balance contains customer information (as does the manual system master), but it does not include a summary of monthly transactions. Only the old balance from the preceding month is punched into this card. In addition to this punched card record, a separate set of records is manually maintained with the many and varied pieces of information which must be saved for each customer. As we shall see, the account processing cycle involves punching a new Master-Balance card with the updated balance.

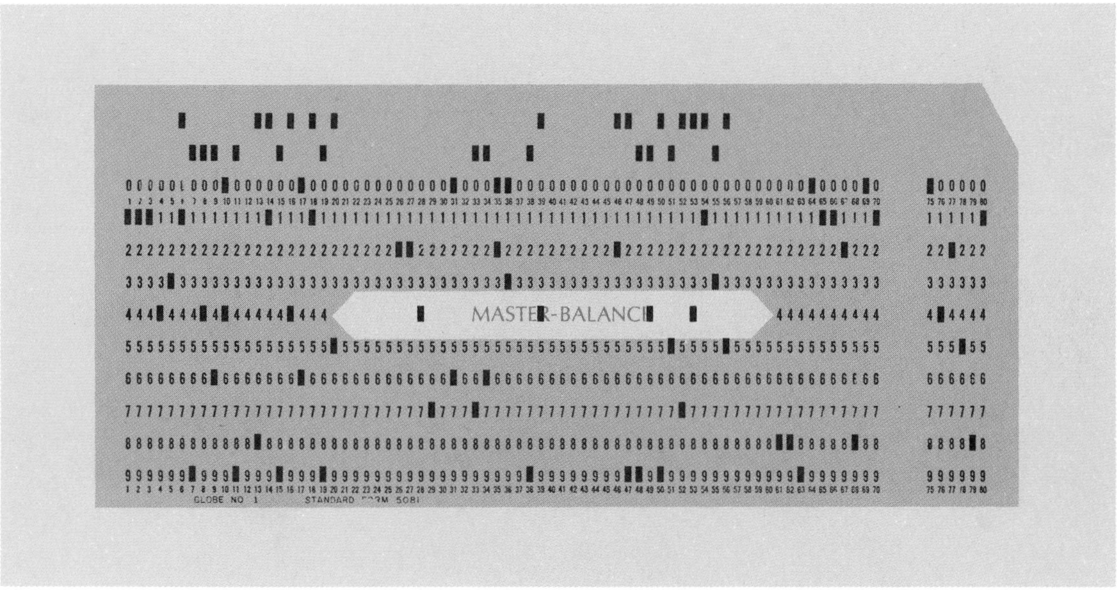

Fig. 2.11 The Customer Master-Balance card.

THE ACCOUNT UPDATING PROCEDURE   In principle, the unit record account updating operation is very similar to the corresponding operation in the manual system. Of course, with the automatic capabilities of the unit record equipment, the versatility of the overall procedure is significantly increased. The following steps are involved in preparing customer account statements.

1. For each Current Charge card, the gross and net are calculated using the previously punched values of unit price, quantity, and cost factor as follows:

    Gross = quantity $\times$ unit price
      Net = gross $\times$ cost factor

    These values are punched into the appropriate positions of the Current Charge card. (This operation is performed on a special calculating punch machine.)
2. The Current Charge and Current Credit Files are sorted on customer account numbers.
3. The sorted Current Charge–Current Credit File is merged with the Master-Balance File. Thus, each master card is followed by the corresponding detail cards for that customer (as illustrated in Figure 2.12). This operation performed on the collator is commonly referred to as *match-merging*.
4. Using the old balance from the master card and transaction data from each of the detail cards, the account is brought up to date as follows:
    a. Total all charges yielding the gross.
    b. Apply the appropriate customer discount to obtain net charge.
    c. Add net charge and old balance.
    d. Subtract credits to obtain new balance.
5. A new master card is punched with an updated account balance.
6. A customer statement of account is printed.

Fig. 2.12 A merged Master-Detail File.

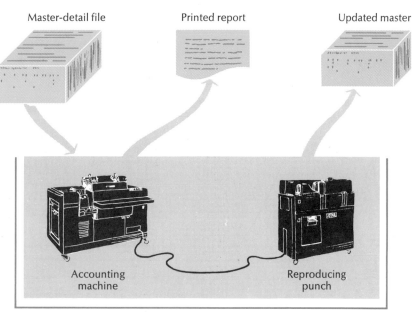

Fig. 2.13 Master-
Detail processing.

In performing a master-detail processing cycle, the accounting machine commonly is connected electrically to a reproducing punch. Thus, each processing cycle produces a new *master deck* with an updated customer balance which can be used as the input for the next processing cycle. This concept is illustrated in Figure 2.13.

THE STATEMENT OF ACCOUNT REPORT   The other output item generated by the account updating procedure is the Statement of Account report as shown in Figure 2.14. Printed on this report we see the customer name, address, and so on as well as the old balance obtained from the master card. Detail lines describing each transaction are printed for each transaction card. The last line, which consists of the totals, represents summary information obtained from both the master and detail.

A secretary preparing a report on a typewriter generally uses $8\frac{1}{2} \times 11$ inch paper; as each page is completed, it is manually removed and a new one is inserted. Since an accounting machine prints at the rate of 150 lines per minute (computer printers are much faster), *continuous feed forms* are commonly used. A continuous form is actually one long piece of paper which is perforated to yield the required size, as shown in Figure 2.15. The results of a processing run (for example, the customer statement of Figure 2.14) are printed continuously from page to page until the processing is completed. The output

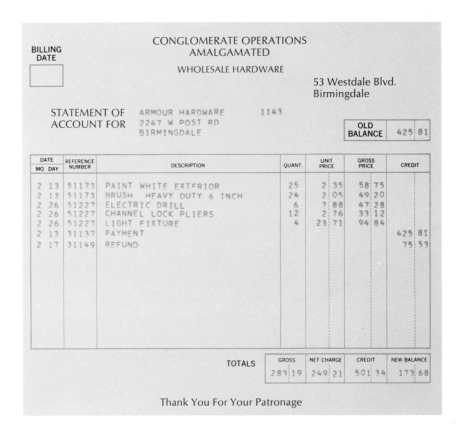

| | | | | CONGLOMERATE OPERATIONS |
| | | | | AMALGAMATED |

BILLING DATE

CONGLOMERATE OPERATIONS
AMALGAMATED

WHOLESALE HARDWARE

53 Westdale Blvd.
Birmingdale

STATEMENT OF
ACCOUNT FOR   ARMOUR HARDWARE   1143
                     2247 W POST RD
                     BIRMINGDALE

| | | | OLD BALANCE | 425 | 81 |

DATE MO. DAY	REFERENCE NUMBER	DESCRIPTION	QUANT.	UNIT PRICE	GROSS PRICE	CREDIT
2 13	51173	PAINT WHITE EXTERIOR	25	2 35	58 75	
2 13	51173	BRUSH HEAVY DUTY 6 INCH	24	2 05	49 20	
2 26	51227	ELECTRIC DRILL	6	7 88	47 28	
2 26	51227	CHANNEL LOCK PLIERS	12	2 76	33 12	
2 26	51227	LIGHT FIXTURE	4	23 71	94 84	
2 13	31137	PAYMENT				425 81
2 17	31149	REFUND				75 53

	GROSS	NET CHARGE	CREDIT	NEW BALANCE
TOTALS	283 19	249 21	501 34	173 68

Thank You For Your Patronage

Fig. 2.14 The Statement of Account Report.

of a given run might consist of only a few pages or of several hundred or even more which are easily separated before use.

In most master-detail processing applications (such as the account updating example), the number of detail cards corresponding to a given master is variable. For instance, one customer might make several purchases and payments requiring a number of detail cards, whereas another customer might make only a single purchase requiring one card (or possibly none at all). As a result, care must be taken when doing the processing to insure that all transaction cards for each customer are properly included in the calculations. To illustrate, let us assume that we are performing the updating operations by hand. The process would likely be as follows:

1. Get the first master card.
2. Record the information from the new master card.
3. Get the next card.

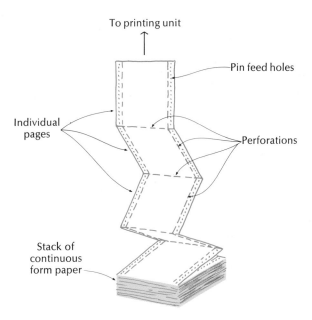

Fig. 2.15 Continuous feed forms.

4. Check to see if the new card is a master or a detail. If it is a master card, skip to step 8; otherwise continue to the next step.
5. Record transaction information.
6. Add the charge or credit to appropriate subtotal.
7. Return to step 3.
8. Since this is the master for the next customer, save it.
9. For the current customer, compute the net charges and new balance, and record it.
10. Go back to step 2.

The logic of these operations is clearly illustrated by the flowchart of Figure 2.16. In carrying out these operations manually, we can easily distinguish between the master and the detail cards by observation. When processing is done by automated equipment, such as an accounting machine or a computer, the unit must be programmed to perform comparing operations. One means of accomplishing this is by using a special identifying code in the master but no code in the detail card. The customer number of the card just read can also be compared to the customer number of the preceding master. (The entire process becomes much more cumbersome if a check is required to insure that no cards are mismatched.)

Master-detail processing of this type is commonly encountered in data processing and encompasses a large bulk of the processing in commercial applications of the computer.

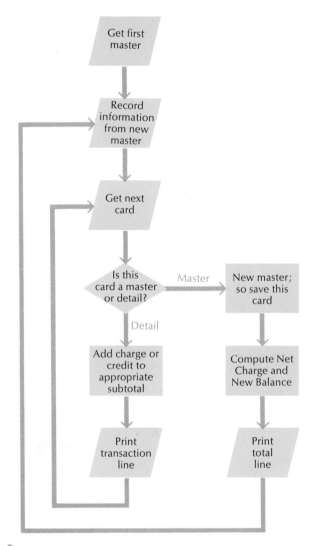

T 8

Fig. 2.16 Master-
Detail processing logic.

Program flow
chart

Exercise

2.7 Referring to the flowchart of Figure 2.16, explain why it is necessary to save the master card (corresponds to step 8 in the verbal description).

2.6

SYSTEM
FLOWCHARTING

THE NEED FOR FLOWCHARTING   Every data processing system involves *flow of data* through a sequence of steps to achieve the final result. For example, sales transactions are recorded on the sales order form, which is transmitted to the data processing department for punching into cards, and so on. The data flow for the manual processing system is pictured in Figure 2.7, in which special symbols are used to represent the various operations. This is called a *system flowchart** and is essential to planning and documenting a data processing system. The great value of a flowchart is that it gives a graphic representation of processing steps and information flow which is difficult to present clearly using word descriptions. For example, it is easy enough to understand a single task of a clerical worker (such as typing a customer information record for the permanent file), but it is not always as simple to visualize how this operation fits into the entire customer accounting system. Nor are the relationships between various functions in a system and the dependency of one step upon another always obvious. Through the use of flowcharts, such as that of Figure 2.7, sequences of steps, utilization of different files, and interfacing of various departments can be clearly illustrated. Often, a set of processing procedures which appear to be feasible "over a cup of coffee" are shown to be completely impractical when the process has been represented in flowchart form.

FLOWCHARTING STANDARDS   A common practice in flowcharting is to use different symbol shapes to represent different functions (as evident by inspecting Figure 2.7). In the interest of standardization of these symbols, the American National Standards Institute (ANSI) has established flowcharting standards. The standards, supplemented with symbols for unit record operations as proposed by the International Standards Organization (ISO) are shown in Figure 2.17. In reading and preparing system flowcharts, one notion that sometimes confuses the beginner is that some of the symbols used in a flowchart represent operations to be performed while others show the general form of the input or output data, whether it be a punched card, a card file, or a printed report. The first three symbols in Figure 2.17 represent the data form, whereas the other eight designate operations to be carried out.

THE CUSTOMER ACCOUNTING SYSTEM FLOWCHART   A system flowchart showing data flow for this application is shown in Figure 2.18. Appropriate descriptions are keyed to the various operations in the cycle. Consideration of this example is left to the reader.

---

*In data processing, two types of flowcharts are commonly encountered: *system* and *program*. Figure 2.7 is a system flowchart, and Figure 2.16 is a program flowchart. This chapter will deal with system flowcharts; with our study of program flowcharts in Chapter 7, the distinction between the two will become apparent.

Symbol	Description
	A deck of punched cards
	A punched card file—example: the Master-Balance File in the COA application.
	A document or printed report—example: the Customer Statement of Account.
↓ →	**Flowline**—represents direction of processing flow which is usually from top to bottom and left to right.
	Manual operation—indicates a manual or clerical operation performed without the use of automatic mechanical aids.
	Keypunching operation—includes both keypunching and verifying (to insure accuracy).
	Processing—represents an operation or group of operations. In a unit record system, this would include gang-punching, interpreting and accounting machine operations.
	Filing—the storage of data records in some logical order.
	Sorting—represents either numeric or alphabetic sorting of data.
	Merging—the bringing together or merging of two data sets as described earlier in this chapter.
	Extracting—the selecting of one or more types of records from a file.
	Match-merging—the merging of two files into a single file as described earlier in this chapter.

Fig. 2.17 System flowchart symbols.

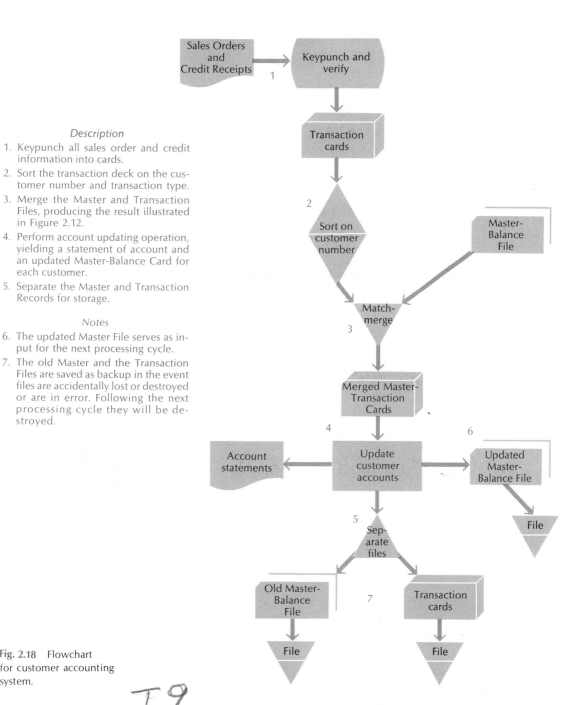

Description

1. Keypunch all sales order and credit information into cards.
2. Sort the transaction deck on the customer number and transaction type.
3. Merge the Master and Transaction Files, producing the result illustrated in Figure 2.12.
4. Perform account updating operation, yielding a statement of account and an updated Master-Balance Card for each customer.
5. Separate the Master and Transaction Records for storage.

Notes

6. The updated Master File serves as input for the next processing cycle.
7. The old Master and the Transaction Files are saved as backup in the event files are accidentally lost or destroyed or are in error. Following the next processing cycle they will be destroyed.

Fig. 2.18 Flowchart for customer accounting system.

Exercise

2.8 Based on the meaning of the system flowcharting symbols, explain, as nearly as possible, what operational sequences are implied by the following sequences of flowcharting symbols.

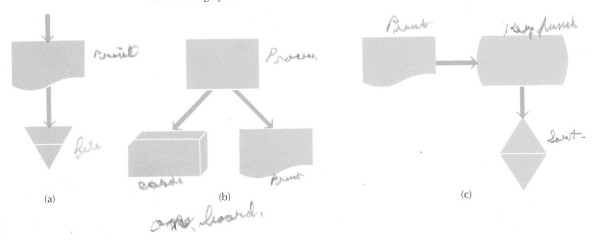

(a)   (b)   (c)

<table>
<tr><td>2.7</td><td rowspan="1">This simple illustration of a customer accounting system illustrates many of the basic principles of data processing. It is significant that we see the meaning</td></tr>
</table>

2.7
IN RETROSPECT | This simple illustration of a customer accounting system illustrates many of the basic principles of data processing. It is significant that we see the meaning of data processing and that no machines or computers are necessarily involved. (A computerized payroll system is described in Chapter 12 to illustrate data processing using modern computers.) The concept of systems, files, records, and fields are four of the very important notions of data processing which are introduced.

The operations involved in a data processing cycle of the type described in this chapter include data recording, sorting, merging, calculating, and summarizing. The reader should recognize that these functions exist in most data processing applications whether they are manual, unit record, or computerized.

Answers to Preceding Exercises

2.1 The Payment Received Record, being a *record*, contains data on a single transaction (in this case, on a payment received). The Monthly Sales File, being a *file*, is a collection of *all* Payment Received Records. It is not especially realistic to contrast one type of file with another type of record. A more realistic question would be: "What is the difference between a Payment Record and a Sales Record?" (They are both transactions, the first a credit and the second a debit.) Another meaningful and related question would be: "What is the difference between the Payment Record and Payment File?"

2.2 The Customer Master File is normally maintained in alphabetic order. The Payment and Sales

Files are placed in alphabetic order to simplify the updating procedure. In this way, all the Payment Records and Sales Records for the first Customer Record are at the front of the respective files. This saves searching through the Payment and Sales Files for each transaction. It speeds up the processing operation and reduces the probability of errors.

2.3 *Record*—a collection of related fields of data which are treated as a basic unit of information; for example, the Customer Master Record. All records of a given type form a file.

   Data base—the collection of all data (that is, all files) around which a system is designed.

2.4 See the definitions in the text.

2.5 a. 5; b. 1, 3; c. 2, 4; d. 1; e. 2 or 4; f. 7; g. 2; h. 6.

2.6 One Current Credit card will be punched for each Credit Receipt. One Current Charge card will be punched for each entry on the Sales Order Form; thus one or several cards can result from one sales order.

2.7 When a new master card is encountered, processing for the preceding master-detail set must be completed and recorded before entering the data from the new customer into the system.

2.8 The operations implied by the symbols are (a) the filing of an output report, (b) a processing function producing a deck of cards and a printed report as output, (c) punching data into cards from a source document, then sorting the cards.

Additional Exercises

2.9 Matching. Match each description in a–h with the most appropriate word in 1–8.

1. merge	2. system	3. file
4. record	5. sort	6. data collection
7. summarize	8. field	

a. Arrange a group of student grade reports in order based upon student numbers.
b. Part of a record.
c. The collection of all the procedures and data files used for customer accounting.
d. Bring two or more data sets together.
e. A clerk writes down an order on a Sales Order Form.
f. All sales and receipts for the day are added up for the day end report.
g. All of the Customer Master Records.
h. A Payment Received Form.

2.10 True-False. Determine whether each of the following is true or false:

a. In performing master-detail processing, both the master file and the detail file must be sorted.
b. A system is a collection of related records.
c. A flowchart is a pictorial means of representing data flow in a system.
d. In a descending sequence of numbers, the numbers are arranged so that the largest is first and the smallest is last; for example, 125, 93, 89, 58, 31, 15 is a descending sequence.
e. Master-detail processing always involves two or more files.
f. Master-detail processing was widely used in manual data processing systems but is relatively uncommon with modern computers.
g. Each block in a system flowchart represents an operation to be performed.
h. The collection of all fields of a given type form a file.

2.11 Multiple Choice. Determine which answer best completes or answers each of the following statements.

a. An example of a transaction record is (1) Sales Order Form, (2) Credit Receipt Form, (3) Customer Master Record, (4) all of the preceding, (5) both 1 and 2.
b. To arrange a data set into a particular sequence is called (1) merging, (2) sum-

marizing, (3) sorting, (4) recording, (5) none of the preceding.

c. A detail file is another name for a (1) updated master file, (2) transaction file, (3) master file with detailed entries, (4) none of the preceding.

d. The collection of all records of a given type form a (1) field, (2) system, (3) procedure, (4) master record, (5) none of the preceding.

e. Bringing two data sets together for processing is commonly called (1) master-detail processing, (2) sorting, (3) merging, (4) updating, (5) all of the preceding.

Note: The following exercises relate specifically to punched card equipment and processing.

2.12   Matching. Match each machine in 1–6 with the corresponding operation in a–f.

1. interpreter   2. reproducing punch
3. card punch   4. sorter
5. collator   6. accounting machine

a. Merge two files.
b. Print information punched in a card onto the card itself.
c. Record handwritten data into cards.
d. Print a daily sales report.
e. Make a copy of a deck of cards.
f. Put a deck of cards in alphabetic order.

2.13   True-False. Determine whether each of the following is true or false.

a. With automatic processing equipment, operations from a manual system such as merging are no longer used.

b. The collator is a useful machine to have in a punched card installation, but the functions it performs are not essential so the machine is generally considered optional.

c. The punched card is commonly used as a document in addition to serving as an input and output medium.

d. The data from each Sales Order Form is punched into one Current Charge card.

e. The data from each Credit Receipt is punched into one Current Credit card.

f. The total of each customer's transactions is punched into his/her Master-Balance card at the end of the day.

g. The Master-Balance card in the unit record system contains exactly the same data as the Customer Master Record in the manual system.

h. Continuous feed forms are commonly used with automated data processing equipment to simplify and speed up the process of printing from page to page.

i. The two primary items of output in a master-detail processing cycle are printed reports and an updated master file.

j. In master-detail processing, once the updating operation is completed and a new master deck is punched, the old one is usually thrown away.

Chapter

3

Principles of Punched Card Data Recording

3.1
EVOLUTION
OF THE
PUNCHED CARD

THE JACQUARD LOOM   In our present highly computerized society, most of us are familiar with the punched card, or IBM card, as it is commonly called. However, few realize that the concept of the punched card goes back over 200 years. During the 1700s much experimentation was performed in using holes on a metal drum or a paper strip to operate a weaving loom. Finally, in 1801, Joseph Marie Jacquard produced the first successful textile loom (of the type shown in Figure 3.1) to operate under the control of punched cards. In this case, the punched holes effectively supplied *instructions* to the loom which controlled the weaving patterns. Although the Jacquard loom revolutionized the weaving industry, it produced considerable hostility because of general "fear of machines." (Interestingly, this is also a commonly expressed concern today because of broad use of the computer, a topic which is discussed in Chapter 1.)

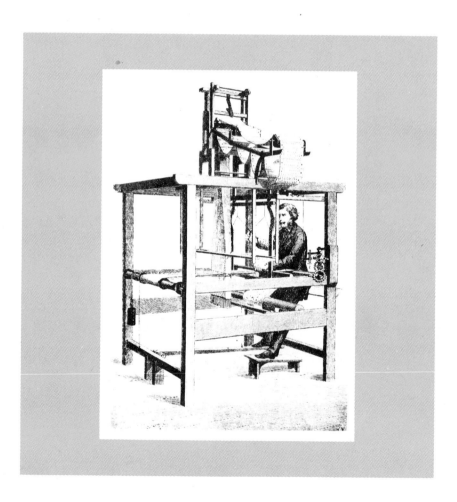

Fig. 3.1   The Jacquard loom. (Engraving, 1877, Bettman Archive)

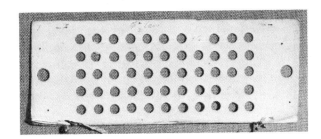

Fig. 3.2 Punched instruction card. (Science Museum, London)

THE ANALYTIC ENGINE During the 1800s Charles Babbage, an Englishman, made a remarkable series of contributions to the development of automated computing devices (see the discussion on Babbage in Chapter 4). His greatest dream, which was never realized, was to construct a mechanical computer, the *analytic engine*, involving many principles virtually unknown in his day. Knowing of Jacquard's work, Babbage proposed that punched cards be used in his analytic engine for the purposes of introducing data into the machine (that is, for *input*) and for storage of data within the machine. Furthermore, control of the machine was to be through specially encoded cards punched with instructions to perform the required processing operations. One such instruction card is shown in Figure 3.2.

THE CENSUS Article I, Section 2 of the Constitution of the United States requires that the census be taken every ten years. It had taken seven years to compile the results from the census of 1880, and it was obvious that soon the census results would require more than ten years to complete. The result would be the permanent and hopeless situation not only of never catching up but of continually getting further behind. The solution to the problem was presented by Dr. Herman Hollerith, a statistician and inventor from Buffalo, New York. He developed a system by which the census data was punched into cards with a hand punch and counted on a tabulating machine which he invented. It is often said that when a worker asked Dr. Hollerith what size the card should be, Dr. Hollerith placed a dollar bill on the table and said, "That large." (Although the size of the dollar bill was changed in 1929, the card has remained the same size.) With this system, the 1890 census was done in one third the time of the 1880 census, in spite of a 25 percent increase in population.

Following the successful use of cards and card processing machines for handling data, Hollerith left the Census Bureau and founded the Tabulating Machine Company. This company was later sold by Hollerith and eventually evolved into the International Business Machines Corporation (IBM).

After Hollerith's departure from the Census Bureau, James Powers, working in their development laboratory, devised a tabulating system similar to Hollerith's but superior in some respects. This system was used to compile the census of 1910. Like his predecessor, Powers also left the Census Bureau to form his own company. Eventually, this company became part of Remington Rand Corporation which presently includes the Univac computer division.

Originally, the Hollerith card contained 45 columns of numeric information, punched with circular holes. Later, additional punches were added to permit the card to hold 45 columns of alphabetic or numeric information, and in 1928 IBM initiated the use of rectangular holes, which would permit 80 columns of information.

Exercise

3.1 For each achievement below, match the names of the following individuals.

1. Charles Babbage	2. Joseph Jacquard
3. James Powers	4. Herman Hollerith

- *4* a. First developed and actually used punched cards for processing of data for the census of 1890.
- *3* b. As a result of his developments formed a company which eventually became a part of the present-day Remington Rand.
- *2* c. Revolutionized the weaving industry through punched card control of weaving looms.
- *1* d. Proposed use of the punched card with the analytic engine, an early proposed mechanical computer.
- *4* e. As a result of his developments formed a company which eventually became part of the present-day IBM.
- *3* f. Devised an improved card processing system for use in compiling the census of 1910.

3.2 THE PUNCHED CARD

UNIT RECORD CONCEPT   The present-day version of the punched card with which most people are familiar is technically known as the *Hollerith coded card*, in honor of Herman Hollerith. (We most commonly refer to it as the *IBM card*.) The card is also known as the unit record because it is normally used to contain all the data for one complete unit of information (record). For example, let us consider the billing form of Figure 3.3 from the Sandon University Bookstore to the University math department for office supplies. We will note that each entry on the invoice (each transaction) is recorded on a single card. Thus, the four items shown on the form are punched into four separate cards. By inspection we see that some of the information will be common to all of these cards (for example, the customer number, which is 1220), and some will be different for each card (for example, the stock number, which is 244187G for the first record and 148945B for the last). One very convenient feature of the unit record relates to the correction of errors. For instance, if we assume that the last entry was incorrectly billed and the unit price should

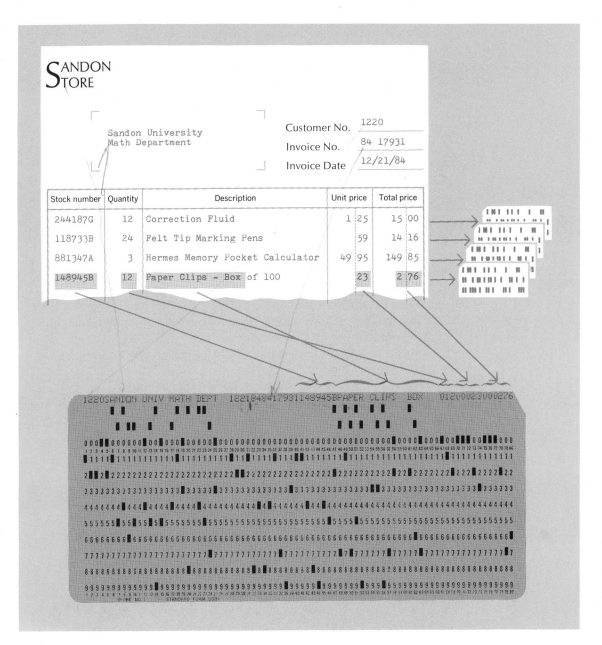

Fig. 3.3 Billing information punched in cards.

have been $0.19 instead of $0.23, then that card could easily be replaced with a correctly punched card without affecting any of the other cards in the deck. On the other hand, a disadvantage of the card is its fixed physical size; that is, the card can contain only 80 columns of information. This is a serious drawback in some applications.

The card itself is a piece of cardboard $7\frac{3}{8}$ inches long and $3\frac{1}{4}$ inches wide. As we can observe, it contains 80 recording positions in the form of vertical columns. Each of these columns consists of 12 punching positions which form 12 horizontal rows across the card. The coding system used for the Hollerith coded cards is capable of representing any letter of the alphabet, the digits 0–9, and certain special characters (for example, the comma and the period). One or more punches in a single column represents a character.

In the average data processing installation, the punched card serves a variety of uses. For instance, the card of Figure 3.3 will be used as an input medium which enters data into the processing machines. Cards are also used as an output medium for recording results of the machine's computations. In other words, the punched card is one technique by which man can communicate with the machine. Second, in most processing systems (unit record systems described in Chapter 2) the card is commonly as a storage medium. For instance, the Customer Master-Balance card was used to store the old balance from month to month. (However, in most computer systems, large files of data are stored on magnetic tape or disk—see Chapter 12.) Third, the punched card is commonly used as a document upon which information punched into the card is also printed so that it is easily read and used by people. In our highly

Fig. 3.4 Card as a document.

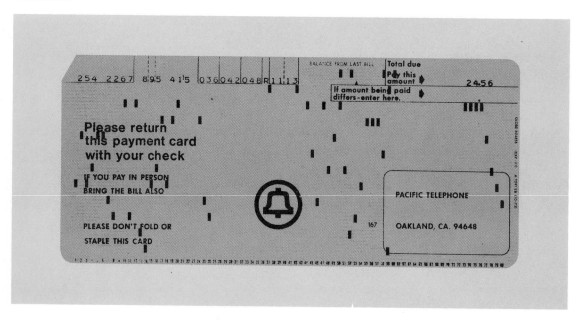

automated society, nearly everyone has seen examples of this system—for instance, payroll checks and telephone or utility bills with the classic inscription, "Please do not fold, spindle, or mutilate." Figure 3.4 is an example of a card that serves as a document.

THE HOLLERITH CODE   The card in Figure 3.5 is punched with the digits 0-9 in columns 15-24, the letters in columns 31-56, and special characters in columns 60-79. Column 8 has been specially punched in all 12 positions specifically to illustrate the twelve punching positions of the card. (The columns are designated by the small numbers between the row of 0s and 1s and also below the row of 9s.) These 12 positions are divided into two portions called the *digit area* and the *zone area*. Beginning from the bottom of the card, the 9, 8, 7, 6, 5, 4, 3, 2, 1, and 0 positions are digit areas; the three rows 0, 11, and 12 are zone areas. Note that 0 is both a digit and a zone. Each number from 0 through 9 is represented by a single punch in the required column. For instance, in Figure 3.5, 3 is punched in column 18 and 0 in column 15. (Note that in this instance, the zero position is considered to be a numeric punch.)

The alphabetic characters are represented by a combination of two punches in a single column. One is a digit punch and the other is a zone punch. Thus, using 0 as a zone punch, we have 27 different combinations with which to represent the 26 letters. The coding, apparent in Figure 3.5, uses the 12 zones and 1-9 digit punches to represent A through I, the 11 zone and 1-9 digit punches to represent J through R, and the 0 zone and 2-9 digit punches to represent S through Z. This alphabetic card code is summarized in Table 3.1.

Fig. 3.5   Hollerith coding.

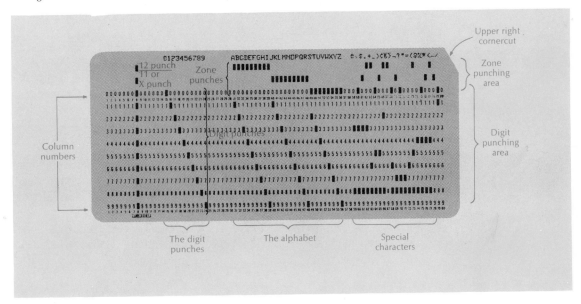

Table 3.1 CARD CODING

		Zone	
Digit	12	11	0
1	A	J	/
2	B	K	S
3	C	L	T
4	D	M	U
5	E	N	V
6	F	O	W
7	G	P	X
8	H	Q	Y
9	I	R	Z

Since there are 27 combinations but only 26 letters in the alphabet, one combination of a zone and digit, the 0–1, is not used for an alphabetic character. A simple aid to remembering just how the letters are divided is that the first and last letters using the 11 zone are J and R or JR, respectively. In addition to the numbers and the alphabet, special characters using one, two, or three punches may be coded.

Exercises

3.2 Why must two holes be used to represent alphabetic information on cards?
3.3 Name the punching positions on a card (from top to bottom of the card).
3.4 How many characters of information may be stored on a single punched card?
3.5 Write out the Hollerith code for each letter of your initials.

CARD FIELDS In some applications, only a few columns of a card are used to store information; in others, special techniques are used to get "double duty" from some of the columns to utilize the card's capacity most efficiently. In almost all cases, the card is divided into various sections or *fields* into which is punched the required information. For example, for each student a school might record the student number, name, current number of units for which enrolled, total units of credit earned, and present grade point average in a card using the following *layout* or *card format*.

Field	Card Columns	Format
Student number	2–6	xxxxx
Name	7–26	
Current units	35–37	$xx\underset{\wedge}{x}$
Total units	38–41	$xx\underset{\wedge}{x}x$
GPA	52–54	$x\underset{\wedge}{x}x$

Under the heading *Format* the notation xxxxx indicates a five-digit number; the notation $xx\underset{\wedge}{x}$ indicates a three-digit number with an understood decimal point between the second and third digits (implied by the inverted V). Figure 3.6 is a card with sample information punched. Relating these to the designated card format yields the following:

Number	12543		
Name	JONESɸɸALFREDɸɸɸɸɸɸɸ*		
Current units	145	implies	14.5
Total units	0725	implies	72.5
GPA	243	implies	2.43

*The character ɸ (lower case b with a slash) will be used in this book to indicate a blank position.

Fig. 3.6 Fields in a card.

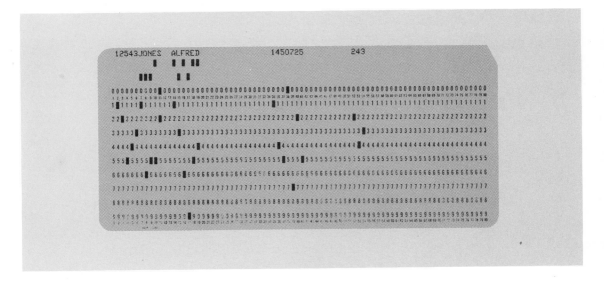

We should note that since the name does not fill the entire field allotted, it is punched in the left-most portion of the field, that is, it is *left-justified*. This is standard practice for alphabetic fields. On the other hand, the total units field is *right-justified*, that is, positioned to the right of the allotted field positions. Although in many instances leading 0s need not be punched with numeric fields, right justification with leading 0s punched is standard practice for numeric fields. Of great significance in this illustration is that two of the fields are punched adjacent to each other in the card. Although the card may be confusing for us to read, the computer has no problem. On the other hand, if the card must be read by people, it is convenient to utilize cards with preprinted areas which are labeled and lined off to designate the locations of various fields. The Student Master and Enrollment-Scholarship cards (Figure 2.11) and the card in Figure 3.3 are good examples of this. However, we must recognize that printing on the card is simply for human convenience since the machine card reader detects only the holes (or no holes) punched in various rows and columns of the card. All card processing equipment must be programmed in one manner or another to process the data contained by the card. Furthermore, whether the program consists of a wired panel board or a set of written instructions, each field must be processed to meet the user's requirements.

Exercise

3.6 Referring to the following format, what is punched in each of the fields in the card of Figure 3.7?

Field	Card Columns	Format
Card code	3	
Inventory code	4–7	
Description	8–26	
Units sold	29–31	xxx
Total cost	35–39	xxxxx

3.3
PUNCHED CARD
RECORDING

THE CARD PUNCH   In some data processing applications, it is possible to use special *porta-punch* cards which are designed to allow manual punching with a simple stylus or a pencil. To facilitate this operation, the punching positions of porta-punch cards are partially perforated and are easily pushed out. However, for general applications, these cards are not practical, and a faster, more efficient method must be used. The most common means for recording source information into a punched card is via the *card punch machine* (commonly referred to as the *keypunch*). Although many units of the older IBM

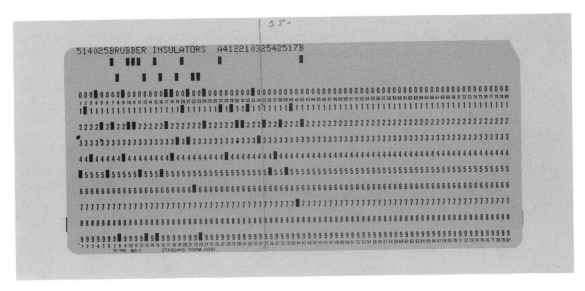

Fig. 3.7 Card for Exercise 3.6.

model 24 and model 26 are still in use, the IBM and model 29 (shown in Figure 2.8) is the one most commonly encountered. As can be seen by referring to the keyboard schematic of Figure 3.8, it is evident that the keyboard is very similar to that of a typewriter. Since no distinction is made between the upper case and lower case characters on punched card equipment, the digits are super-imposed in the reverse of a ten-key adding machine arrangement. Digits (and special characters) are punched by depressing the *numeric* shift key, an operation analogous to depressing the upper case shift of a typewriter.

In using the keypunch machine, blank cards are placed in the *card hopper*. A single card is fed from the hopper to the *punching station* by depressing appropriate keys. Punching begins in column 1 and continues through column

Fig. 3.8 Model 029 keyboard schematic.

Fig. 3.9 A program drum. (Courtesy IBM Corporation)

80 as data is entered; columns which are to remain blank are easily skipped by depressing the space bar. When punching has been completed for a given card, the card is transported to the *reading station*. If entirely new data is to be recorded into the next card (now at the punch station), then the card at the reading station is ignored. However, if certain columns are to be duplicated for all of the cards, this can quickly be accomplished by using the automatic duplication feature. By depressing the DUP key, information in the card at the reading station is automatically duplicated into the corresponding columns of the card at the punching station. After a card passes through the reading station, it is moved into the *card stacker*.*

AUTOMATIC OPERATION OF THE KEYPUNCH   Since recording source data into machine readable cards is a time-consuming, error-prone task, special means have been incorporated into the keypunch machine to provide for a certain amount of automatic operation. The device which controls this is the *program drum* (Figure 3.9); by proper coding, the operations of duplicating, skipping columns and shifting to and from numeric are performed automatically. The keypunch machine is "programmed" for these functions by preparing a control card with codes corresponding to the required functions. For example, assume that a deck of cards is to be punched as follows:

Columns	Description of Field
1–6	Numeric field to be punched by operator
7–33	Field to be duplicated from preceding card
34–40	Do not punch—skip this field
41–60	Alphabetic field to be punched by operator
61–63	Numeric field to be punched by operator
64–80	Do not punch—skip remainder of card

The program card of Figure 3.10 will control these functions when mounted on the program drum of the keypunch.

VERIFICATION OF RECORDED DATA   From the point of view of accuracy, the weakest link in a data processing system is the point at which data is entered from the source document. Present-day computers have a number of built-in error-checking features which render undetected machine errors highly unlikely. However, no matter how expert a keypunch operator may be, errors are bound to occur in punching. The use of a control card to position cards automatically during the punching process greatly reduces but does not elim-

---

*A detailed description for using the card punch is included in Appendix I.

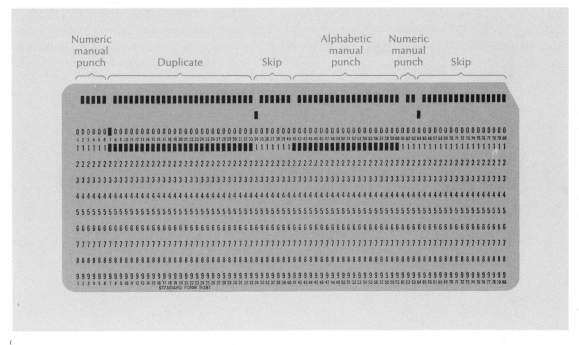

Fig. 3.10   An
example program card.

inate the chances of errors. To ensure the data is entered correctly, another machine called the *verifier* is commonly used. The verifier is similar to the keypunch except that its function is to perform a checking rather than a punching operation. After a set of data has been punched, the source document and the newly punched cards are given to a verifier operator who places the cards in the verifier and keys in exactly the same information which was originally punched into the cards. If the verifier operator keys a different character than that which is punched, an error is indicated by an edge notch above the column. If no errors are detected in the entire card, the right edge of the card is notched.

Exercise

3.7   Why is the verifying process important?

3.4

THE IBM
SYSTEM/3
UNIT RECORD

In 1969, IBM introduced a new small computer line called the System/3. This low-cost, card-oriented computer system combines the convenient characteristics of card equipment with the processing advantages of the computer. Among the innovations of System/3 is the use of a new 96-column card designed to optimize the utility of System/3.

THE SYSTEM/3 CARD CODE Although the 96-column card retains the basic characteristics of the Hollerith code, a more condensed code is used to reduce the card size. The 96-column card includes two zone positions, the B and the A, and four numeric positions, the 8, 4, 2, and 1. The digits 1–9 are coded by using multiple indication as is done with letters in the Hollerith code. That is, using the digits 8, 4, 2, and 1, the nine digits 1–9 can be represented as follows.

1	4	$7 = 4 + 2 + 1$
2	$5 = 4 + 1$	8
$3 = 2 + 1$	$6 = 4 + 2$	$9 = 8 + 1$

This can also be represented as shown in Table 3.2 if the dot is considered equivalent to a punch on a card.

Table 3.2

	Digit								
	1	2	3	4	5	6	7	8	9
8								●	●
4				●	●	●	●		
2		●	●			●	●		
1	●		●		●		●		●

The three zone positions of the Hollerith code are represented by the B and A zone positions of the 96-column card; Table 3.3 summarizes the equivalence between these two methods for representing the zone positions. Now, by combining Tables 3.2 and 3.3, the 96-column card code for the letters and digits is obvious (Figure 3.12).*

Table 3.3

	Zone		
	12	11	0
B	●	●	
A	●		●

---

*Anyone familiar with the IBM 1401 computer, a predecessor of the System/3, will quickly recognize this as the coding method used for internal storage on that computer.

Fig. 3.11 The IBM System/3. (Courtesy IBM Corporation)

Exercises

3.8 As in Exercise 3.5, write the Hollerith code for your initials; also convert this to the System/3 card code.

THE SYSTEM/3 CARD   The 96-column card consists of two sections, as shown in Figure 3.13: the upper section or *print area* and the lower section or *punch*

Fig. 3.12 The 96-column card code.

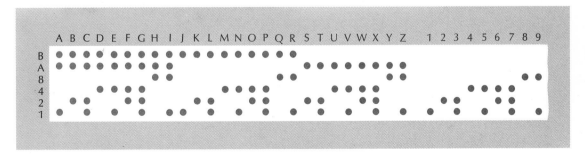

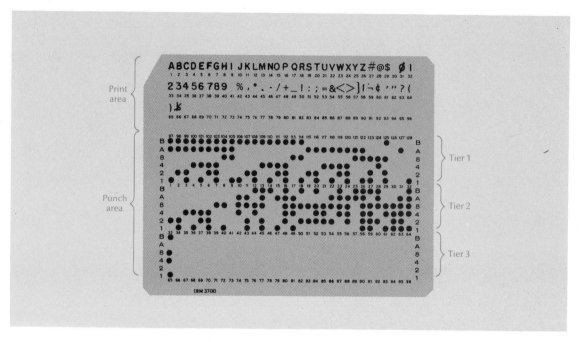

Fig. 3.13 The 96-column card.

area. The punch area, in turn, is divided into three horizontal sections called *tiers*. Each tier consists of 32 columns, each containing six punching positions (B, A, 8, 4, 2, and 1). Thus, in contrast to the 80 columns of the Hollerith coded card (all effectively in a single horizontal section), the 96-column card consists of three tiers, each consisting of 32 columns, yielding the specified 96-columns of information.

As with 80-column cards, System/3 equipment reads only the holes punched in the cards and not printed information. The printing is for the convenience of people. The print area of the card is divided into *four* rows, each consisting of 32 print positions. The first three print lines are numbered 1–96 to correspond to the columns in the punch area. Positions in print line 4 (numbered 97–128) are reserved for special codes and do not correspond to any particular column of the punch area. The card of Figure 3.13 shows the alphabet, the digits, and the special characters and illustrates the punched and printed information on a card. The reader will note that the 96-column card holes are round rather than rectangular as with the 80-column card.

RECORDING DATA   Data is recorded into the 96-column card using a punch machine (technically called a *data recorder*) in much the same manner as with 80-column cards. However, where the 80-column card keypunch is a serial machine (punches one column at a time), the System/3 data recorder is a *parallel machine* (punches all columns only after all the data has been keyed in). As each character is keyed, it is recorded in a special storage unit; then, upon depressing a special key, all of the information is punched in the card. An error detected during the keying operation can easily be corrected before punching, thus eliminating the need to repunch the entire card as with 80-column card punch machines.

Courtesy Field Newspaper Syndicate.

Answers to Preceding Exercises

3.1 a. 4; b. 3; c. 2; d. 1; e. 4; f. 3.

3.2 Since the card consists of only 12 rows (rather than 26 or 36), it is necessary to use multiple punches when coding more than 12 characters.

3.3 12, 11, 0, 1, 2, 3, 4, 5, 6, 7, 8, 9.

3.4 80.

3.5 For the author, it is WTP or 0,6; 0,3; 11,7.

3.6	Field	Contents
	Card code	4
	Inventory code	025B
	Description	RUBBER INSULATORS
	Units sold	1221
	Total cost	254.25

3.7 Entering data into the system via manual operations is the "weak link" in accuracy. Every effort must be made to insure accuracy prior to entering information into an automatic system for permanent retention.

3.8 Letter	Hollerith	96-column
W	0,6	A,4,2
T	0,3	A,2,1
P	11,7	B,4,2,1

Additional Exercises

3.8 Matching. Match each item in 1–8 with the corresponding description in a–h.

1. verifier
2. zone
3. Hollerith code
4. porta-punch card
5. program card
6. card format
7. program drum
8. 96-column card

8 a. A card used with the IBM System/3.

4 b. A card which can be easily punched with a special stylus (without the need of a keypunch machine).

6 c. Pertaining to the arrangement of data fields on a card.

2 d. Punching positions on the card which are used in conjunction with the digit punches to represent alphabetic data.

5 e. A card which is used for setting up automatic operation of the keypunch.

3 f. A system of punching with which alphabetic and numeric data can be encoded on cards.

1 g. A machine similar to the keypunch which is used to ensure the accuracy of information punched into cards.

7 h. A feature of the keypunch which can be used to automate many operations of the keypunch.

3.9 True-False. Determine whether each of the following is true or false.

T a. The commonly used 80-column card (IBM card) is often called the "Hollerith coded card" after Herman Hollerith, an early pioneer in the use of punched cards.

T b. The 0 row serves as both a numeric punching position and a zone punching position.

F c. The letter T is stored in a punched card by punching holes in the 0 row and the 2 row of the same column.

F d. If a three-digit number such as 628 is to be stored in a card, all three digits, 6, 2, and 8, may be punched in the same column to save space.

F e. Usually a blank column is left between adjacent fields to make it easier to read what is punched in the card.

T f. The format of a card means the columns allotted to each field to be punched in the card.

F g. The format description xxxxx represents a five-digit number with the decimal point between the third and fourth digits. This would require six card columns, five for the digits and one for the decimal point.

T h. The automatic duplicating feature of the card punch simplifies the process of duplicating fields from one card to another.

T i. Operations such as duplication, skipping fields, and shifting can be "programmed" on the keypunch.

T j. The 96-column card includes six punching positions (two zone and four digit) in contrast to the twelve punching positions in the 80-column card.

3.10 Multiple Choice. Determine which answer best completes or answers each of the following statements.

5 a. The 80-column card is commonly referred to as (1) the System/3 card, (2) the Hollerith coded card, (3) the unit record, (4) all of the preceding, (5) both 2 and 3.

4 b. In automated data processing systems, the punched card is commonly used as (1) an input medium, (2) an output medium, (3) a document, (4) all of the preceding, (5) only 1 and 2.

1 c. The zone punching positions make up the (1) top three rows of the card, (2) top two rows of the card, (3) bottom three rows of the card, (4) bottom two rows of the card.

2 d. The combination of a 0 and a 1 punch in a given column (1) represents the letter S, (2) is not used for a coding letter, (3) represents the letter J, (4) represents the letter A, (5) none of the preceding.

4 e. Which of the following groups of letters uses the nine-punch in addition to a zone when coded with the Hollerith code? (1) I,R,S (2) A,J (3) A,J,S (4) I,R,Z.

2 f. The letters of the alphabet are coded with (1) two-digit punches in the same column, (2) one-digit punch and one-zone punch in the same column, (3) two-zone punches in the same column, (4) a two-digit code using two adjacent columns.

g. A field on a Hollerith card (1) cannot exceed 80 positions, (2) corresponds to the concept of a field in the manual system of Chapter 2, (3) may occupy only one card column, (4) all of the preceding.

h. With reference to punched cards, the term "justify" refers to (1) checking information punched in a card to ensure its accuracy, (2) placing leading 0s in a numeric field so that it occupies all the allocated card columns, (3) positioning fields within the allocated columns of a card, (4) none of the preceding.

i. In a punched card application, a unit price amount (dollars and cents) is to be punched in columns 21–24 according to the format xxxx. If ¢ represents a blank column, which of the following represents the way $6.53 would usually be punched? (1) 6.53, (2) $6.53, (3) 0653, (4) ¢653.

j. The data recorder used to punch IBM System/3 cards (1) is commonly termed a parallel punching machine, (2) is exactly like the IBM model 29 card punch, (3) can handle both 80-column and 96-column cards, (4) none of the preceding.

Chapter

4

Introduction to the Modern Digital Computer

4.1
EVOLUTION
OF THE
COMPUTING
DEVICE

During the 1940s the first electronic digital computers were making news. The next decade saw computers installed by private business and industry for a wide variety of applications. During the 1960s the computer industry, although still relatively new, truly came of age. At present, computer installations number in the thousands, with a value measured in billions of dollars. Small computers are now available that rent for a few hundred dollars per month; a large computer might rent for over $100,000. Almost every discipline has been affected by the computer. To those who work with computers, it is apparent that only the surface has been scratched and that the computer is still in its infancy. Prior to learning what a computer is and how it works, let us pause for a historical perspective of computing devices and computers.

There are no bounds to the ingenuity of man in adapting the computer to serve his needs.

Reprinted with permission of THE Journal—Technological Horizons in Education.

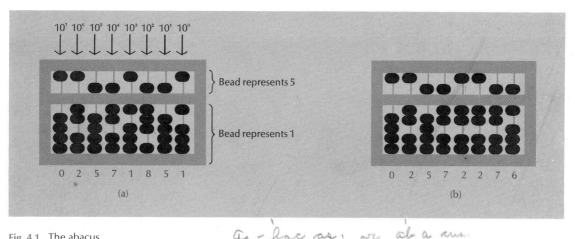

Fig. 4.1   The abacus.

EARLY COMPUTATIONAL DEVICES   Undoubtedly one of the earliest developed computational devices is the abacus, which has been in use some 2000–3000 years yet is still commonly encountered today. Figure 4.1(a) is an illustration of a Japanese Soroban in which the number 2571851 has been stored. Each row of beads is used to represent one digit of a number; having eight such rows, this abacus can hold an eight-digit number. Note the coding scheme which is used. Referring to any given string, each of the four lower beads can be used to represent 1 whereas the upper bead may represent 5. Beads positioned toward the inner bar are counted, and those positioned away are not counted. The operation of adding another number, say 425, is easily accomplished by moving the required beads in each string with the result shown in Figure 4.1(b). Note that in the third string from the right (100s position), a carry resulted, so beads were returned and the carry of one is propagated to the next string. This is a manual operation and must be carried out by the operator.

The actual mechanical carry did not come into being until 1642, when a 19-year-old French boy constructed the first true adding machine in hopes of alleviating the tiresome work of his accountant father. Blaise Pascal, later to become widely known in mathematics and physics, marked the digits 0 through 9 around the edges of circular dials. He then connected the dials by gears so that at the end of each revolution of a dial, a tooth would mesh with the gear connected to the next dial on the left and advance it $\frac{1}{10}$ revolution. Figure 4.2 shows Pascal's adding machine. Note that each wheel can be positioned at any of ten positions, thus representing one decimal digit. These same principles are used in such modern devices as adding machines and gas and electric meters; anyone who has driven an automobile has noted the odometer (mileage gauge) which is fundamentally a Pascal-type adding machine. Although these principles have been developed to a high degree of efficiency in

Fig. 4.2 Pascal's adding machine.

present-day electromechanical calculating devices, any mechanical device is severely restricted by its relatively low speed. For example, mechanical operations which take place in hundredths or thousandths of a second might appear to be very fast. But when considered in view of millions of such operations required in common data processing applications, such slow-speed methods become quite impractical.

THE WORK OF CHARLES BABBAGE   Undoubtedly the most remarkable contributor to the development of computing devices was an Englishman, Charles Babbage, who spent his entire life in the effort of building computing machines. Around the year 1812 Babbage proposed a machine which he called the *difference engine,* which would be capable of rapidly calculating logarithm tables, a slow and painstaking task when performed by hand. Without completing the difference engine (Figure 4.3 shows a replica built for IBM), he terminated work on this machine to build an even larger one which he called the *analytic engine.* This machine was to be capable of storing 1000 fifty-digit numbers in its "store" and performing arithmetic operations in its "mill." Still other parts of the engine would print answers and read and punch holes in pasteboard cards. But probably most unique of all was its ability to hold, execute, and modify its instructions internally—all significant characteristics of the modern digital computer. Babbage had attempted to build, but never completed, the mechanical equivalent of the modern electronic digital computer.

**4.2
DEVELOPMENT
OF THE
MODERN
DIGITAL
COMPUTER**

During the later 1800s and early 1900s, many calculating devices were developed and later marketed. With the advent of punched card processing by Herman Hollerith and others, machines were developed which could perform many data processing functions beyond simple addition and subtraction. The evolution of these devices and of the modern computer is illustrated in Figure 4.4

Fig. 4.3 A replica of Babbage's difference engine.

ELECTROMECHANICAL MACHINES   During the 1940s electronic components were developed on a mass-produced, low-cost basis, which made possible giant strides in the computer field. Although a great many computers were built on a one-of-a-kind basis and countless people contributed to their success, a few machines in particular seem to be the highlights of the story. From 1937 to 1944, Howard Aiken, with the support of IBM, built the Mark I computer at Harvard University. It was the first completely automatic electromechanical computer to be built. By "electromechanical" is meant that all internal operations, such as performing arithmetic and comparing numbers, were performed by a series of electrically driven mechanical relays and switches. This is in contrast to modern computers which are electronic in nature, giving them far greater speed and capacity. However, Mark I was a very reliable computer and was used at Harvard for more than ten years. It is felt by some that Mark I was the first realization of Babbage's dream of an analytic engine, although it was not until the Mark I was almost complete that Howard Aiken became aware of Babbage's work.

I. Abacus, 2000–3000 years ago

II. Pascal's adding machine, 1642

III. Babbage's difference and analytic engines, 1812–1871

IV. Punched card processing (Census Bureau), 1890

V. Punched card processing

VI. Mark I–first electro-mechanical computer

VII. The ABC computer, 1942

VIII. Eniac–first electronic digital computer, 1946

IX. Univac 1–first commercially available computer, 1951

X. IBM 650–first generation computers, 1954

XI. IBM 1401–second generation computers, 1959

XII. IBM System/360–third generation computers, 1964

XIII. Honeywell 6080–continued evolution of computers, 1970

XIV. DEC 11V03–minicomputer; 1975

XV. First Altair Computer Kit–computers for hobbyists, 1975

Fig. 4.4 The evolution of machine-aided computation. (Photos IV, V, X, XI, XII courtesy IBM Corporation; VII reprinted with permission of Datamation®, copyright 1974 by Technical Publishing Company, Greenwich, Conn. 06830; VIII, IX courtesy Sperry Rand Corporation; XIII courtesy Honeywell Information Systems; XIV courtesy Digital Equipment Corporation; XV courtesy MITS Corporation)

ELECTRONIC MACHINES   For many years, the work of Dr. John V. Atanasoff, an associate professor of physics and mathematics at Iowa State College from 1930 to 1942, remained relatively obscure. However, the recent decision of a lawsuit relating to the invention of the automatic electronic digital computer concluded that the basic principles were the work of Dr. Atanasoff. Interestingly, his work in electronic computers stemmed from the need of his physics graduate students for calculating devices capable of solving complex mathematical equations. During the period 1935 to 1939, Atanasoff evolved the basic principles of using vacuum tubes for the internal "thinking" circuitry and capacitors for information storage. In December, 1939 he produced an operating model of his machine which proved the soundness of his ideas. With this encouragement, Dr. Atanasoff, assisted by an Iowa State graduate student, Clifford Berry, commenced work on the so-called Atanasoff-Berry Computer, or ABC. In 1942, shortly after Atanasoff left Iowa State for the Naval Ordnance Laboratory, work on the ABC machine was discontinued. The photograph in Figure 4.4 of the ABC was taken in 1942 at Iowa State College.

Everything has been around for a long time, you know. Nobody really invents anything. We all lean on the work of others.*

During development of the ABC, one of the visitors to Atanasoff and his machine was John W. Mauchly. Using the basic principles of the ABC machine, Dr. Mauchly, working with J. Presper Eckert at the Moore School of Engineering of the University of Pennsylvania, began development work on an electronic computer. During the period 1939 to 1946, their working group designed and built the *Eniac* computer (Eniac is an acronym for Electronic Numeric Integrator and Calculator). The Eniac contained 18,000 vacuum tubes and weighed about 30 tons. A picture of a portion of it may be found in Figure 4.4. Through use of vacuum tubes for performing arithmetic operations, Eniac could perform 5000 additions in one second, a truly astonishing speed at that time. (A modern computer can perform in the order of 5,000,000 additions in one second.) An idea of the significance of using vacuum tubes, as in the ABC machine and Eniac, as opposed to electromechanical relay switches, as in the Mark I, can be gained by recognizing that operation of a relay involves physical movement of a mechanical part where switching a vacuum tube involves purely an electronic operation with no moving parts. Eckert and Mauchly filed a patent application for the Eniac on June 25, 1947.

Many features of the Eniac were utilized in the design of another machine which represented one of the great milestones in the evolution of the computer. The *Edsac* (Electronic Delayed Storage Automatic Computer), which was completed in 1949 at Cambridge University in England, included as its basic

*John Atanasoff, *Datamation*, February, 1974.

design feature internal storage of the program of instructions for directing operations. Prior to this, programming of a computer to perform desired operations involved external wiring of the machine for that particular task. By storing all of the operating instructions together with data quantities internally by electronic means, the versatility of the machine was greatly increased.

Meanwhile, Eckert and Mauchly resigned their positions at the University of Pennsylvania in 1946 to form the Eckert-Mauchly Computer Corporation with the intent of designing computers for commercial use. In 1949 their company, together with the patent on Eniac, asserted to be "the invention of the automatic electronic digital computer," was acquired by Remington Rand Corporation. Using the principles of Eniac and their later-developed Edvac, Remington Rand developed and marketed the first large-scale stored program computer under the name *Univac*, for Universal Automatic Computer. (The computer company begun by Eckert and Mauchly eventually became the Univac division of the Sperry Rand Corporation.)

Through a series of threatened lawsuits and countersuits, Sperry Rand and IBM entered into a "technological merger" granting IBM a license to the Eniac patent. This agreement, together with relatively high potential royalty rates on the Eniac patent that other manufacturers might be forced to pay Remington Rand, had a stifling effect on the evolution of the computer industry. In fact, a recent lawsuit brought against Honeywell Corporation by Sperry Rand sought $250 million for infringement of this patent. The case, tried in the U.S. District Court, began on June 1, 1971 and was completed on March 13, 1972. The result: The Eniac patent was invalid, and John Atanasoff, rather than Eckert and Mauchly, was the inventor of the "automatic electronic digital computer."*

Exercise

4.1 Match the following terms with the corresponding descriptions.

1. abacus	2. analytic engine
3. Eniac	4. ABC machine
5. Univac	6. Edsac
7. Mark I	8. Pascal adding machine

5 a. The first commercially available electronic computer (1951).

1 b. One of the earliest and most commonly used calculating devices.

6 c. The first stored program electronic digital computer.

---

*Two highly interesting articles on this subject may be found in *Datamation*, a monthly computer and data processing magazine: "How the Judge Looked at the IBM-Sperry Rand ENIAC Pact," January, 1974, p. 78; and "Will the Inventor of the First Digital Computer Please Stand Up," February, 1974, p. 84.

   d. First mechanical calculating device to utilize the principle of the mechanical
carry (1642).

   e. The proposed mechanical equivalent of the modern digital computer; conceived by Charles Babbage approximately 100 years ago.

   f. The first computing machine to use vacuum tubes for internal circuitry.

   g. The first large-scale electronic computer, built in 1946.

   h. The first electromechanical computer, considered by many to be the "realization" of the Charles Babbage dream.

4.3
COMPUTER
GENERATIONS

Evolution of the modern computer is commonly considered in terms of *generations* of computers. For instance, as mentioned in the preceding section, the Univac I and IBM 650 are characteristic of the *first generation*. Some think of the one-of-a-kind machines built prior to Univac (including Mark I, Eniac and Edvac) as representing the *zero generation* of computers. Over the past 20 years, we have seen three distinct generations of computers (excluding generation zero) and, in the eyes of many, a further improvement which represents the *fourth generation*. On the average, each new generation has seen the following changes in computer characteristics:

- Speed increased over 10 times
- Storage capacity increased 20 times
- Reliability increased 10 times
- System cost reduced 2.5 times

Let us consider some of the characteristics of each generation.

THE FIRST GENERATION   Introduction of the Univac I in 1951 marked the beginning of the first generation. General features of these computers are:

1. Typical computers: Univac I, IBM 650, Burroughs 220.
2. Electronic circuitry characterized by use of the vacuum tube.
3. Relatively unreliable due to failure of vacuum tubes, solder joints, and so on. The average time between failures of the computer itself was measured in hours.
4. Primitive devices for feeding information into the computer and getting results out.
5. The primary storage units utilized relatively primitive devices, such as magnetic drum and mercury delay line. The capacity of a large machine was typically 20,000 positions. Although this is very large when compared to the 80-position capacity of the punched card, it is quite small by present-day computer standards.
6. Relatively high cost for given capacity. For example, the cost per binary number of main storage was approximately $2.50.

7. Generally, machines were designed for either commercial or scientific processing.
8. Oriented toward batch processing, where the entire machine is dedicated to a particular job until completed.
9. Programming performed in internal codes of machines requiring extensive knowledge of the machine. Programs written for one model of computer could not be run on another model of computer.

The versatility of the IBM 650 made a notable impression on business and industry. In fact, the original marketing forecast of IBM called for 50 computers as compared to the actual 2000 which were manufactured and sold. The popularity of the 650 set the trend for domination of the computer market by IBM.

THE SECOND GENERATION   The transistor, invented by Bell Telephone Laboratories in 1948, formed the basis for the second generation of computers which were introduced beginning in 1959. Through use of the transistor, these computers were much faster, far more reliable, and more versatile than corresponding first-generation computers. Some principal characteristics of the second generation are:

1. Typical computers: IBM 1400 series and 7000 series, Control Data 3600, General Electric 635.
2. Electronic circuitry characterized by use of the transistor.
3. Much more reliable than vacuum tube machines; average length of time of operation without an internal error occurring was measured in tens of hours.
4. High-speed card readers, line printers, and magnetic tape units provided vastly improved devices for input and output of data.
5. Storage capacity was greatly increased by wide use of the magnetic core device; the storage capacity of a large system might be in excess of 100,000 characters.
6. The transistor and core storage provided for a reduced overall cost of maintaining one binary digit of storage to approximately $0.85.
7. Although these machines were significantly more versatile, the trend of designing one type of computer for business applications and another for scientific applications continued.
8. Oriented toward far more versatile types of applications in which multiple users were capable of using the machine concurrently.
9. Programming performed using symbolic languages requiring the use of special translating programs. These relieved the programmer of much detail. However, such programs written for one model of computer could not be run on another. This generation of computer also

marked the introduction and wide acceptance of high level languages (notably Fortran and later Cobol) which were machine-independent and negated the requirement of a detailed knowledge of the computer.

Of all the second-generation computers, the IBM 1401 was by far the most commonly used. In fact, it is generally accepted that by the time the third generation was introduced in 1964, there were more IBM 1400 series computers in use than all other computers put together.

THE THIRD GENERATION   Although the third generation of computers, introduced in 1964, included significant advances in machine hardware, they were specifically designed with heavy emphasis on *software*, the computer programs designed to make the machine work. These included special operating systems which provided capabilities for automatically proceeding from one job to the next without human intervention and for multiprogramming, which makes it possible for a machine to perform several different jobs concurrently. For hardware, the notion of families of computers—where an entire series of machines provided compatibility from very small computers to very large ones—was introduced. Summarizing the main features of third-generation computers, we have the following:

1. Typical computers: IBM System/360, Honeywell 200, National Cash Register Century series.
2. Electronic circuitry characterized by microelectronic, or integrated, circuits which although microscopic in size contained the equivalent of many transistors.
3. Improved reliability with an average time between internal errors measured in hundreds of hours.
4. A broad range of devices commonly used for input and output of information including machines capable of reading characters printed with magnetic ink and plotting complex graphs and charts.
5. Storage capacity further increased; up to one half million characters of main storage.
6. A dramatic cost reduction occurred in machine computational capabilities per dollar. The cost of storage further decreased to approximately $0.20 per binary digit.
7. General-purpose machines were designed to perform business processing functions and scientific functions equally well.
8. Designed around sophisticated operating systems capable of handling several jobs concurrently. Used extensively in real-time applications, where results of a process are fed to a computer which in turn controls the process.
9. Heavy emphasis on applications-oriented languages such as Fortran and Cobol.

FURTHER EVOLUTION (FOURTH GENERATION?)   In 1970 and 1971 a number of new computers were introduced which are considered by some to represent the fourth generation. These computers introduced some significant improvements over the classic third generation, but many in the computer industry consider them evolutionary rather than revolutionary. Consequently, it is somewhat debatable whether or not they truly represent a new generation of machines. Regardless, let us consider their characteristics.

1. Typical computers: IBM System/370, Honeywell 6000 series.
2. Further miniaturization in which complete circuits are reduced to virtually microscopic sizes. Hundreds of circuits may be placed in a chip the size of a pinhead.
3. Further improvement in reliability with average times between internal occurrence of errors measured in several hundreds of hours. Internal circuitry for error detection provides for automatically retrying an operation in which an error occurs and recording the occurrence in a system log for the maintenance engineer to check.
4. Further refinement of input and output devices.
5. Integrated circuits with their greater speeds begin replacing the magnetic core for data storage. Internal storage capacities range to one million positions.
6. Further cost reductions see even more computational capability per dollar, with internal storage costs decreasing to $0.05 per binary digit.
7. Continuation of general-purpose machines capable of performing a broad spectrum of functions.
8. Further sophistication of operating systems capable of *virtual storage*, in which the machine can operate as if its main storage were several times its actual size.
9. The beginning of broad use of special software for managing large data bases.

It should also be noted that this further evolution marked the wide use of minicomputers, small low-priced machines with capabilities exceeding the capacities of the medium- and large-scale machines of the first and second generation.

Exercise

4.2 Make a brief summary table of the main characteristics of computers, by generation.

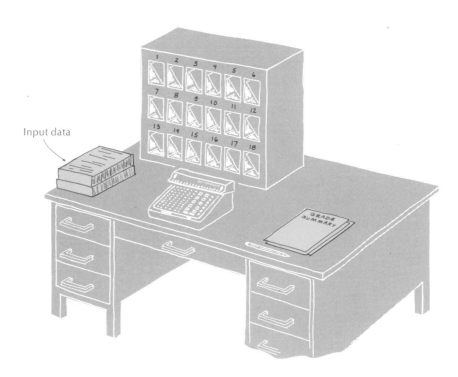

Input data

Fig. 4.5 A human-operated computer system.

AN ANALOGY Before discussing the basic components of the computer, let us consider a familiar data processing example, calculating grade point averages. We will assume that a sequence of steps must be defined that describe grade point average calculations sufficiently to allow an untrained clerk to perform the task. For this we set up a work desk complete with a "pigeon-hole box," a calculator, data records, and a grade summary form as shown in Figure 4.5. The input data consists of one set of data cards for each student. The first card of the set is called the *master card* and those following it are called the *detail cards*. Such a grouping of data records is commonly referred to as a *master-detail* set and is illustrated in Figure 2.12. The master record for each student contains three fields: the student number, the total units completed to date, and the total points earned. Following each student master record are the corresponding scholarship records, each containing the student number, the number of units for the course, and the grade received in the course; these are illustrated in Figure 4.6(a). The grade summary form includes one entry for each student, that is, the student number, the updated cumulative (total) units and points, and the GPA; these are illustrated in Figure 4.6(b). (Note that for simplicity, the Grade A is recorded as 4, B as 3, C as 2, D as 1, and F as 0 to simplify calculations.)

The pigeonhole box consists of 18 slots numbered 1–18, each containing one information card in it; some of these slots are used to store information and some to store instructions describing operations to be performed. The contents of the card are:

Card Number	Content
1	Get first input record.
2	Write the information from input record on pigeonhole cards as follows: first field (student number) to card 15 second field (cumulative units) to card 16 third field (cumulative points) to card 17
3	Get next input record.
4	Compare first field (student number) of card just read to number on card 15; if different, skip to step 9.
5	Add the second field (course units) to number on card 16 with the sum replacing previous contents of card 16.
6	Multiply second field (units) by third field (grade) with product remaining in calculator.
7	Add product from calculator to number on card 17 with the sum replacing previous contents of card 17.
8	Go back to step 3.
9	Set aside input record just read.
10	Divide number on card 16 into number on card 17 with quotient remaining in calculator.
11	Record results on summary form as follows: card 15 recorded under student number card 16 recorded under cumulative units card 17 recorded under cumulative points quotient in calculator recorded under GPA
12	Retrieve input record set aside in step 9.
13	Replace cards 15, 16, and 17 with blank cards.
14	Go back to step 2.
15	Blank.
16	Blank.
17	Blank.
18	Not used.

At the beginning of the work cycle, the clerk is instructed to start with the card in slot 1, to do whatever it says, then to proceed to card number 2, and so on.

PERFORMING THE OPERATIONS Let us act as the clerk and perform this task to get a better feeling for what is required. In doing so, we shall use the input records illustrated in Figure 4.6(a). Card 1 directs us to obtain an input

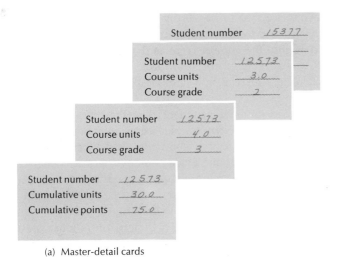

Student number	15377
Student number	12573
Course units	3.0
Course grade	2

Student number	12573
Course units	4.0
Course grade	3

Student number	12573
Cumulative units	30.0
Cumulative points	75.0

(a) Master-detail cards

GRADE SUMMARY FORM

Student Number	Cum Units	Cum Pts.	GPA
06531	55.0	110.0	2.00
08925	63.5	129.5	2.04
12468	25.0	81.5	3.26
12573	37.0	93.0	2.51

(b) Grade summary form

Fig. 4.6 (a) Master-Detail Records; (b) Grade Summary Form.

record and card 2 to record the three fields on cards 15, 16, and 17, respectively. Their contents are then as follows.

#15   #16   #17

12573   30.0   75.0

Card 3 tells us to get the next input record, and card 4 tells us to compare the first field to the number on card 15. Since they are identical (both are 12573), we continue to card 5, which directs us to add the second field to card 16, yielding $30.0 + 4.0 = 34.0$. Multiplying the second field from the input record by the third gives $4.0 \times 3 = 12.0$ (by direction of card 6); then, adding this product to card 17 (per instruction on card 7) gives $75.0 + 12.0 = 87.0$. The results on cards 16 and 17 are now as shown.

#16   #17

~~30.0~~   ~~75.0~~
34.0   87.0

Card 8 directs us to go back to card 3, causing the sequence to be repeated with the following results.

#16   #17

~~30.0~~   ~~75.0~~
~~34.0~~   ~~87.0~~
37.0   93.0

Upon returning to step 3 again and reading the next input record, we find that the first field (student number) differs from that on card 15, that is, 15377 as compared to 12573. Thus, we skip to step 9 (by direction of step 4) and set aside the input record just read (as directed by step 9). In step 10 we divide the number from card 16 into the number from card 17, giving 93.0/37.0 = 2.51. By step 11, we record the numbers from cards 15, 16, and 17 and the quotient from the calculator; these results are shown as the last entry in Figure 4.6(b).

It is important to recognize the nature of this illustration; that is, it includes a set of clearly defined *instructions* which describe, in a step-by-step fashion, operations to be performed. A prior knowledge of the fact that cumulative grade records are being updated and grade point averages are being calculated is *not* necessary to perform the required operations. It is only necessary that we have the capability for following a sequence of steps and for operating a calculator. As we shall learn, the computer functions much the same; it has the capacity to follow instructions, to perform arithmetic operations, and to make decisions based on clearly defined criteria. It does *not* possess the ability to use what we call "value judgment" in making decisions.

Exercise

see p. 111 for answer

4.3 In the pigeonhole analogy, change the program to begin the sequence of instructions on card 4 and put the blank cards used in the calculations in slots 1, 2, and 3.

4.5 THE COMPUTER

Not only does this example illustrate the nature of a computer program, but it also embodies the basic components of the stored program computer. These are:

1. *Input/output* as illustrated by the input records and output summary record.
2. *Storage* as illustrated by the pigeonhole box which stores instructions and data side by side.
3. *Arithmetic unit* corresponding to the calculator.
4. *Control unit* as illustrated by the function of the clerk who oversees the entire process.

INPUT/OUTPUT   Means for communicating with computers have always posed a formidable problem to computer designers, since all input/output devices involve some type of mechanical linkage and, in general, mechanical methods are relatively slow. This undoubtedly has contributed to the many and varied means used to get information into and out of a computer. A number of commonly used devices for input and output of data, many of which are described in detail in Chapter 5, are listed on the following page.

Computer Input Devices	Computer Output Devices
Console typewriter	Console typewriter
Card reader	Card punch
Paper tape reader	Paper tape punch
Optical mark reader	Line printer
Magnetic ink character reader	Video display unit
Optical character reader	Plotter
Magnetic tape unit	Audio response unit
Magnetic disk unit	Magnetic tape unit
	Magnetic disk unit

Note that many devices are used for both input and output. Although magnetic tape and magnetic disk are most commonly used to store large quantities of data, they also serve as input and output devices, especially on large computer systems. Typically, a large data processing installation will utilize a large computer for its principal calculation and processing operations. Input to the machine is via magnetic tape or disk; input data from cards is recorded on the tape or disk by a smaller computer. Similarly, output from the large machine is via tape or disk, and reports are prepared and printed on a smaller machine from the tape or disk.

In spite of many recent advances in input devices, the 80-column punched card used with the high-speed card reader is still a very commonly encountered medium. Card readers are available with speeds ranging from a few hundred to over 1000 cards per minute. For output, high-speed printers capable of printing entire lines at a time at rates up to 2000 lines per minute are commonly used. A variety of these units is shown in Figure 4.7.

STORAGE Computer *storage,* the single component of computers that is probably most glamorized, is often referred to as a memory analogous to the human memory. However, we shall use the term "storage" rather than "memory," since the popular representation can be misleading. The storage unit is better compared to the pigeonhole box (of the analogy), which is capable of storing information in an orderly fashion, than to human memory. The analogy can further illustrate how the computer uses storage. As we can see, the box contains 18 separate slots or storage positions. To distinguish one from the other, each was given a unique number or a storage address; note that this address has nothing to do with the information which is stored on the card but merely distinguishes one slot from another. Furthermore, each position is capable of storing one number or one instruction; the slots containing numbers have no distinguishing characteristics from those containing instructions. (In fact, the numbers could as well have been stored at the beginning of the program of instructions, that is, in slots 1-3, with appropriate changes in the

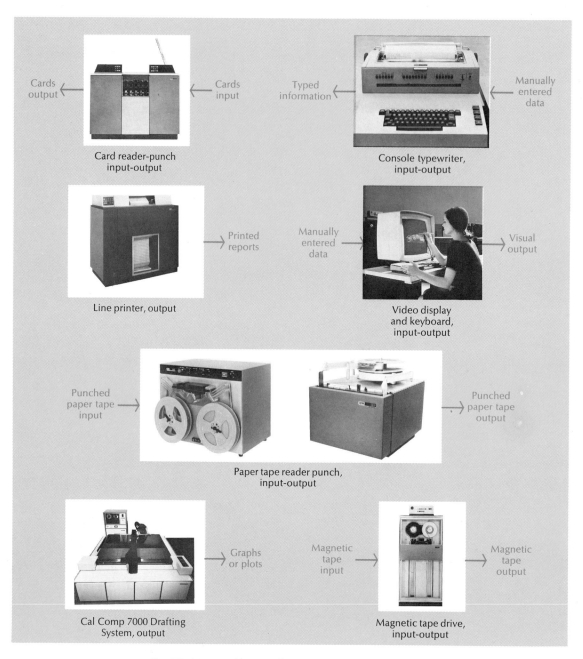

Fig. 4.7 Input and output devices. (Plotter courtesy California Computer Products, Inc.; other photos courtesy IBM Corporation)

address references of each instruction.) These notions are directly applicable to storage devices used in the modern electronic digital computer.

Storage capacity and speed of digital computers have increased remarkably in the past 20 years. Early computers had capacities of a few hundred to a few thousand storage positions. (For simple comparison purposes, we can consider one storage position as being analogous to one card column.) A small modern computer will commonly be available with a storage capacity in the range of 4000–20,000 positions, a medium-sized machine will likely have a capacity of approximately 100,000 positions, and a very large computer may have in the order of 1 million positions.

In addition, auxiliary storage devices which have vast capabilities for storing information are frequently used with computer systems of almost all sizes. The most common of these are magnetic tape, magnetic disk, and magnetic drum.

THE ARITHMETIC UNIT   The primary purpose of every digital computer is to perform computations of one type or another with numbers. The arithmetic/logic unit of the computer contains the electronic switches and circuits necessary for these computations. These correspond to the desk calculator of the analogy and provide the capability to perform, directly or indirectly, operations of addition, subtraction, multiplication, and division. As noted earlier in this chapter, it is in the area of computational speed where the capabilities of man have been most remarkably extended through the computer. For instance, if we were to consider the multiplication of two five-digit numbers (for example, 52381 and 26552), typical times required to perform the operation manually and on relatively small computers would be as follows:

Method of Calculation	Approximate Time	
Man (manual calculation)	60 seconds	
Burroughs E101 early wired panel computer	0.25 second	$\frac{1}{4}$
IBM 1620 (second-generation computer)	0.005 second	5 thousandth
Digital Equipment Corporation PDP 11 (1974)	0.000001 second	1 millionth

In other words, a modern computer is capable of performing such operations at speeds in excess of 1 million per second. The computer has provided man an increase in computational speed of approximately 100 million times. This is truly an amazing accomplishment.

CONTROL UNIT   The task of directing operations within the computer is the function of the automatic control unit. This portion of the computer can be considered analogous to a combination of traffic officer and automatic telephone switchboard. It obtains instructions from storage, interprets them, and makes certain that they are carried out as required. These functions require opening and closing appropriate circuits, starting and stopping input/output devices and, in general, directing the flow of information within the computer.

In the pigeonhole analogy, the control function was served by the clerk. The normal sequence was to progress from a given instruction to the next sequential one unless explicitly directed otherwise. By carefully following this sequence, there was never any difficulty such as looking for an instruction in a slot containing data or vice versa.

THE CENTRAL PROCESSING UNIT   The control unit, storage, and arithmetic units make up what is usually called the *central processing unit* (CPU) of the computer. Figure 4.8 is a schematic representation of these logical components together with the input and output units. To illustrate the basics of data flow, let us assume that we have placed a program of instructions in the storage and that the computer is about to perform the following sequence: read a data record, perform some calculations, and print the results. Referring to Figure 4.8, we see that the following would take place.

1. The control unit obtains from storage the instruction to read data and begins the reading process.
2. Under direction of the control unit, the data is read from the input device into storage.
3. The next instruction (for a calculation, in this case) is obtained from storage by the control unit.
4. Under direction of the control unit, the needed fields are transmitted from storage to the arithmetic/logic unit where the calculation is per-

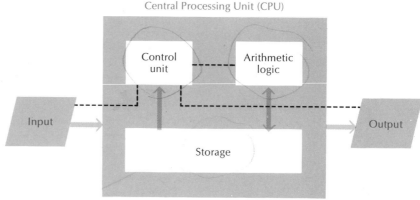

Fig. 4.8   The logical structure of a computer.

formed. The results are transmitted back to storage from the arithmetic/
logic unit.

5. Each calculation required in the program is performed as in steps 3 and 4.

6. Upon encountering a print statement, the control unit transfers the desired quantities to the output device, which performs the required output operation.

Exercises

4.4 Name the logical "blocks" of a computer and describe their functions.

4.5 Do the corresponding logical blocks exist in the desk or pocket calculator? If so, describe them.

4.6 INTERNAL STORAGE

In the short history of electronic computers, many different devices have been used for internal storage of information. These include *mercury delay lines* on early computers, *magnetic drum*, and the relatively long-lived *magnetic core*. More recently *thin film* and *plated wire* storage devices have been used to a limited extent. With the announcement of the IBM System/370, Model 145, IBM introduced into their line *monolithic* storage, which uses semiconductor devices. Semiconductor technology for computer storage has been developed to a high degree and is now commonly used in computers, both large and small. Many new and exotic devices are at various stages of research and development with the emphasis on higher speed, greatly increased storage capacities, and lower cost. However, the magnetic core is still commonly used, and an understanding of how it functions provides the beginner with a useful insight as to how a computer works.

THE MAGNETIC CORE   The relationship between an electrical current and magnetism is an important physical principle. That is, electric current flowing through a conductor will produce a magnetic field with a direction dependent on the direction of current flow. Furthermore, under certain conditions a magnetic field can cause an electric current to flow through a wire. These principles are fundamental to nearly every type of electrical and electronic equipment today and are the basis for the design of modern computer storage units. It is well known that if the current within a wire is shut off, the magnetic field will disappear. However, the effects of it will remain if the wire is near a piece of iron, since the field caused by the current will produce a magnetism within the iron. The effect is even more pronounced if the material is a small core made from a ferromagnetic material through which the wire has been threaded. Such a magnetic core is now commonly used as a storage device for electronic digital computers, mainly because of its following properties and characteristics:

1. It can easily be magnetized in either of two directions.
2. It will retain its magnetism indefinitely if not disturbed.
3. A minimum or "threshold" current will change magnetization.
4. It can be manufactured in extremely small sizes (some barely larger than the period at the end of this sentence).

The concept of the magnetic core is shown in Figure 4.9. In Figure 4.9(a) the current is being applied and a magnetic field results according to the conventional laws of physics. After the current flow has ceased the field remains as shown in Figure 4.9(b). Reversal of the current flow causes reversal of the field, which again is retained after the current is stopped, as illustrated in Figures 4.9(c) and (d). If magnetism in one direction is equivalent to being 'off" or "0," then magnetism in the other direction can be considered "on" or "1," thus representing any on-off device or a binary number. In large computers, millions of such cores are used to store data and instructions. They are incorporated into the computer by stringing each core on a pair of wires as illustrated in Figure 4.9(e). (This takes on the appearance of a screen with a core located at each point of crossing of a pair of wires, as illustrated by the core plane in Figure 4.10.) Any given core can be turned "on" or "off" by the

Fig. 4.9 Magnetic cores.

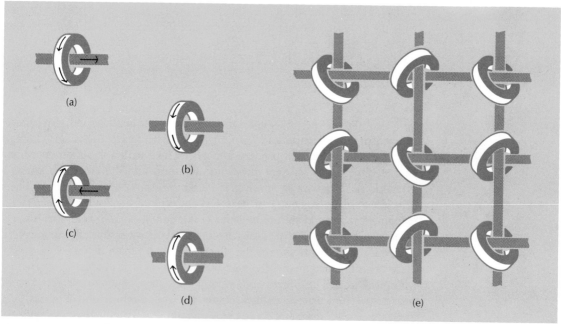

(a)

(b)

(c)

(d)

(e)

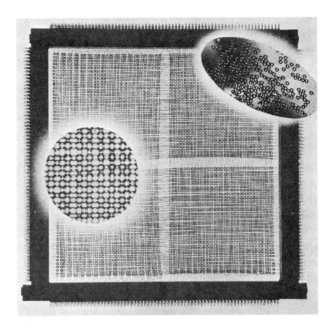

Fig. 4.10 Magnetic core plane. (Courtesy IBM Corporation)

pair of wires running through its center. The pair of wires which pass through each core obviously serves the need for placing information in storage; additional wires are used to read it out again.

Exercise

4.6 What are the characteristics of magnetic cores that make them useful as computer storage devices? *magnetive rotation in either of two direction small size*

MONOLITHIC STORAGE With the advent of third-generation computers, microminiature electronic circuits (termed *monolithic integrated circuits*) came into common use. These exceedingly small units replaced the transistorized circuits of the second generation (which had replaced the large and bulky vacuum tubes of the first generation) in forming so-called logic circuits. These logic circuits provide the basic arithmetic and decision-making ability. With the IBM System/370, Model 145, which was introduced in 1970, monolithic circuitry was adopted for internal storage use. By employing the now commonly used solid state technology, small chips measuring about one eighth of an inch square contain 128 storage bits (equivalent to 128 cores) and the associated circuitry. As shown in Figure 4.11, two storage array chips are mounted on a half-inch-square module. Thus, one of these small modules has storage capacity of 512 bits. These modules are, in turn, mounted on $4\frac{3}{4}$ inch cards as shown

Fig. 4.11 Mono-
lithic storage array
module. (Courtesy IBM
Corporation)

in Figure 4.12. With present-day chip technology, the size of such units has
been further reduced.

Significant advantages of the monolithic storage over core storage include
increased speed, lower cost, reduced space requirements, and simpler serviceability. On the other hand, one disadvantage is that power is required to
maintain the state of the circuit, so data is lost when the electrical power is
turned off. Core storage, as we have learned, retains its magnetized state even
if the power is removed.

**4.7
AUXILIARY
STORAGE DEVICES**

THE NATURE OF AUXILIARY STORAGE   Modern data processing techniques
require large storage capabilities and high-speed input and output devices to
take full advantage of the phenomenal internal speed of computers. A student
information system is a prime example of a system with large storage requirements. To store all of the required information in main storage of even a very
large computer would be impractical. This becomes apparent if we consider
that a typical-size student information record consists of approximately 1000
characters (equivalent to a "1000-column card"). Using the entire storage of a

Fig. 4.12 Mono-
lithic storage array card.
(Courtesy IBM
Corporation)

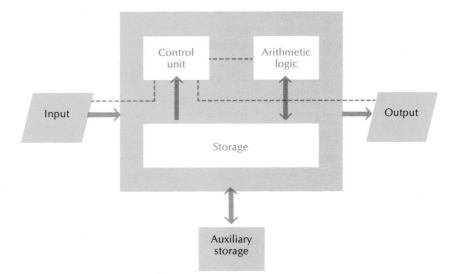

Fig. 4.13 Computer with auxiliary storage.

very large computer with 1 million storage positions, it would be possible to accommodate only 1000 students. Due to the high cost of main storage, it is currently impractical to maintain large data bases in this way.* As a result, auxiliary storage devices are commonly used, the three most frequently encountered being magnetic tape, magnetic disk, and magnetic drum. Figure 4.13 is a schematic representation of a computer equipped with auxiliary storage. The principal advantage of auxiliary storage is high capacity at a relatively low price; auxiliary storage devices will commonly have a capacity of 100 to over 1000 times the capacity of main storage. The principal disadvantage lies in its low speed relative to the speed of main storage. Note that information stored in auxiliary storage must first be read into main storage before it is processed in the system. Transfer of information from main storage is typically ten or more times faster than transfer from auxiliary storage. In addition, mechanical features of auxiliary devices further degrade their speeds when used as storage mediums.

MAGNETIC TAPE   Magnetic tape units function in much the same manner as ordinary home tape recorders. That is, a tape drive machine is used to transport a magnetic tape strip while the recording or reading of information takes place. The tape reel contains 2400 feet of half-inch-wide tape and has the capacity to

---

*Many techniques currently in the research and development stages are intended to provide tremendous increases in main storage capacity at low cost. However, as users become more sophisticated, data processing needs appear to stay continually at least one jump ahead of technological developments.

store approximately 250,000 fully punched cards. A typical tape drive with a tape mounted in place is shown in Figure 4.14.

The relatively low cost of storing vast quantities of information is a distinct advantage of magnetic tape. However, its principal disadvantage lies in the fact that records in a tape file must be in a particular sequence and must be processed in that sequence. In a student grade processing system, records are processed sequentially beginning with the lowest student file number and proceeding through the highest. This is an ideal tape application. On the other hand, nonsequential, or *random,* processing is impractical with tape. For instance, assume that a student information file is stored sequentially on tape and the computer has just completed answering a request from a typewriter for information on James Anderson. If a counselor keys in a request for information on Alfred Zener, it would·be necessary to search the entire tape, which might require a minute or more. For a system servicing several hundred such requests per hour, this slow speed would be totally impractical. For such *random processing* applications, magnetic disk (described in the next section) is commonly employed.

In addition to serving as an auxiliary storage device, magnetic tape is commonly used for input/output. Although slow compared to core storage,

Fig. 4.14 Magnetic tape drive. (Courtesy IBM Corporation)

2 5 tamu an fuit on Carole

magnetic tape is very fast compared to card readers; a typical tape input speed would be equivalent to a card reader speed of 25,000 cards per minute. It is quite common for a data processing installation with a large computer to utilize one or more small computers for input and output operations exclusively. Typically, data from cards is read by the smaller computer and written on tape for input to the large machine; likewise, output from the large computer is written on high-speed tape which is used by the smaller computer for printing reports.

MAGNETIC DISK   A magnetic disk unit consists of rotating metal disks coated with a magnetic material capable of storing information is much the same way as magnetic tape. Due to design of the disk and the associated disk drive, information can be read or written in other than a sequential manner; thus, the disk is commonly referred to as a *direct access* or *random access device.* A magnetic disk unit consists of a stack of disks (resembling a set of phonograph records in appearance) rotating on a common shaft. A removable disk pack and a disk drive are shown in Figure 4.15.

The disk surfaces, which rotate at a high speed, are read and written upon by a movable read-write mechanism which provides the disk with its versatility. Any given piece of information can be located and read from the surface of a

Fig. 4.15 Magnetic disk unit and closeup of the disk. (Courtesy IBM Corporation)

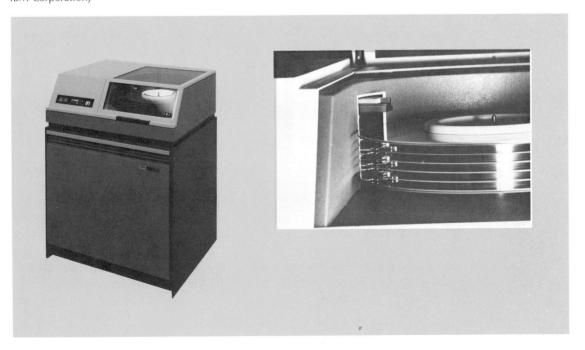

disk in less than one tenth of a second, which provides the disk with a significant advantage over tape for many types of applications. Depending upon the type of disk system, capacities range from 2 million to 100 million characters, which compares favorably with magnetic tape. However, the cost of the removable disk packs is approximately 20 times the cost of a reel of tape.

Both magnetic tape and disk are commonly encountered, and each has its place in the computer system. For many business data processing applications, tape is completely adequate (and cheaper); for other applications, disk is necessary. In Chapter 12, we will study magnetic tape and disk in more detail.

Exercise

4.7 What is meant by auxiliary storage? Distinguish between sequential processing and random processing; give an example of each, and specify which type of auxiliary storage device is most commonly used for each.

4.8
**CATEGORIES OF
COMPUTERS**

THE GENERAL PURPOSE MACHINE Preceding descriptions relate to the general-purpose stored program digital computer—computers which can be programmed to perform a variety of operations, from calculating paychecks to computing satellite orbits. A very common practice in the industry is to classify computers by their cost and size. Although there are no hard and fast rules for classifying computers, the following figures are typical.

	Purchase Price	Monthly Rental
Small	$ 200,000	$ 4,000
Medium	800,000	16,000
Large	2,000,000	40,000
Super	5,000,000	100,000

In general, as the size and cost go up, so do the capabilities of the machine in a number of areas. For instance, a small computer might have a maximum internal storage capability of 50,000 positions, the input and output devices might be relatively limited in versatility and speed, and the auxiliary storage capacity might be fairly limited in size and speed. (In descriptions of this type it is somewhat "dangerous" to quote figures, since what is universally true today can be untrue tomorrow. Technology advancements in this field seem to come at a breathtaking pace.) A large computer will commonly have in excess of a million positions of storage, the capability for handling a huge variety of input/output devices, and auxiliary storage devices with capacities in excess of a billion positions. In fact, it is common practice with a large computer to use one or more medium-sized computers to perform all the input and output operations. For example, a medium computer might be used to load data from slow-speed input devices onto magnetic disk. The data is then read from high-speed disk into the large machine. Conversely, the large computer writes output to disk which the medium or small machine prints for ordinary reports.

Summarizing, we can conclude that the progression from a small or medium computer to a large or super computer includes the following improvements.

1. Speed of operation increases.
2. Storage capability, both internal and auxiliary, increases.
3. Operating systems for automatically controlling the computer become more powerful and flexible.
4. A broader selection of more powerful languages becomes available.
5. Greater versatility is present for a broader base of applications.

MINICOMPUTERS We can hardly read a magazine or newspaper without encountering some mention of a minicomputer doing one thing or another. One problem in discussing minicomputers is in deciding upon a proper definition of just what a minicomputer is. Minicomputers are generally categorized as physically small, inexpensive computers with limited input/output and storage capabilities. Furthermore, they are characterized by a relatively small basic data unit size within the storage.* Where a medium or small computer might be capable of handling several different types of jobs concurrently, the true mini is much more limited in this respect. Characteristically, the mini has fewer types of instructions, which decreases both its capability and its overall speed. However, with rapidly changing technology, to define in detail the characteristics of a minicomputer is not too practical (any such definition appears to be constantly changing). On the other hand, in 1970 the following would have been reasonably descriptive of a minicomputer.

1. Input and output tend to be limited to relatively basic devices such as typewriter-like units, paper tape reader punches and television-like terminals. Generally, the larger the mini, the greater variety of devices.
2. Limited storage capacity ranging from 8000 to 16,000 positions.
3. Relatively low-speed and low-capacity auxiliary storage devices.
4. Relatively crude operating systems, if any at all, and a limited selection of programming languages.

Computers such as the Digital Equipment PDP 11 family further compound the confusion. The smallest computer in this series, the 11/05, is

---

*Most minis use between 8 and 16 binary digits for the internal storage word, although one mini is currently available with 32. The concepts of bits and words is described in Chapter 6.

Fig. 4.16 The Digital Equipment Classic minicomputer. (Courtesy Digital Equipment Corporation)

definitely a mini in its price, size, and performance. However, the larger 11/70 has a price tag in the small computer range and has some of the capabilities of computers in the low end of the medium range. Although Digital Equipment does not advertise the larger members of the PDP 11 family as minicomputers, they are commonly referred to as such in the field.

Similarly, the Hewlett-Packard HP3000, which is termed a mini by the manufacturer, is mini only in the sense that it is a miniature sophisticated computing system complete with a large variety of versatile input/output devices, large internal storage capability, large high-speed auxiliary devices, and a sophisticated operating system. Furthermore, its price is in the $100,000 -200,000 range. The price and performance is definitely within the small computer range.

Regardless of what a mini is, they have found wide acceptance and are used for a broad range of applications. This is illustrated by the following article captions taken from *Computerworld,** a weekly computer and data processing newspaper. In each case, the computer manufacturer and the computer model are indicated in parentheses.

- Insurance Firm's Mini System
  Cuts Plan Revision Costs
  (Digital Equipment Corporation)

- Minis Process Member's Tabs
  at Two Country Clubs
  (Basic/Four Corporation—Model 400)

- Minis Play Part in Army,
  Air Force Ordnance Tests
  (Hewlett-Packard HP2100)

- *Build around Twin Minis*
  Calif. Police System Proves
  Match for "Bad Guys"
  (Digital Equipment Corporation—PDP 11/40)

- Mini Performs Administrative
  Functions for College
  (Varian Data Machines—V73)

- *For a Net of Catalog Showrooms*
  Real-Time Mini System Watches
  Inventory in 500-Mile Area
  (Digital Equipment Corporation—PDP 11/40)

- *City Outgrew Batch*
  Mini Ends Search for
  Data Base System
  (Microdata 1600)

- Mini Keeps Track of Electronics
  Parts for Company
  (Data General Corporation—Nova 1200)

The mini has indeed come of age.

MICROPROCESSORS With the coining of the term "minicomputer," can the microcomputer be far behind? (And what comes after the micro?) Where

---

*The last caption was taken from the March 1, 1976 issue of *Computerworld;* all the others are from the February 23, 1976 issue.

the mini has been with us in concept (if not in name) since 1959, the *micro-computer* or *microprocessor* is a result of recent advances in Large Scale Integrated circuits (LSI). Introduced by Intel Corporation in 1971, microprocessors have had a huge impact on not only the computer industry but on many other industries as well. Basically, a microprocessor is the control unit and arithmetic logic unit of a computer, all on a single chip less than one quarter of an inch square. It is difficult to conceive that the several thousand electronic components which require a cabinet the size of an ordinary desk can be etched onto such a chip. The low cost (as little as $10) and small size of microprocessors has made it possible to put a "brain" in all sorts of machines. We can even buy a sewing machine controlled by a microprocessor; within a very short time, microprocessors will be used in automobiles to optimize the control of the engine and provide better pollution control. There appears to be no end to the possibilities of this amazing device. Within the computer field itself, the microprocessor is causing much head scratching about computer design philosophy. Where a large central system appeared to be the practical, economical way to satisfy data processing needs in 1970, the microprocessor is now providing distributed processing capability on the spot at a lower cost. By combining microprocessor chips, it is possible to construct microcomputers with the capacity of many small minis. The Texas Instruments 990 micro/minicomputer family (Figure 4.17), which is designed around the TMS9900 microprocessor, is typical. The Model 990/4 Microcomputer, which is a complete computer on a single printed circuit board, is designed as a controlling device for other computer components (control of terminals and other devices). The cost of this unit with 8000 positions of storage is $512. The upper end of this family, still designed around the 9900 microprocessor, is the Model 990/10, which is classified as a general-purpose minicomputer. With its 16,000 positions of storage, the 990/10 costs $1968. Amazingly, this computer includes an operating system and the languages Fortran, Cobol, and Basic. On the other hand, it should be recognized that these costs are for the computer itself. Where on

Fig. 4.17 (a) The TI 990 microprocessor; (b) the Model 990 minicomputer. (Courtesy Texas Instruments, Incorporated)

(a)

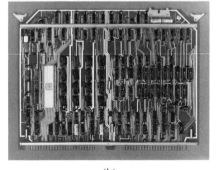

(b)

one hand computer costs have dropped dramatically, the cost of peripheral equipment such as terminals and disk storage devices has not. (The cost of a TV-like terminal might be as much as the computer itself.) The overall cost of a computer "system" will thus be considerably higher than the price tag for the computer itself. However, there is no doubt that the microprocessor and microcomputer will find a burgeoning use in our society.

Answers to Preceding Exercises

4.1 a. 5; b. 1; c. 6; d. 8; e. 2; f. 4; g. 3; h. 7.

4.2 See descriptions in Section 4.3.

4.3
1. Blank card.
2. Blank card.
3. Blank card.
4. Get first input record.
5. Write information as follows:
     first field to card 1
     second field to card 2
     third field to card 3
6. Get next input record.
7. Compare first field of card to number on card 1; if different, skip to step 12.
8. Add second field to number on card 2 with sum replacing previous contents of card 2.
9. Multiply second field by third field with product remaining in calculator.
10. Add product from calculator to number on card 3; record sum on card 3.
11. Go back to step 6.
12. Set aside input record just read.
13. Divide number on card 2 into number on card 3 with quotient remaining in calculator.
14. Record results on summary form as follows:
     card 1 recorded under student number
     card 2 recorded under cumulative units

card 3 recorded under cumulative points quotient in calculator recorded under GPA
15. Retrieve input record set aside in step 12.
16. Replace cards 1, 2, and 3 with blank cards.
17. Go back to step 5.

4.4 Input, output, arithmetic-logic, control, and storage.

4.5 Yes.
Input—keyboard.
Storage and output—display indicators from which the results may be read by the user.
Arithmetic logic—internal wheels and gears or electronic circuits.
Control—the operator.

4.6 The core is easily magnetized in either of two directions; it will retain its magnetism indefinitely if not disturbed; a threshold current will change the magnetization; and it can be manufactured in very small sizes.

4.7 Auxiliary storage is storage which is used to supplement the main storage of a computer. Its capacity is usually much greater than that of main storage, but its access time is greater. Commonly used devices are magnetic tape and disk.

Additional Exercises

4.8 Matching. Match each item in 1–8 with the corresponding description in a–h.

1. second-generation computer
2. microprocessor
3. magnetic disk
4. third-generation computer
5. magnetic core
6. magnetic tape
7. first-generation computer
8. central processing unit (CPU)

7 a. Characterized by the use of vacuum tubes.
6 b. Requires the use of sequential processing methods.
8 c. Consists of the arithmetic/logic and control portions of the computer.
1 d. Marked by wide acceptance of higher-level languages.
3 e. Provides fast access to large data files.
5 f. Used for internal storage in computers.
2 g. Is virtually a computer on a chip.
4 h. Hardware designed for use with operating systems.

4.9 Matching. Referring to the pigeonhole example, match each instruction type in 1–5 to the corresponding instruction taken from the example in a–h.

1. input   2. arithmetic
3. output   4. unconditional branch
5. conditional branch

4 a. Go back to step 3.
1 b. Get next input record.
2 c. Add product from calculator to number on card 17 with . . .
5 d. . . . If different, skip to step 9.
3 e. Record results on summary form as follows:
2 f. Multiply second field (units) by third field (grade) with . . .
4 g. Go back to step 2.
1 h. Get the first input record.

4.10 True-False. Determine whether each of the following is true or false.

T a. The term "software" refers to programs used with computers.
F b. Computers have evolved through three generations of machines, and, because of the high quality of current machines, further significant evolution is highly unlikely.
F c. Some commonly used computer input devices are the card reader, paper tape reader, optical character reader, and magnetic core.
F d. The speeds of modern card readers and printers have increased to the point where the input and output devices are far faster than the computer itself.
T e. The task of directing operations within the computer is the function of the control unit.
F f. The control unit, storage, and auxiliary storage make up what is commonly referred to as the central processing unit (CPU) of the computer.
T g. Magnetic tape, magnetic disk, and magnetic drum are commonly used auxiliary storage devices.
T h. Auxiliary storage is commonly used to greatly increase the storage capacity of a computer at a moderate cost.
F i. An advantage of magnetic tape over magnetic disk is that records can be processed either sequentially or randomly on tape.
F j. To be classed as a minicomputer, a machine must have no more than 16,000 positions of storage.

4.11 Multiple Choice. Determine which answer best completes or answers each of the following statements.

3 a. One of the earliest known computational devices is the (1) electromechanical computer, (2) Pascal's adding machine, (3) abacus, (4) Mark I.
4 b. Charles Babbage is known for his work with (1) the analytic engine, (2) the mechanical equivalent of the modern digital computer,

(3) the difference engine, (4) all of the preceding, (5) none of the preceding.

c. Third-generation computers are characterized by (1) special operating systems to improve their overall efficiency, (2) heavy emphasis on the use of high-level languages, (3) typically the IBM System/360, (4) all of the preceding, (5) both 1 and 3.

d. In computer terminology, a sequence of instructions is commonly referred to as (1) a pigeonhole analogy, (2) a program, (3) an unconditional branch, (4) data.

e. The basic components of the modern digital computer are (1) storage, input, output, and the control unit, (2) storage, input, output, the control unit, and the sorter, (3) the central processing unit, storage, input, output, and the arithmetic unit, (4) storage, input, output, the control unit, and the arithmetic unit.

f. Some commonly used output devices are (1) video display unit, plotter, card punch, and accounting machine, (2) magnetic tape unit, line printer, audio response unit, and video display unit, (3) paper tape punch, line printer, reproducing punch, and plotter, (4) plotter, console keyboard, video display unit, and interpreter.

g. One of the following is *not* a characteristic of the monolithic integrated circuits for use as internal storage devices: (1) increased speed over core storage, (2) simplified serviceability, (3) retains storage information even when current is turned off, (4) employs solid state technology, (5) all of the above are characteristic of monolithic integrated circuits.

h. Auxiliary storage devices (1) consist primarily of additional core storage units, (2) are no longer commonly used because of the widespread availability of core and semiconductor storage, (3) have capacities of one hundred to one thousand times the capacities of internal storage units, (4) use the latest in semiconductor storage techniques.

i. The primary disadvantage of magnetic tape for use in computers is that (1) records must be stored and processed sequentially, (2) the tape easily breaks during processing runs, (3) due to the required high quality the tape is very expensive, (4) the data recorded on the tape can easily be erased.

j. One of the following is not descriptive of the microcomputer: (1) can use operating systems, (2) can use high-level languages, (3) was first introduced with the third-generation microelectronic technology found in the IBM 360, (4) very expensive due to extremely small size, (5) both 3 and 4.

4.12 Other Problems and Projects

a. Research and prepare a report on one of the following events or people significant to the development of the modern computer: Charles Babbage, John von Neumann, Mark I, Eniac, Edvac, or Univac I.

b. A principle (P) when compounded at an annual rate (r) for a given number of years (n) will yield an amount (A) as computed by the following formula:

$$A = P(1 + r)^n$$

For example, if $P = \$500$, $r = 00.5$ (5%) and $n = 7$ years, then

$$A = 500(1.05)^7$$

This exercise involves preparing a set of instructions similar to those of the pigeonhole analogy. In this case, each input record consists of the principle P, the interest rate r and the number of years n. Write a detailed set of directions to calculate the amount A for each input record. Use as many of the slots 1–6 as required to record data and any needed constants and slots from 7 on for the instructions. Remember that each instruction must involve one simple operation.

c. Operation of computers and computer components are commonly measured in terms of milliseconds (0.001 second) and microseconds (0.000001 second), and now even in terms of nanoseconds (0.000000001 second). If electricity travels at the rate of 186,000 miles per second, how far will it travel in one nanosecond? Conjecture on the implications of such short times regarding the electronic design of computer components.

d. Obtain information from one of the computer manufacturers listed below and summarize the general characteristics of the computers which they manufacture. Include descriptions of storage capacity ranges, input/output units, auxiliary storage devices and other pertinent data. (*Note*: Most of this general descriptive data is available from local sales offices of the computer manufacturer.)

Burroughs Corporation
6071 Second Ave.
Detroit, Mich.   48232

Control Data Corporation
8100 34th Ave. So.
Minneapolis, Minn.   55420

International Business Machines Corporation
112 East Post Road
White Plains, New York   10601

Univac Division of Sperry Rand Corporation
1290 Avenue of the Americas
New York, New York 10019

Digital Equipment Corporation
Maynard, Mass.   01754

Honeywell Information Systems
200 Smith St.
Waltham, Mass.   02154

National Cash Register Company
Main and K Streets
Dayton, Ohio   45409

Hewlett-Packard
1501 Page Mill Road
Palo Alto, Ca.   94304

Chapter

5

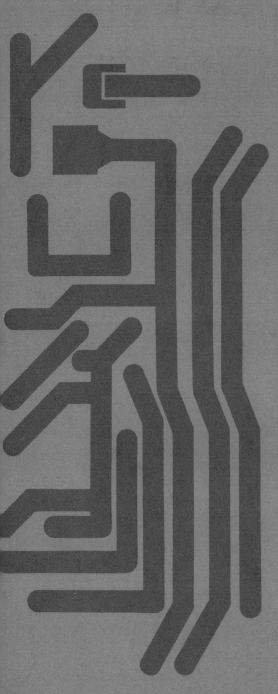

Communicating with the Computer

5.1

BASIC INPUT/
OUTPUT MEDIA

CHANGING CIRCUMSTANCES   Concurrent with explosive evolution of the computer we are now seeing a huge growth in the general area of *data entry*. For many years the punched card served as the basic means for entering data into the computer. In many cases, a very large computer might use one or more small computers to read data from cards onto magnetic tape. Then that data could be read from the tape into the larger computer at a very high rate of speed. (Indeed, this method is still commonly used.) However, in recent years a number of factors have arisen, such as:

1. The high cost of recording data in punched cards.
2. The widespread need for recording data in the field in a machine readable form.
3. The wide use of telecommunications.
4. The widespread availability of low-cost minicomputers.

These factors have spawned an entire industry within the computer industry in which we see everything from machines capable of reading handprinted characters, to voice recognition devices, to bar code (supermarket) readers, to pressure sensitive pens, and so on. All of this new equipment has been developed in an effort to provide information to the computer in the simplest and most direct manner possible.

On the other side of the computer process, *output,* we have the traditional printed page for getting information from the machine to us humans. Again, circumstances and evolving technology spell a changing environment. For one thing, the cost of computer paper has increased several times in the past few years—to the point where a small company might be spending thousands of dollars per year for paper. (Prior to the rapid paper price increases in the early 1970s, many schools operated their instructional computer centers using surplus paper or obsolete forms donated by local industrial and business firms. To a large extent, those surpluses and obsolete forms are now used by the firms themselves rather than being given away. The reason: high paper cost.) Other factors have also come into play:

1. The storage of extensive records printed on paper can be a severe space problem.
2. Handling extensive volumes of printed output can lead to a clumsy and inefficient bookkeeping task.
3. The wide use of telecommunications yielding a direct link-up to the computer simply requires other means than the printed page for getting information out of the machine.

As a result of these many factors, the use of microfilm as a printed page replacement is widespread. Furthermore, the common use of telecommunications is seeing ever-increasing use of video display units.

THE CARD READER   However, we must not get the idea that the card reader generally is ready for the junk pile. On the contrary, use of the punched card for computer input is still very common. Card readers are available with speeds ranging from a few hundred to 2000 cards per minute. The readers shown in Figure 5.1 are typical of the two different types available. The unit in 5.1(a) is a combination card reader and punch. Input data punched in cards is read in the right half of the machine, and output is punched into cards in the left half of the machine. This particular unit is commonly referred to as a *parallel reader* since the card is read row by row; that is, the card proceeds through the machine as illustrated below (usually 9-edge, or the bottom, first).

Parallel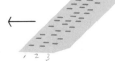

As each row comes under a group of 80 reading units (one for each column), that row is read and stored in an internal buffer storage within the card reader. After the complete card is read into the buffer, it is then transmitted to the computer storage.

The other two units in Figure 5.1 are *serial readers*. That is, the card progresses through the reader column by column as illustrated below.

serial

As the 12 positions of a given row are read, the information is transmitted directly to the internal storage of the computer. Such a serial card reader will read and store one card column at a time.

Fig. 5.1   (a) Card read/punch; (b), (c), serial card readers. [(a) and (c) courtesy IBM Corporation, (b) courtesy Digital Equipment Corporation]

MACHINE READING   Like most specialized areas, the field of data processing includes its own terminology which is not very meaningful to the person not

(a)   (b)   (c)

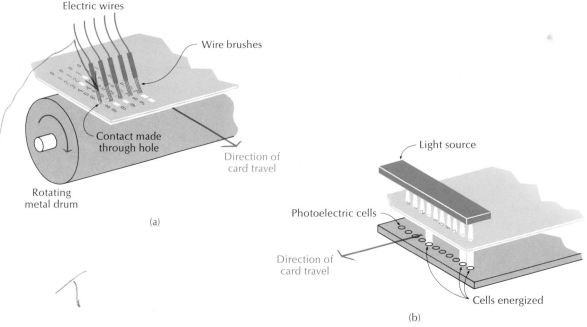

Electric wires

Wire brushes

Contact made
through hole

Direction of
card travel

Rotating
metal drum

(a)

Light source

Photoelectric cells

Direction of
card travel

Cells energized

(b)

Fig. 5.2   Reading a card:
(a) brush reader; (b)
photoelectric reader.

wears out

familiar with the field. In this and preceding chapters, the ability of machines to read a card has been referred to. In Chapter 2, it was pointed out that only the punched holes in the card, not the printing, is read; obviously, the notion of a machine reading a card is not to be equated to the manner in which a human reads a page. Most machines "read" the holes in a card by either of two methods: (1) with earlier machines, such as the reader in Figure 5.1(a), the card passes between a wire brush (or set of brushes) and a metal roller as shown in Figure 5.2(a); (2) with most modern computers, the card passes between a set of light sources and corresponding photocells as shown in Figure 5.2(b). (A photocell is a light-sensitive device which will generate electricity when exposed to a light source.) In Figure 5.2(a) the unpunched portion of the card acts as an insulator which allows no electrical current to flow. Similarly, the card in Figure 5.2(b) screens the photocell from the light source, with no current resulting. However, in the punched portion of the card where the brush contacts the roller through the punched hole, current flows until contact is broken by the continually moving card. In a similar fashion, the light source shines through only the punched holes in 5.2(b), thus generating a current in the photocells. The parallel reader of Figure 5.1(a) uses wire brushes, where the serial readers of Figures 5.1 (b) and (c) use photocells.

Many card readers are designed with two reading stations. The card is read at the first station, then reread at the second, and the readings are compared. If there is a difference, then an error has occurred and the reader will stop.

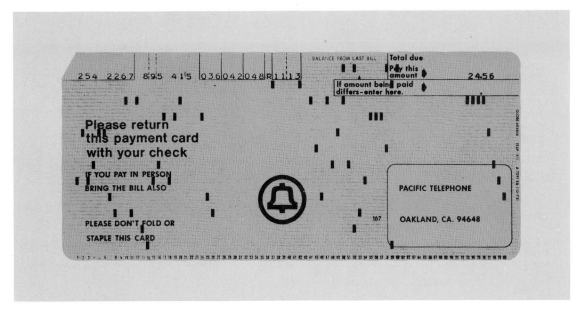

Fig. 5.3 Punched card output.

CARD OUTPUT   In addition to serving as an input medium, the punched card is also used for output. The telephone bill shown in Figure 5.3 is an instance where the computer output is punched into a card and that card is used as a document. In many earlier computers and in some small business systems, the punched card is used as the basic input medium, for storage of files, and as an output medium. For example, consider a card-oriented master-detail system for maintaining inventory control. In Figure 5.4 each inventory master record is followed by its corresponding transaction records (indicating sales and receipts). Processing produces, as output, summary reports and an updated master for storage of results and use during the next processing cycle. This concept is familiar from the unit record principles presented in Chapter 2. In spite of rapidly evolving electronic techniques, some types of applications remain well suited for card processing. Figure 5.5 is a card-oriented computer system (using the 96-column card) with all the capabilities, and more, of the unit record equipment described in Chapter 2.

Exercise

5.1 In preparing a data set, a student incorrectly punched the digit 3 in a column instead of 8. Being thrifty, he put a small piece of mending tape over the 3 punch and repunched the column with an 8. Will this work? Explain.

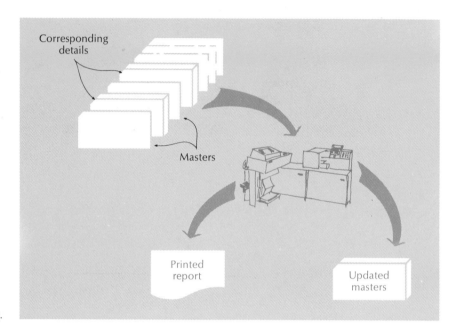

Fig. 5.4   Card processing.

Fig. 5.5   A card processing computer. (Courtesy IBM Corporation)

PUNCHED PAPER TAPE   Punched paper tape is another old standby I/O (input/output) medium for use with the computer. In fact, it is used in some cases for input, output, and offline storage in much the same way as cards are. The tape itself is a continuous strip of paper into which information may be punched. One commonly used type consists of 8 channels which are used for data coding (as compared to 12 rows on the punched card). Figure 5.6(a) is a short strip punched with the 8-channel character set, and 5.6(b) shows a reel of tape. A little detective work here will show that the code used is essentially equivalent to the card code where the combination punched X, O is equivalent to the 12 punch, X to the 11 punch and O to the 0 punch. (Referring to Tables 3.2 and 3.3 of Chapter 3, we see that this code is identical to the IBM 96-column card code.) The small sprocket holes are used for feeding the tape through the reading and punching machines and contain no coded information. Into each position or *frame* on the tape, one character can be coded; thus a frame corresponds to a card column. However, unlike the card, tape is not limited to a maximum of 80 characters per record. In fact, a record may be as short or as long as required; the end of a record is signaled by a punch in the EL, or end of line, channel.

Although earlier mechanical paper tape readers were relatively slow, modern photoelectric readers will read at speeds up to 2000 frames per second, equivalent to 25 cards per second. However, punches operate at less than one tenth this speed, which is relatively slow. Figure 5.7 shows an inexpensive tape reader and a tape punch. Because of the relatively low-cost readers and punches available, paper tape is commonly used on small computers for input

Fig. 5.6   (a) Eight-channel paper tape code; (b) a reel of paper tape.

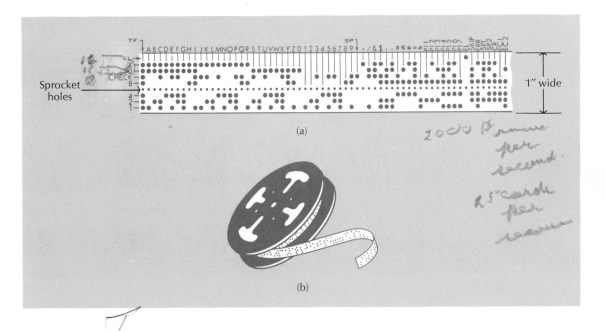

(a)

(b)

Fig. 5.7 Paper tape units: reader and punch. (Courtesy IBM Corporation)

and output. In particular, timesharing systems have made wide use of paper tape partially because of the ease with which data from paper tape can be transmitted over telephone wires.

Another common use for paper tape is for recording source data at the point of origin for later entry into the computer. For example, a computer service company might contract with a number of small businesses to process their records. Through use of special cash registers or accounting machines, a record of all transactions is punched into paper tape. At the end of the day, these tapes are delivered to a computer service company, the records are processed, and the finished reports delivered the next morning. Because of the convenience of paper tape and its relative compactness, such tapes are easily and cheaply sent by mail. Figure 5.8 illustrates this concept.

As we can see, the continuous form of paper tape provides a distinct advantage over punched cards: that is, the record length is not limited to 80 characters. Furthermore, tape is far less bulky, an advantage for handling and mailing, and considerably cheaper than cards. However, the continuous nature of tape also contributes to its major shortcoming. That is, the unit record concept is lost and with it goes the convenience relating to correcting an incorrect entry and adding or deleting records. With a card file, the incorrect record is replaced with a corrected card; with paper tape, it is necessary to splice in the correction or else repunch the entire tape. However, in spite of these limitations, paper tape finds an important niche as an input/output medium even today.

Exercise

5.2   A paper tape reader reads at the rate of 1200 frames per second. What card reader speed is this equivalent to in cards per minute? $\frac{1200 \times 60}{80} = 900$

5.2
PRINTED OUTPUT

Computer printers come in all sizes, types, and prices. For this description, we will consider them in three categories: *serial*, which print a character at a time like a typewriter; *line*, which print a full line at a time; and *page*, which print an entire page much like a printing press.

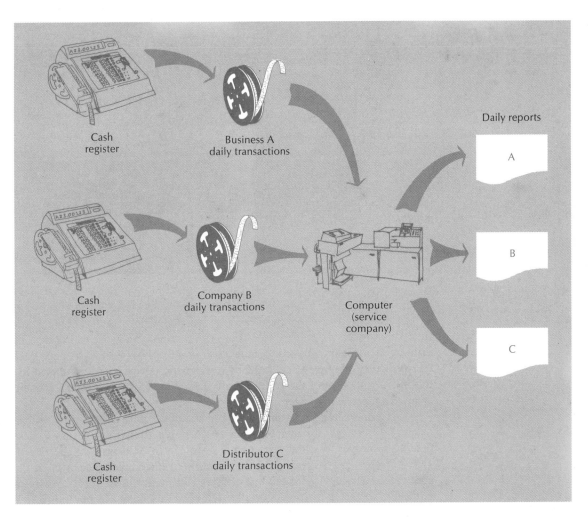

Fig. 5.8 A centralized processing system using paper tape.

SERIAL PRINTERS The most basic of the serial printers are little more than electric typewriters, which fall in the general category of *impact printers* since they print through a printing element which impacts against the paper. The Teletype was one of the earlier devices used, especially with small computer systems and shared systems whereby the user communicates directly with the computer (this procedure, called timesharing, is described in Chapters 9 and 13). With the introduction of the IBM Selectric typewriter in the 1960s, IBM and a large number of other computer manufacturers adapted it to the computers. The Teletype and an IBM unit, which print at the rates of 10 and 15.5 characters per second, respectively, are shown in Figure 5.9. We will note that both of these include keyboards so that they may be used for input as well as output.

Fig. 5.9 (a) Teletype model 33 ASR data terminal; (b) console keyboard-printer. [(a) courtesy Teletype Corporation, (b) courtesy IBM Corporation]

In recent years, *matrix* printers have become widely used. These devices function in much the same way as the printing unit of a keypunch does. The printing element of a matrix printer consists of a 5×7 array of pins, each of which may be pressed forward by a magnetic device, thereby imprinting through a ribbon onto the page. Figure 5.10 illustrates the printing element array and a set of characters printed by one such device.

A printing speed of 30 characters per second is quite common for matrix printers, so we can see that blinding speed is not the strong point of these devices. However, the unit shown in Figure 5.11(b) will print at the rate of 180 characters per second. (This is somewhat remarkable since it is in the speed range of many low-speed line printers.) The unit shown in Figure 5.11(a) is the Decwriter II (manufactured by Digital Equipment Corporation); it is widely used by a large number of other computer manufacturers. Some inexpensive portable devices utilizing the matrix principle require special heat-sensitive paper and imprint by contact between selected heated wire ends and the paper. Although these units, termed *thermal* printers, are somewhat lower priced than impact printers, the high cost of thermal paper can add up over a period of time. The speed of most of these units is 30 characters per second.

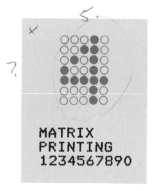

Fig. 5.10 Matrix printing.

LINE PRINTERS   Overall, the line printer (Figure 5.12) is the old standby for computer output. As the name implies, each print operation of a line printer involves printing an entire line. This contrasts to serial printers, where characters in a line are printed one after the other. One of the distinguishing features of any given line printer is its number of print positions—that is, how many printing positions there are on one line. The most commonly encountered

Fig. 5.11 (a) The Decwriter II printer/keyboard; (b) high-speed serial matrix printer. (Courtesy Digital Equipment Corporation)

sizes are 120 and 132. Modern line printers have speeds of up to 2000 lines per minute.

The two most common types of line printers are the *chain* printer and the *drum* printer. In a chain printer, an endless loop chain device into which are mounted the printing characters moves continually past the paper. Each print position consists of a print hammer which, when activated, will cause the desired character to be printed. Thus, as each chain character to be printed moves into position opposite the desired printing position, the hammer is "fired," thus causing the required character to be printed. (The noise created by each of the 132 hammers and the revolving chain is considerable when the printer unit is opened.) For many years the standard of comparison for quality printing was the IBM 1403, the chain printer introduced with the IBM 1401, a widely used second-generation computer.

A drum printer uses a rotating cylindrical drum with rows or bands of characters engraved, one band for each printing position. As with the chain printer, a series of hammers is positioned, one for each band or printing position. As the drum rotates and the paper moves by the printer, hammers are activated in turn, thus causing the printing. The action of the hammer causes the paper to be pressed against the engraved drum through a ribbon to effect the printing operation. Both chain and drum printers are widely used in business and industry. As described in Chapter 2, computer printers employ special

Fig. 5.12 High-speed line printer. (Courtesy IBM Corporation)

continuous-feed forms which are actually one long piece of paper perforated at intervals, as illustrated in Figure 5.13. A special pin feed mechanism allows the use of multiple copy and/or preprinted forms with or without carbon paper. A large number of labor-saving forms have been devised to increase the utility of the printed report. For instance, many companies use so-called *data mailers* to print W2 income tax withholding forms. These are special mailing envelopes completely sealed with selected portions of the various layers of paper coated with carbon material. The impact of the printer thus prints only on those areas of the envelope and the withholding information on the inside. (The next time you get such an envelope, take it apart and see for yourself.) Most companies have a large inventory of preprinted forms for various applications.

PAGE PRINTERS   For most computer systems, the line printer is completely adequate to handle all printed output. However, in some instances, huge volumes of printed output are required. To satisfy this need, a number of page printers capable of printing an entire page at a time are available. In general, these devices use some type of photographic or electronic technique, and some have speeds in excess of 50,000 lines per minute.

In April, 1975, IBM announced their IBM 3800 Printing Subsystem. Using laser and electrophotographic techniques to create the printed images, this system can print at the rate of 13,000 lines per minute. One important feature of the 3800 is its versatility in print size. Where line printers commonly print 10 characters per inch, this system can use any of three sizes: 10, 12, or

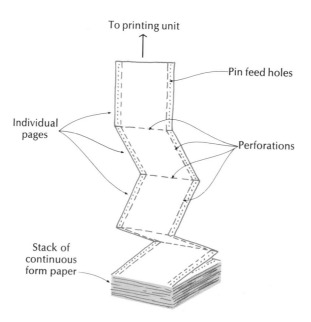

Fig. 5.13 Continuous-form paper.

15 characters per inch. The use of 15 characters per inch makes it possible to print normal computer reports on standard $8\frac{1}{2} \times 11$ inch paper rather than the normal 11×15 inch computer paper. Another significant feature of the 3800 is its ability to create the preprinted form. That is, through use of a special overlay which can be inserted into the machine, both the business form and the desired computer output can be printed simultaneously on plain paper. Unlike many of the earlier high-speed page printers, the quality of the printed results is very good. However, as with all nonimpact printers, it is not possible to use multiple-part forms, thus producing two or more copies. If several copies are required, then the machine must print each page the required number of times (much the same as an ordinary printing press). Although each copy will be an original (in quality), the overall speed is slowed significantly; that is, two copies effectively cuts the machine speed in half.

Exercise

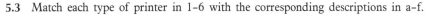

5.3 Match each type of printer in 1–6 with the corresponding descriptions in a–f.

1. matrix	2. impact	3. thermal
4. chain	5. page	6. serial

3 a. Requires the use of specially treated paper.
5 b. The fastest type of printer available.
1 c. Forms characters by an array of dots (much like a football scoreboard).
6 d. Similar in principle to a typewriter.
2 e. Includes both serial and line printers; prints by pressing the paper against a print element (or vice versa).
4 f. Each operation of the printer causes one full line to be printed.

'He Died From an Overdose of Data'

COMPUTER OUTPUT MICROFILM   The storage of records by photographing and reducing the size, commonly referred to as *microfilming*, has been used in business and industry for many years. In recent years, devices have become available which provide for recording printed material to microfilm via magnetic tape: these are termed *Computer Output Microfilm*, or simply COM, devices. Typically a page of computer output is reduced in size from $\frac{1}{24}$ to $\frac{1}{42}$ of the original with the result that an equivalent of 270 computer output pages may be stored on a single 4 × 6 inch sheet of film. Due to the high cost of COM devices, this medium was not widely used except for installations with huge quantities of output and/or those with relatively sophisticated operations. However, during the early 1970s several factors forced many companies to reassess their output needs:

1. Serious paper shortages evolved, resulting in rapidly soaring prices.
2. The storage, handling, and retrieval of ever-growing numbers of computer-generated reports was becoming extremely clumsy and expensive.
3. Increasing postage rates escalated the cost of mailing computer-generated reports. (For instance, Petrolane Corporation, Long Beach, California mails 4.5 million pages per year of computer printouts to 300 branch offices.*)

The case for COM is made very well by the accompanying article from the weekly newspaper *Computerworld*.

AS PAPER COSTS CLIMB, COM SAVINGS MORE SIGNIFICANT

INDIANAPOLIS, Ind. — "Our decision to go to computer output microfilm (COM) encoded for fast retrieval . . . seemed to be a cost-effective measure that would bring us in step with current trends in the DP field.

"But as paper costs skyrocketed, our savings became much more significant," according to R. Michael Ahern, a DP officer with Merchants National Bank and Trust Co. here.

The bank, using COM-generated microfiche instead of conventional paper printouts, along with encoded rolls of microfilm, trimmed an estimated $70,000 in paper costs and saved 9,555 hours of computer time during the first six months of operation, Ahern said.

There are three primary uses for COM at Merchants Bank.

"All reports, except the daily exception reports, are produced in microfiche," Ahern explained. "Our biggest runs are in trial balances for different areas of our operations. For demand deposits, the report, printed on paper, amounted to 4,000 pages a day, stood two feet high and required $2\frac{1}{2}$ hours to print. The same information can be generated on microfiche in 25 minutes from the time the computer tape is loaded until the 17 microfiche masters are produced."

Merchants Bank's Kodak KOM-80 microfilmer uses a 42-to-1 reduction ratio

*Source: *Datamation*, January, 1974.

to produce masters from which circulating duplicates are made. Original fiche remain in the data processing library.

"Our reports fall mostly into the very high-volume, very low-activity category," Ahern said. "Having them on microfiche is extremely important to us in terms of storage and production time. Many of our correspondent banks, for whom we do data processing, have very limited storage areas, which are normally inundated with stacks of paper printout. Now, they can have the same material in a usable form near the person who needs to use it."

Bottleneck Eliminated

A second application for COM is the creation of archival storage of documents such as demand deposit account statements. In the past, documents were filmed using a Recordak Rotoline microfilmer.

"The old procedure added an additional mechanical step to our operation," Ahern said. "Now, we've eliminated a clerical bottleneck and produced some labor savings."

The third COM application involves use of an automatic key index system that eliminates manual searching for microfilmed records.

"Very few banks have their trust department accounting entirely on microfilm," said Gary Kyle, trust department assistant operations officer at Merchants Bank.

10-Second Retrievals

Efforts to automate accounting began with on-line data entry direct from the trust department to the bank's IBM computer. From there, output goes to the microfilmer which produces microfilm encoded for high-speed retrieval. With all the account information stored in plastic magazines containing encoded film, retrieving reports takes as little as 10 seconds, he added.

A typical COM configuration is shown in Figure 5.14, in which computer output is written to a magnetic tape drive which in turn is processed by the COM device from the tape. Whenever the film is to be read, special display units are commonly used which magnify the film image and project it to a screen. A microfilm recorder and corresponding tape unit are shown in Figure 5.15.

With the many advantages of COM, there is little doubt that its use as a computer output medium and even as an input medium will continue to increase rapidly.

Fig. 5.14 Typical COM configuration.

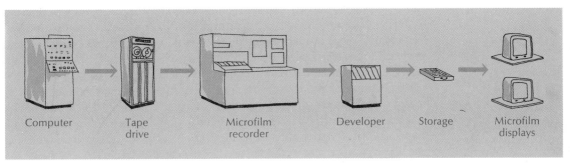

| Computer | Tape drive | Microfilm recorder | Developer | Storage | Microfilm displays |

Fig. 5.15 The Eastman Kodak KOM-90 system. (Courtesy Eastman Kodak Company)

5.3
MAGNETIC
RECORDING
MEDIA

MAGNETIC TAPE AND DISK   As described in Chapter 4, magnetic tape and disk are commonly used input/output media. For instance, data files which are stored on tape or disk can be read into storage at a very high rate of speed for processing and/or updating. Since a single computer is capable of controlling several tape or disk units, results of the processing run can be written out to one or more other tape or disk units. In recent years, computer tape and disk technology have produced two relatively inexpensive media for data input/output: the *tape cassette* and the *diskette*, commonly referred to as the *floppy disk*.

The tape cassette, identical to that of the ordinary home recorder tape cassette, has a capacity of 145,000 characters, which is nearly equivalent to a box of 2000 fully punched cards. Inexpensive cassette input/output units such as the one shown in Figure 5.16 are finding wide use with computers of all sizes.

The "small brother" of magnetic disk storage devices, the floppy disk, is a circular piece of plastic coated on one side with a magnetic material and enclosed in a special envelope 8 inches square. The capacity of a single disk of 250,000 characters is approximately equivalent to that of a box of 2000 cards. Because of its nature, that is, a magnetic recording medium, a single disk may be reused again and again. In comparison to cards which may not be reused, the disk price of two to three times that of a box of cards is quite a bargain. This is clearly a device with great potential in data processing. From the first announcement of the floppy disk (so-called because the disk itself is a thin, flexible piece of plastic), myriad applications and improvements have

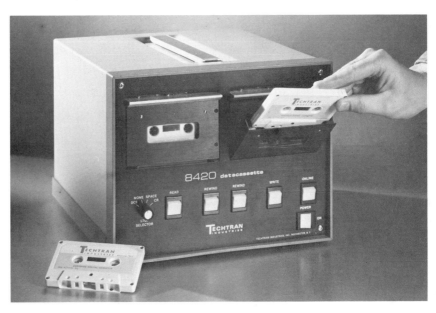

Fig. 5.16 Techtran 8420 Datacassette unit. (Courtesy Techtran Industries)

4b00 cards

appeared. For instance, dual-density floppy disk systems are currently available which provide twice the storage capacity of previous models (that is, 500,000 positions of storage as opposed to 250,000). Since the plastic disk itself is very thin, it has been possible to record only on one side. New developments now allow recording on both sides. One manufacturer refers to this as the "flippy floppy." There is no question that the floppy disk will find ever increasing use in all areas of data processing. Figure 5.17(a) is a photograph of a disk and a deck of cards with a corresponding capacity. A dual floppy disk drive is shown in 5.17(b).

FLOPPY DISKS BOOMING BABY OF DP INDUSTRY

Although still in its product life infancy, the floppy disk drive has already left a legacy in the industry. . . .

Floppy disk drive makers come in all sizes, showing a wide divergence in their dependence on the revenue-generating power of their product.

Control Data Corp., California Computer Products and Memorex Corp. have other larger products creating revenue to sustain operations until the mass market for floppies really opens up, which should be in '75 or '76, according to various estimates.

REPLACEMENTS FOR THE PUNCHED CARD   In 1965 a *data recorder* designed to record keyed data directly onto magnetic tape was introduced amid predictions that the keypunch machine and the wide use of punched cards would

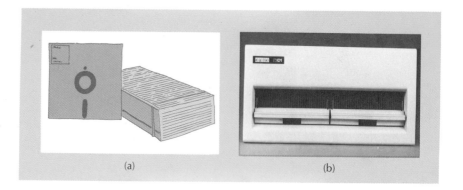

Fig. 5.17 (a) One floppy disk will hold approximately 2000 cards (b) dual floppy disk drive. (Courtesy Digital Equipment Corporation)

(a)   (b)

Flippy from Floppy

Right now you use only one side of your Floppy Diskettes. Why not use both? Simple conversion kit changes your Floppy to a Flippy. Satisfaction guaranteed or return kit within 45 days for refund.

Special Introductory Price **$34.95**

Available from COA

rapidly become obsolete. Almost ten years later, an extensive survey by Datapro Research Corporation,* which involved over 2700 users of punches, showed a high level of satisfaction with their keypunch operations. This was especially true of those using buffered keypunches, such as the IBM 129. Furthermore, over 50 percent indicated no plans to change to another medium.

However, over the past several years a number of factors have arisen, causing a continual and gradual increase in the number of computer installations replacing their punched card input with other methods. This is occurring for a number of reasons, such as:

1. The limitation of the card to 80 characters per record.
2. The relatively slow rate at which data can be entered into the computer via cards.
3. The ever-increasing cost of cards and handling of them.

---

*A survey summary was published in *Computerworld*, October 30, 1974, pp. 23–24.

All of these factors boil down basically to a single consideration: economics. With improved technology, other methods have become available which, for many applications, are more cost effective in the overall consideration—in some cases, much more so. As a result, we see a proliferation of keyboard entry devices which encode information directly onto conventional magnetic disk or tape, or to the floppy disk or tape cassette. The three preceding shortcomings of cards are resolved by use of these devices.

1. Records may be as short or as long as required and thus are not restricted to 80 positions.
2. Encoding the data directly to tape or disk then produces a medium which can be read at very high speeds by the computer. The often-used method of loading cards to a tape on a small computer for subsequent loading to a larger computer is not necessary.
3. The media costs are significantly reduced, since the tapes or disks can be reused when appropriate.

Another extremely important factor relates to noise generated by keypunches: one keypunch is noisy; a room full of them is a disaster. By contrast, data recorders are virtually noiseless, resulting in a far more pleasant work atmosphere and, consequently, better operator efficiency.

A large number of different units are available from a variety of manufacturers. For instance, the unit shown in Figure 5.18 is an early key-to-tape machine; the tape drive unit is clearly visible in this photograph. By contrast, the key-to-disk system shown in Figure 5.19 involves a number of key stations, all of which enter data to a disk storage unit via special controller [refer to the schematic in 5.19(b)]. This is actually a small data entry computer system which not only provides for entry but also verification, accumulation, and editing.

Figure 5.20(a) is a picture of a dual data entry station for recording data directly to floppy disks. Once data is recorded on floppies, the disks may be stacked (like cards) and transferred to magnetic tape by the converter shown in 5.20(b). The converter may in turn communicate directly with a computer.

If it is not possible to bring the source data to the data recorder, then one solution is to bring the recorder to the data. The portable cassette unit shown in Figure 5.21 can easily be carried by a shoulder strap. Data entered via the keypad is stored on a tape cassette. Once the data recording process is completed, the cassette-stored data can be read into the computer via a cassette reader such as the one shown in Figure 5.16.

Fig. 5.18 Magnetic tape encoder. (Reprinted with Permission of Tally Corporation)

Exercise

5.4 What is the storage capacity in characters of a floppy disk? Of a tape cassette?

(a)

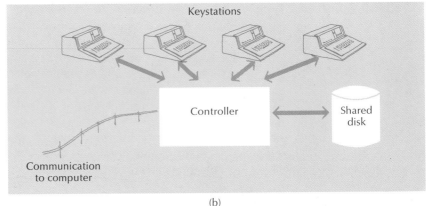

Keystations

Controller

Shared disk

Communication to computer

(b)

Fig. 5.19 (a) Key-to-disk data entry system (Courtesy Mohawk Data Sciences Corporation); (b) schematic representation of a key-to-disk data entry system.

5.4

OTHER I/O DEVICES

In spite of many disadvantages associated with the punched card, it still finds wide use in a number of areas. For instance, Figure 5.3 shows a card punched with billing information which is used as a document and sent to the customer. Upon return of the card with the payment, it can be read into the computer just like any other punched card. However, one serious drawback exists for cards used as documents that are handled by the public. That is, people are not always too careful with them; for example, cards have coffee spilled on them, they get stepped on or sat on, they get stapled, and so on. Unfortunately, card readers are highly sensitive machines and simply cannot cope with other than near-perfect cards. Consequently, *character recognition* devices have evolved which can read information printed on a page. These fall in two broad categories: *magnetic ink character recognition* and *optical character readers.*

(a)

(b)

Fig. 5.20 (a) Dual data entry stations; (b) data converter—floppy disk to tape. (Courtesy of IBM Corporation)

Fig. 5.21 Portable cassette recorder. (Courtesy Checkpoint Systems, Incorporated)

MAGNETIC INK CHARACTER RECOGNITION (MICR)   To the average American, a checking account and the ordinary personal check are a convenient way of life. We give little thought to the fact that a personal check is an important data processing document. Consider the travels of a typical check drawn on XYZ Bank of San Francisco by Arnold Average during his trip to Disneyland.

1. The check is written to Anaheim Curio Center for an amount of $23.57.
2. It is then deposited to the account of Anaheim Curio Center at the ABC Bank of Anaheim.
3. The ABC Bank sends the check to a Federal Reserve clearing house.
4. The Federal Reserve clearing house forwards the check to the XYZ Bank in San Francisco.
5. The XYZ Bank deducts $23.57 from Arnold's account.
6. The cancelled check is returned to Arnold.

At each of these steps, the entries on the check (data) are processed. If we recognize that each family of the millions in this country will write approximately 10–40 checks per month, we see that this becomes a staggering data processing operation involving billions of checks per year. Obviously, some sort of mechanization is absolutely necessary. In the mid-1950s an automated system was devised for Bank of America, and in 1959 the American Banking Association agreed upon a standard for recording numeric information on checks. This standard involves printing critical information along the bottom of the check in special magnetic ink using a standard type font (designated the E-13B font). The ten digits and four special symbols which make up this code are shown in Figure 5.22.

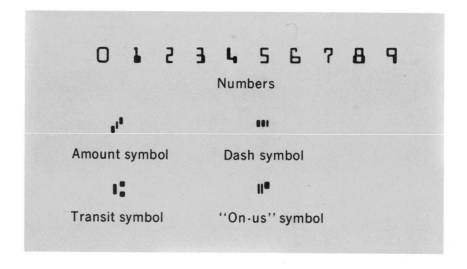

Fig. 5.22   The E-13B type font.

The processing of any check actually takes place one step prior to its being written. Upon opening an account, an individual is assigned an account number. This account number, together with other bank information, is preprinted with the E-13B font on the bottom of each check, as shown in Figure 5.23(a). Then, after the check is written and eventually deposited in a bank (step 2 in the preceding description of Arnold Average), the amount of the transaction is encoded on the bottom right of the check from the handwritten amount [Figure 5.23(b)]. From that point on, all processing of the check may be by MICR machines which are specially designed to read the magnetically imprinted characters. For instance, the IBM 3890 Document Processor shown in Figure 5.24 will both read and sort magnetically encoded checks. This machine may be operated *online* (connected directly to the computer), or *offline* (not connected directly to the computer but outputting to magnetic tape). Thus data

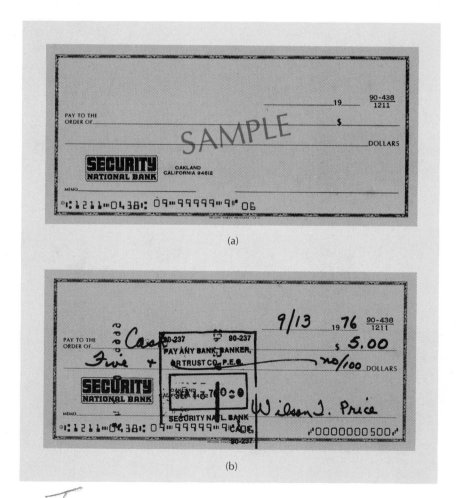

(a)

(b)

Fig. 5.23 (a) A blank check; (b) a processed check. (Courtesy Security National Bank)

Fig. 5.24 The IBM 3890 Document Reader. (Courtesy IBM Corporation)

read may be immediately routed to the computer with an online system, or written to magnetic tape and later read into the computer with a offline system.

Although MICR has served the banking industry well, the small size of the character set (limited to the digits and four special characters) has been a barrier to more general use. Furthermore, the magnetic ink does not retain its full magnetic properties for a long period of time after printing, especially if the document is handled extensively. As a result, Optical Character Recognition (OCR) systems were developed to satisfy a wide spectrum of needs.

Fig. 5.25 Mark sense card.

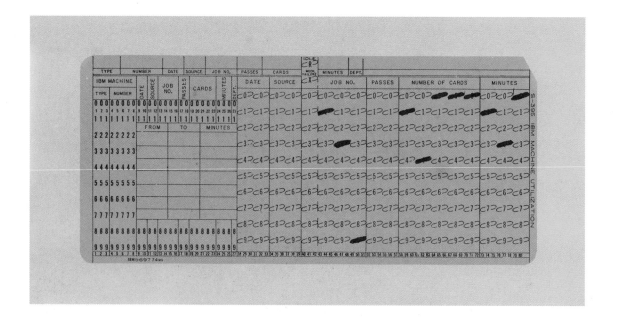

OPTICAL READERS   In Chapter 2 and again in the earlier portion of this chapter, it was emphasized that the card reader senses only the holes punched into the card. However, some of the early card processing machines were capable of reading special mark sense cards similar to that shown in Figure 5.25. In this type of card, appropriate positions are filled in with a pencil and the marks were machine read by completing an electrical current through the graphite mark. Modern machines are capable of reading mark sense cards by optical means, then punching the information read directly into that same card. Some inexpensive computer card readers include a mark sense feature whereby the mark sense coded information may be read directly into the computer. The mark sense medium is a very popular one because of its simplicity in recording data with the use of no equipment other than a pencil. As a result, mark sense processing machines are available which will read a variety of document sizes ranging from a card to a full-size sheet of typing paper. Most of us have encountered questionnaires and/or school examinations where results are entered on a mark sense page by entering a mark in the appropriate position. (Figure 5.26 is an example of one such form.)

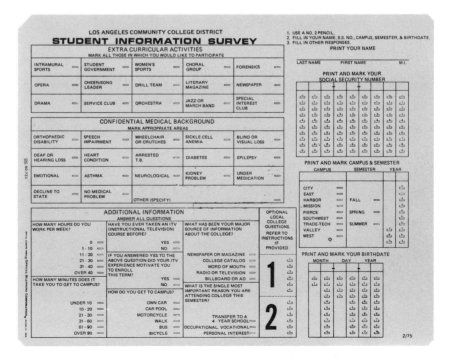

Fig. 5.26 Mark sense form. (Courtesy Optical Scanning Corporation)

Although the mark sense method is quite practical in certain situations, it does lack a degree of versatility. The more versatile *Optical Character Readers* (OCR) find wide use in data processing. A wide variety of OCR devices are available which can read printed information from a computer printer or from an ordinary typewriter using a special machine readable font (type style). For the purpose of industrywide standardization, the American National Standards Institute (ANSI) has defined the OCR-A font which is now commonly used. The character set, which includes the letters, digits and special characters together with an example, is shown in Figure 5.27.

```
ABCDEFGHIJKLMNOPQRSTUVWXYZ
0123456789
$%|&*.-+='";:/?{},


1      OPSCAN 37   $42,500.00
```

Fig. 5.27 The OCR-A character font.

Although several other type fonts are in use, OCR-A font is rapidly becoming the industry standard. In addition to standardized type fonts, most OCR devices can also read hand-printed numbers which conform to a specific format. However, care must be taken to ensure that each digit is carefully printed—the average scribbling by 50 percent of us remains unintelligible to the machine. The OCR reader shown in Figure 5.28 can read the OCR-A font, hand-printed numeric characters, and mark sense forms. Output can be either directly to a computer or to magnetic tape for later entry to the computer.

With the original introduction in the mid-1950s of OCR, the prevalent theory was that typewriters and hand printing used in an OCR environment would replace all or most keypunches. This has obviously not occurred and, in all probability, will not occur. Each different input technique has its own advantages and disadvantages for each application, and we are likely to continue to see a wide proliferation of these devices in the future. However, with standardization of the type font and reduced prices of OCR devices, we can expect a gradually increasing use of this medium.

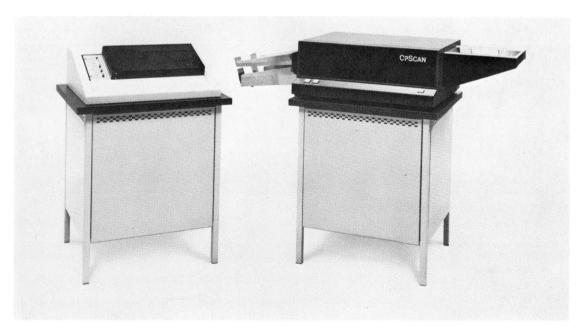

Fig. 5.28 The OpScan 17 Optical Character Reader with magnetic tape. (Courtesy Optical Scanning Corporation, Newtown, Pa.)

CRT TERMINALS Most of the devices described in the preceding sections provide the user the ability to get large quantities of data into and out of the computer at very high rates of speed. In contrast, many applications require that the user communicate directly with the computer (in spite of the low-speed capabilities of humans). This is commonly accomplished using ordinary typewriter-like devices such as those shown in Figure 5.9. With these, the keyboard is used for input and the printed page for output. In some applications, a special-purpose keyboard is used; for instance, stockbrokers use a keyboard entry system designed especially for stock market transactions. With highly sophisticated computer hardware and software systems, one computer is generally capable of handling many terminals concurrently. (This concept is described in detail in Chapter 13.)

Another very common output device is the *cathode ray tube* (CRT), which is very much like an ordinary television. Basic models of CRTs are capable of displaying ordinary alphanumeric data output which we might print on a line printer. Commonly used general-purpose units provide for displaying either twelve or twenty-four 80-character lines on the screen [Figure 5.29(a)]. More sophisticated terminals have the capability for displaying graphic material as well as ordinary printed output [Figure 5.29(b)]. In fact, phenomenal improvements in the capabilities of CRTs have taken place over the past several years (even while the prices have been decreasing—a paradox in today's living).

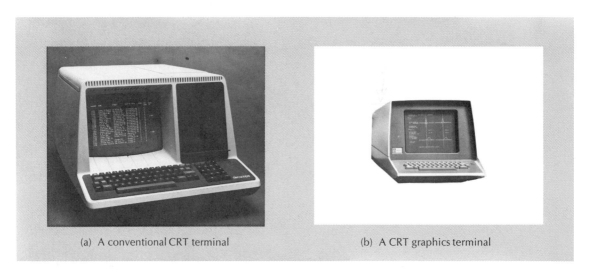

(a) A conventional CRT terminal   (b) A CRT graphics terminal

Fig. 5.29 CRT terminals.
[(a) courtesy Digital
Equipment Corporation,
(b) courtesy Tektronix,
Inc.]

In general, the CRT terminal is referred to as a *soft copy device* since it produces no permanent printed record. (This is in contrast to typewriter-like terminals, known as *hard copy devices* since they do yield a printed record.) For many applications, the soft copy CRT is quite adequate. And because of the nature of the CRT, information can be flashed to the screen at extremely high speeds: for instance, at rates ranging up to 2000 characters per second. At this rate, one full screen of 24 lines (a *page*) can be displayed in less than one second. Through appropriate control keys on the keyboard, the user can direct the computer to display the next page of output as required by the particular job requirements. Needless to say, this is accomplished by programming the computer to operate within the limitations of the CRT terminal.

Early CRTs were basically typewriter terminal equivalents; that is, they could be used to perform the basic functions of typewriter-like terminals. In a sense, they were "dumb"; all "thinking" was performed by the host computer. With the advent of microprocessors, the "smart" or *intelligent terminal* made its appearance. In brief, an intelligent terminal is essentially a microcomputer capable of limited data storage and program handling capabilities. These are invaluable for many types of applications, such as those in which it is necessary to edit and/or reformat data or to control other I/O devices without "bothering" the CPU. There is much that could be said about CRT terminals. This is a rapidly expanding area of the computer field, one in which significant developments seem almost to appear daily.

PORTABLE TERMINALS   Both the hard and soft copy terminals described in the preceding section can be connected directly to the computer, or they can communicate via telephone lines. For example, a bank might include a main

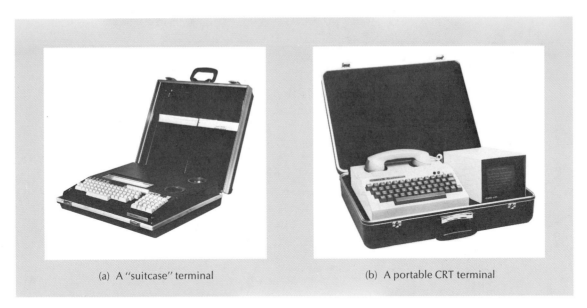

(a) A "suitcase" terminal   (b) A portable CRT terminal

Fig. 5.30 Portable
terminals. [(a) courtesy
Dataproducts, (b)
courtesy Digi-Log
Systems, Inc.,
Horsham, Pa.]

office with a central computer and several branch offices. Terminals in the main office might access the computer directly where those in branch offices might access via telephone lines. Some applications have a need for portability of terminals—for instance, an engineer might desire to take a terminal home to work on an especially urgent program. A number of such portable units are available which can operate from an ordinary telephone simply by dialing the computer's number and inserting the handset in a special receptacle as illustrated in Figure 5.30.

Exercises

5.5   What are the shortcomings of MICR?

5.6   What is the difference between a mark sense reader and an optical character reader?

5.7   What is the difference between an intelligent terminal and a dumb terminal?

5.5
BAR CODES FOR
DATA ENTRY

By now most of us are familiar with the series of vertical lines together with a group of digits encoded on most items in the grocery store. The lines, termed *bar codes*, might mean little to us, but they carry descriptive information which can be read by computer equipment. Although the grocery store bar codes are relatively new (1973), bar codes were first implemented by the railroad system in 1967 for automatic car identification purposes. Since that time, the number of applications using bar codes has mushroomed and numerous codes have been devised for different purposes. As seen in Figure 5.31, most codes include human-readable characters alongside.

THE PULSE WIDTH MODULATED CODE   *8 4 2 1* Although most of the bar codes themselves are difficult to decipher, one of them (commonly termed a *Pulse Width Modulated Code*) uses a grouping of four bars to represent each character in a manner reminiscent of the digit portion of the 96-column code described in Chapter 3. As we will see in Chapter 6, it bears a strong resemblance to the base 16 number system. In this code, each of the four positions represents a power of two as illustrated in Figure 5.32(a). (The reader might refer to Table 3.2, which illustrates the 96-column code for coding digits, and compare these techniques.) The 16 possible combinations which represent the entire character set for this code are shown in Figure 5.32(b).

An example of a student card with an encoded strip is shown in Figure 5.33.*

THE UNIVERSAL PRODUCT CODE   The bar code most of us are familiar with is that found on grocery items, the *Universal Product Code* (UPC). This code is far more complex than the preceding Pulse Width Modulated Code so it will not be explained in detail. However, a few characteristics are significant; for these let us refer to the example shown below:

1. The code consists of the left half (048001) and the right half (265684).
2. Each digit is coded by two bars and two spaces. The total width of a digit consists of seven "unit" widths. Each bar and each space can be 1, 2, 3, or 4 basic units in width.
3. The code on the left half is exactly the opposite of that on the right half. (The industrious reader who is inclined to decipher this code should keep this factor in mind.)

As a check to ensure that the code is read properly, the last digit is used as a check digit. When the code is read, the computer sums the odd and even positioned digits as follows:

- Add odd position digits: $0 + 8 + 0 + 2 + 5 + 8 = 23$
  Add even position digits: $4 + 0 + 1 + 6 + 6 = 17$
- (excluding the last one)
- Add odd sum times 3 to even sum: $23 \times 3 + 17 = 86$
  Subtract this sum from next higher multiple of ten: $90 - 86 = \underline{4}$

---

*The perceptive reader will note that the coding of the first group of four bars is not printed above the bar codes nor is anything printed beyond the extra-wide bar (the fifth from the right). These are used to indicate the beginning and end, respectively, of the encoded data.

Fig. 5.31   A variety of bar codes.

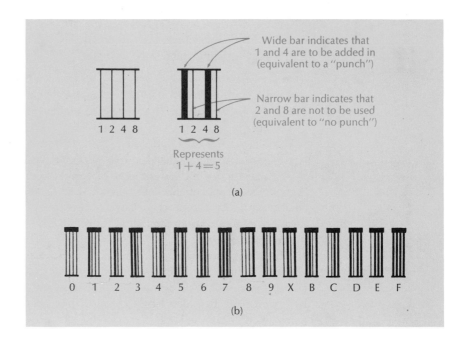

Represents
1 + 4 = 5

(a)

(b)

Fig. 5.32 The Pulse Width Modulated bar code.

Fig. 5.33 A Student Identification card (actual size). (Courtesy Checkpoint Systems, Inc.)

The check digit is 4 and is encoded in the last position of the code. If the label is misread by the machine, the computed check digit will differ from the encoded digit and an error will be signalled.

BAR CODE PROCESSING DEVICES   Basically two devices (in addition to a computer) are required to use bar codes: one unit to imprint bar code labels and another to read them. Due to close tolerances in most bar codes, it is essential that the bar widths and spacings be precise. Figure 5.34 shows a small bar code printer which encodes onto self-adhesive labels.

A large variety of different types of devices to read bar codes are available. A typical supermarket checkout unit which includes a reader that functions in tandem with a cash register is shown in Figure 5.35. The cash register is, in turn, linked to a central computer. (This concept is described in more detail in the next section.)

In many cases, such as a warehouse where careful inventory control of all items in stock is required, it is not practical to bring the data items to the reader; therefore, the reverse is done—the reader is brought to the data source. In Figure 5.36, bar code labels are read by a special reading wand and the information is recorded on a tape cassette incorporated into the portable unit. The cassette-stored data can later be read into a computer through a cassette reader such as that shown in Figure 5.16. Key to this unit is a hand-held pencil-like unit which actually reads the bar code. Figure 5.37 is a schematic of one

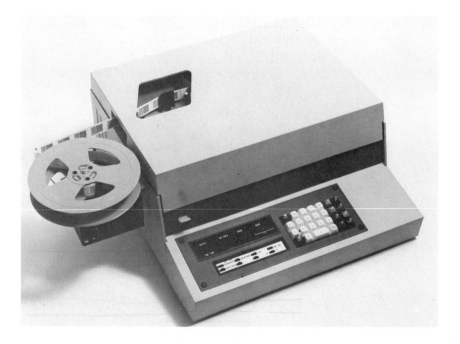

Fig. 5.34 The Intermec 8124 bar code printer. (Courtesy Interface Mechanisms, Inc.)

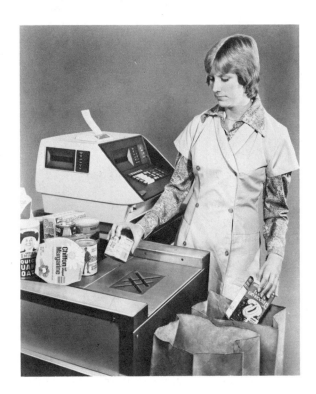

Fig. 5.35 The Sweda UPC scanner linked to a cash register. (Courtesy Sweda International)

Fig. 5.36 Using a CI portable bar code processor. (Courtesy Computer Identics Corp.)

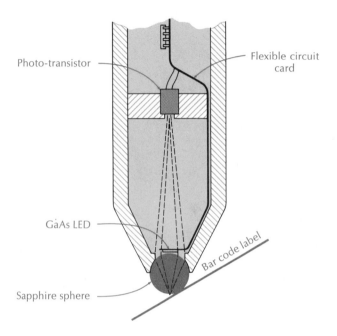

Photo-transistor

Flexible circuit card

GaAs LED

Bar code label

Sapphire sphere

Fig. 5.37   The Model 1230 Ruby Wand bar code reader. (Courtesy Interface Mechanisms, Inc.)

such reader which is capable of reading bars and spaces as narrow as 0.0075 inch with high reliability.

Exercise

5.8   The following is a Pulse Width Modulated coded label (the beginning and ending codes have been removed). Decipher the information which is coded.

5.6

POINT OF TRANSACTION APPLICATIONS

A variety of low-cost, on-the-spot input/output devices have resulted in some very significant changes in processing data. Many applications which were once batch-oriented, with subsequent undesirable time delays, are no longer so restricted. (Remember, batch processing involves accumulating a "batch" of transactions during a predetermined period of time, then making an update run.) In a *point of transaction* system, the transaction is entered directly into the computer for immediate processing. To illustrate, let us consider an automated library system.

AN AUTOMATED LIBRARY CIRCULATION SYSTEM   A typical system is based on bar-coded labels which are affixed to (1) books and other loan material, and (2) library users' identification cards (see Figure 5.33). Through the use of bar code reading devices, book loan and return information may be quickly read and transmitted to a central computer, as illustrated by the network of Figure 5.38. To check out a book involves the following steps:

1. The borrower's card is placed in the charge terminal.
2. The light pen is drawn across the borrower's card and then the book, thus transmitting the information directly to the computer (see Figure 5.39).
3. The book is hand stamped with the due date.

Fig. 5.38 An automated library system.

To return a book, it is only necessary to draw the light pen across the bar code in the book which transmits the information directly to the computer.

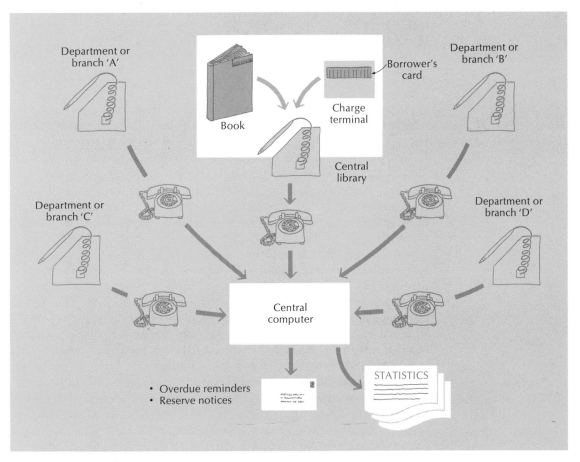

The many advantages of such a system include:

1. Simplicity and speed of operation.
2. Automatic and instant records on whereabouts of all books.
3. Computerized control and handling of all clerical tasks.
4. Automatic printout by computer of overdue notices.

The net effect is better overall service to the users of the library resource.

Fig. 5.39 Checking out a book. (Courtesy Checkpoint Systems, Inc.)

AUTOMATING THE GROCERY STORE During the past few years, many retailers have begun using *Point of Sale* (POS) methods whereby all transactions are fed directly to a computer via an automated cash register or some other such device. The central computer can then handle all of the bookkeeping as well as up-to-the-minute inventory control. (The schematic representation in Figure 5.38 of the library system is equally representative of an automated POS system.) Suddenly the grocers burst onto the scene (1973) with their Universal Product Code and plans to streamline supermarket operations. The UPC and automated checkout stands were no overnight dream. In 1970 the manufacturing and distribution sides of the food industry, in a rare burst of cooperation, agreed to a study which eventually led to UPC. Management consultants, graphic arts experts, computer specialists, and even the Massachusetts Institute of Technology were utilized to ensure that the planning and implementation of UPC would leave no stones unturned. By 1974 the grocery industry was receiving the praise of many other industries for the careful planning and cooperation that had gone into this sophisticated step forward. Briefly, the plan works like this: Each food manufacturer—for example, General Mills—is assigned a unique five-digit code (the left portion of the UPC); the manufacturer then assigns a unique five-digit code (the right portion of the UPC) to each product in the line, for example, a five-pound bag of flour. The reader will note that this is not price information, it merely represents an inventory code. However, stored within the computer is a table of these codes together with appropriate pricing and descriptive information for each product on the shelf. At the checkout stand, the scanner reads the code and transmits it to the computer, the computer looks up the price information, and that information is automatically rung up on the cash register (see Figure 5.35).

Let us consider some of the advantages which are championed by the supermarkets.

1. By marking the price on the shelf rather than on the individual item, labor costs are significantly reduced. Item price marking is estimated to cost $1 per thousand items marked and $3 per thousand items remarked.
2. Checkout time can be reduced by an estimated 50 percent, thereby resulting in fewer delays for the customer and reduced labor costs for the store.
3. Accuracy is improved with prices retrieved from the computer, and the shopper will always benefit from special sales or promotional prices. With weekly and even daily promotions, many of these are accidentally overlooked at the conventional checkstand.
4. The receipt will contain far more information for the shopper; refer, for instance, to the following example.

```
HOMETOWN FOOD MART
STORE 123    04/20/7-


GRO    .54F CEREAL
NFD   3.90H WINSTON
GRO    .57F CHILI
MT    1.13F T BONE
NFD    .43C KLEENEX
PRO    .47F BANANA
NFD    .19C DOG FOOD
NFD    .35C GLAD WRAP
GRO    .07F KOOL AID
GRO    .07F KOOL AID
GRO    .06F KOOL AID

     .06  TAX

    7.84  TOTAL

   10.00  CASH

    2.16  CHANGE

0007 02  4  4.22PM
```

Now this sounds very impressive; so what is all of the shouting about? The primary bone of contention relates to removal of individual prices. A number of consumer groups and labor unions have registered strong opposition. In May, 1974, *Consumer Reports* published an article attacking the elimination

'Apparently It's More Than Just a Psychological Barrier. . .'

of individual pricing as making it more difficult for the consumer to compare prices in different parts of the store. The alleged remark of one consumer, evidencing a basic mistrust of computers, was: "The worst thing they can do is take off all the prices. If that thing is not set right it could be eating me alive and I would never know it." As a result, bills have been introduced in several legislatures to require item marking. The upshot of all this is a slowdown in the implementation of UPC processing. As is so often the case with automation, the human factors ran a poor second to the technology factors in the early planning of UPC. In retrospect, the ensuing controversy was quite predictable (hindsight usually is much more accurate than foresight).

Answers to Preceding Exercises

5.1 The tape, if securely attached, will "correct" the mispunch since it will prevent contact between the reading brush and roller. However, this is unwise since a small piece of tape could cause a machine jam. Furthermore, the cost of an IBM card is approximately one-tenth of a penny; so such economizing is, by and large, a waste of time. On the other hand, cards which are used as documents and are not conveniently replaceable are sometimes corrected in this manner (for example, utility bills).

5.2 A rate of 1200 frames per second is equivalent to 900 cards per minute.

5.3 a. 3; b. 5; c. 1; d. 6; e. 2; f. 4.

COM Computer Output Microfilm

5.4 Floppy disk capacity = 250,000 characters; tape cassette capacity = 145,000 characters.

5.5 The character set is relatively small in numbers (14), and the ink loses its magnetic properties with handling.

5.6 A mark sense reader detects the presence (or absence) of a simple mark in somewhat the same fashion as a card reader detects the presence (or absence) of a punched hole. An optical reader can interpret the shapes of machine-printed or hand-printed characters and read the data directly without the need for a coding technique.

5.7 A dumb terminal has the capability for accepting data from a keyboard and transmitting as is to the host computer and, conversely, for receiving results from the computer and displaying them. An intelligent terminal has limited capability to be programmed and operate semi-independently of the host computer prior to or after transmitting or receiving data.

5.8 12300001300C4.

Additional Exercises

5.9 Matching. Match each item in 1–8 with the corresponding description in a–h.

1. thermal printer
2. data recorder (keydisk)
3. CRT terminal
4. floppy disk
5. COM
6. OCR
7. UPC
8. tape cassette

a. A magnetic storage medium.

b. Displays computer output on a television-like screen.

c. Provides the capability for recording source data directly to magnetic disk.

d. A coding method adapted by the grocery industry for labelling items in the grocery store.

e. These devices provide the capability for the computer to read hand-printed characters.

f. Uses photographic techniques for storing large amounts of computer output.

g. A portable recording medium which can be used in the field for recording source data.

h. Requires heat-sensitive paper.

5.10 True-False. Determine whether each of the following is true or false.

a. One disadvantage of paper tape is that it does not provide the unit record flexibility of punched cards.

b. In general, serial printers tend to be faster than line printers.

c. The use of COM is diminishing somewhat because special film readers are required to read what is saved on the film.

d. One disadvantage of the diskette (floppy disk) as compared to a regular disk is that the diskette cannot be reused after data has been stored on it.

e. In spite of many new highly efficient methods, the punched card and keypunch machines are still commonly used.

f. MICR is commonly used by the banking industry.

g. OCR is an abbreviation of Online Character Recognition.

h. Some keyboard type machines allow data to be entered directly to magnetic tape or disk.

i. Bar codes are commonly used by the grocery industry but have not been widely used in other industries.

j. With a Point of Sale (POS) system, data can be entered directly into a computer in the next room or miles away at another location.

5.11 Multiple Choice. Determine which answer best completes or answers each of the following statements.

a. A serial card reader reads cards (1) one row at a time, (2) the same way as a parallel reader, (3) one column at a time, (4) none of the preceding.

b. Ranking printers according to speed (slowest to fastest), we would have (1) drum, serial, page, (2) line, serial, page, (3) serial, line, page, (4) page, line, serial, (5) none of the preceding.

c. In a computer system, paper tape can be used for (1) input, (2) internal storage, (3) output, (4) all of the preceding, (5) both 1 and 3.

d. Which of the following is not a commonly used computer output device? (1) COM, (2) magnetic tape, (3) MICR devices, (4) CRT devices, (5) all of the preceding are output devices.

e. Which of the following does not use some type of magnetic method for storing data? (1) floppy disk, (2) tape cassette, (3) paper tape, (4) MICR, (5) both 3 and 4.

f. One reason Computer Output Microfilm (COM) has come into common use is (1) low cost of paper, (2) shortage of printers, (3) high cost of handling printed reports, (4) increased speed of computers, (5) none of the preceding.

g. One problem with MICR is (1) the ink dries too slowly, (2) a small character set, (3) it can only be used on bank checks, (4) reading machines are slow, (5) both 1 and 3.

h. An advantage of using the Universal Product Code in grocery stores is (1) reduced costs, (2) easier for consumer to compare prices, (3) improved accuracy, (4) all of the preceding, (5) both 1 and 3.

i. OCR devices are most commonly used in (1) the banking industry, (2) automated supermarkets, (3) library systems, (4) a broad range of applications, (5) are not commonly used.

j. Which of the following is not descriptive of a POS system? (1) provides immediate inventory control, (2) improved accuracy, (3) involves batch processing, (4) automates many clerical tasks, (5) none of the preceding.

Chapter

6

Internal Codes
for Computers

The concept of using a symbol to represent a value or quantity has been a basic notion to man since the earliest attempts to communicate. Printed characters such as 13, -7, $\frac{4}{5}$, and 3.1416 are immediately recognized as numbers and are as much a part of our everyday language as the words on this page. Let us briefly consider the basic characteristics of our decimal number system before studying number systems which are typical of computers.

6.1
CHARACTERISTICS OF
DECIMAL NUMBERS

EXPONENTS   Exponents are a commonly used shorthand form of mathematics. For instance, the exponent form as illustrated below can be used to save considerable writing:

$$a \times a \times a \times a \times a = a^5$$

or

$$10 \times 10 \times 10 \times 10 \times 10 \times 10 = 10^6$$

Generalized, the relationship is

$$\underbrace{a \times a \times a \times \cdots \times a}_{n \text{ times}} = a^n$$

where a is any number, called the *base*, and n is any number, called the *exponent*. The use here is obvious, the exponent n merely indicating how many times the base a should be included as a factor in the expression. We should recognize that this is a symbolism arrived at by definition, and that the product of eight values of a can be defined as a^8. This is much the same as defining the symbol $ to represent dollars, or # to represent pounds. Although detailed properties of exponents are not covered in this book, the exponent can be zero or negative, as well as positive. By definition, any quantity raised to the zero power is equal to 1. For example,

$$10^0 = 1$$
$$2^0 = 1$$
$$16^0 = 1$$

PLACE VALUE   One very important characteristic which is fundamental to the decimal system is the principle of *place* or *positional* value. Since the decimal system includes only nine distinct digits and 0, it is necessary to use the principle of place value in counting above 9. A multiple-digit number such as 4378 uses four of the ten available digits, yet each of them has a different significance. What is actually implied by the symbolism 4378 is

implies $4000 = 4 \times 1000$
implies $\ 300 = 3 \times 100$
implies $\ \ 70 = 7 \times 10$
implies $\ \ \ \ 8 = 8 \times 1$

4378

$$4378 = (4 \times 1000) + (3 \times 100) + (7 \times 10) + (8 \times 1)$$

Thus, the value of each digit is represented not only by the digit itself but also by its place or position. The inclusion of 0 in the number system is important here since it serves the purpose of a *place holder*. Obviously, there is a considerable difference between the numbers 352 and 3520. Were it not for the use of place value it might be necessary to incorporate many hundreds of different symbols into our number system. Using exponential forms, numbers such as 4378 and 13905 may be expressed as

$$
\begin{aligned}
4378 &= 4 \times 1000 + 3 \times 100 + 7 \times 10 + 8 \\
&= 4 \times 10^3 + 3 \times 10^2 + 7 \times 10^1 + 8 \times 10^0 \\
13905 &= 1 \times 10000 + 3 \times 1000 + 9 \times 100 + 0 \times 10 + 5 \\
&= 1 \times 10^4 + 3 \times 10^3 + 9 \times 10^2 + 0 \times 10^1 + 5 \times 10^0
\end{aligned}
$$

Although our decimal system uses a base of 10, the choice of a number system base is arbitrary and, as we will learn in this chapter, base 10 leaves much to be desired in computer applications.

OTHER BASES   Actually we need not view number systems with bases other than 10 as completely new to us, since we often use at least one of them without realizing it. For instance, consider one of the more common methods for tallying results, in which a line is drawn for each tally and the tallies are marked off in groups of five. Thus a total of 17 attempts to run a computer program might appear as

$$\cancel{||||} \quad \cancel{||||} \quad \cancel{||||} \quad ||$$

In essence, this is a base 5 (quinary) number system* in which the following correspondence between the decimal number system and the tally system exists:

1	|
2	||
3	|||
4	||||
5	$\cancel{||||}$

---

*A variation of the base 5 number system, a so-called biquinary system, was used on the IBM 650, an early computer, as a basis for displaying numbers.

Thus, we might count three groups of 5 plus 2 left over for the total. We could write this as 32_t, where the first digit represents the number of groups of 5, the second digit represents the number of marks left over, and the subscript t tells us that this is in the tally system base. Thus, 32_t would really represent $3 \times 5 + 2 = 17_{10}$, as previously defined. It is of utmost importance to recognize that the physical occurrence (that is, attempts to run a program) that had taken place a certain number of times is independent of the method for representing it.

Exercise

6.1 Using the tally notion of this section, what does each of the following represent in terms of base 10 numbers?

     a. 23_t b. 41_t c. 53_t d. 42_t

6.2
BASE 2
BINARY NUMBERS   The rapid evolution of the computer field has involved the use of several number systems in computing equipment. For instance, the IBM 650 display panel uses a biquinary (basically a base 5 system), and the Univac an octal or base 8 system. However, arithmetic operations in these computers are done in a *binary* or *base 2* system. In fact, nearly all computers operate in the binary mode because of its ability to describe an electrical circuit as being either on or off, or a magnetic core as being magnetized either in one direction or in the other. However, we should not get the idea that a base 2 number system is something new and unique to the computer. There is evidence that a binary system was recognized 5000 years ago in China, but it was only within the last 300 years that Baron Gottfried von Leibnitz delved into the system and documented his work.

The reader will recall from Chapter 3 that the IBM System/3 96-column card uses the digits 1, 2, 4, and 8 to code the nine decimal digits 1–9. The choice of these four digits and the associated coding (Table 3.2) was not a chance one; it is directly related to the binary number system. To illustrate, we will consider one column (digit position) "turned on its side," as shown in Figure 6.1. Let us use the convention that a darkened position indicates that the value is to be included; otherwise, it is to be excluded. Then the number coded in Figure 6.1 is $4 + 1 = 5$. Obviously, the same message can be conveyed by using the digit 1 to represent the *on* condition and 0 the *off*. Now it is possible to represent this value as 0101, but we must remember the *positional significance* of each 0 or 1. Mathematically, this actually represents

$$0 \times 8 + 1 \times 4 + 0 \times 2 + 1 \times 1 = 0 + 4 + 0 + 1$$
$$= 5$$

One more careful observation and we have "arrived." That is, the digit values used here and in Figure 6.1 are actually the first four powers of 2, or

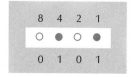

Fig. 6.1   Binary coding.

$$1 = 2^0$$
$$2 = 2^1$$
$$4 = 2^2$$
$$8 = 2^3$$

Then the representation becomes

$$0 \times 8 + 1 \times 4 + 0 \times 2 + 1 \times 1 = 0 \times 2^3 + 1 \times 2^2 + 0 \times 2^1 + 1 \times 2^0$$

Note that this is precisely the polynomial type form which our familiar base 10 number system exhibits. Thus, we have established an intuitive basis for further consideration of a base 2 number system. That is, the system incorporates the two distinct digits 0 and 1, and utilizes the principle of positional value which is based on powers of the number system base 2. However, we must take care to distinguish between a binary and a decimal number. For example, is 101 the decimal quantity "one hundred one" or the binary quantity (without its leading zero) which is equivalent to the decimal quantity "five"? The standard practice is to use subscripts whenever it is not clear by context. Then the binary quantity is 101_2 is easily distinguished from the decimal quantity 101_{10}.

COUNTING IN BINARY To gain more insight to the nature of binary numbers, consider Table 6.1, which shows binary quantities and their decimal equivalents.

Table 6.1 BASE 2 AND BASE 10 NUMBERS

2^3	2^2	2^1	2^0		Base 10	
8	4	2	1			
0	0	0	0	→	0000	0
0	0	0	1	→	0001	1
0	0	1	0	→	0010	2
0	0	1	1	→	0011	3
0	1	0	0	→	0100	4
0	1	0	1	→	0101	5
0	1	1	0	→	0110	6
0	1	1	1	→	0111	7
1	0	0	0	→	1000	8
1	0	0	1	→	1001	9
1	0	1	0	→	1010	10
1	0	1	1	→	1011	11
1	1	0	0	→	1100	12
1	1	0	1	→	1101	13
1	1	1	0	→	1110	14
1	1	1	1	→	1111	15

We can see that these both represent "counting sequences" (from 0 through 15). Of course, when counting with decimal numbers we "use up" all of the digits after reaching 9, so we start the familiar cycle again: that is, 0,1,2,3,4, 5,6,7,8,9,10,11,12,· · ·. In counting with a binary system, a similar situation arises, except that we use up all of the digits much more rapidly. With the digits 0 and 1 we can see in Table 6.1 that the repetition is begun with the binary equivalent of 2_{10}. A careful study of this table will show that effectively the same technique is involved in binary counting as in decimal counting.

For convenience, this exploration of binary numbers has focused on quantities consisting of four digits. (Since they are binary as opposed to decimal, they are commonly referred to as *binary digits* or *bits*.) However, we must not get the impression that binary quantities are aways limited to four bits. For instance, the quantities 10110_2 and 10011101_2 actually represent*

$$10110_2 \equiv 1\times2^4 + 0\times2^3 + 1\times2^2 + 1\times2^1 + 0\times2^0$$
$$\equiv 1\times16 + 0\times8 + 1\times4 + 1\times2 + 0\times1$$
$$\equiv 16 + 4 + 2$$
$$\equiv 22_{10}$$
$$10011101_2 \equiv 1\times2^7 + 0\times2^6 + 0\times2^5 + 1\times2^4 + 1\times2^3 + 1\times2^2$$
$$+ 0\times2^1 + 1\times2^0$$
$$\equiv 1\times128 + 0\times64 + 0\times32 + 1\times16 + 1\times8$$
$$+ 1\times4 + 0\times2 + 1\times1$$
$$\equiv 128 + 16 + 8 + 4 + 1$$
$$\equiv 157_{10}$$

---

*Throughout this text, the notion of equivalence will be used extensively; for example, 9_{10} is equivalent to 1001_2. This will be represented mathematically as $9_{10} \equiv 1001_2$ where the symbol $\equiv$ means "is equivalent to."

Because large binary numbers with their strings of 1s and 0s are often confusing to read, they are commonly grouped in threes or in fours as follows:

	in fours			*in threes*	
	1	0110		10	110
or	0001	0110	or	010	110
	1001	1101	010	011	101

(handwritten above "in fours": 16 8421)

As we shall learn later in this chapter, these groupings are related in a very important way to the base 16 and 8 number systems, respectively, and essentially provide the basis for the classification of computers as base 16 or 8 machines.

Exercise

6.2 Extend the counting sequence in Table 6.1 to produce the binary equivalents of the decimal numbers 16–25.

see Page 163

6.3
COMPUTER STORAGE CODING

THE TWO STATES OF THE MAGNETIC CORE   At this point the reader may well wonder what the relationship is between cores which can be magnetized in either of two directions, binary number systems, and the storing of information such as student file numbers and names. However, if we carefully consider the punched-card method of storing information, we see that character storage is accomplished by an indicator which can be yes or no; in other words, a binary indication which, in the case of a card, takes the form of a punch or no punch. For instance, if 9 is to be stored in column 70 of a card, a hole is punched in that position of the card; otherwise, there is no hole punched.

Since computer storage devices are best suited to coding methods using the on-off principle, the Hollerith code appears to be an attractive means for internal storage coding also. The coding system used in many computer systems is fundamentally the same as the Hollerith code, although differences do exist because of practical considerations in designing the computer. The card column uses 12 rows, one for each of the 10 digits and all 12 for letters and special characters. The use of 12 positions on the card is no problem, since cardboard is relatively inexpensive. On the other hand, the computer core storage consists of thousands of very expensive components. As a consequence, it is desirable to use the most efficient coding method possible in order to get the most out of the given equipment.

By considering magnetism in one direction equivalent to a punch (or we could refer to it as an *on-state* or a *1-state*) and in the other direction equivalent to no-punch (or correspondingly an *off-state* or a *0-state*), we can easily devise the core storage equivalent of the 80-column card. We see in Figure 6.2 that

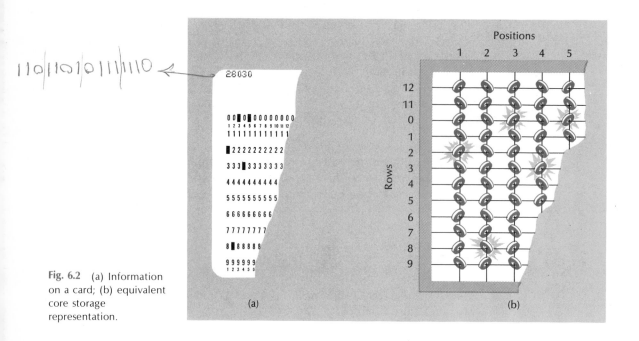

Fig. 6.2 (a) Information on a card; (b) equivalent core storage representation.

the number 28030 is stored in columns 1–5 of the card. Correspondingly, we see that same number stored in what we might term an equivalent 80-position "core storage card." Note that each storage position in this hypothetical unit consists of 12 cores and serves precisely the same function as the punching position on the card. In addition, each group of 12 cores can be referred to by its position number (corresponding to card column) or its *address*, as it is commonly called in computer terminology. Thus, the five-digit number can be spoken of as being stored in storage locations 1–5. Note that the storage address itself has nothing to do with the information which is stored; thus, the five-digit field 28030 could as well have been stored in locations 76–80. We can see by this that many of the basic principles regarding storage of information in cards apply to storage of information in magnetic cores. Of course, core storage provides a number of advantages, among them that (1) the core may be easily and very quickly changed from the "on" to the "off" state and vice versa, and (2) the capacity is not limited to 80 "columns." For instance, minicomputers are typically available now with 8000 and more storage positions.

BINARY CODED DECIMAL   Although the preceding example is convenient to illustrate the basic principle of core storage, various coding methods other than the Hollerith code itself are commonly used to store data within the computer. Most of them employ, in one way or another, some form of a binary number representation. For example, most modern general purpose computers

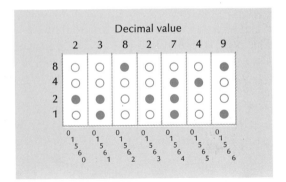

Fig. 6.3 Information in storage.

have some type of capability for handling decimal (base 10) numbers. One common method used is similar to that used in the IBM System/3 96-column card (Chapter 3). That is, by use of four positions with values of 8, 4, 2, and 1, the nine nonzero decimal digits can be represented as

1	4	$7 = 4 + 2 + 1$
2	$5 = 4 + 1$	8
$3 = 2 + 1$	$6 = 4 + 2$	$9 = 8 + 1$

Thus, instead of ten-digit rows with this coding method, it is possible to represent each decimal digit of a number using four bits. This coding method is illustrated in Figure 6.3, where the seven-digit number 2382749 is represented in storage locations 01560 through 01566 (analogous to seven adjacent columns on a card). Since a set of four binary indicators is used to represent each decimal digit, this coding method is commonly called *binary coded decimal* (BCD). Although it is efficient for representing and manipulating numeric information, alphabetic data storage requires additional bit positions as described in the next section.

EXPANDED BINARY CODED DECIMAL One very common method for coding alphanumeric data involves using the four-digit positions and, in addition, two zone positions. The result is a coding method which is identical to the System/3 96-column card code. That is, the digit positions consist of 8, 4, 2, and 1 bits, and the zone positions consist of the B and A bits, with the following correspondence to the Hollerith zones.

Hollerith	On Bit	
Zone	B	A
12	•	•
11	•	
0		•

Thus, a student number and name punched in a card, as shown in Figure 6.4(a), might appear in storage (locations 671–680) as shown in Figure 6.4(b).

This code is technically called extended binary coded decimal although it is usually referred to as simply binary coded decimal; it is also called the *seven-bit alphanumeric* code (the seventh bit is the parity bit, which is described in the next section). As we have seen, this code is identical to the 96-column card code; it is commonly used for punched paper tape coding and for some types of magnetic tape systems. It is also used, with minor variations, in a number of computers, including the following:

IBM 1401
  (second generation)
Burroughs B200
  (second generation)
Honeywell H200
  (second generation)
Honeywell H6000
  (third generation)
International Computer Ltd.
  ICL 1900 (third generation)

Exercise

6.3 Write the seven-bit alphanumeric code for the word COMPUTER.

Fig. 6.4 (a) Information in a card; (b) equivalent core storage representation

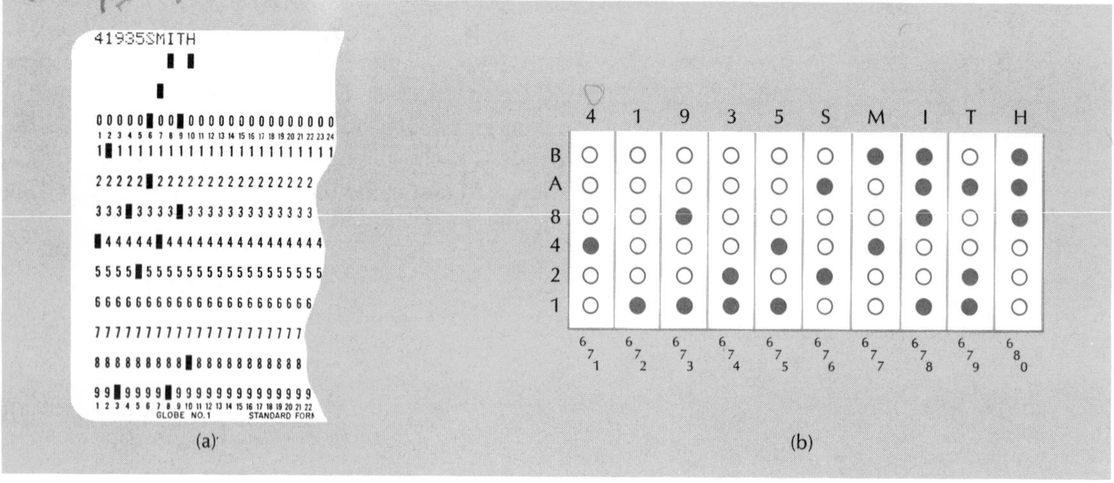

(a)

(b)

THE PARITY BIT   Virtually all digital computers employ a special error-control bit as part of each storage position; the sole purpose of this *parity-check bit* is to detect certain machine errors. Whenever a character is placed in storage— whether it is a letter, number, or special character—the number of 1-bits is checked. If there is an even number of them, the computer automatically turns on the parity bit to give an odd number of them in the 1-state; if an odd number already exists, the parity bit is left in the 0-state. This is commonly referred to as *odd parity*; although odd parity is most commonly encountered, *even parity* is used in magnetic tape coding and in some computers.

Whenever any characters are moved or operated upon, the number of 1-bits is checked to make certain there is an odd number of them (an even number for even parity). If by chance there is an even number, a machine malfunction has occurred and the computer will indicate the error. This method of checking for internal errors in the computer is called *parity checking*. The seven-bit alphanumeric code with parity is illustrated for the letters A-I in Table 6.2.

Table 6.2

Letter	Parity	Zone		Digit				
	C	B	A	8	4	2	1	
A	0	1	1	0	0	0	1	3 1-bits
B	0	1	1	0	0	1	0	3 1-bits
C	1	1	1	0	0	1	1	5 1-bits
D	0	1	1	0	1	0	0	3 1-bits
E	1	1	1	0	1	0	1	5 1-bits
F	1	1	1	0	1	1	0	5 1-bits
G	0	1	1	0	1	1	1	5 1-bits
H	0	1	1	1	0	0	0	3 1-bits
I	1	1	1	1	0	0	1	5 1-bits

Exercise

odd

6.4 Write the equivalent seven-bit alphanumeric code, including the parity check bit (odd parity), for the word COMPUTER. (For example, the letter G would be B,A,4,2,1 and the letter K would be C,B,2.)

6.4
IBM 360/370
CODING
THE IBM 360/370 BYTE   The basic unit of storage in the IBM 360/370 is the *byte,* which consists of eight bits plus a parity bit which is normally ignored in descriptions of the byte.* However, unlike most earlier computers, the byte

---

*The concept of the storage byte has also been employed in the design of other computers, such as the RCA Spectra 70, the Univac 9000, and the English Electric Computers System 4.

can be coded and interpreted in a number of ways, depending upon the types of operations to be performed and the instructions which are used. These include both fixed word length capabilities and variable field length capabilities which are described in a later section of this chapter.

THE EXTENDED BINARY CODED DECIMAL·INTERCHANGE CODE   One of two computer codes commonly used today is the *Extended Binary Coded Decimal Interchange Code (EBCDIC)* adopted by IBM as the standard code in their System/360 and also used in the later System/370. Since the code consists of eight bits, each of which may be in the 1-state or the 0-state, this coding scheme allows 256 (2^8) different code combinations. For example, the letter *A* could be placed in one storage byte as 11000001. To be consistent with the Hollerith card code, the first four bits of the byte correspond to the zone portion of the card and the second four bits to the digit portion. (A half-byte is sometimes referred to as a "nibble.") Thus, the letter *A* may be represented in one storage byte as follows:

Zone   Digit

1 1 0 0 0 0 0 1

1 byte

EBCDIC codes for the letters, digits, and some of the special characters are summarized in Table 6.3.

Table 6.3   A PARTIAL CHARACTER LIST EXTENDED BINARY CODED DECIMAL INTERCHANGE CODE

Character	Code	Letter	Code	Letter	Code	Letter	Code	Digit	Code
blank	0100 0000							0	1111 0000
.	0100 1011	A	1100 0001	J	1101 0001			1	1111 0001
(	0100 1101	B	1100 0010	K	1101 0010	S	1110 0010	2	1111 0010
+	0100 1110	C	1100 0011	L	1101 0011	T	1110 0011	3	1111 0011
&	0101 0000	D	1100 0100	M	1101 0100	U	1110 0100	4	1111 0100
*	0101 1100	E	1100 0101	N	1101 0101	V	1110 0101	5	1111 0101
)	0101 1101	F	1100 0110	O	1101 0110	W	1110 0110	6	1111 0110
#	0111 1011	G	1100 0111	P	1101 0111	X	1110 0111	7	1111 0111
@	0111 1100	H	1100 1000	Q	1101 1000	Y	1110 1000	8	1111 1000
=	0111 1110	I	1100 1001	R	1101 1001	Z	1110 1001	9	1111 1001

If we look carefully at this table, we will see that the digit portion of the code (right four bits) have binary values equal to the digit portion of the card code. Furthermore, we can observe the following correspondence between the zone bits (left four bits) and the Hollerith zones.

C = parity bit

Hollerith	EBCDIC
12 zone	1100
11 zone	1101
0 zone	1110
no zone	1111

A – I
J – R
S – Z

7 Bit

A + B C 1100 positive sign
B 5 1101 negative sign
A 1111 no sign

The information in the partially punched card used to illustrate the seven-bit alphanumeric coding (Figure 6.4) is shown in 360/370 storage locations 4050 through 4059 in Figure 6.5.

Exercise

6.5 Write the EBCDIC code for the word COMPUTER.

C 1100 0011
O 1101 0110
M 1101 0100
P 1101 0111
U 1110 0100
T 1110 0011
E 1100 0101
R 1101 1001

NUMERIC FIELDS   A beginner's reaction to storing negative numbers within the computer probably would be simply to use a minus sign. For circuit design reasons, it is far more practical to position the indication of sign to the right

Fig. 6.5 (a) Information in a card; (b) equivalent EBCDIC representation.

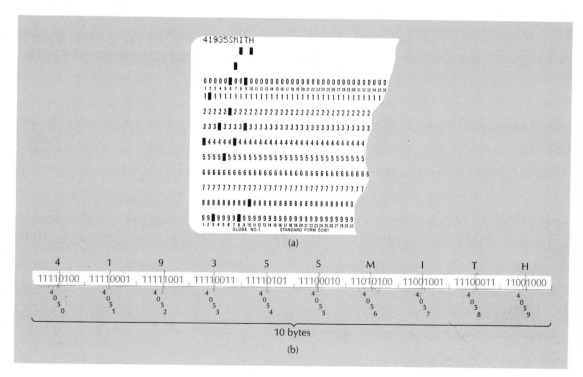

4	1	9	3	5	S	M	I	T	H
11110100	11110001	11111001	11110011	11110101	11100010	11010100	11001001	11100011	11001000
4050	4051	4052	4053	4054	4055	4056	4057	4058	4059

10 bytes

(b)

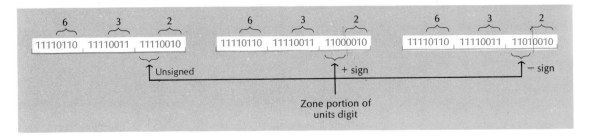

Fig. 6.6 Zoned decimal format.

of the number rather than to the left. A commonly used convention, carried over from punched card processing, involves indicating a negative field by use of an 11-zone over the units position (rightmost digit) of the number. In general, numeric fields within 360/370 storage use the zone half-byte of the units digit to indicate sign as follows:

Sign	EBCDIC	Hollerith
positive	1100	12 zone
negative	1101	11 zone
unsigned	1111	no zone

For instance, the three-digit numbers 632, +632, and −632 would appear in storage as illustrated in Figure 6.6. Numbers stored in this form of EBCDIC are commonly said to be in *zoned decimal format*.

However, before any variable field length arithmetic operations can be performed on numeric data, it must be converted to the more compact *packed decimal format*. With this format, *both* half-bytes are used to store digits and the zone portion of the EBCDIC code is discarded, except for the sign, which is stored in the extreme right half-byte. To illustrate packed decimal, the three examples, 632, +632, and −632, are shown in Figure 6.7.* The reader will note that only two bytes are required to store the three-digit number in packed format. As we can see, a numeric field stored in packed format requires, in addition to an extra half-byte for the sign, one half the number of bytes as it does when stored in zoned decimal format. Packed decimal fields of variable length are used by the RPG and Cobol languages in the System/360 and the System/370.

---

*Within the IBM 360/370, all packed fields are considered as either negative or positive, with a number of zone configurations which are interpreted as positive. Whenever the result of an arithmetic operation produces a positive result, it is stored with a 12-zone. A no-zone condition only occurs within the machine as the result of an unsigned field being read from a card.

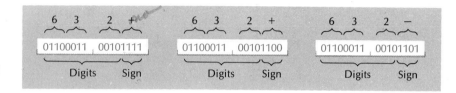

Fig. 6.7 Packed decimal format.

Exercise

6.6 Using binary representation, show the numbers 231, +231, and −231 in zoned decimal format as they would appear in storage; also show them in packed decimal format.

VARIABLE LENGTH FIELDS IN THE COMPUTER   As we have learned, computers such as the IBM 360/370 have the capacity for storing data fields in much the same manner as information is stored in a card. For example, a student name field occupying columns 7–26 of a punched card would be stored in 20 consecutive storage positions of the computer. In Figure 6.5 the name SMITH is shown in storage positions 4055–4059; presumably the entire 20-position name field would occupy locations 4055–4074. Now if in writing a program we desire that this name field be moved to some other portion of storage, we would have to provide the computer with sufficient information to determine both the beginning and the end of the field. This notion is familiar from our study of unit record processing; for instance, we might refer to the "parts description field in columns 11–34," or to the "nine-digit Social Security number field beginning in column 4," or to the "invoice number field in print positions 13–21 of an output document."

   To illustrate field definition within a computer with variable field length, let us consider the following 10-position field as it would appear in storage.

That portion of storage of interest to us (locations 7816–7825) is shaded for convenient reference. The reader will note that storage preceding position 7816 and following position 7825 contains other information which is not part of the name field. This is virtually identical to the punched card, where fields are punched side by side with no separating blank columns. Since the computer does not recognize the ending of one field and the beginning of the next by the context in which they are used, the designers must build into the machine special provisions for specifying this information.

FIELD LENGTH DESIGNATION   In many computers, variable-length fields are referred to by the address of the leftmost position of the field. For instance, the data field in the preceding example would be addressed by location 7816. The fact that the data actually occupies locations 7816 *through* 7825 is indicated by designating the actual number of locations to be included in the field as a part of the instruction itself. For instance, in the IBM 360/370 and the RCA Spectra 70 (no longer manufactured), the actual length of the field is included as part of the machine instruction; in the Honeywell 6030, the machine instruction refers to information elsewhere in storage which describes the location of the field and its length.

CHARACTERISTICS OF THE IBM 360/370   Generally speaking, second-generation computers were designed for either scientific processing or for business data processing. The typical scientific requirements involve extensive high-speed computational ability with limited alphabetic data manipulation capacity. In contrast, business processing involves extensive input/output and data manipulation operations with only a limited computational requirement. Categorically speaking, the scientific need lends itself well to the fixed word length computer and the business need to the variable field length machine. One of the important features of most third-generation computer systems is the combination of the fixed and variable field length features, yielding computers that are well suited for both scientific and business processing. The IBM 360/370, using the concept of the 8-bit storage byte, is the most commonly used computer of this type. Fixed-length capabilities in the 360/370 are provided by combining four adjacent storage bytes to form the *fullword* (32 bits). A special set of machine instructions allows the programmer to manipulate fixed word length data.

For business applications, special instructions can be employed which operate on variable field length data. In this mode of operation, each byte is treated individually and, for practical purposes, is equivalent to one card column.

6.5
MORE ON BINARY
—BINARY
OPERATIONS

BINARY TO DECIMAL CONVERSION   Occasionally the programmer will find it necessary to convert a binary representation from the machine to decimal representations or, conversely, to convert a decimal quantity to binary. From Section 6.2, we recall that conversion from binary to decimal can easily be performed by expanding the binary number in the powers of its base. That is,

$$101101_2 \equiv 1 \times 2^5 + 0 \times 2^4 + 1 \times 2^3 + 1 \times 2^2 + 0 \times 2^1 + 1 \times 2^0$$
$$\equiv 32 + 8 + 4 + 1$$
$$\equiv 45_{10}$$

This is a convenient method to remember and use because it relies on the basic characteristic of the number systems we have studied and involves no "gimmicks." When converting whole numbers, it is usually a simple matter to scan the binary number from right to left, writing down appropriate powers in the process.

DECIMAL TO BINARY CONVERSION To perform the inverse operation, that is, to convert from base 10 to base 2, it is convenient to write out a table of powers of 2. For instance, 93_{10} is readily converted by reference to the following table:

$2^0 = 1$	$2^4 = 16$	$2^8 = 256$	$2^{12} = 4096$
$2^1 = 2$	$2^5 = 32$	$2^9 = 512$	$2^{13} = 8192$
$2^2 = 4$	$2^6 = 64$	$2^{10} = 1024$	$2^{14} = 16384$
$2^3 = 8$	$2^7 = 128$	$2^{11} = 2048$	$2^{15} = 32768$

Since the number to be converted is between 2^6 (64) and 2^7 (128), 6 will be the largest power of base 2 which will be required. The process now consists merely of breaking the number 93 into a sum of powers of 2 with the largest being 64. This gives

$$
\begin{array}{rl}
93 & \\
-64 & \quad 2^6 \\
\hline
29 & \\
-16 & \quad 2^4 \\
\hline
13 & \\
-8 & \quad 2^3 \\
\hline
5 & \\
-4 & \quad 2^2 \\
\hline
1 & \quad 2^0 \\
\end{array}
$$

or

$$93 = 64 + 16 + 8 + 4 + 1 = 2^6 + 2^4 + 2^3 + 2^2 + 2^0$$

In order to include all powers of 2 from 0 through 6, this would be written

$$93 = 1 \times 2^6 + 0 \times 2^5 + 1 \times 2^4 + 1 \times 2^3 + 1 \times 2^2 \\ + 0 \times 2^1 + 1 \times 2^0$$

Thus $93_{10} \equiv 1011101_2$

Once we understand the basic nature of the number systems we are dealing with, conversion from one system to another is a straightforward, although somewhat cumbersome, task. To facilitate conversion, both to and from decimal, a number of techniques have been developed; however, we shall not consider them in this book.

Exercises

Using the method of the preceding sections, convert the following decimal numbers to binary.

6.7 0, 4, 9, 27, 63, 64, 91, 593

6.8 1, 8, 13, 36, 127, 128, 129, 427

Using the method of the preceding sections, convert the following binary numbers to decimal.

6.9 1, 10, 101, 1111, 10000, 10001, 1011010

6.10 0, 11, 111, 11101, 100000, 11111, 100001, 1010101

6.11 Why is it meaningless to speak of the binary number 102_2?

BINARY ARITHMETIC   The common arithmetic operations, such as addition and subtraction, are as easily performed on binary numbers as on decimal numbers. For example, the basic rules of addition are

$$0 + 0 = 0$$
$$0 + 1 = 1$$
$$1 + 0 = 1$$
$$1 + 1 = 0 \text{ with a carry of } 1$$

The operation of adding two binary numbers is much the same as adding two base 10 numbers. For example, consider the addition of two decimal numbers 392 and 469:

```
1 1     carries
3 9 2   addend
4 6 9   augend
8 6 1   sum
```

Whenever the sum of a pair of digits exceeds 9, only the units digit is recorded, and a high-order carry of 1 is propagated to the next position. The addition process in binary arithmetic is essentially the same, as the binary numbers 11001 and 1011 illustrate.

```
1 1   1 1     carries
0 1 1 0 0 1   addend
    1 0 1 1   augend
1 0 0 1 0 0   sum
```
$2^5 + 2^2 = 32 + 4 = 36$

Converting each of these to base 10 gives the following check:

$$11001_2 \equiv 25 \qquad 25 + 11 = 36$$
$$1011_2 \equiv 11$$
$$100100_2 \equiv 36$$

Two simple rules of thumb are apparent from this example. First, if a column including the carry consists of an odd number of 1-digits, a 1 should be placed in the sum position of that column; otherwise, a 0 should be recorded. Second, if there are two or three 1-digits (including a carry) in a column, a carry should be placed in the next column. Although binary addition is sufficiently simple that memorization of such rules is of little or no value, techniques similar to this are used in computer arithmetic units to simplify electronic equipment.

Exercise

6.12 Add the following binary numbers.

a. 101
   10

b. 1101
   101

c. 11101
    11

d. 11111
     1

e. 101101
   011101

f. 100
  10
  11

FIXED WORD LENGTH CONCEPTS For binary arithmetic operations, most computers involve the concept of a *fixed-length word* of binary data. For example, the IBM 1130 and the Digital Equipment Corporation PDP 11 machines utilize a *16-bit* word, and the IBM 360/370 uses a *32-bit* word. The internal capacity of a machine such as the IBM 1130 might consist typically of 8000 16-bit words; the PDP 11/70 (a small-scale computer) is available with up to one million words of storage. Each of these words is identified by a unique *address* within storage (somewhat analogous to the pigeonhole example of Chapter 4). It is thus possible to reference the contents of a selected storage word by its address. Within a 16-bit word machine, we might view the word as illustrated in the examples of Figure 6.8. (For the sake of clarity, place values are indicated directly above each binary digit.) It is common practice to use the leftmost bit as a sign bit where the digit 0 represents a positive number

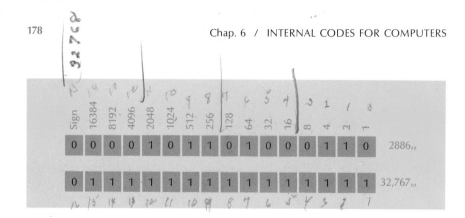

Sign	16384	8192	4096	2048	1024	512	256	128	64	32	16	8	4	2	1	
0	0	0	0	1	0	1	1	0	1	0	0	0	1	1	0	2886_{10}
0	1	1	1	1	1	1	1	1	1	1	1	1	1	1	1	$32{,}767_{10}$

Fig. 6.8   Storage words.

and the digit 1 represents a negative number. For negative numbers, however, the notion of the *arithmetic complement* is used, in which case all negative numbers are stored in a complement form with a sign bit of 1.* Under these conditions, the range of numbers for a 16-bit word is $+32767_{10}$ (as illustrated in Figure 6.8) to -32768_{10}. Whenever larger numbers are required in a 16-bit machine, a number of coding methods are commonly employed to expand this basic capacity.

Exercise

6.13   What would be the largest numbers which could be stored (using the first bit for sign) with a 6-bit register? With a 12-bit register?

6.6

OCTAL AND
HEXADECIMAL
NUMBERS

CORRESPONDENCE WITH BINARY AND DECIMAL   Although all digital computers operate in a binary mode in one manner or another, the binary number system is not the only one of importance in the study of computers. Where the binary system—with 0 and 1 corresponding to the on and off states of electronic components—is ideal for use in the computers, the large binary numbers are often cumbersome for the programmer. For example, communication from one programmer to another is hardly enhanced when the topic is a binary number within the computer such as 1001010110101110. Although the communication problem would be improved by converting to base 10, the binary-decimal conversion is a cumbersome process. As a result, two other number bases, 8 and 16, are commonly used with computers because of their important relationship to binary (that is, both 8 and 16 are powers of 2).

Whereas the base is 10 in our decimal system and 2 in the binary system, the base in an *octal* (base 8) system is 8 and in a *hexadecimal* (base 16) system is 16. Since an octal system requires eight distinct digits, the digits 0 through 7 are used. On the other hand, a hexadecimal system requires 16 unique digits;

---

*For an explanation of binary complements, the reader is referred to Price and Miller, *Elements of Data Processing Mathematics*, 2nd ed., Holt, Rinehart and Winston, 1970, Chapter 3.

thus, the 10 digits used in decimal are insufficient. Rather than generating new and strange "hieroglyphics," the ten digits and the first six letters of the alphabet are most commonly used. The correspondence between decimal, hexadecimal, binary, and octal is shown in Table 6.4. In the counting sequence, when the digit 7 is reached in octal and F (15_{10}) in hexadecimal, all the digits have been "used" in the respective systems. At this point, a high-order carry to the next digit is necessary in each instance, exactly as in decimal and binary counting.

Table 6.4 OCTAL AND HEXADECIMAL NUMBERS

Decimal	Hexadecimal	Binary	Octal	Decimal	Hexadecimal	Binary	Octal
0	0	0000	0	16	10	1 0000	20
1	1	0001	1	17	11	1 0001	21
2	2	0010	2	18	12	1 0010	22
3	3	0011	3	19	13	1 0011	23
4	4	0100	4	20	14	1 0100	24
5	5	0101	5	21	15	1 0101	25
6	6	0110	6	22	16	1 0110	26
7	7	0111	7	23	17	1 0111	27
8	8	1000	10	24	18	1 1000	30
9	9	1001	11	25	19	1 1001	31
10	A	1010	12	26	1A	1 1010	32
11	B	1011	13	27	1B	1 1011	33
12	C	1100	14	28	1C	1 1100	34
13	D	1101	15	29	1D	1 1101	35
14	E	1110	16	30	1E	1 1110	36
15	F	1111	17	31	1F	1 1111	37

In their structures, all four of these number systems are the same in that they all use the concept of place values representing powers of the number system base. For example, the quantity 101 would normally be interpreted as the decimal quantity "one hundred one." However, consider its meaning in each of the four number systems which we have studied.

$$101_2 \equiv 1\times2^2 + 0\times2^1 + 1\times2^0 \rightarrow 4 + 1 = 5_{10}$$
$$101_8 \equiv 1\times8^2 + 0\times8^1 + 1\times8^0 \rightarrow 64 + 1 = 65_{10}$$
$$101_{10} \equiv 1\times10^2 + 0\times10^1 + 1\times10^0 \rightarrow 100 + 1 = 101_{10}$$
$$101_{16} \equiv 1\times16^2 + 0\times16^1 + 1\times16^0 \rightarrow 256 + 1 = 257_{10}$$

Perhaps the curious reader wondered about the comment earlier that base 8 and 16 are commonly used in computers because of their important relationship to binary. That is, 8 and 16 are both integer powers of 2, since $8 = 2^3$ and $16 = 2^4$. (Note that 10 is *not* an integer power of 2.) As a result, the eight octal digits and the sixteen hexadecimal digits may be represented by exactly three and four binary digits, respectively, as shown in Table 6.5.

Table 6.5   OCTAL AND HEXADECIMAL REPRESENTATIONS

Octal	Binary	Hexadecimal	Binary	Hexadecimal	Binary
0	000	0	0000	8	1000
1	001	1	0001	9	1001
2	010	2	0010	A or X	1010
3	011	3	0011	B	1011
4	100	4	0100	C	1100
5	101	5	0101	D	1101
6	110	6	0110	E	1110
7	111	7	0111	F	1111

CONVERSION—BINARY TO OCTAL AND HEXADECIMAL   To convert from binary to octal or from binary to hexadecimal, it is only necessary to group the binary digits in groups of three (for octal) or four (for hexadecimal) and substitute the appropriate octal or hexadecimal digits. For example, consider converting the binary number 1101011011.

$$1101011011_2 = \underline{001}\ \underline{101}\ \underline{011}\ \underline{011} \qquad 1101011011_2 = \underline{0011}\ \underline{0101}\ \underline{1011}$$

$$\qquad\qquad\qquad 1 \quad 5 \quad 3 \quad 3 \qquad\qquad\qquad\qquad 3 \quad 5 \quad B$$

$$\equiv 1533_8 \qquad\qquad\qquad\qquad \equiv 35B_{16}$$

The reader will note that in both cases the grouping of digits proceeds from the right to the left.

CONVERSION—OCTAL AND HEXADECIMAL TO BINARY   Needless to say, converting from octal to binary or from hexadecimal to binary is every bit as simple. It is only necessary to expand each octal digit into its three-bit binary form or each hexadecimal digit into its four-bit binary form as follows:

$$2607_8 \equiv 010\ 110\ 000\ 111 \qquad 29CA_{16} \equiv 0010\ 1001\ 1100\ 1010$$

$$\equiv 10110000111_2 \qquad\qquad \equiv 10100111001010_2$$

With this convenient relationship between binary and hexadecimal, a programmer or operator can easily look at a row of lights on a computer console which shows 1s and 0s (for example, 0001100111000010), group them in fours, and record the value as the hexadecimal number 19C2.

As we have seen earlier in this chapter, the basic unit of storage in the IBM 360/370 (and in many other computers) is the *byte*, which consists of eight bits. Because of the versatility of the eight-bit storage unit, which has virtually become a standard, hexadecimal is commonly used. The contents of an eight-bit unit can easily be represented by two hexadecimal digits.

Although many computers are classified as octal or as hexadecimal machines, it is important not to be misled by this terminology. The octal or hexadecimal numbers are used simply as a convenient device to represent binary quantities (usually storage addresses). Within the computer, operations take place in binary and storage addresses appear in binary form.

Exercises

6.14 Convert the following binary numbers to octal.
  a. 101001101   b. 101111011
  c. 1101011001   d. 1110111101

6.15 Convert the following octal numbers to binary.
  a. 617   b. 526
  c. 103   d. 240

6.16 Convert the following binary numbers to hexadecimal.
  a. 10011100   b. 11100011
  c. 1110101101   d. 100011110

6.17 Convert the following hexadecimal numbers to binary.
  a. C14   b. B09
  c. 1D80   d. 27A5

Answers to Preceding Exercises

6.1 a. 13; b. 21; c. 28; d. 22.

6.2

Binary	Decimal
10000	16
10001	17
10010	18
10011	19
10100	20
10101	21
10110	22
10111	23
11000	24
11001	25

6.3

Letters	Hollerith	Seven-Bit Alphanumeric
C	12,3	B,A,2,1
O	11,6	B,4,2
M	11,4	B,4
P	11,7	B,4,2,1
U	0,4	A,4
T	0,3	A,2,1
E	12,5	B,A,4,1
R	11,9	B,8,1

6.4

Letters	Seven-Bit Alphanumeric
C	C,B,A,2,1
O	B,4,2
M	C,B,4
P	C,B,4,2,1
U	C,A,4
T	A,2,1
E	C,B,A,4,1
R	B,8,1

6.5

Letters	EBCDIC
C	1100 0011
O	1101 0110
M	1101 0100
P	1101 0111
U	1110 0100
T	1110 0011
E	1100 0101
R	1101 1001

6.6

	Zoned decimal			Packed decimal	
231	11110010	11110011	11110001	00100011	00011111
+231	11110010	11110011	11000001	00100011	00011100
−231	11110010	11110011	11010001	00100011	00011101
	1st byte	2nd byte	3rd byte	1st byte	2nd byte

6.7 0, 100, 1001, 11011, 111111, 1000000, 1011011, 1001010001

6.9 1, 2, 5, 15, 16, 17, 90

6.11 To speak of 102_2 is meaningless, since a binary system includes only two digits, whereas 102 includes three.

6.12 a. 111; c. 100000; e. 1001010

6.13 6-bit register; 31; 12-bit register; 2047

6.14 a. 515; c. 1531

6.15 a. 110001111; c. 1000011

6.16 a. 9C; c. 3AD

6.17 a. 110000010100; c. 1110110000000

Additional Exercises

6.18 Convert each of the following sets of numbers from one base to the other as indicated.
- a. Decimal to binary: 9, 13, 44, 255, 256, 257
- b. Binary to decimal: 11, 101, 1101, 111111, 1000000, 1000001
- c. Octal to binary: 1627, 152, 146, 777, 1001
- d. Binary to octal: 101, 100110, 1101111, 1011011, 10001101, 10111111
- e. Hexadecimal to binary: 7, D, 20, A5, 1B3, 2C3
- f. Binary to hexadecimal: 101, 100110, 1101111, 1011011, 10001101

6.19 Add the following pairs of binary numbers.

a. 1101	b. 1011011
110	110101

c. 1100001	d. 11001110
111111	1101011

6.20 Convert each letter of the word FORMAT to its corresponding seven-bit alphanumeric code (with odd parity).

6.21 Convert each letter of the word FORMAT to its corresponding EBCDIC code; your result may be either in binary or hexadecimal.

6.22 The evolution of the computer has seen a number of different codes. As we have learned, the binary coded decimal method uses the four digits 1, 2, 4, and 8 for coding the decimal digits 1–9. With the two-of-five code, each storage position consists of five bits and each digit is represented by having two of the five bits in the on-state. Select a combination of five digits 0–9 for the place values of such a coding scheme to yield the nine nonzero decimal digits. (Note that one of the digit position values will necessarily be 0.) An advantage of this coding method is that a parity bit is not required because all characters are represented by two on-bits.

Note: The following two exercises relate mainly to number systems described in Sections 6.1, 6.2, 6.5, and 6.6.

6.23 True-False. Determine whether each of the following is true or false.

a. The binary number system has been developed within the past 30 years for use with the computer.

b. The term *bit* is a commonly used contraction of "binary digit."

c. When adding two binary numbers, carries are handled in much the same way as they are in decimal arithmetic.

d. As computer technology has progressed, the use of binary within the computer is being replaced largely with octal and hexadecimal.

e. Octal and hexadecimal refer to number systems with bases of 8 and 16, respectively.

f. The principal reason for using an octal or hexadecimal system instead of a decimal system in the design of a computer is the convenient relationship to the binary system.

g. The letters A, B, C, D, E, and F are used in hexadecimal to represent the decimal quantities 10, 11, 12, 13, 14, and 15.

h. Each hexadecimal digit represents four bits.

i. In a counting sequence the next numbers following $9F_{16}$ and 77_8 are $A0_{16}$ and 100_8, respectively.

j. Both the octal and hexadecimal systems can be used as "shorthands" for displaying binary numbers.

6.24 Multiple Choice. Determine which answer best completes or answers each of the following statements.

a. In the representation 10^4, the quantity 4 is referred to as the (1) cipherization value, (2) exponent, (3) base, (4) place holder.

b. The binary, or base 2, number system, (1) was developed for use with modern computers, (2) includes the digits 0, 1, and 2, (3) is similar in its structure to the decimal

number system, (4) none of the preceding, (5) both 1 and 3.

c. Arithmetic operations in most modern computers involve the use of (1) decimal numbers, (2) binary numbers, (3) base 16 numbers, (4) additional tables.

d. The term *bit* refers to (1) small particles of waste which lodge in computer components, causing failures, (2) digit, (3) decimal digit, (4) binary digit, (5) none of the preceding.

e. The decimal equivalent of 101101_2 is (1) 35, (2) 36, (3) 63, (4) none of the preceding.

f. The binary equivalent of the decimal number 93 is (1) 10111010, (2) 1011111, (3) 1011101, (4) none of the preceding.

g. The range of numbers which can be stored in an eight-bit register which uses the leftmost bit for sign is (1) -128 to $+127$, (2) -128 to $+128$, (3) -99999999 to $+99999999$, (4) cannot be determined without knowing the type of computer.

h. A number system which consists of the digits 0, 1, 2, and 3 would (1) be totally impractical to use, (2) be termed as base 4 system, (3) not allow for arithmetic operations, (4) not allow for conversion to other number systems.

Note: The remaining exercises relate mainly to computer coding concepts described in Sections 6.3 and 6.4.

6.25 Matching. Match each item in 1-6 with the corresponding description in a-h.

1. binary coded decimal
2. bit
3. EBCDIC
4. seven-bit alphanumeric
5. byte
6. parity bit

a. The internal code used for storing alphanumeric information in the IBM 360/370.

b. Pertaining to a commonly used code for storing alphanumeric data using two zone bits and four numeric bits.

c. The means used by the computer to check for errors during internal manipulation of data.

d. The basic addressable storage unit of the IBM 360/370.

e. The method by which decimal digits may be coded using binary digits.

f. Referring to the basic two-state storage unit with the computer.

6.26 True-False. Determine whether each of the following is true or false.

a. The binary coded decimal system uses the four digits 1, 2, 4, and 7 for coding the nine nonzero decimal digits.

b. The seven-bit alphanumeric coding method includes two zone bits and four numeric bits for coding alphabetic information.

c. The parity bit is used primarily to ensure that data is correctly read from an input device into storage.

d. Using even parity, the digit 5 would be coded as 4,1, but the digit 8 would be coded as C,8.

e. The basic unit of storage in the IBM 360/370 is the seven-bit byte.

f. The Extended Binary Coded Decimal Interchange Code (EBCDIC) was introduced by the American National Standards Institute and is used by most computer companies; IBM is a notable exception.

g. In principle, the EBCDIC code is completely different from the Hollerith code.

h. One common means for classifying computers is as variable field length or as fixed field length.

i. The most common means for referring to a given field in a variable field length machine is to specify both the beginning address and the ending address of the field.

j. Virtually all fixed word length computers use 32-bit words.

k. Most modern computers, such as the IBM 360/370 are basically fixed word length because of the greater speed of fixed length operations.

Chapter 7

Program Planning and Preparation

7.1
ON SOLVING
PROBLEMS

BASIC STEPS   With the widespread use of computers in virtually all disciplines, the average person, when faced with a burdensome computational or data processing problem, will frequently respond with, "Let the computer do it." Such a comment usually reflects a basic misunderstanding on two points: (1) The computer is not capable of "thinking" in the usual sense; it can operate only when given a set of detailed instructions written by a programmer. Thus, a complete understanding of the problem and of how to solve it must be possessed by the computer user. (2) Not all problems lend themselves to practical solution on a computer. As we shall see, there are criteria for judging whether or not a given application is, in fact, a realistic "computer application."

By this time, the reader has probably recognized that the programmers themselves must "solve" the problem and that the computer is capable of only the most basic arithmetic and logic operations. The creative portion of the overall process remains the task of people; the machine simply follows basic instructions. However, the coding of instruction sequences for the computer is only one phase of the overall task of problem solution. The general steps can be loosely categorized as:

1. Defining the problem.
2. Planning and analyzing the solution of the problem.
3. Programming or coding the problem in a computer-intelligible language.
4. Testing the program.
5. Documenting the problem solution and the program.
6. Running the program for production purposes.

Figure 7.1 shows a simplification of these steps on a time sequencing scale. In reality, the relationship of these individual phases is usually much more complex than illustrated.

PROBLEM DEFINITION   The average student of programming seldom recognizes the significance of the problem definition phase since, in a conventional programming course, problems are carefully defined by the instructor. This

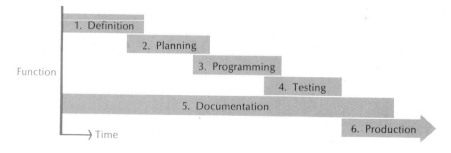

Fig. 7.1 Steps of a
problem solution.

is hardly the case in an actual business environment. The programming department is commonly faced with such needs from other departments as, "We require a system to report and perform statistical analyses on student entrance examinations." Upon questioning, it frequently becomes apparent that persons making requests are (1) not really aware of what they want, (2) uncertain of how their needs can be fulfilled, (3) not very convincing in their need for the results, and/or (4) totally unaware of whether or not the job is economically justifiable. It is the job of the *systems analyst* to resolve these unknowns.

First of all, a careful evaluation must be made of whether or not the problem is actually worth doing. This might sound strange, but in any data processing installation, a significant number of job requests are received that are totally impractical. This can occur for a number of reasons, such as:

- The desired output simply cannot be clearly defined, nor can the exact use to which the results are to be put be pinpointed.
- No realistic method of solution is available for the problem. It is important to recognize that the computer itself usually adds little or nothing to conceiving a method of solution. Whereas most problems *can* be solved, the point here is whether or not a *realistic* solution is available.
- It is economically impractical to use a computer. For instance, the value of the results simply might not warrant the cost of preparing and running the program. Sometimes the management of a company, in anxiously computerizing their operations, will fail to recognize that some tasks are more efficiently performed manually.

During the later steps of the problem definition phase, program planning usually begins.

PROGRAM PLANNING   Once the general method of problem solution has been determined, then the actual process of laying out the sequence of events can begin. At this stage, details of the input data and output reports are carefully spelled out and documented (another phase of the overall operation which is taking place concurrently). Here the fine points of the solution method are analyzed; occasionally results of this work will require that ground rules conceived during the definition phase be modified. It is usually during this phase that the choice of a programming language is made. The end result of the planning phase is a set of flowcharts which describe the overall logic of the problem solution. We have studied system flowcharts in earlier chapters; a portion of this chapter is devoted to preparing and using program flowcharts.

PROGRAMMING   Once the program logic is clearly defined, it is practical to begin writing the actual computer program to perform the desired operations using the flowcharts as a guide. In some instances, particular techniques which

appeared practical during the planning phase will be obviously impractical
when the coding is attempted, necessitating modifications to the program logic.
If the program planning phase has been carefully completed and a good set
of flowcharts is available, the coding phase is considerably simplified. In many
cases, the program planning phase is performed by a systems analyst, and the
actual programming by a *coder* or *programmer*, a person with less training and
experience. *or writing a program*

TESTING   Once the beginner finally "persuades" the computer to accept a
program, process the data, and print results, he/she commonly breathes a sigh
of relief and concludes, "On to the next problem!" However, we must never
trust the output of a computer simply because it comes from a computer. This
is not to imply that the computer is a clumsy, error-prone oaf. To the contrary,
modern computers are so designed that very few machine errors go undetected
by the computer itself. The problem lies with the programmer in preparing
the set of instructions. For example, suppose a program is being written to
update customer charge accounts and the following directions are to be given
to the computer:

NEW BALANCE = OLD BALANCE − PAYMENTS + CHARGES

Now if the programmer inadvertently coded this as

NEW BALANCE = OLD BALANCE + PAYMENTS + CHARGES

the computer would not complain, but the customers certainly would. Errors
such as these are detected and corrected through preparing and running test
data.

DOCUMENTATION   Where each of the preceding phases overlaps one another slightly, documentation should be an ongoing process from the beginning.
The end result of the documentation should be a carefully written program
report. Although each computer installation in business or industry has its
own rules and format, most will include such items as those that follow:

- *Problem definition:* a complete description of the problem for which
  the program is written.
- *Methods:* means and methods used in the program.
- *Program:* a listing of the source program.
- *Flowchart:* mainline and detailed flowcharts for the program (flowcharting will be discussed in detail later in this chapter).
- *Program usage:* a detailed description of how to use the program,
  including switch settings (if any), input format, output format, and
  special limitations.

6 • *Sample run:* a sample run showing expected output from the sample input.

All too frequently, programmers will complete problems and, in their anxiety to proceed to others, will write incomplete reports, if any at all. In documenting work that has been completed, programmers should continually consider these reports from the point of view of a person who needs to use the program but knows nothing about it.

PRODUCTION   Programmers will often be ecstatic over the shrewd coding techniques they have used, but everyone else is normally preoccupied with but one thing, the end results. Once a program is completely tested, then it can be made available as a production program to perform the job for which it was designed. Although we might expect all the preceding phases to end at this point, it does not necessarily follow. Programs are commonly in a nearly constant state of expansion and improvement, sometimes even requiring a redefining of the basic problem.

The overall process of problem definition through production is illustrated in Figure 7.2 (see the following page).

Exercise

7.1 Describe the six phases in preparing a program.

see Ap. 215 or 188

7.2 ALGORITHMS WHAT IS AN ALGORITHM?   The pigeonhole example of Chapter 4 involved a detailed set of steps to be performed in calculating grade point averages (page 92). This program of instructions is commonly referred to as an *algorithm*. An algorithm, broadly speaking, is no more than a set of rules or instructions for doing something. In this sense, a recipe for baking a cake is an algorithm; calculating interest for a bank account involves an algorithm; solving a set of equations involves an algorithm; computing a satellite orbit involves an algorithm and so on. Of foremost importance to the programmer is that programming itself involves the preparation of algorithms (programs) for the computer. Without a systematic approach, programming of any complexity becomes virtually impossible.

EXAMPLES OF ALGORITHMS

To gain insight into algorithms, let us consider the simple task of calculating interest.

Algorithm

Add the interest rate (expressed in hundredths) to 1.00; raise this sum to the fifth power and multiply by 200. Repeat this process for each of the interest rates.

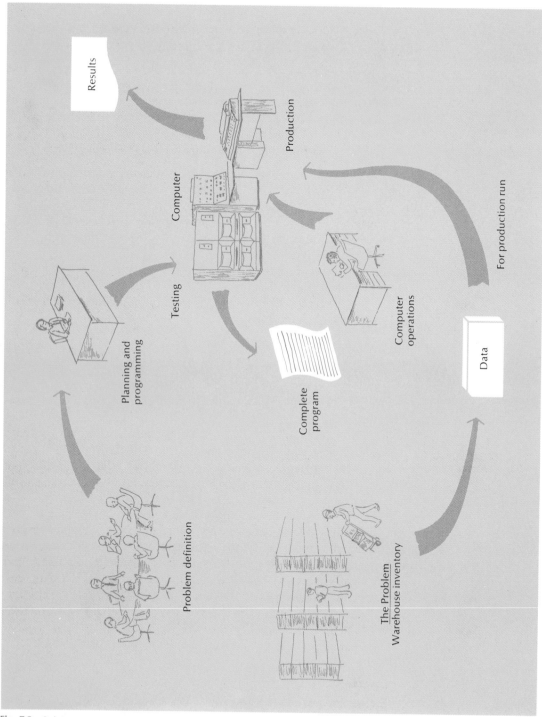

Fig. 7.2 Solving a problem.

Although this description is complete, an individual with no prior knowledge of compound interest would probably find it somewhat confusing. Notice how much clearer the language of algebra is for expressing this algorithm in the following alternate solution.

EXAMPLE 7.1

Algorithm

Calculate the interest on $200 invested for five years compounded annually at each of the four interest rates 4, 6, 8, and 10 percent.

Algorithm (alternate)

Calculate interest using the formula

$$I = 200(1.0 + i)^5$$

for values of $i = 0.04, 0.06, 0.08,$ and 0.10.

What is confusing and sometimes even ambiguous when written in ordinary English becomes obvious when written in algebraic form. The use of algebra in expressing mathematical operations to be performed in a computer program is often invaluable. In fact, the Fortran programming language is designed to appear as similar to the language of algebra as possible.

On the other hand, algorithms are hardly restricted to the field of mathematics, as Example 7.2 illustrates.

EXAMPLE 7.2

Turn on a gas furnace.

Algorithm

First turn the fan on, then check the pilot light. If it is burning, turn the gas valve on; if it is not burning, turn off the pilot light valve, wait five minutes, turn the valve on, and light the pilot light. Then turn the gas valve on.

Virtually all of us have encountered such a set of instructions at one time or another and have found it necessary to reread them several times to understand their meaning. Frequently the problem is compounded by ambiguities; for example, what is to be done if the furnace has several valves and the main valve is not clearly obvious? (Of course, it is possible to go overboard on clarity, as many parents will attest after attempting to assemble junior's new toy in which "flange C is overlapped with the interior of column A and connected by the inverted hexagonal crossbolt.") However, consider the clarity introduced in the task of lighting the furnace when the algorithm is stated as follows:

Algorithm (alternate)

1. Turn on the fan.
2. Check the pilot light. If it is on, skip to step 7; otherwise continue to step 3.

3. Turn off pilot light valve (small valve with "P" imprinted on handle).
4. Wait five minutes.
5. Turn on pilot light valve.
6. Light pilot light.
7. Turn on main gas valve (red-handled valve near bottom of furnace).

Obviously this detailed, step-by-step approach is far less likely to be confusing. Very often we can get by with writing vague and sometimes ambiguous instructions to another person because a human being can exercise a degree of judgment in carrying out the operations. However, in writing computer programs, we must be much more precise, because the computer has no means for exercising judgment to determine what we think; it can only do as it is explicitly told.

EXAMPLE 7.3

An employer plans to pay a bonus to each employee. Those earning $6000 or over are to be paid 5 percent of their salary; those earning less than $6000 are to be paid $300. Prepare a set of instructions (algorithm) for performing this operation.

Algorithm

1. Obtain next employee folder.
2. Compare salary to $6000; if less, go to step 5.
3. Calculate bonus as

   bonus $= 0.05 \times$ salary

4. Go to step 6.
5. Set bonus to $300.
6. Record bonus on employee ledger.
7. Return to step 1.

Note that this sequence differs from the sequence for lighting a furnace in that it is repetitive in nature. That is, the sequence of steps is carried out for one employee and then the same set of operations is performed for the next employee. Of course, the difference between successive executions of the loop involves the numbers which are used in the calculations.

Exercises

Write an algorithm for each of the following problems.

7.2 A paint touch-up job is to be done in a home. The original color was obtained by adding small amounts of red and blue paint to a can of white paint. Mix some paint to match the present color.

7.3 From a set of examination papers, find the paper with the highest score.

7.2 sort from highest score to lowest score

Pg. 215

7.4 Working as a clerk, you accept one dollar for the purchase of an item. Determine what the change should be in terms of half dollars, quarters, dimes, nickels, and pennies for a given amount of purchase.

7.3 FLOWCHARTING PRINCIPLES

WHY FLOWCHARTS? The three examples of the preceding section and the pigeonhole example of Chapter 4 serve to illustrate the basic nature of algorithms. These English descriptions appear to be adequate for the relatively simple tasks of the examples. However, as a given problem becomes more complex, the algorithm can become more cumbersome. This is commonly due to the fact that the extensive and detailed descriptions, together with the ambiguous nature of the English language, tend to disguise the basic logical structure of the algorithm. This was especially true of Example 7.2, which consisted of descriptions of how to light a furnace. The problem was partially resolved by listing steps 1, 2, 3, and so on. However, a long and confusing sequence of steps can very often be clearly illustrated by a flowchart (consistent with the notion that "a picture is worth a thousand words"). Flowcharts fall in two broad categories, *system flowcharts* and *program flowcharts*. The system flowchart was used in Chapter 2 to describe the logical flow of data through all parts of an overall data gathering and processing system.

As the name implies, a program flowchart describes what takes place in a computer program (the program flowchart is often referred to as a *block diagram*). It displays specific operations and decisions, and indicates their sequence within the program. One of the most important uses of the program flowchart is to provide the programmer with the means of visualizing during development of a program the sequence in which operations occur. Further, it serves to display the relationship of one portion of a program to another. An entire program flowchart is commonly represented in a system flowchart as a single phase of the overall operation. In this chapter and those that follow, primary emphasis will be on programming and program flowcharts.

Because of the importance of using flowcharts in programming, they will be widely used in chapters which follow. In perusing data processing literature, the reader commonly encounters the same geometric symbol used by different authors to illustrate different operations. In the interest of standardization, all flowcharts in this book will conform to the ANSI (American National Standards Institute) flowcharting standards as adopted by IBM.

Exercise

7.5 Distinguish between a program flowchart and a system flowchart.

The flowcharting standards define a set of several *basic symbols* which are common to both system and program flowcharting and *symbols related to programming* which are related specifically to program flowcharting. The basic symbols which we shall study in the following paragraphs are processing, input/output, connector, and flowline; those related to programming which we shall study are decision and terminal. Three of the basic symbols, processing, input/output, and flowline, are illustrated in Figure 7.3.

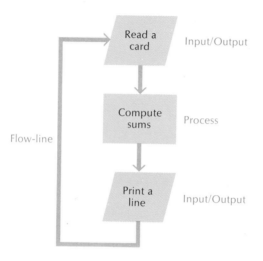

Fig. 7.3   A simple flowchart.

FLOWLINES   The *flowline* symbol represents the direction of processing flow, which is generally from top to bottom and left to right. However, most programs involve decisions that result in multiple courses of action. Frequently, the net effect is a complicated flowchart. In order to avoid ambiguity, flowlines are usually drawn with an arrowhead at the point of entry to a symbol. Good practice also dictates that flowlines should not cross each other and that "jogs" be avoided whenever possible.

Flowlines

PROCESSING   The *processing* symbol is used to represent general processing functions not represented by other symbols. These functions are generally those that contain the actual information processing operations of the program, such as arithmetic and data movement instructions.

Process

INPUT/OUTPUT   The *input/output* symbol is used to denote any function of an input/output device in the program. In addition, making information available for processing is generally considered an input function and recording processed information, an output function.

Input/Output

CONNECTOR   Another of the basic symbols that will be useful is the *connector* symbol. Whenever a flowchart becomes complex enough that the number and direction of flowlines is confusing, it is useful to utilize the connector symbol. This symbol represents an entry from, or an exit to, another part of the flowchart. A pair of identically labeled connector symbols is commonly used to indicate a continued flow when the use of a line is confusing. Its use is illustrated in Section 7.4, where the bonus calculation is flowcharted [Figure 7.8(b)].

Connector

DECISION   The *decision* symbol is used to indicate a point in a program at which a branch to one of two or more alternative points is possible. As shown in the three examples of Figure 7.4, the criterion for making the choice should be indicated clearly. Also, the condition upon which each of the possible exit paths will be executed should be identified and all the possible paths should be accounted for.

Decision

TERMINAL   The *terminal* symbol represents any point at which processing originates or terminates. With normal program operations, such points will be at the start and completion of the sequence and sometimes at a terminal point under error conditions. For example, an employee payroll program might be written to terminate if an employee time card is found out of sequence.

Terminal

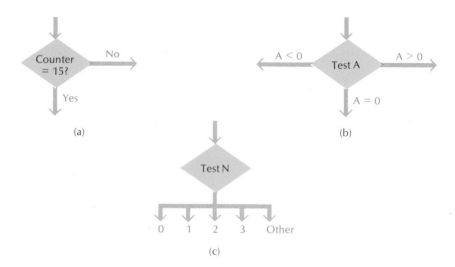

Fig. 7.4 (a) A simple conditional branch; (b) and (c) two or more alternate paths.

FLOW CHARTING TEMPLATE To promote standardization in the use of flowchart symbols, various types of flowcharting templates are available, such as the one shown in Figure 7.5. Note that grid lines are provided as an aid to centering the symbols. In addition to the programming symbols, standard system symbols are included.

USING THE FLOWCHART One of the primary uses of a flowchart is to aid the programmer in determining the basic flow of logic in a problem. By

Fig. 7.5 IBM flowcharting template.

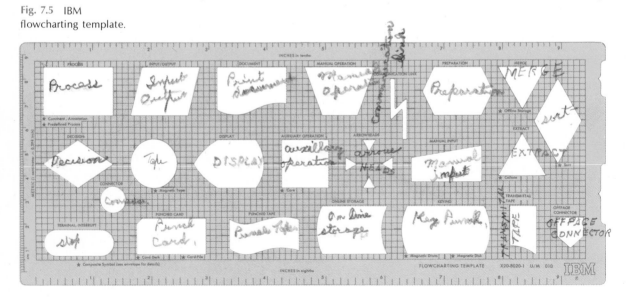

flowcharting, the sequence and relationships among the various parts of the program can be seen. The flowchart provides a means of experimenting with various approaches to laying out program logic. It is much easier to move and to rearrange logic by moving blocks of flowchart than by rewriting segments of a program. Many programmers draw their charts on a chalkboard to facilitate continuous changing.

Once the overall picture or overall mainline logic has been developed, detailed flowcharts of large segments may be charted. After the mainline and detailed flowcharts are completed, they should serve as a guide for writing the program. Here it is important to remember that the flowchart is a working device. As the problem is coded, it is frequently necessary to make changes in program logic because of such things as machine logic, incorrect flowcharting and so on. However, when changes in logic become apparent, the flowchart should be changed accordingly. Otherwise, its value as a programming aid is lost.

In drawing flowcharts, the programmer should keep in mind that the primary functions of the flowchart are to provide a better insight into the problem while preparing the program and to document and explain the program to others who might want to use it. The following points may frequently be of help in producing useful results:

1. First chart the main line of logic, then incorporate detail.
2. Do not chart every detail or the chart will only be a graphic representation, step by step, of the program. A reader who is interested can refer to the program itself.
3. Use descriptive titles written in English rather than in machine-oriented language.
4. Use the flowchart as a genuine reference while coding, not as something to be discarded once coding is begun; do not be afraid to change it when necessary during the program coding.
5. Put yourself in the position of readers and try to anticipate their problems in understanding your chart.

The importance of flowcharting cannot be overemphasized. Usually, the most complex part of programming a problem is determining the basic logic required. Recognizing this, some large business firms employ trained individuals to reduce problems for computer solution to a series of flowcharts. From there, the somewhat less difficult task of coding is performed by someone with a lesser degree of training.

Exercise

7.6 Name and describe the flowchart symbols discussed in this chapter.

$p_{\wedge}$ 198

7.4
FLOWCHARTING
EXAMPLES

FLOWCHARTS OF EXAMPLE ALGORITHMS The sequence of operations involved in lighting the furnace (Example 7.1) is illustrated in the flowchart of Figure 7.6. Note that this is a simple sequence of steps which progresses from the beginning to the end without repetition (although it involves one decision point).

In contrast, the algorithm of Example 7.2 flowcharted in Figure 7.7 includes a repetitious process. The flowchart clearly illustrates the sequence of operations to be followed in calculating the accumulated amount A. It also shows that termination will occur after a given number of passes, or *iterations,* through the loop.

Similarly, the algorithm of Example 7.3 is clearly illustrated by the flowchart of Figure 7.8. In (a) we see the usual flowlines, causing a return to process the next employee file. An alternate flowchart (b) is included to illustrate use of the connector symbol to avoid drawing the flowline. Although the presence of the connector symbol provides no advantage in this case, it is commonly used when a large number of lines may appear confusing in a complex flowchart.

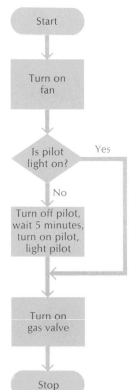

Fig. 7.6 Flowchart for algorithm of Example 7.1.

A FLOWCHARTING APPLICATION To further illustrate use of the symbols described in this chapter as well as more complex flowcharting principles, consider the following example.

EXAMPLE 7.4

A deck of personnel cards is to be examined to find all persons who (1) have either been with the company 25 years or more or are 65 years of age or over, and (2) have 120 days or more of accumulated sick leave. Each card includes the employee number, age (in years), service (in years), sick leave (in days), and monthly salary. When a card of a person meeting the above requirements is found, the accumulated sick leave must be calculated and the employee's name and accumulated sick leave printed.

A FLOWCHART In this problem it will be necessary to examine each card to determine if the employee meets the age requirement or the length-of-employment requirement. In either case the employee may be eligible. Then, in addition, he or she must also meet the days-of-sick-leave requirement. Note that it is not necessary to satisfy all three conditions in order to qualify; a minimum of two is sufficient.

Figure 7.9 is a flowchart illustrating the logic involved in this problem. Note the use of connector symbols to avoid many confusing flow lines. An important part of the logic of this problem is represented by the decision symbols. The decisions labeled number 1 and number 2 represent a parallel construction. If the employee qualifies by either 1 or 2, then he/she may be further

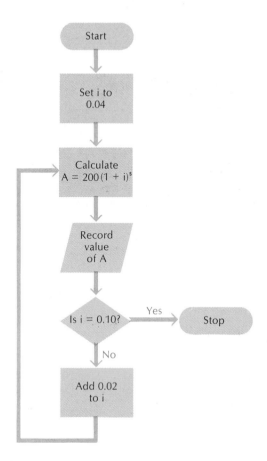

Fig. 7.7 Flowchart for algorithm of Example 7.2.

considered. In addition, he/she must qualify under condition number 3; that is, he/she must qualify according to 1 or 2, and 3.

Exercises

Draw a flowchart for the following:

7.7 A deck of student information cards is to be searched and the names printed for each student meeting the following requirements: (a) carries 15 units or more, (b) is a senior, and (c) has a grade point average of 3.2 or better.

7.8 Each salesperson's card contains an account number, commission, amount of sales, minimum commission, and maximum commission. The program is to check the sequence of the cards by account number and stop if any are out of sequence. The actual commission paid will depend upon the maximum or minimum in the following way: (a) if the commission is less than the minimum, the minimum is paid;

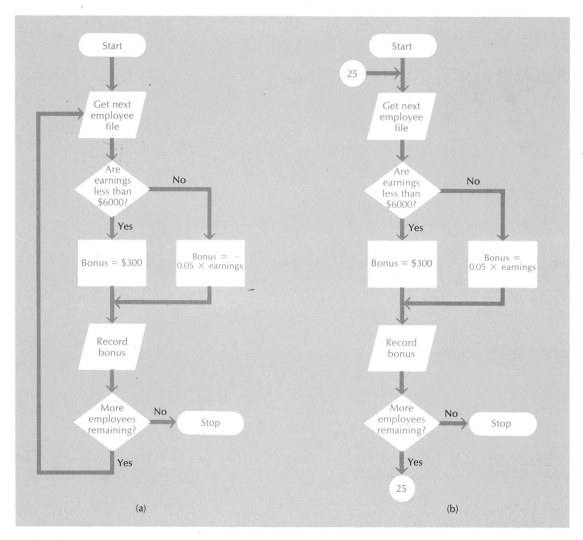

Fig. 7.8 Flowcharts for algorithm of Example 7.3.

(b) if the commission is over the maximum, the maximum is paid; and (c) if the commission is between the maximum and minimum, the calculated commission is paid. The printed line is to contain the salesperson's name, plus the appropriate commission.

7.5 COMPUTER LANGUAGES

Once the flowcharting of a problem is complete, the programming or coding task can begin. A wide variety of programming languages (some very specialized) are currently available to ease the programming burden. The choice of a particular language usually depends upon the nature of the job being performed and the language capabilities of the computer being used. This

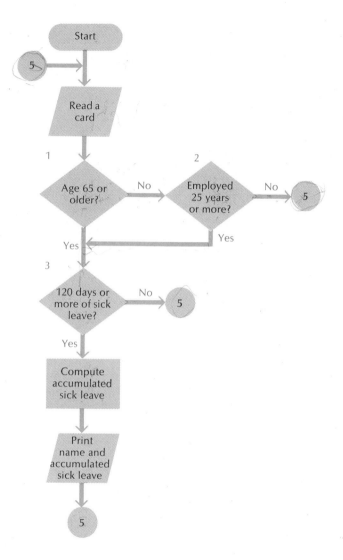

Fig. 7.9 Flowchart for
Example 7.4.

will become more meaningful as we study characteristics of commonly used languages. However, let us first consider a historical perspective of the evolution of languages.

As soon as the first electronic digital computers were built, it became obvious that the means by which man could communicate with the machine were inadequate and that better methods had to be found. In the beginning, man had to learn the machine's language and prepare instructions to the machine in exactly that language. Over the next twenty years, through the use of what has become known as *programming systems* (often informally referred to as *software* in contrast to the machine hardware), the situation has become reversed to the point where the machine in a sense understands the human languages of English and mathematics. The development of these high-level languages has been a major factor in the advance of computer technology.

MACHINE LANGUAGE   Regardless of which programming language we use in solving a problem, the program must ultimately be converted to its machine language equivalent for execution by the computer. When programming with a user-oriented language such as Fortran, we may use a form which looks much like an algebra equation in directing the computer to perform computations. However, in machine language, each operation such as addition and subtraction must be defined explicitly. Furthermore, programs written for one machine will not work on another machine because of design differences. For example, the following is an example of a typical machine language instruction for a variety of computers to add two numbers together.

124130144300	Burroughs B200
A4733BC	IBM 1401
210538618772	IBM 1620
1010100000000111	Varian 620 minicomputer
0101101010100000110000000001111000	IBM 360/370

ASSEMBLER LANGUAGE   In the next chapter we shall study the general nature of instructions in their machine language forms, the actual format which the computer requires to carry out its operations. Because of the immense amount of detail required, few programs are ever written in machine language. More often, special *symbolic assembly languages* are used which free the programmer from most of the exacting detail. However, before such a program can be run on a computer, it must be converted to machine language using a special *assembler program*. The term *assembler* has its origin in the function of these programs to assemble the various parts of an instruction, such as an operation code, one, two, or three addresses, index register tags, flags, or indicators, and so on, into a single machine-language instruction. In the case of binary computers, they are extremely helpful in converting decimal addresses and constants written by the programmer to the binary values needed by the machine.

Next, assemblers were written that permitted the use of symbolic operation codes and symbolic addresses. By no means the first of this type, but significant because of its widespread use, was the Symbolic Optimal Assembly Program (Soap) for the IBM 650 data processing system. This program was written in 1956 by Stan Poley of IBM's Service Bureau Corporation and, like most assemblers, greatly decreased the time required to write a program, simplified the debugging of the program, and provided better documentation.

Programming time was improved through the use of this symbolic system. With symbolic operation codes, it was easier to remember that multiply was MPY rather than 19; with symbolic addresses, it was easier to remember that a constant 5 had been stored in location FIVE rather than at some numeric address such as 1732; and it was certainly much simpler to use blanks in places where the assembly program could assign addresses much more easily than the programmer could.

Checking a program was simplified because the symbolic program was easier to follow and because no erroneous duplication of address assignments could occur, since the bookkeeping was performed by the assembler. Documentation was greatly improved by the use of remarks and comment cards, and even the mnemonic symbolic addresses were very helpful.

In addition to these functions, which are common to almost all assemblers, Soap also optimized the program. Because the IBM 650 had its main storage on the surface of a revolving drum, gaining access to data or the next instruction was much like catching the brass ring on a merry-go-round. If you reach without looking, you might catch the ring immediately, or you might just miss it and have to wait a whole revolution. Similarly, a 650 program would be fast or slow depending upon whether the data and instructions were placed in good or poor locations. The Soap program automatically placed them in nearly optimum locations.

The development of programming systems has been greatly influenced by computer users' groups. These are organizations of computer installations that use the same type of computer and find it advantageous to share their programs. When the largest of these groups, aptly named SHARE (sometimes said to stand for the Society to Help Alleviate Redundant Effort), was formed, it found that its members could not communicate with each other. Although they all used IBM 704 computers, they were using different symbolic assembly languages. For example, General Electric had its Cage (Compiler and Assembler for General Electric), United Aircraft has its Sap (Symbolic Assembly Program) and IBM had its Nyapl, the first assembly program written by the New York group. It was obvious that the organization needed to settle on a single language, and a vote by the members selected United Aircraft's Sap written by Roy Nutt.

COMPILER LANGUAGES   A compiler is a much more powerful programming tool than an assembler. In an assembler, one symbolic instruction must be written for each machine language instruction assembled, but in a compiler, one statement will produce a multitude of machine language instructions. Another difference between an assembler and a compiler is that the assembler language is so closely tied to the computer's machine language that it is impossible to use the assembler language of one computer on any other computer. This is not the case with compiler languages, which are generally considered procedure oriented or problem oriented rather than machine oriented.

The first compiler was the A-O compiler written by Dr. Grace Murray Hopper for Univac in 1952. This program compiled subroutines from a magnetic tape library into complete computer programs. In or about 1957 the

IT (Internal Translator) language of A. J. Perlis, J. W. Smith, and H. R. Van Zoeren was made available for both the IBM 650 and the Burroughs 205 Datatron computers. Here for the first time was a computer language that not only ran on two different machines but cut across manufacturer's lines as well.

In summary, the compiler has many features of the assembler plus multiple instruction per statement and machine independence. This latter quality permitted systems programmers to take the concept one step further. Why couldn't this machine-independent language be algebra or English?

FORTRAN   In 1954 John W. Backus of IBM proposed the idea of a FORmula TRANslating compiler with statements that were as near to algebraic expressions as the keypunch would permit. A working committee was formed, including Backus, R. A. Hughes of the University of California Radiation Laboratory at Livermore, R. Nutt of United Aircraft, and ten others from IBM. In early 1957 Fortran was running on the IBM 704. Since that time IBM has written a Fortran compiler for each of its new computers, and in September of 1960 Burroughs released a version of Fortran for its Datatron 205 which they called Fortocom. This started a major trend in manufacturer-independent languages, leading to Fortran's becoming the most universally used scientific computer language. Presently, the most commonly used version of the language is called Fortran IV and is described in Chapter 10.

COBOL   In May 1959, the U.S. Department of Defense called together representatives from government agencies and computer manufacturers to discuss the possibility of adopting a common language for business data processing. At this meeting, the Conference On Data Systems Languages (Codasyl) was established, and in January 1960 this group completed its specifications for a COmmon Business-Oriented Language (Cobol).

- The new language was to be machine-independent and written in English.
- Automatic documentation was to be provided by a program that could be read by a nonprogrammer. No longer would programmers have to write comments about what their programs were doing. It could almost be said that they kept the comments and threw away the coding.
- Communication between the business executive who requests the program and the programmer who wrote it was to be improved, since both could read the program.
- The time required to write the program was to be decreased by leaving the detail code to the Cobol compiler.
- The debugging time was to be decreased by having the Cobol compiler print diagnostic messages indicating possible programming errors.

- Once written, the program should be able to run on a computer of another model or manufacturer by recompiling after only minor changes.
- The education of a Cobol programmer should be applicable to any computer.

These were all valuable objectives for the Department of Defense, because of the variety of computers that it uses and the mobility of its programmers, and were equally valid for the entire computer industry as well.

The original Cobol specifications published in 1960 became known as Cobol 60. This version was implemented by both RCA and Sperry Rand's Univac Division. Most other manufacturers waited until Codasyl updated the language the next year and published it as Cobol 61. Since then, Cobol compilers have been written for almost every tape-oriented computer in operation. In the years since 1960, Cobol has undergone extensive refinement and standardization. Through the efforts of the American National Standards Institute (ANSI), an industrywide association of computer manufacturers and users, the American National Standard (ANS) Cobol has been approved.

COMPARISON OF LANGUAGES   With the greater convenience provided the computer user by compiler languages such as Fortran and Cobol, we might wonder why assembly languages are used at all. From the overall point of view, compiler languages are far more commonly used in applications areas than assembly languages. However, for certain types of applications with specialized needs and for preparing system software, assembly languages are more frequently required. This is largely due to the features of these languages that allow programmers to make the most complete and efficient utilization of the computer they are working with. The advantages characteristic of compiler languages and of assembly languages are summarized in Table 7.1.

As computers become larger and faster, and compilers become more efficient, the notion of program efficiency becomes less of a factor. Although a clever programmer can indeed produce a better specific program than is obtained through a general purpose language, the additional programming time and cost is usually unjustified. Overall, the needs and requirements of a given task usually dictate whether a compiler language or an assembly language is most appropriate.

Exercises

7.9   What is the advantage of using a symbolic language over a machine language?

7.10   List and compare the features of assembly languages and compiler languages.

Table 7.1   ADVANTAGES OF COMPILER AND ASSEMBLY LANGUAGES

COMPILER LANGUAGE ADVANTAGES

Item of Consideration	*Explanation*
Program preparation cost	Generally, the cost of all phases of program preparation (coding, correcting and documenting) is lower with a compiler language than with an assembly language.
Machine knowledge required	Actually, most compiler languages such as Fortran and Cobol can be used without a knowledge of the given computer on which the program will be run. Thus, the programmer need not know the machine instructions, the data format, and so on. However, such a knowledge is desirable since it allows the programmer to utilize the system more efficiently.
Generality of language	Languages such as Cobol and Fortran are industry-wide standards and are not machine oriented. Knowledge gained in a compiler language on one machine is almost 100 percent transferable to the same compiler language used on another machine.

ASSEMBLY LANGUAGE ADVANTAGES

Versatility	An assembly language provides programmers access to all the special features of the machine they are using. Certain types of operations which are impractical to attempt using a compiler language are easily programmed using the machine's assembly language.
Program efficiency	Generally, a program prepared by a good assembly language programmer will require less storage and less running time than one prepared by a good compiler language programmer.

**7.6
LANGUAGE
TRANSLATION**

A SIMPLE ANALOGY   Although assembly and compiler languages differ in many respects, both yield programs which must first be converted to the machine language of the computer to be used before they can be run. This program translation phase is done on the computer by special *language processor* programs which are normally furnished by the computer manufacturer. For compiler languages, these translators are termed *compilers* and the translating operation is termed *compiling*; for assembly language, the corresponding terminology is *assembler* and *assembling*. Throughout the following discussion, the all-inclusive term *processor* will usually be used. To gain an insight into the language processing function, we will consider a simple analogy.

Let us assume that we have a large garden that we desire to have cared for by a professional gardener. Furthermore, our neighbor (a close friend) knows an excellent Japanese gardener. Since the gardener speaks no English, our friend, being versatile in both Japanese and English, volunteers to act as a translator. Thus, we establish the following procedure:

1. We write the daily instructions in English.
2. The friend translates them from English, the language convenient for us to use, into Japanese, the only language which the gardener understands.
3. Assuming that everything has been translated properly, the gardener carries out the required functions.

The function of the translator is to convert the description and accounts written in English into like descriptions and accounts written in Japanese and record them for the gardener. Whether or not our friend has an extensive background in gardening would be unimportant. The primary requirement would be that he have the capability to translate from English to Japanese. Note that the functions of our friend do not contribute directly to garden care. His only purpose is to perform the translation, *not* to carry out the enumerated tasks. These notions can be represented by diagrams as shown in Figure 7.10. The idea of changing from a language which is easy for the writer to one which is easy for the user via a translator cannot be overemphasized. This is precisely the notion of converting from an assembly or compiler language program to a machine language program via a processor. In the case of the computer language, the translating function is performed by the computer rather than by a helpful neighbor. However, just as the neighbor must have learned the art of translating, so must the computer "learn" how to assemble or compile. This consists of loading the special language processor program into the computer.

Fig. 7.10 Analogy for language translation process.

Daily gardening instructions

(a)   (b)   (c)

Then, under control of the processor, the computer will translate the entire program to machine language. During the processing phase (as during translation in the analogy) none of the instructions are being carried out, they are merely being translated. In essence, the language processor program is treating the assembler or compiler program, usually referred to as the *source program*, as data and is producing as output a machine language program, usually referred to as the *object program*. This can be presented by diagrams as shown in Figure 7.11.

ERRORS   One important feature of assembler and compiler language processors is their ability to detect certain types of errors. Unfortunately, these errors fall only in the "use of language" area and do not provide a thinking capability for the programmer.

The gardener analogy can be expanded to illustrate error detection capabilities of the language processor. For example, let us assume that we desire to have a particular tree trimmed and we record the instruction, "Trim the tree." Upon encountering this statement, the translator would recognize that the required tree is not specified and would so indicate on the instruction before returning it to us for correction. Thus, the translator has detected an error and has aided us; of great importance is the type of error. This one is simply a statement which is not completely descriptive of the function to be performed. The translator realized that all of these details must be provided and was capable of quickly and easily detecting such an omission. However, consider two variations of an error of a different type. Assume we had inadvertently

Fig. 7.11   The language translation phase.

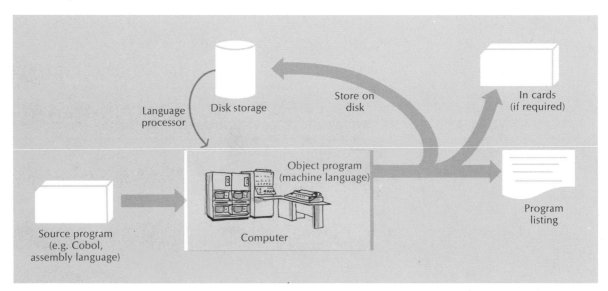

stated "cut down" instead of "trim" and the statement was, "Cut down the third tree from the left." To the translator, this is a clearly defined, valid task which he would translate into Japanese. Upon encountering this instruction, the gardener would perform the task and continue to the next chore, all the while assuming that we knew what we were doing. On the other hand, if it were illegal to cut these trees without a special permit from the city, the gardener, upon encountering this instruction, would indicate that an error had been made and would not carry it out. These are two distinct types of errors, both of which have their important corollaries in programming.

Exercises

7.11 What is the purpose of the language processor (the assembler or compiler)?

7.12 What is the difference between a source program and an object program?

7.13 In preparing a program, the programmer erroneously instructed the computer to calculate the perimeter of a rectangle by adding the width and twice the length (that is, $p = w + 2l$). Would you expect the language processor to detect this error? Explain.

LANGUAGE PROCESSOR DETECTED ERRORS   As programmers, we will do well to become accustomed to *diagnostic messages* such as the following:

UNDEFINED OPERATION CODE	Assembly language
01) DUP. LABEL	Fortran
IMPROPER CONTINUATION OF AN LITERAL	Cobol

The first is a 360 assembler language error in which the programmer has specified the operation code of an instruction to be ADD instead of the correct form, which is simply A. The second illustrates an error in a Fortran program where the programmer has used the same statement number (label) twice. In the third example, a programmer has not followed the Cobol language rules for continuing so-called literals and the compiler has detected this. Error-detecting capabilities of language processors are of great importance in programming and partially relieve the programmer of much painstaking, detailed checking. However, these types of errors are not the only ones which cause the programmer headaches.

OTHER TYPES OF ERRORS   A program free of processor diagnostic errors will not necessarily run correctly (or at all, for that matter). In general, remaining errors can be classed in two broad categories. First are errors in program logic. This is a serious type of error and one that often results from insufficient planning in setting forth the basic program requirements. For instance, a programmer might prepare a testing and branching sequence of instructions incorrectly, causing execution of a loop to occur 25 times instead of the required 24.

The second type is in the "bonehead" category, such as defining a discount rate as 52 percent instead of 25 percent. The advice here is to take a deep breath, for such mistakes will always be with us. However, in both instances, these errors can produce either of two effects: (1) an invalid directive to the computer can result which will cause termination of the program, or (2) the computer can be misdirected, producing invalid results (analogous to the gardener cutting the tree we did not want cut). The process of eliminating errors from a program is commonly called *debugging*. Prior to coding, the programmer should exercise care in defining the problem (on paper) and in preparing a flowchart. Once the program is complete, he/she should proceed through it step by step. Each path should be traced where multiple paths occur as a result of a conditional branch and each condition investigated. Prior to assembling or compiling the program, the source deck should be listed and checked for keypunching errors. If these practices are followed, many programming errors will be eliminated before they can cause any difficulty.

However, when the program does not run, the programmer has problems. Finding the "bugs" is frequently a painstaking, exasperating chore and there is no set formula for doing it. Perhaps the best general rule in debugging is to run a set of simplified data and, when the program functions improperly, to study the results and the program (this falls under the category of program testing, the subject of the next section). Many techniques may be used, but usually each is peculiar to a given situation, and the learning of these techniques comes from many hours of experience.

Exercise

7.14 After correcting a program so that all language processor errors are eliminated, a user runs the program and gets printed results. The user therefore concludes that the program is complete. Comment.

7.7 PROGRAM TESTING

GENERAL CONSIDERATIONS   The average beginning student usually breathes a gigantic sigh of relief when finally he or she ceases to obtain discouraging error messages from the language processor, and observes the computer pouring forth results with great humility. The great fallacy is, of course, related to whether or not the results are correct. The fact that a program runs (that is, it does not "blow up" and it yields output) means that the program is performing operations as defined by the programmer (that is, the sequence of instructions). Now the important question arises, "Is this the set of operations that was originally intended by the programmer?" For example, each card in a data deck might be punched with the length and width of a rectangle. If our job includes calculating the perimeter of each rectangle, we would use the relationship

$$P = 2l + 2w$$

That is, the perimeter equals twice the length plus twice the width. Now if we forgot to double the length and width, we would be calculating the perimeter as

$$P = l + w$$

Assuming no bugs, the program would run like a charm; for each card read, something would be printed. Furthermore, the results would appear reasonable unless we checked them carefully. Of course, this perimeter example represents a rather gross error on our part and one which is easily detected. However, a complex program involving many conditions can include very subtle errors which are not easily detected. Such programs require careful preparation of test data to insure that all aspects of the program are tested. Let us consider some factors to be taken into account in preparing test data for our previously studied example programs.

AN EXAMPLE TEST CASE   Basic flowcharting techniques are illustrated earlier in this chapter by Figure 7.9, which involves searching a deck of personnel cards for employees who (1) have been with the company 25 years or more *or* are 65 years of age or over, *and* (2) have 120 days or more accumulated sick leave. Considering the three conditions to be tested, the test data should include cards fulfilling the conditions in Table 7.2.

Table 7.2

	25 Years Employment	or	65 Years of Age	and	120 Days Sick Leave	Qualify
1	Yes		Yes		Yes	Yes
2	Yes		Yes		No	No
3	Yes		No		Yes	Yes
4	Yes		No		No	No
5	No		Yes		Yes	Yes
6	No		Yes		No	No
7	No		No		Yes	No
8	No		No		No	No

Since three conditions are to be tested, each with the two possible values of "yes" or "no," there exist eight combinations as summarized in the table. Although test data (2), (3), (5), and (7) would probably give an excellent indication of whether or not the program is error-free, inclusion of the other cases would further increase our confidence in the program. Furthermore, they would indicate any undesired (and unlikely, but possible) interaction of test sequences. Although not shown in Table 7.2, the test data should also test for the "equals" as well as for the "exceeds" conditions. For example, for the age criterion, one card should include an age of 64 (not qualifying), another card an age of 65 (minimum requirement), and yet another card an age of 66 (qualifying).

As we can see, this task of testing can become a time-consuming part of the overall job. However, it is usually time well spent. As an aid to testing, it is often possible to write a short, simple program to generate the test data. This program, however, must be relatively simple and straightforward, lest it in turn require extensive testing. It would appear that the primary value of such a circular sequence would be to perpetuate the programmer's job (at least until he/she is fired). Actually, the very serious question of when to stop testing usually involves a subjective answer which evolves from, among other things, a good understanding of the programmed problem and a knowledge of the data characteristics. Probably the most important three factors (on the part of the programmer) are experience, experience, and experience.

Exercise

7.15 Exercise 7.7 involves determining a student honor list (refer to the flowchart shown in the answer to Exercise 7.7). Tabulate a set of data values which could be used as a program test.

Answers to Preceding Exercises

7.1 The six steps in preparation of a program (see Figure 7.2) are (a) problem definition, (b) planning, (c) programming, (d) testing, (e) documenting, and (f) production. For a description of each phase, refer to the discussion in Section 7.1.

7.2 a. Add small amount of red paint to can of paint.
b. Compare paint to original color;
   if not red enough, go to step (a);
   if not blue enough, go to step (c);
   if proper, match then stop.
c. Add small amount of blue paint to can of paint.
d. Go to step (b).

7.3 a. Set aside the first examination paper.
b. Get the next exam paper.
c. If score of this paper is not higher than score of paper set aside, then skip to step (e).
d. Replace paper previously set aside with the latest paper.
e. If no more papers then stop (paper set aside contains highest score).
f. Return to step (b).

7.4 a. Subtract cost of item from $1.00.
b. If difference $\geq$ 50¢, give half dollar and subtract 50¢ from remainder.
c. If difference $\geq$ 25¢, give quarter and subtract 25¢ from remainder.
d. If difference $\geq$ 10¢, give dime and subtract 10¢ from remainder, then perform step (d) again.
e. If difference $\geq$ 5¢, give nickel and subtract 5¢ from remainder.
f. Give remainder of change in pennies.
g. Stop.

7.5 A program flowchart diagrams the processing steps and logic of a computer program. A system flowchart diagrams the flow of work, documents, and operations in a data processing application.

7.6 Flowline, processing, input/output, connector, decision, and terminal. For descriptions, see Section 7.3.

7.7

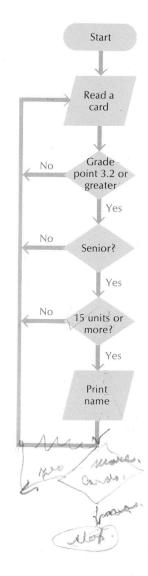

language processor
language translator

7.8

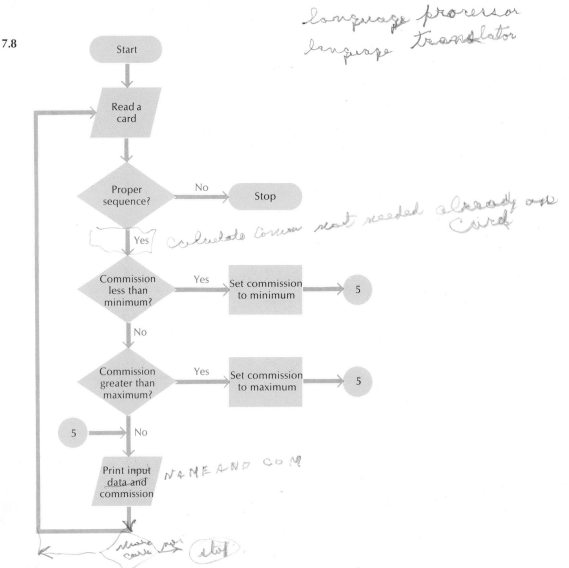

calculate commun not needed already on card

NAME AND COM

7.9 Simplicity of use. The programmer need not remember various machine codes and determine addresses, since those operations are handled by the assembler program.

7.10 *Compiler Languages*
   a. Machine independent.
   b. Require little or no knowledge of computer.
   c. Impractical to perform certain functions.
   d. Programs can be coded more quickly than in assembly language.
   e. Normally yield good machine language programs.
   f. Yield many machine language instructions per statement.

Assembly Languages
   a. Machine oriented.
   b. Require thorough understanding of computer.
   c. Provide access to valuable machine features not available through compiler languages.
   d. Much time-consuming detail required in preparing programs.
   e. Can produce better, more efficient programs than compiler languages.

f. Produce one machine language instruction per assembly language instruction.

7.11 The language processor converts programs from the assembler or compiler language to the machine language.

7.12 The source program is one written in an assembler or compiler language (a *user-oriented* language); the object program is the machine language program resulting from machine translation of the source program.

7.13 The compiler will not detect this as an error, since it does not "know" the context of the problem;

that is, that the perimeter of a rectangle is determined by adding twice the width to twice the length.

7.14 The programmer has not necessarily completed the program since there may still be logic errors. For instance, the program may be directing the computer to subtract interest from a customer account rather than add it. The only way this will be detected is by carefully checking the results. The reader should refer to the section on program testing.

7.15

GPA:	3.1	3.2	3.3
Senior:	Yes	No	
Units:	14.9	15.0	15.1

Additional Exercises

7.16 Matching. Match each item 1–8 with the corresponding description a–h.

   1. block diagram   2. algorithm
   3. debug   4. flowcharting
   5. assemble   6. compile
   7. documentation   8. program testing

   a. Usually necessary to insure that a program properly performs the operations for which it was designed.
   b. To convert a Fortran program to machine language.
   c. To detect and correct all errors in a program.
   d. The same as a program flowchart.
   e. That phase of preparing a problem for computer solution in which the program logic is first laid out.
   f. A set of rules or instructions for doing something.
   g. The preparation of a report which describes a computer program and its use.
   h. A translation process in which each source instruction produces one object instruction.

7.17 True-False. Determine whether each of the following is true or false.

   a. An algorithm can be defined as a set of instructions to perform a required task.
   b. A program flowchart is an illustration of the overall operations to be carried out in a computer program.

   c. The recommended procedure in preparing a program is first to code the program in the selected language, then to prepare the flowchart for documentation purposes.
   d. After the overall logic has been flowcharted, details of the program should be defined in the form of a more detailed flowchart.
   e. A compiler is a prewritten program designed to translate programs written in a machine-independent language into machine language.
   f. Fortran is a specialized language designed by IBM exclusively for use on the IBM 360.
   g. Cobol is a commonly used machine-independent language for business data processing applications.
   h. One disadvantage of using an assembly language is that programs written for one computer will not run on other types of computers.
   i. The primary differences between a source program and an object program is that the source program includes the data to be processed.
   j. Logic errors, such as subtracting bonus pay from an employee's paycheck rather than adding it, generally cannot be detected by the compiler.

7.18 Multiple Choice. Determine which answer best answers or completes each of the following statements.

a. In the overall process of preparing a computer program for use in a system, two of the important early steps in the process are (1) programming and testing, (2) programming and compiling, (3) documentation and testing, (4) problem definition and planning.

b. Which of the following would probably not be included in a program report? (1) the program punched into a deck of cards, (2) a program flowchart, (3) a problem definition, (4) a description of how to run the program on the computer, (5) all of the preceding would be included.

c. Generally speaking, an algorithm may be defined as a (1) special programming language which eliminates the need for knowledge of the computer in order to program, (2) type of computer used for scientific applications, (3) weakness in a program which can produce errors, (4) program written in the Fortran language, (5) none of the preceding.

d. The most significant difference between the flowcharts of Figures 7.6 and 7.7 (pp. 200 and 201) is (1) in 7.7, a yes condition produces an immediate end of operation, (2) the flowchart of 7.7 consists of seven blocks, but that of 7.6 consists of only six, (3) the flowchart of 7.6 does not illustrate any calculations to be performed, (4) the flowchart of 7.7 involves a repetition of the sequence, whereas that of 7.6 does not.

e. Referring to the flowchart of Figure 7.9 (p. 203) employees will not qualify who (1) are not 65 years of age or older, (2) have not been with the company 25 years or more, (3) have 120 days of sick leave, (4) do not satisfy all three requirements, (5) none of the preceding is completely true.

f. An example of a machine-independent language is (1) the IBM 650 Symbolic Optimal Assembly Program language, (2) the IBM System/360 Assembly language, (3) Cobol, (4) Univac.

g. A source program (1) is one written to process source data, (2) is a program written in a compiler type language, (3) must first be translated into a machine language program before it can be run, (4) is converted to a compiler language by the programmer.

h. The operation of debugging a program is (1) aided by the language translator, (2) most commonly done after the program is placed in production, (3) an optional part of programming, (4) never necessary if the programmer is careful, (5) none of the preceding.

i. The primary purpose of program testing is to (1) ensure that the program correctly performs the job for which it was designed, (2) test the running speed of the program, (3) ensure that the language translator has not failed to detect the errors, (4) be certain that the program will not damage the computer under full load conditions.

j. An error in a program where a programmer divided rather than multiplied by allowed discount would (1) usually be detected by the language translator, (2) be detected through careful program testing, (3) produce a diagnostic message during language translation, (4) normally be detected during production runs.

7.19 Flowcharting Problems. Prepare a flowchart for each of the following.

a. A set of examination papers which have been graded with scores from 0 to 100 is to be searched to find how many of them are above 90. Prepare a flowchart to illustrate this job.

b. Each paper in a set of examination papers includes a grade of A, B, C, D, or F. A count is to be made of how many papers have grades of A and how many have grades of F. Prepare a flowchart to perform this function.

c. Each employee pay record includes the hours worked and pay rate. Gross pay is to be determined and recorded as hours worked times pay rate. For all hours worked in excess of 40, pay the overtime rate, which is $1\frac{1}{2}$ times the regular rate. Draw a flowchart to illustrate the problem logic.

d. A water company bills certain customers according to the following schedule:

Flat rate $1.00
plus   0.20/unit for the first 20 units
plus   0.225/unit for the next 30 units
plus   0.30/unit for all in excess of
           50 units

Draw a flowchart to illustrate calculating the charge based on the number of units used.

e. Experimental data is recorded on a set of cards with one data point per card. Draw a flowchart to illustrate the process of inspecting each card to find the card with the largest data value.

7.20 Devise a set of test data for each of the three flowcharting problems 7.19(c), (d), and (e) which would be adequate to test completely the logic of your flowchart.

See solution M-35

Do 7.19

a or b.

c or d.

Do 7.20 for c or d.

Complete by Feb 27.

```
        D
C  0.0   0
   39.9  19
   40.0  20
   40.1  21
         50
         51
```

Chapter

8

Computer Programming Concepts

8.1
A SIMPLE
COMPUTER

In Chapter 4, we considered a pigeonhole analogy to illustrate basic features of the computer, including the nature of instructions and the basic computer components: input/output, storage, control, and arithmetic/logic. With a computer, as in the analogy, before any processing of data can be performed, a detailed sequence of instructions must be prepared and read into the computer. Although characteristics of computers vary widely from one machine to another, a basic understanding of how an electronic digital computer works and of programming principles applies to all computers. In this sense, it is important that the beginner gain some idea of each of the following:

1. What a computer instruction actually is and does.
2. How instructions are combined to form a program.
3. The appearance of instructions and data within storage.
4. How data is brought into storage and results are printed out.
5. The process of repeating a program over and over.
6. The process of testing results.

A wide number of methods are used in approaching this topic, varying from "ignore it—go directly to user oriented languages" (such as those described in the following three chapters) to "study a subset of a real computer" to "devise an imaginary computer." The latter approach is that taken in this chapter. Although the hypothetical computer described here does not exist, it includes features which illustrate basic characteristics of the stored program computer. Without a doubt, it is lacking in many, many features considered essential to most modern data processing applications. (For instance, the hypothetical computer can only work with numbers; it cannot handle alphabetic data.) However, it does present the *basic principles* of the *stored program computer*. Furthermore, by omitting many of the modern features, the machine and its concepts are kept simple and straightforward. With a minimum of effort, the reader can gain an insight into the basics of a stored program computer and preparing programs.*

THE COMPUTER STORAGE   The simple computer to be considered in this chapter consists of 100 storage positions with addresses of 00 through 99. Each storage position is capable of storing one number consisting of up to four digits, or else one instruction. Whenever a storage location contains a number, that number will also include a sign to indicate whether the quantity is positive or negative. Since an extra sign bit is provided in the rightmost digit of each storage position for the sign, it will always appear over the units digit of the field. For example, the following schematic form will be used throughout this chapter to represent one or more positions of storage and the contents.

---

*Through the use of a special simulator program and operating procedures listed in Appendix III, all programs described in this chapter can be run on any computer equipped with Fortran.

$$\underset{22}{\underline{\;0\;|\;1\;|\;6\;|\;\overset{+}{5}\;}} \qquad \underset{23}{\underline{\;3\;|\;8\;|\;2\;|\;\overset{-}{9}\;}} \qquad \underset{24}{\underline{\;0\;|\;0\;|\;0\;|\;\overset{+}{7}\;}}$$

In this case, the contents of three storage locations are as follows:

Location	Contents
22	165
23	−3829
24	7

In general, the storage can be thought of as a large housing project with 100 identical houses. Their addresses, which range from 00 to 99, are the only means for distinguishing among them. Moreover, the occupants of any given house are independent of the address; in fact, occupants come and go without changing the house or its address. In computer storage, the address of a given position remains unchanged, but its contents are easily changed. This is very similar to the pigeonhole box which consists of 18 slots, each capable of storing one number or one instruction.

In addition to the 100 storage positions, our computer includes a number of special purpose *registers*. The one to which we shall focus our attention is the *accumulator register* or simply the *accumulator*. The accumulator, which is in the control section of the computer, is similar in nature to each of the storage positions. As we shall see, it is the center of all processing within the machine. Information can be placed in storage from the accumulator, or the accumulator contents can be replaced with information from any part of storage. Furthermore, whenever arithmetic is to be performed on two quantities, one of them must be in the accumulator and the other in storage. For example, an addition operation would cause a designated number in storage to be added to the number in the accumulator.

CATEGORIZING COMPUTERS   In the short history of computers, many concepts have appeared. From the point of view of instruction format, most machines can be classed as *one-address, two-address,* or *three-address* computers. The distinction is easily made by considering a particular machine instruction such as the Add, which causes two numbers to be added together. Whenever an addition is to take place, there are three numbers of importance: the two quantities to be added (the addend and the augend) and the result (the sum). In a one-address computer such as the one we are considering in this chapter, the number in a specified storage location is added to the number in the accumulator. Thus, the Add instruction includes the address of one of the numbers, and the other is understood to be in the accumulator. The sum remains in the accumulator, replacing the original contents. In a typical two-address computer, both numbers are in storage and the instruction includes two addresses, one for each of the fields. The resulting sum commonly replaces one of the two fields in storage. For example, an Add instruction might add the contents of location 62 to the contents of location 47 and replace the original contents of location 47 with the sum. In both one-address and two-address computers, the machine carries out instructions (that is, *executes* instructions) consecutively as they are obtained from storage, as illustrated in the analogy of Chapter 4. However, some three-address computers function differently in this respect. That is, the addition would take place as in the two-address machine, but the third address might designate the location of the next instruction to be executed.

Although these characteristics of two-address and three-address computers are typical, they are not universal. Indeed, even within a given computer, the manner in which each address portion of the instruction is used varies from instruction to instruction. In fact, all instructions in a given computer often do not use each component of the instruction. In some systems, this can result in wasted space.

DATA INPUT As we learned in Chapter 3, the placement of each field on a card for a given application is a matter of format design. For example, in Chapter 2, Figure 2.11, the decision to use columns 2–5 for the account number and 6–25 for the name (in the master-balance card) was an arbitrary choice; columns 1–4 and 21–40 could as easily have been used. However, to simplify the hypothetical computer, input data will be read from cards according to a rigid, fixed format. Accordingly, data cards will be divided into 9 five-position fields as follows:

Field	Card Columns
first	1–5
second	6–10
third	11–15
fourth	16–20
fifth	21–25
sixth	26–30
seventh	31–35
eighth	36–40
ninth	41–45

Figure 8.1 illustrates a data card that has been punched with a number in each field. Note that the first column of each field is reserved for the sign,

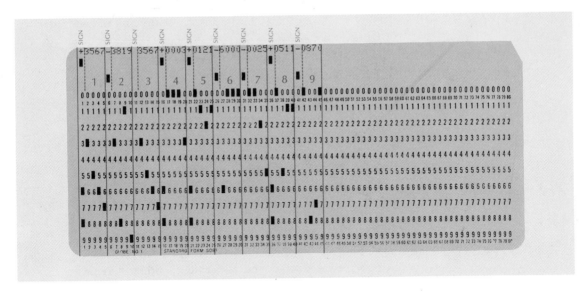

Fig. 8.1 Fields in a card.

which may be − or + or omitted (which will automatically result in a positive field). The nine fields that will be read into storage from this card are

Field	Value	In Storage
1	+3567	3 5 6 7⁺
2	−3819	3 8 1 9⁻
3	+3567	3 5 6 7⁺
4	+3	0 0 0 3⁺
5	+121	0 1 2 1⁺
6	−6000	6 0 0 0⁻
7	−25	0 0 2 5⁻
8	+511	0 1 5 1⁺
9	−870	0 8 7 0⁻

We can see that the first and third fields will both result in a positive 3567 being placed in storage. Also, fields 4, 5, 7, 8, and 9 include less than four digits but leading 0s have been punched to avoid accidentally misplacing the field.

Exercises

8.1   What can be stored in storage location 53?

8.2   Referring to the card of Figure 8.2, how many fields are punched, and what are the values? Sketch each as it would appear in storage.

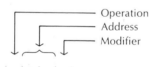

GENERAL CHARACTERISTICS OF INSTRUCTIONS   The computer is directed to perform our operations through a program of instructions similar to the instructions of the pigeonhole analogy from Chapter 4. As in that illustration, we shall deal with input and output instructions, with arithmetic instructions and with branching instructions. Each instruction, which will direct the computer to perform a particular operation, will consist of four digits (the size of the storage word) as follows:

one-digit operation code—indicates the operation to be performed
two-digit address operand—indicates where in storage the data is
to be found
one-digit modifier—used by some instructions but not others.

The general format is as follows:

```
            ┌──────── Operation
            │ ┌────── Address
            │ │ ┌──── Modifier
            ↓ ↓ ↓
      └─┴─┴─┴─┘
```

DATA INPUT   The first two instructions we shall study provide us with the ability to bring data into the computer and print results out.

READ A CARD

Operation code   *1*

The Read a Card instruction causes the computer to read one card from the card reader as follows: (1) the one-digit modifier specifies how many fields are to be read from the card, according to the card format of Figure 8.1; (2) the address operand specifies the storage position into which the first field is to be read; successive fields from the card are stored in successive storage locations. The original contents of the designated storage locations will be lost.

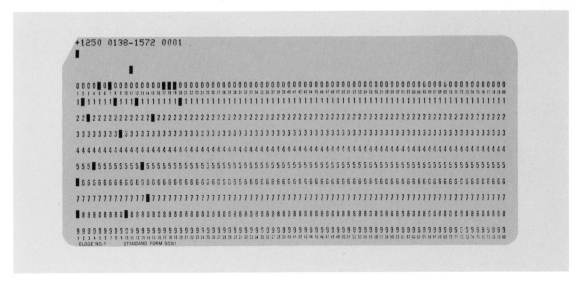

Fig. 8.2 Fields in a card.

The following is an example of the Read a Card (or Read) instruction.

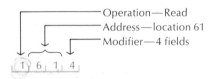

Operation—Read
Address—location 61
Modifier—4 fields

This instruction causes a card to be read and four fields to be placed into storage locations 61–64. For example, if the card of Figure 8.1 were read, the 3567 would be placed in location 61, −3819 in location 62, 3567 in location 63, and 3 in location 64. Since the modifier of this instruction indicates that four fields are to be read, the remaining fields punched in the card will be ignored.

DATA OUTPUT   The instruction to print one line of results is essentially the reverse of the read.

WRITE A LINE

Operation code   *2*,

The Write a Line instruction causes the computer to print from storage the specified number of fields on a single output line as follows: (1) the one-digit modifier specifies how many fields are to be printed from storage, (2) the address operand specifies the storage position from which the first field is to be obtained; contents of successive storage positions are printed as controlled by the modifier. Storage contents are unchanged by execution of this instruction.

The following Write instruction will print one line of output.

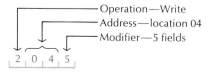

As an illustration, let us assume that the contents of storage locations 04–08 are

Location	Contents
04	+ 3 0 0 5
05	+ 0 0 2 7
06	− 5 1 1 8
07	0 0 0 0
08	+ 0 7 3 4

The printed output for this instruction will be

3005	27	−5118	0	734

Note that on output, leading 0s are not printed.

Exercise

8.3   Four fields are to be read from a card into storage positions 92–95.

    a. Into which card columns must these fields be punched in the data cards?

    b. Write the Read instruction to perform this operation.

8.3

DATA

MOVEMENT

LOADING DATA INTO THE ACCUMULATOR   As noted earlier, the accumulator is the center of all activity in a one-address computer. Prior to performing any arithmetic operation, one of the quantities must be placed in the accumulator; after completing an arithmetic operation, the result is commonly transferred to storage from the accumulator. Operations of loading information into the accumulator from storage in preparation for performing arithmetic operations and storing results into storage from the accumulator are accomplished by the *Load Accumulator* and *Store Accumulator* instructions, respectively.

LOAD ACCUMULATOR

Operation code   *3*

The Load Accumulator instruction causes the contents of the specified storage location to be placed in the accumulator. Previous contents of the accumulator are lost; storage contents are unchanged. The modifier portion of the Load Accumulator instruction is not used.

The Load Accumulator instruction is illustrated by the following example, which shows the accumulator and addressed storage location contents before and after execution of the instruction.

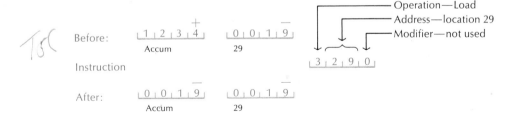

As we see in this example, execution causes the field at location 29 to be loaded into the accumulator. The field in storage is *not* changed by this operation but the original quantity in the accumulator is lost. Since the Load instruction does not use the modifier, a value of 0 is entered (any value may be used but it will be ignored).

SAVING DATA FROM THE ACCUMULATOR   The reverse operation, that of placing the value from the accumulator into storage, is accomplished with the *Store Accumulator* instruction.

STORE ACCUMULATOR

Operation Code   *4*

The Store Accumulator instruction causes the contents of the accumulator to replace the contents of the storage location specified by the instruction.

The accumulator contents are unchanged. The modifier portion of this instruction is not used.

The following example illustrates the Store Accumulator instruction.

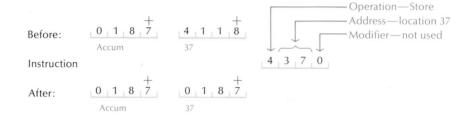

Note that the original accumulator contents are *not* changed, but the original field in storage is lost. It is of utmost importance to recognize that *all* instructions consist of four digits, which provides for a one-digit operation code, a two-digit address operand, and a one-digit modifier. Even though the modifier is ignored by the computer for some instructions (such as Load and Store), a digit *must* be included in that portion of the instruction.

Exercise

8.4 Write a sequence of instructions to read one field from a card into storage location 01, move it to location 24, and print it from 24.

1 0 1 1 Read   4 2 4 0 Store   2 2 4 1 Print
3 0 1 0 load.

8.4
ARITHMETIC
INSTRUCTIONS

ADDITION   A computer would not be of much value to us if all we could do is read data into storage, move it around, and then print it. Of course, the big feature of the computer is its uncanny speed in performing arithmetic operations.

ADD

Operation code   5

The Add instruction causes the quantity in the storage position specified by the instruction to be added to the accumulator contents. The storage quantity is unchanged, but the accumulator contents are replaced with the sum.

The following example illustrates the Add instruction.

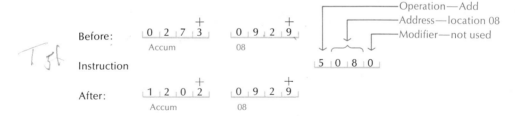

Here we see that the original contents of the accumulator have been replaced by the sum (273 plus 929), but the original storage contents are indeed unchanged.

SUBTRACTION   The Subtract instruction is similar to the Add instruction.

SUBTRACT

Operation code   6

The subtract instruction causes a quantity in the storage position specified by the instruction to be subtracted from the accumulator contents. The storage quantity is unchanged, but the accumulator contents are replaced by the resulting difference.

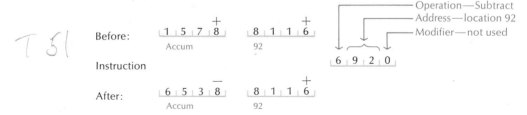

Since the quantity to be subtracted is the larger of the two (8116 as opposed to 1578), the result will be negative (-6538). The result of any valid arithmetic operation will always include the correct sign. Thus either or both of the fields to be operated upon may be negative.

MULTIPLICATION   The last arithmetic operation which we shall consider is multiplication.

MULTIPLY

Operation code   7

The Multiply instruction causes the contents of the accumulator to be multiplied by a quantity in the storage position specified by the instruction.

The storage quantity is unchanged, but the accumulator contents are replaced by the resulting product.

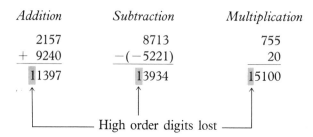

Before: $\overset{+}{\underline{0\;|\;0\;|\;2\;|\;5}}$ $\overset{-}{\underline{0\;|\;1\;|\;2\;|\;2}}$ ┌─────Operation—Multiply
            Accum   48   ┌────Address—location 48
                                                      └──Modifier—not used

Instruction $\underline{7\;|\;4\;|\;8\;|\;0}$

After: $\overset{-}{\underline{3\;|\;0\;|\;5\;|\;0}}$ $\overset{-}{\underline{0\;|\;1\;|\;2\;|\;2}}$
            Accum   48

Here we see the product of a positive field in the accumulator and a negative field in storage producing a negative result in the accumulator.

OVERFLOW   When performing arithmetic operations, care must be taken to insure that the magnitude of the result will not exceed the capacity of the accumulator (four digits). Whenever this occurs, it is called an *arithmetic overflow condition* and digits beyond the accumulator capacity (to the left) are lost. For example, consider the following three examples.

Addition	*Subtraction*	*Multiplication*
2157	8713	755
+ 9240	−(−5221)	20
11397	13934	15100

───────────── High order digits lost ─────────

In other words, the resulting quantities in the accumulator would be 1397, 3934, and 5100, respectively. Whenever this condition occurs, excess digits to the left are simply lost with no indication. Thus, it is the responsibility of the programmer to exercise care to insure that this condition does not occur. (Most modern computers include provisions for indicating to the programmer when such an overflow condition occurs, thereby giving the programmer the capability for including corrective action in the program.)

Exercise

8.5   Write a sequence of instructions to subtract the field at location 02 from the field at location 03, then multiply this difference by the field at 13; store the result at 41.

TERMINATING PROCESSING   Whenever processing is to be ended in a program, the *Halt* instruction is used; it terminates processing and allows the computer to continue to the next job.

HALT

Operation code   *0*

The Halt instruction terminates execution of a program and returns control to the computer system. Neither the address nor the modifier portions of the instruction are used.

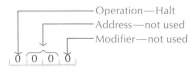

Operation—Halt
Address—not used
Modifier—not used

Instruction   0   0   0   0

Exercise

8.6 What will occur with execution of each of the following instructions?
   a. 0000   b. 0150   c. 0153   d. 0999

AN EXAMPLE PROGRAM   To illustrate how individual instructions are used to construct a program, let us consider the following simple program to read and process one data card.

EXAMPLE 8.1

A foundry keeps a record of each type of casting it manufactures; for each casting, one card is punched with the following information:

Field	Contents
First	Part number
Second	Quantity on hand (beginning of month)
Third	Quantity shipped during month
Fourth	Quantity manufactured during month
Fifth	Quantity lost, damaged, etc., during month

For this first illustration of programming, write a program to process one data record by calculating how many units of that part are on hand at the end of the month. Print the part number, the quantity on hand at the beginning of the month, and the quantity on hand at the end of the month.

Before we write this program, a certain amount of planning is required. For example, we must recognize that the updated quantity on hand is to be calculated as follows:

Updated quantity on hand = previous quantity on hand
+ quantity manufactured
− quantity shipped
− quantity lost, etc.

One of the first steps in preparing the problem for computer solution is to determine where in storage we desire to place the various quantities. If we arbitrarily read the first card field into storage location 01, then the remaining fields will be placed in the following locations.

Storage Address	Field
01	Part number
02	Quantity on hand
03	Quantity shipped
04	Quantity manufactured
05	Quantity lost

Since the program requires that the part number and the quantities on hand at the beginning and end of the month be printed, the following three locations will be used for output.

Storage Address	Field
11	Part number
12	Quantity on hand (beginning of month)
13	Quantity on hand (end of month)

(The reader will note that these choices are purely arbitrary and could as easily have been 00-04 for input and 05-07 for output.)

A sequence of instructions to perform this operation is shown in Figure 8.3. To illustrate execution of this program, let us assume that the data card to be processed contains the following information.

Instruction			Remarks
Op	Addr	M	
1	0 1	5	Read a record.
3	0 2	0	Load beginning balance to accum.
5	0 4	0	Add number manufactured.
6	0 3	0	Subtract number shipped.
6	0 5	0	Subtract number lost.
4	1 3	0	Store result (new balance) to location 13.
3	0 1	0	Move part number
4	1 1	0	to location 11.
3	0 2	0	Move beginning balance
4	1 2	0	to location 12.
2	1 1	3	Print part number, old and new balances.
0	0 0	0	Terminate processing.

Fig. 8.3 Instruction sequence for Example 8.1.

Part number	9255
Quantity on hand	352
Quantity shipped	100
Quantity manufactured	500
Quantity lost, etc.	13

Table 8.1 (which is on the following page) illustrates storage contents after execution of each instruction in this program. Note that whenever execution of a given instruction does not affect the contents of a register, the letters *nc* are used to indicate *no change*. Upon completion of the sequence, storage contents will remain as indicated by the shaded quantities in Table 8.1.

Exercise

8.7 The program of Figure 8.3 uses locations 01–05 for data input and 11–13 for output. Modify it to continue reading the input to 01–05 but to use 01–03 as the output area.

Table 8.1

| | | Storage Contents | | | | | | | |
Instruction	ACC	01	02	03	04	05	11	12	13
Initial Contents	?	?	?	?	?	?	?	?	?
1015 (Read)	?	9255	352	100	500	13	nc	nc	nc
3020 (Load)	352	nc	nc	nc	nc	nc	nc	nc	nc
5040 (Add)	852	nc	nc	nc	nc	nc	nc	nc	nc
6030 (Subtract)	752	nc	nc	nc	nc	nc	nc	nc	nc
6050 (Subtract)	739	nc	nc	nc	nc	nc	nc	nc	nc
4130 (Store)	nc	nc	nc	nc	nc	nc	nc	nc	739
3010 (Load)	9255	nc	nc	nc	nc	nc	nc	nc	nc
4110 (Store)	nc	nc	nc	nc	nc	nc	9255	nc	nc
3020 (Load)	352	nc	nc	nc	nc	nc	nc	nc	nc
4120 (Store)	nc	nc	nc	nc	nc	nc	nc	352	nc
2113 (Write)	nc	nc	nc	nc	nc	nc	nc	nc	nc
0000 (Halt)	352	9255	352	100	500	13	9255	352	739

**8.5
UNCONDITIONAL
BRANCHING**

INSTRUCTION STORAGE ASSIGNMENT   In the pigeonhole analogy of Chapter 4, we saw that the storage consisted of 18 cells and that instructions as well as data were stored in these units. Perhaps the most important single feature of the modern digital computer is that instructions are placed in storage in exactly the same way as data. In fact, the computer has no way of knowing whether something we place in storage is intended to be a data field or an instruction. Since each instruction is four digits in length, each storage position may contain either one data field or one instruction. Whenever we code a program, we must decide which storage areas we intend to use for data and which areas for the program of instructions. Although this decision is arbitrary, once it has been made care must be taken to ensure that data does not overlay a portion of our program. Also, the instructions must appear one after the other in storage. For instance, if the program of instructions is to begin at location 15, then the Read instruction (Figure 8.3) would be at location 15, the first Load instruction at 16, and so on through the Halt instruction, which would be at location 26.

THE BRANCH INSTRUCTION   Needless to say, the program of Figure 8.3 is of little practical value with its ability to read, process, and print for one data record. (One such set of calculations could be done manually very quickly.) This problem of updating an inventory becomes a practical computer application only if the process is to be repeated many times, once for each record in the file. In order to accomplish this, we must make use of an instruction which will break the normal sequence of proceeding from one instruction to the next and cause the computer to *jump* or *branch* to some designated instruction. This was done in the pigeonhole analogy by an instruction directing the "human computer" to go to a particular storage location for the next instruction. It is done in the computer in exactly the same way through use of the *Branch* instruction.

BRANCH (unconditional)

Operation Code   9

Modifier   0

The unconditional Branch instruction causes the normal sequential execution of instructions to be broken and the next instruction to be taken from the location specified by the Branch instruction. Note that the modifier for the unconditional Branch *must be 0*.

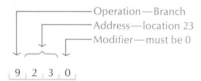

Instruction

Execution of this instruction causes the computer to branch to location 23 for the next instruction.

To simplify the process of preparing the program, it is customary to use special *coding sheets* upon which all of the needed information can be recorded. The program of Figure 8.3 has been modified to include the branch instruction necessary to process an entire data file; storage assignments together with the instructions are shown in Figure 8.4.

Exercise

8.8 What would occur in the program of Figure 8.4 if each of the following coding errors were made?

    a. The address portion of the Branch instruction was 16 instead of 15.

    b. The address portion of the Branch instruction was 17 instead of 15.

    c. The Add and the first Subtract instructions were interchanged. This would give the instruction sequence

        6030
        5040   *no error for c*
        6050

1. Read
2. Write
3. Load
4. Store
5. add
6. Substract
7. Multiply
8. Compare
9. Branch
10. Halt

CODING SHEET

Program _Program Loop_   Programmer _C. D. Clark_   Date _Today_

Load addr	Instruction Op	Addr	M	Remarks
1 5	1	0 1	5	Read a record.
1 6	3	0 2	0	Load beginning balance to accum.
1 7	5	0 4	0	Add number manufactured.
1 8	6	0 3	0	Subtract number shipped.
1 9	6	0 5	0	Subtract number lost.
2 0	4	1 3	0	Store result (new balance) to location 13.
2 1	3	0 1	0	Move part number
2 2	4	1 1	0	to location 11.
2 3	3	0 2	0	Move beginning balance
2 4	4	1 2	0	to location 12.
2 5	2	1 1	3	Print part number, old & new balance.
2 6	9	1 5	0	Branch back to the beginning.

Fig. 8.4 Processing a data file—Example 8.1.

8.6 OTHER USEFUL FEATURES

TERMINATION OF PROCESSING   As we can see by carefully inspecting the program in Figure 8.5, this program of instructions represents an endless loop. Although in reality the computer will stop when no more input records are available to be read, there is no *logical* end to the program. This is quite obvious from the program flowchart of Figure 8.5(a). Most modern computers utilize very complex sets of programs to monitor all operations within the computer and to progress from one job to the next. One of the features of many monitoring systems is to provide for termination of a program whenever the last data record has been processed. The simplest way of doing this is to follow the last data record in the file with a record containing a special code. Unfortunately, no industrywide standard exists for indicating the end of a data file; each manufacturer has a different code. Similarly, different programming languages use different techniques to sense the end-of-data indicator. However, in most cases, the test for end-of-data is automatically performed by the monitoring system whenever a Read operation is performed. Consistent with that concept, the simple machine of this chapter also employs an automatic end-of-data check whenever a card is read. (The actual means for doing this are discussed in Appendix III.) Consequently, the flowchart for the program of Figure

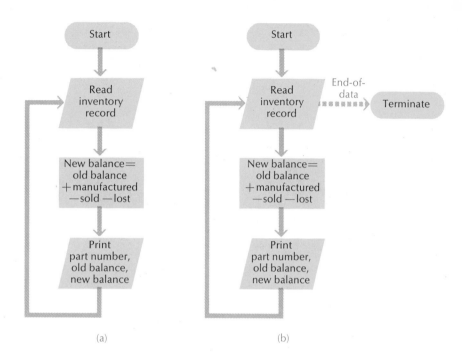

Fig. 8.5 Flowchart for Example 8.1.

(a)   (b)

8.4(a) would be modified as in Figure 8.5(b). Note that the end-of-data alternate is shown by a broken line. The use of a broken line rather than a solid one indicates a segment of the flowchart which is *not* programmed by the user.

THE STORAGE DUMP Occasionally, the programmer will encounter a situation where, try as he/she may, the program simply will not function properly. In such a situation, it is convenient to have a complete printout of all storage contents. Figure 8.6 is a *storage dump* which shows the contents of each storage position after execution of the program in Figure 8.4 has been terminated. Note that the sequence of instructions appears in storage positions 15–26 exactly as required (compare the program of Figure 8.4 to this storage dump). Furthermore, the values in the accumulator and storage locations 1–5 and 11–13 remain exactly as they were after processing the last data card. (For an indication of the processing sequence, refer to Table 8.1.)

<table>
<tr><td>8.7
CONDITIONAL
CAPABILITIES</td><td>TEST INDICATORS In addition to the 100 storage positions and the accumulator, the computer includes a number of other special-purpose registers. Of interest to us are the three binary *arithmetic/compare indicators*. These are used to provide an indication of whether the result of an arithmetic operation is positive, zero, or negative. These are termed the *high/positive* (H/P), *equal/zero* (E/Z), and *low/negative* (L/N) indicators, respectively. Each of</td></tr>
</table>

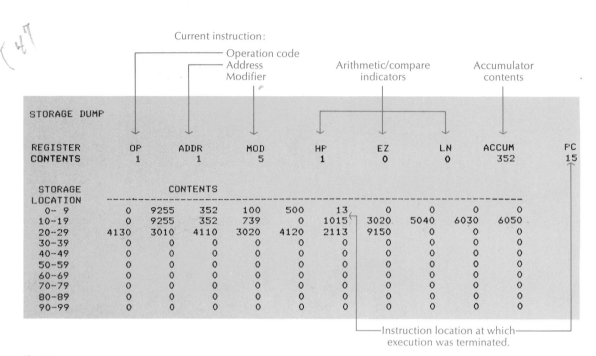

Fig. 8.6   Storage dump.

these three consists internally of a single bit which will be either ON or OFF. Whenever an arithmetic instruction is executed, each of them is set to a state which reflects the nature of the result in the accumulator. The set of examples illustrates the effect of adding two fields for a variety of data values.

Storage	+	Accum (initial)	→	Accum (final)		Indicators		
						H/P	E/Z	L/N
0 3 1 2 (+)		4 7 5 1 (+)		5 0 6 3 (+)		ON	OFF	OFF
0 4 5 2 (−)		0 4 5 2 (+)		0 0 0 0		OFF	ON	OFF
8 1 5 3 (−)		4 0 0 1 (+)		4 1 5 2		OFF	OFF	ON
8 7 1 1 (−)		3 6 5 0		2 3 6 1		OFF	OFF	ON
5 0 0 0 (+)		5 0 0 0 (+)		0 0 0 0		OFF	ON	OFF

Note that only the final value in the accumulator affects the indicators; although arithmetic overflow occurs in the last two cases yielding an invalid result, the appropriate indicators are turned on according to the accumulator contents.

Within a program, these indicators remain as set (either ON or OFF) until another arithmetic instruction is executed. Then each of the indicators is reset according to the result of that operation.

Exercise

8.9 The contents of selected storage words are as follows:

+					−					+					−			
0	8	7	6		0	8	7	6		9	8	1	0		0	0	0	4
Accum					25					37					44			

What indicator will be turned on by each of the following instructions?
a. 5250   b. 6370   c. 5370   d. 7440

THE COMPARE INSTRUCTION   Frequently the programmer will find it necessary to compare two quantities within a program and perform different functions, depending upon which field is larger. For example, when bringing customer charge accounts up to date it might be necessary to print the name of each customer whose account exceeds $1000. Thus, it would be necessary to compare each account balance to 1000. This common type of programming function is performed with the *Compare* instruction.

Compare

Operation Code   8

The Compare instruction causes the quantity in the storage position specified by the instruction to be compared to the accumulator contents. Neither the accumulator nor the storage contents are affected, but indicators are turned on as follows:

Accumulator contents greater than storage contents	High/Positive (H/P)
Accumulator contents equal to storage contents	Equal/Zero (E/Z)
Accumulator contents less than storage contents	Low/Negative (L/N)

In the following example, the contents of storage location 26 are compared to the accumulator contents. The resulting effect on the indicator is shown.

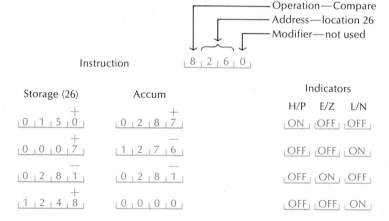

Instruction

Operation—Compare
Address—location 26
Modifier—not used

8 2 6 0

Storage (26)	Accum	Indicators
		H/P E/Z L/N
+ 0 1 5 0	+ 0 2 8 7	ON OFF OFF
+ 0 0 0 7	− 1 2 7 6	OFF OFF ON
− 0 2 8 1	0 2 8 1	OFF ON OFF
+ 1 2 4 8	0 0 0 0	OFF OFF ON

In each case, neither the storage contents nor the accumulator contents are affected by the Compare instruction.

Exercise

8.10 The instruction 8630 is to be executed in a program. Assuming that the accumulator contains 1922, which indicator will be turned on if location 63 contains each of the following?

     a. 1922   b. −0433   c. −2157   d. 3000

CONDITIONAL BRANCHING   Whenever indicators have been set by an arithmetic or a Compare instruction, they remain in their respective settings until reset by another arithmetic or Compare instruction. In the meantime, they can be tested by the Branch instruction, thereby providing the programmer with a conditional branching capability. The Branch instruction (operation code 9) that we studied in the preceding sections provides the ability to branch conditionally as well as unconditionally. The modifier digit of the instruction specifies whether conditional or unconditional and, if conditional, which of the arithmetic indicators to test. If that indicator is on, the branch will occur; if it is off, the next sequential instruction will be executed. The complete definition of the Branch instruction is as follows.

Branch

Operation Code   8

Modifier   *0, 1, 2, or 3*

The Branch instruction serves as an unconditional Branch if the modifier is 0; if 1, 2 or 3 it becomes a conditional Branch. When the designated indicator is on, execution branches to the instruction specified by the address portion of the Branch instruction. If the indicator is off, the next sequential instruction is executed. The indicators and their corresponding instruction modifier codes are as follows.

Indicator	Modifier Code
High/Positive (H/P)	1
Equal/Zero (E/Z)	2
Low/Negative (L/N)	3

Since the conditional Branch instruction is usually used in conjunction with an arithmetic or Compare instruction, the following examples illustrate such a usage.

Instructions		
8 0 5 0	(Compare)
9 3 1 3	(Branch if L/N on)

	Storage (05)	Accum	Indicators H/P E/Z L/N	Results
(a)	+ 2 8 8 1	+ 1 5 3 7	OFF OFF ON	L/N ON; branch to location 31
(b)	+ 2 8 1 7	+ 2 8 1 7	OFF ON OFF	L/N OFF; no branch; continue to next instruction

The Branch instruction modifier has a value of 3, designating the L/N indicator. Since this indicator is turned on in (a), the branch will occur causing the next instruction to be taken from location 31. In (b), execution will continue to the instruction following the branch, because the L/N indicator is not on.

Instructions		
5 2 3 0	Add
9 4 5 2	Branch if E/Z ON
9 6 2 0	Unconditional branch

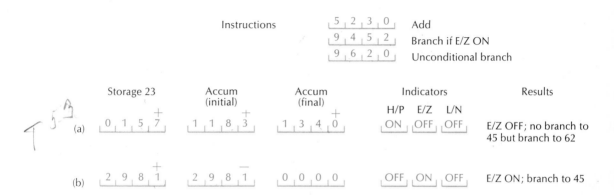

	Storage 23	Accum (initial)	Accum (final)	Indicators H/P E/Z L/N	Results
(a)	+ 0 1 5 7	+ 1 1 8 3	+ 1 3 4 0	ON OFF OFF	E/Z OFF; no branch to 45 but branch to 62
(b)	+ 2 9 8 1	− 2 9 8 1	0 0 0 0	OFF ON OFF	E/Z ON; branch to 45

In this example, a conditional Branch is followed by an unconditional Branch. The overall effect is a branch to location 45 if the E/Z indicator is ON as in (b); otherwise, branch to location 62 (caused by the next sequential instruction), as in (a).

Exercise

8.11   What will occur with execution of each of the following instructions?
  a. H/P indicator ON.   Instruction: 9432
  b. L/N indicator ON.   Instruction: 9283
  c. E/Z indicator ON.   Instruction: 9283
  d. E/Z indicator ON.   Instruction: 9370
  e. H/P indicator ON.   Instruction: 9091

**8.8
EXAMPLE
PROGRAMS**

SEQUENCE CHECKING   To illustrate various branching techniques, let us study two example programs, the first involving sequence checking.

EXAMPLE 8.2

Each card in a deck includes an identification number in columns 1–5; the cards should be in ascending sequence based on this number. Write a program that will read each card and print the number; then check to ensure that the sequencing is correct. If a card is found out of sequence or if two cards contain the same number, terminate execution of the program.

This program will involve reading cards and comparing identification numbers. If the number on the card read is larger than the number on the preceding card, the cards will be in their proper sequence and another card can be read. If this is not the case, the cards are out of sequence and execution should be terminated. However, special handling of the first data card is required, because no card will precede it for comparison purposes. This logic is illustrated by the flowchart of Figure 8.7.

The logic is reflected directly in the program of Figure 8.8. Note that the accumulator is used to store the preceding identification number. If the number from the current card (read into location 01) is greater than the preceding one (in the accumulator), then a low compare occurs. This causes a return to location 12 (via the conditional branch at location 16) which saves this number, then proceeds to read the next card. If a low compare does not occur, execution "falls through" to the Halt instruction at location 17 and execution is terminated.

Professor **Cheney**

Date Submitted **12-14-7?**

Date Required **12-15 am**

Instructions:

Type from end of Chapter 11.

This is a test!

20 COPIES

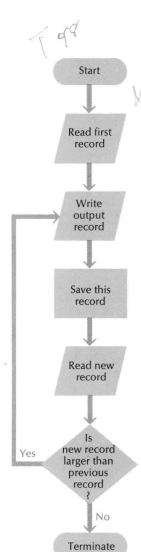

Fig. 8.7 Flowchart for Example 8.2.

Fig. 8.8 Sequence checking—Example 8.2.

Exercise

8.12 Modify the program of Figure 8.8 to terminate processing only when the next identification number is smaller than the preceding number. (In other words, two consecutive cards with the same number do *not* represent a sequencing error.)

CONTROLLED LOOPS Another commonly encountered technique involves breaking out of a loop after a designated number of passes. This involves a counting procedure and results in a *controlled loop*; as an illustration, consider the following example.

EXAMPLE 8.3

Each card in a deck contains one field in columns 1–5. Write a program that will add the fields from 12 consecutive cards, print the total, process 12 more cards, and so on. Assume that the number of data cards is a multiple of 12.

In this program, it will be necessary to set up a counting device in order to control the loop. We might note that it will be necessary to initialize work areas after processing each group of 12 cards. A flowchart illustrating the program logic is shown in Figure 8.9. In preparing this program, we must recognize the need for two work areas, one in which to store the card count during processing and the other to store the total. In addition, certain *program constants* will be required; that is, a value of 0 will be necessary for initializing the work areas prior to processing each group of 12 cards, a value of 1 will

CODING SHEET

Program *Sequence Check*   Programmer *I.B. Miller*   Date *Today*

Load addr	Instruction			Remarks
	Op	Addr	M	
1 1	1	0 1	1	Read first record.
1 2	2	0 1	1	Print the record.
1 3	3	0 1	0	Save new record.
1 4	1	0 1	1	Read next record.
1 5	8	0 1	0	Compare new record to accum.
1 6	9	1 2	3	If new record larger, branch.
1 7	0	0 0	0	Otherwise, halt.

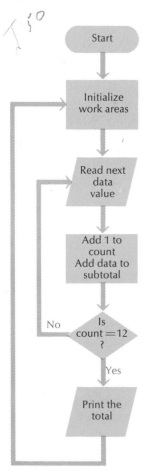

Fig. 8.9   Flowchart for Example 8.3.

be required for incrementing a "counter," and a value of 12 will be needed for comparing purposes. When a number of work areas and constants are required in a program, it is convenient to tabulate them and their storage assignments to avoid confusion when coding the program. For this program, the required working storage areas will be

Location	Use in Program
91	Input area for Read instruction
92	Storage position containing constant 0
93	Storage position containing constant 1
94	Storage position containing constant 12
95	Work position for storing card count (for loop control)
96	Work position for storing sum of card fields

A program to perform the required operations is shown in Figure 8.10. Note that the program constants 0, 1, and 12 are included on the coding sheet in the same manner as the instructions. As do the instructions, each constant has its assigned loading address. Thus, they will be loaded into positions 92–94, whereas the program will be loaded into positions 01–15. Execution of the program involves loading the constant 0 into the accumulator and storing it into positions 95 and 96 which are used as work areas. As each card is read, the constant 1 is added to the counter (location 95) and the data field is added to the total (location 96). If fewer than 12 cards have been processed, the loop repeats itself; otherwise, the sum is printed from location 96, the work areas are initialized, and the sequence repeats.

Exercise

8.13   What would occur in this program (Figure 8.10) if the Branch instruction at location 15 (9010) were written to branch to the Read instruction (that is, if it were 9040)?

8.9
IN RETROSPECT

The capabilities of the hypothetical computer studied in this chapter, although simple and limited, illustrate many of the characteristics of computer programming. Undoubtedly, the reader has noted many shortcomings of this simple system. A particularly serious restriction, especially for business data processing applications, is the inability to handle alphabetic information. As we have seen, this restricts the preparation of useful data processing reports. Virtually all modern digital computers have some provision for storing and manipulating alphabetic as well as numeric data. (Remember that coding methods for various computers were described in Chapter 6).

CODING SHEET

Program __Subtotals__   Programmer __D.E. Clay__   Date __Today__

Load addr	Instruction			Remarks
	Op	Addr	M	
0 1	3 9	2 0		Load 0 to accum to initialize
0 2	4 9	5 0		card count and
0 3	4 9	6 0		subtotal to 0.
0 4	1 9	1 1		Read next field. from Card put in 91
0 5	3 9	6 0		Add new field load 0 from 96 to accum
0 6	5 9	1 0		to subtotal then store data from 91 add accum.
0 7	4 9	6 0		back to subtotal area. Accum to location 96
0 8	3 9	5 0		Add 1 to
0 9	5 9	3 0		card count,
1 0	4 9	5 0		store back to card count area,
1 1	8 9	4 0		then compare to 12.
1 2	9 1	4 2		If count = 12, then branch to output
1 3	9 0	4 0		else branch to get next record.
1 4	2 9	6 1		Write subtotal.
1 5	9 0	1 0		Branch back to start again.
9 2	0 0	0 0		These are the constants
9 3	0 0	0 1		0, 1, and 12 for use in
9 4	0 0	1 2		the program.

Fig. 8.10   A controlled loop—Example 8.3.

In addition, the reader probably found coding using numeric operation codes, addresses, and modifiers somewhat cumbersome. Only the slightest imagination is required to recognize that coding a large, complex problem would be a painstaking task. To this end, a variety of languages are available which are much more oriented toward the computer "nonexpert." Three such languages are described in the next three chapters.

Answers to Preceding Exercises

8.1 Storage location 53 is exactly like the remaining 99 (00–99). Each can store one instruction or one four-digit number with sign, ranging from −9999 to +9999.

8.2 The four fields 1250, 138, −1572, and 1 are punched. In storage, they would appear as follows:

$$\begin{array}{|c|c|c|c|}\hline 1 & 2 & 5 & \overset{+}{0} \\\hline\end{array}$$

$$\begin{array}{|c|c|c|c|}\hline 0 & 1 & 3 & \overset{+}{8} \\\hline\end{array}$$

$$\begin{array}{|c|c|c|c|}\hline 1 & 5 & 7 & \overset{-}{2} \\\hline\end{array}$$

$$\begin{array}{|c|c|c|c|}\hline 0 & 0 & 0 & \overset{+}{1} \\\hline\end{array}$$

8.3 a. Card columns 1-5, 6-10, 11-15, and 16-20
     b. 1924

8.4 1011 (Read)
     3010 (Load)
     4240 (Store)
     2241 (Write)

8.5 3030 (Load)
     6020 (Subtract)
     7130 (Multiply)
     4410 (Store)

8.6 The operation code indicates a Halt instruction; since the Halt does not use the address or modifier, all four of these will terminate processing.

8.7

Instruction			Remarks
Op	Addr	M	
1	01	5	Read a record.
3	02	0	Load beginning balance to accum.
5	04	0	Add number manufactured.
6	03	0	Subtract number shipped.
6	05	0	Subtract number lost.
4	03	0	Store result (new balance) to location 03.
2	01	3	Print part number, old & new balances.
0	00	0	Terminate processing.

8.8 a. The program would read only the first card and continually recalculate with the same data. The output for the first record would be repeated continually until someone stopped the machine.
     b. The program would read only the first card. In this case, the instruction at location 16 which loads the accumulator with the beginning balance would *not* be executed repeatedly. However, the output would be the same as in part (a). Why?
     c. The arithmetic sequence is not critical; this is no error.

8.9

Accumulator Contents	Indicator On
0000	Equal/Zero (E/Z)
−8934	Low/Negative (L/N)
0686 (overflow)	High/Positive (H/P)
−3504	Low/Negative (L/N)

8.10 a. E/Z; b. H/P; c. H/P; d. L/N

8.11 a. Branch if E/Z ON; therefore, no branch.
      b. Branch if L/N ON; therefore, branch to location 28.
      c. Branch if L/N ON; therefore, no branch.
      d. Unconditional branch to location 37.
      e. Branch if H/P ON; therefore, branch to location 09.

8.12

Load addr	Instruction			Remarks
	Op	Addr	M	
1 1	1	0 1	1	Read first record.
1 2	2	0 1	1	Print a record.
1 3	3	0 1	0	Save new record.
1 4	1	0 1	1	Read next record.
1 5	8	0 1	0	Compare new record to accum.
1 6	9	1 8	1	If new record smaller, branch to halt.
1 7	9	1 2	0	Branch to print instruction.
1 8	0	0 0	0	Halt.

8.13 The program would function properly in processing the first 12 cards. However, neither the count (at 95) nor the total (at 96) would be initialized. The thirteenth card would be read, the count incremented by 1 to 13, and the card field added to the total, which would include the first 12 cards as well. Since the equal indicator would be set off as the result of the Compare (at location 11), execution would fall through. The summary line for the first 12 cards would be the only line printed, since the equal condition for the card count would not occur again.

Additional Exercises

8.14 Matching. Match each item in 1–8 with the corresponding description in a–h.
1. accumulator
2. logical end
3. operation code
4. modifier
5. arith/compare indicators
6. dump
7. overflow
8. one-address computer

a. The basic work register in a single address computer.
b. The last executable instruction in a program.
c. A condition produced when the sum of two numbers exceeds the accumulator capacity.
d. Can be tested by the branch instruction.
e. Used by some instructions but not by others.
f. Involves operating on data through use of a special accumulator register.
g. Indicates which operation is to be carried out during execution of an instruction.
h. A printout of the entire storage contents of the computer.

8.15 True-False. Determine whether each of the following is true or false for the computer described in this chapter.
a. Instructions are four digits long except those that do not use the modifier, which are three digits long.
b. The 100 storage positions have addresses of 1–100.
c. Each storage position can hold one four-digit number plus a sign.
d. A single Read instruction can read a record containing from one to nine fields.

e. The computer always gets the next instruction from the storage location immediately following the current one.

f. Every instruction consists of exactly three parts.

g. When data is loaded from storage into the accumulator, the storage area is left blank.

h. If the result of an arithmetic instruction is too large for the accumulator, the computer stops.

i. The following instructions can all change the indicator settings: Add, Subtract, Multiply, Compare, and Branch.

j. The branch instruction can be used to jump either "backward" or "forward" in the program.

8.16 Describe what will occur with execution of each of the following instructions or groups of instructions.

a. 2732	h. 3220	k. 1602
b. 4250	5220	3600
c. 5210	i. 8670	5610
d. 8880	9281	l. 3510
e. 9312	j. 3870	4500
f. 0123	5920	3520
g. 3250	4870	4510
6720		3500
		4520

8.17 Write an instruction or a sequence of instructions to perform each of the following operations.

a. Print three fields punched in an input record.

b. Add the first two fields punched in an input record and put the result at location 25.

c. Branch to location 67 if the number at location 38 is less than the number at 23.

d. Change the sign of the quantity in the accumulator (that is, if it is positive, make it negative; if it is negative, make it positive).

e. Set the contents of location 67 to 0.

f. Read the first two fields punched in a card and place the first one at location 61 and the second at location 60.

g. Halt if the value in location 25 is equal to the accumulator contents; otherwise branch to location 59.

h. Branch to location 85 if the value in the accumulator is less than the value in location 20 or greater than the value in location 21.

8.18 Programming Problems. Write a simple machine language program for each of the following.

a. Each record in a salesperson work file includes the following:

> Salesperson number
> Units sold
> Commission/unit
> Bonus

Write a program to calculate gross pay which is:

> Gross pay = units sold × commission/unit + bonus

Print one line per salesperson as follows:

> Salesperson number
> Gross pay
> Units sold

b. A teacher has grade examination information punched into cards as follows:

> Student number
> First hour exam grade
> Second hour exam grade
> Third hour exam grade
> Final exam grade

Two quantities are to be calculated:

> Hour exam total = first hour exam grade
> + second hour exam grade
> + third hour exam grade
> Total points = hourly exam total
> + 2 × final exam grade

For each student, print the following:

> Student number
> Hour exam total
> Total points

c. Each customer of a clothing store has an account record with the following information:

> Customer number
> Old balance
> Payments
> Other credits
> Charges
> Service charges

Write a program to calculate the new balance as

New Balance = old balance + payments
             + other credits
             − charges − service charges

For each customer print three lines as follows:

First line	Customer
Second line	Old balance and new balance
Third line	Blank

d. The input record of Exercise *c* has been expanded as follows:

> Customer number
> Old balance
> Payments
> Other credits
> Charges
> Service charges
> Credit limit

Calculate the new balance as in Exercise *c* and for each customer whose new balance is equal to or greater than the credit limit, print the following:

First line	Customer number
Second line	Old balance, new balance, and credit limit
Third line	Blank

e. Each salesperson has a sales record in the sales file with the following information:

> Salesperson number
> Total commissions
> Commission quota
> Bonus

Total pay for each salesperson is to be calculated as:

> If total commissions are less than commission quota,
> then gross pay = total commissions;
> otherwise, gross pay = total commissions + bonus

Print the following for each salesperson:

> Salesperson number
> Gross pay

f. Each record in a file contains three fields. Write a program to sort them into an ascending sequence; for each record, print the following:

First line	Original three fields
Second line	Fields in sorted sequence
Third line	Blank

Compare terms as indicate

Chapter

9

The Elements of Programming in Basic

9.1 FUNDAMENTAL CONCEPTS OF BASIC

INTRODUCTION   The extent to which nonprofessional programmers make use of the computer is directly related to the simplicity of programming the computer. In the early 1960s, a simplified language was devised at Dartmouth University called Basic (meaning Beginners' All-purpose Symbolic Instruction Code). Three important features of this language are: (1) it is easy for beginners to learn because of its similarity to ordinary algebra and English, (2) it allows many users to use one computer concurrently through terminals, and (3) it provides an interactive capability whereby the user and the computer can communicate directly through a terminal. Basic, like every computer language, provides the programmer with the means to do input/output operations, data manipulation, calculations, and conditional and unconditional branching. Whereas in a machine or assembly language the programmer must write on the detailed instruction level, in higher level languages such as Basic most of the detail is automatically handled by the Basic compiler. Although the capabilities of Basic as originally implemented were somewhat limited in scope, the language has been expanded to give it powerful computational capabilities and adequate features for business data processing. The absence of an industry-wide standard for the past 15 years has seen a variety of differences evolve in the language structure from manufacturer to manufacturer. Thus, for example, a program written for a Digital Equipment computer might require some modification to run on a Honeywell computer. However, most of the fundamental concepts described in this book are common to all versions of Basic. The purpose of this chapter is to show programming examples written in Basic to illustrate the language; although they will be sufficient to provide

---

ANSI PUBLISHES BASIC, FORTRAN STANDARDS

by Don Leavitt

WASHINGTON, D.C.—Proposed standards for two programming languages—Basic and Fortran—have recently been published by the American National Standards Institute (Ansi).

Public comments on each will be accepted until early July, according to Robert Brown, secretary of Ansi's X3 committee on information processing.

Basic has not been through the standardization process before. The proposed standard was the direct result of a suggestion made nearly five years ago by Prof. J.A.N. Lee, then of the University of Massachusetts, who argued that without the formality of standardization, the language would become so "enhanced" it would lose its usefulness as a teaching tool. . . .

Basic was developed by professor John Kemeny and Thomas Kurtz of Dartmouth College as a vehicle by which students there could communicate easily with a computer. Kemeny is now president of the college. Kurtz, head of Kiewit Computation Center at Dartmouth, chaired the Ansi X3 technical committee (X3J2) that drafted the current proposal.

The draft standard is entitled "Minimal" Basic and "that is exactly what is is," Kurtz explained recently. One or more sets of enhancements may be proposed later, he said, but for now X3J2 wants to get general agreement on the elemental language.

the reader with the ability to write a few simple programs, this discussion is far from a complete study of Basic.

A BOOKSTORE INVENTORY   Let us assume that we work for a bookstore with a large stock of books and that keeping a check on the number of each title in stock has become a problem. In view of the fact that the bookstore management is very backward regarding modern inventory techniques using the computer, we decide to prepare a simple demonstration program to show what can be done. Before we can do the programming job, we must first figure out what results we want from the computer, then determine if the necessary data is available. After some digging, we decide simply to calculate the number of copies on hand at the end of each month. To be complete, we formally define the job as follows.

EXAMPLE 9.1

Prepare a program to calculate the number of copies of each book in the inventory given the following information:

> Book identification number
> Inventory balance at beginning of month
> Copies received during the month
> Copies shipped during the month
> Copies lost or destroyed during the month

The printed results must include

> A line count
> Book identification number
> Inventory balance at beginning of month
> Updated inventory balance

We can see that the operations are relatively simple; the sequence involves reading a data record, performing the calculations, then printing a line. The calculations are

New balance = old balance
+ copies received
− copies sold
− copies lost and destroyed

In view of the fact that this program is to be used to demonstrate simple inventory processing to the bookstore manager, we elect to use a few typical records from the inventory file. Following is the data which will be incorporated into the test case.

Table 9.1   TEST DATA FOR EXAMPLE 9.1

Book Number	Old Balance	Copies Received	Copies Sold	Copies Lost
4451	453	150	313	2
4892	512	0	186	4
5118	82	500	160	1
6881	0	200	0	0
7144	147	180	60	1

Expected results from the processing run are illustrated below

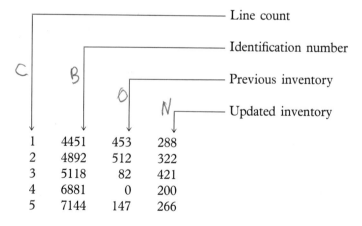

- Line count
- Identification number
- Previous inventory
- Updated inventory

1	4451	453	288
2	4892	512	322
3	5118	82	421
4	6881	0	200
5	7144	147	266

A PROGRAM–EXAMPLE 9.1   A complete program as printed by a computer is shown in Figure 9.1. We should note that this sequence of Basic statements

Descriptive remarks
about the program

Program statements

Input data

```
100 REM      EXAMPLE 9.1
110 REM      PROGRAM TO UPDATE AN INVENTORY
120 REM      INPUT QUANTITIES AND NAMES ARE
130 REM      B - BOOK NUMBER
140 REM      O - OLD BALANCE
150 REM      R - COPIES RECEIVED
160 REM      S - COPIES SOLD
170 REM      L - COPIES LOST AND DESTROYED
180 REM      CALCULATED QUANTITIES AND NAMES ARE
190 REM      C - LINE COUNT
200 REM      N - NEW BALANCE
210 READ B,O,R,S,L
220 LET N = O + R - S - L
230 LET C = C + 1
240 PRINT C,B,O,N
250 GO TO 210
260 DATA 4451,453,150,313,2
270 DATA 4892,512,  0,186,4
280 DATA 5118, 82,500,160,1
290 DATA 6881,  0,200,  0,0
300 DATA 7144,147,180, 60,1
310 END
```

Fig. 9.1 Updating an inventory—Example 9.1.

is illustrated in three different groups: descriptive remarks, the program statements directing the computer to carry out particular operations, and the data to be used in calculations. The similarity to ordinary English and algebra make the function of this program and of individual statements intuitively apparent. Comparing the program statements to what we know of the problem requirements and programming itself, we can surmise the following:

READ B,O,R,S,L	Read input data
LET N = O + R − S − L	Calculate new balance
PRINT C,B,O,N	Print results
GO TO 210	Branch to read next data set

One feature of the Basic language is that each program statement begins with a verb which directs the computer to carry out some action. This characteristic and many other important concepts of Basic are illustrated by the program of Figure 9.1. The important features which it will reveal are:

1. Statement numbers in Basic
2. Remarks in the Basic program
3. Basic constants and variables
4. Basic expressions
5. Input and output capabilities
6. The LET statement
7. The transfer statement
8. The END statement

In the following sections of this chapter, we shall study each of these features and relate them to the fundamental principles of Basic.

LINE NUMBERS*   Each line which we see in the program of Figure 9.1 is called a *statement* and has a *line number* associated with it. Whenever we write a program in Basic, we must assign a unique line number to each line which we enter into the computer. Furthermore, these line numbers must be selected so that they fall in the order in which we want the computer to consider each statement. For instance, let us assume that we forgot to enter the second LET statement into the computer and we had keyed the following:

```
21Ø   READ B,O,R,S,L
22Ø   LET N = O + R − S − L
23Ø   PRINT C,B,O,N
24Ø   GO TO 21Ø
```

If we realized our error at this point, rather than "erasing" everything following statement 220 to make the correction, we could simply enter the forgotten statement as follows.

```
21Ø   READ B,O,R,S,L
22Ø   LET N = O + R − S − L
23Ø   PRINT C,B,O,N
24Ø   GO TO 21Ø
```

```
31Ø   END
225   LET C = C + 1
```

When we request the computer to run our program, it will automatically re-arrange the statements according to the numbers and place statement 225 following statement 220. This also illustrates why the statements are numbered

---

*In Basic it is common practice to distinguish between the letter O and the digit 0 by slashing the digit. By this standard, the digit zero would appear Ø. However, the computer printer used for the examples in this book (e.g., Figure 9.1) does *not* slash zeroes.

by 10s in Figure 9.1: always leave plenty of room between statement numbers for later corrections.

In general, these numbers may be chosen by the programmer; in Figure 9.1, they could as well have been 50, 100, 150, 200, ... The only restriction is in size. Most computers allow up to five digits for them; many small computers allow less, so the reader should check the machine being used.

REMARKS IN BASIC   By placing REM at the beginning of the statement, that entire line may be used by the programmer for descriptive comments. Although the remarks line is ignored by Basic during running of the program, it will still be printed or displayed with the program. The remarks included in this program adequately describe the purpose of the program. The value of using extensive remarks in a program cannot be overemphasized. Programmers commonly find that they must modify or expand an extensive program after completing it and progressing to another job. Even though they have written it themselves, much of the program can be very confusing unless remarks are used liberally. Although the program of Figure 9.1 uses remarks only as the first statements, they may be inserted at any point in the program.

Exercises

9.1   Which types of statement entries in a Basic program do not require line numbers?

9.2   How is a descriptive remark indicated in a Basic program?

9.2
VARIABLES AND CONSTANTS IN BASIC

Inspecting the program statements in Figure 9.1, we see input, calculations, and output. Together with descriptive remarks, statement 210 almost explains itself:

    21Ø   READ B,O,R,S,L

That is, we are directing the computer to read data into storage for the *variables* B, O, R, S, and L (book number, old balance, and so on).

VARIABLES IN BASIC   The term *variable* has much the same meaning in Basic as in algebra; it is a symbolic name given to a quantity that may change in value during running of a program. Each variable in a program will be assigned by the Basic system to some internal storage area into which a number may be stored. In Figure 9.1 we see the following variable names to represent the designated quantities:

Variable	Field
B	Book identification number
O	Old inventory balance
R	Number received
S	Number shipped
L	Number lost
C	Line count
N	New inventory balance

Whereas in algebra variables are usually represented by a single letter, Basic variable names are not so restricted; they may consist of a single letter or a letter followed by a digit. The following are examples of valid and invalid choices for variable names.

Valid	Invalid	
A	2N	Letter must be first
Z	ID	May not be two letters
B1	X25	Only one letter and one digit allowed
N9	6	Cannot be a single digit
B8	P–5	Only letters and digits allowed

In contrast to Basic, most other languages allow variable names to be several characters in length. For instance, in Fortran the name LOST could be used to store the number of copies lost where L is used in this example. Although this feature of Basic somewhat restricts the programmer, the choice of variable names should be made to give an indication of the quantity it represents. For instance, R is selected for copies *Received*, N for *New* balance, and so on.

VARIABLES IN STORAGE   Each variable used in a program will cause the Basic system to reserve one storage area into which a number may be stored. Thus, the program of Figure 9.1 would require seven storage areas, one for each of the variables used. Each such storage area may contain one number at any given time. However, we can easily change the contents of a storage area by placing a new number in it, either by bringing in a new data value through an input operation or by performing a calculation. Prior to execution of any program, the Basic system sets all numeric variables to zero. Then execution of the program places values in them as needed. For instance, let us consider the first data set for which this program is written:

Book number	4451
Old balance	453
Copies received	150
Copies sold	313
Copies lost	2

The contents of the assigned storage areas would appear as follows.

Initial contents

0	0	0	0	0	0	0
B	O	R	S	L	N	C

After reading first record

4451	453	150	313	2	0	0
B	O	R	S	L	N	C

After performing calculations

4451	453	150	313	2	288	1
B	O	R	S	L	N	C

CONSTANTS IN BASIC   In contrast to variables, constants are simply quantities which appear as numbers within the expressions of Basic statements. For instance, statement 230

230 LET C = C + 1

contains the constant 1 in addition to the variable C. Like variables, each constant occupies a storage area; of course, the Basic system places the value in storage for us and leaves it unchanged. In general, constants may be used with or without a decimal point and may include a sign if needed. However, no other punctuation, such as the comma or dollar sign, is allowed. In this respect, the following are examples of both valid and invalid representations for constants.

Valid	Invalid	
25	16,258	Comma not allowed
−25.0	$25.33	Dollar sign not allowed
25.6831		
−687.2		
0.0001875		

Virtually all Basic systems have a set limit on the number of digits allowed for constants (and for variables). Although the limit varies widely from one computer to another, most computers allow for seven significant digits. If the storage area capacity (size of a variable or constant) becomes questionable, then the reader should obtain the specifications of the computer being used.

Exercises

9.3 What value is stored in each variable of a Basic program prior to execution of a program?

9.4 Identify each of the following as a valid variable, a valid constant, or as invalid as a variable or constant.

B	3,685.21
Q293	9
12.62	LOW
5D	12587
D5	Z

9.3
INPUT/OUTPUT
OPERATIONS

THE DATA STATEMENT   There are a number of means for providing input data for a Basic program. One simple method which provides a user the ability to "converse" with the computer is through the keyboard at the request of the computer. Another involves including the data as part of the program. In still another, data files stored on magnetic disk or tape can be read. Example 9.1 uses the DATA statement, with which the data is included as part of the program. Following are two of the DATA statements from Figure 9.1.

```
26Ø   DATA 4451,453,15Ø,313,2
27Ø   DATA 4892,512,  Ø,186,4
```

As do all Basic statements, the DATA statement is preceded by a line number. The keyword DATA is then followed by a list of numbers which represent the input data to be processed. For example, comparing the test data from Table 9.1, we see that the fields listed in each DATA statement represent the inventory information for one book. In contrast to punched cards, where each field is assigned particular columns, adjacent fields in a DATA statement need only be separated by a comma. If it helps to make the program more readable, one or more blank spaces may be inserted whenever appropriate. Although each DATA statement in this example includes exactly one complete record, the DATA statement is not so limited. The fields from each DATA statement in a program are placed in order into a *data pool*, one field after the other. Thus even though the data is arranged in Figure 9.1 in a manner similar to records of file, the fields will be placed one after the other within the computer system awaiting reading by an input statement. Thus, statements 260 and 270 could be replaced by the following.

```
262   DATA 4451
264   DATA 453
266   DATA 15Ø,313,2
272   DATA 4892,512
274   DATA Ø,186,4
```

 DATA 15°, 3/³, 2

Exercise

9.5 Write a sequence of DATA statements to define the data fields of the preceding DATA statements 260 and 270. Define two data values with each statement.

THE READ STATEMENT Data is brought into the computer by use of the READ statement. For example:

```
21Ø   READ B,O,R,S,L
```

This statement will cause the computer to bring the next five fields of data from the data pool into storage, placing the first in the storage area reserved for B, the second in the area reserved for O, and so on. Execution of this statement a second time will cause the next five fields to be brought into storage. This procedure is illustrated in Figure 9.2. The results shown in Figure 9.2

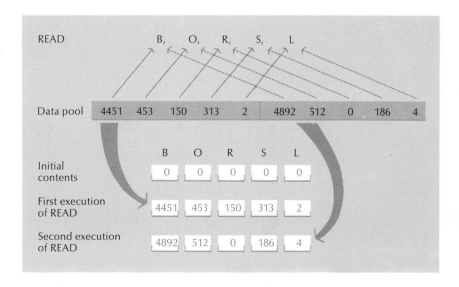

Fig. 9.2 Reading data into storage.

would be identical whether the input data is defined with two DATA statements (260 and 270 in Figure 9.1) or with five (statements 262, 264, 266, 272, and 274) as illustrated in the preceding discussion. In fact, the READ statement of Figure 9.1 could be replaced with the following pair of statements giving exactly the same results.

```
212   READ B,O
214   READ R,S,L
```

The first statement would read the first two fields from the data pool (4451 and 453) and the second statement would read the next three (150, 313, and 2). A number of fields will be read from the data pool by each READ which corresponds exactly to the number of variables listed. Data brought into the computer in this way is commonly referred to as a *data stream.*

The general form of the READ statement is as follows:

The READ Statement
General form: *n* READ *Variable list*

where: *n* is the line number, and
        Variable list is a sequence of variable names separated by commas, which correspond to the data to be read.

Each time the READ statement is executed in a program, a new set of data will be brought into the program. Whenever a READ is executed and no more data remains, the program will automatically be terminated. Thus, using the example data for the program of Figure 9.1, after the fifth (and final) line has been printed, the sixth attempt to read will cause execution of the program to be terminated.

Exercise

9.6 Following is a READ statement and sequence of DATA statements. What will be read into the listed variables with each execution of the READ?

```
150   READ A,B
  .
  .
  .
200   GO TO 150
210   DATA 25,13.3,271,1.287
220   DATA 0,28,17.5
230   DATA 53.35
240   END
```

THE PRINT STATEMENT Information in storage can be printed using the PRINT statement, which essentially performs the reverse operation of the READ. For instance, the PRINT statement from Figure 9.1

24Ø   PRINT C,B,O,N

will cause the current values in storage areas reserved for the variable C, B, O, and N to be printed. Figure 9.3 is the printed output for the example data used with this example. When the PRINT statement is used as it is here, the output will be printed according to a predetermined fixed format. Each output field is allocated 15 positions on the printer and each quantity is left-justified within the 15-position area. (This is in contrast to normal data processing procedures in which numeric fields are right-justified and alphanumeric are left-justified. However, Basic includes other provisions for output to enhance the appearance of printed results.) Obviously, the number of fields which can be printed on a single line depends upon the printer. An ordinary Teletype or equivalent provides for five such 15-position areas. If a given PRINT statement includes a list consisting of more than the single line capacity of the printer, Basic automatically continues printing on subsequent lines until all variables have been printed. As a result, the statement

6ØØ PRINT A, B, X2, B7, Z, L, D2, C3, C4, C5, M, M5

would cause three lines to be printed on a Teletype (five printing areas per line) as follows:

line 1   values of A, B, X2, B7, and Z
line 2   values of L, D2, C3, C4, and C5
line 3   values of M and M5

A partial definition of the PRINT statement is as follows.

The PRINT Statement
General form: *n* PRINT *Variable list*

C	B	O	N
1	4451	453	288
2	4892	512	322
3	5118	82	421
4	6881	0	200
5	7144	147	266

Fig. 9.3 Printed results from Example 9.1.

where: *n* is the line number,

Variable list is a list of variables, separated by commas to be printed, and PRINT defines the operation to be performed.

Exercise

9.7 The statement

    PRINT N2, N4, N6

is executed. Where will each field be printed on the page?

**9.4
PERFORMING
CALCULATIONS
IN BASIC**

ARITHMETIC EXPRESSIONS Basic includes five elementary arithmetic operations: addition, subtraction, multiplication, division, and exponentiation (raising to a power). Examples in this chapter will not deal with exponentiation. Each of these operations is signified by an *operational symbol* as follows:

Addition   +
Subtraction   −
Multiplication *
Division   /

exporentiation ↑ *or power + roots*

The reader will note that these symbols are identical to those of ordinary arithmetic with the exception that a * is used to denote multiplication.

The term *expression* carries much the same meaning in Basic as in algebra, that is, any collection of constants and variables which are related by arithmetic operations. The program of Figure 9.1 includes the following two arithmetic expressions.

    O + R − S − L
    C + 1

The reader should note that blanks are included on either side of the addition symbol (+), but are not required. With only a few exceptions, the Basic system ignores all blanks in the program. Thus, the above expressions could be written as follows.

    O+R−S−L
    C+1

The following additional examples further illustrate Basic expressions.

Description	Algebra	Basic
Perimeter of rectangle	$2l + 2w$	2*L + 2*W
Simple interest amount	$P + Prt$	P + P*R*T
or	$P(1 + rt)$	P*(1 + R*T)
Simple discount amount	$\dfrac{P}{1 - dt}$	P/(1 − D*T)

Note the similarity of each Basic expression to the corresponding algebra expression. In writing expressions, the programmer must keep in mind that each operation is explicitly indicated with an operational symbol. Whereas in algebra the multiplication is commonly implied (for instance, $2w$ means $2 \times w$) this is never true in Basic. *An arithmetic operation must always be signified by an operational symbol.* Even parentheses are used in Basic strictly to group terms and *not* to indicate a multiplication (as in algebra).

The rules for evaluating Basic expressions are much the same as the rules for evaluating algebraic expressions. That is,

1. All expressions within parentheses are evaluated first.
2. Multiplications and divisions are then performed.
3. Additions and subtractions are performed last.

The following examples illustrate this concept.

```
L = 52        2*L + 2*W
W = 28        2 × 52 + 2 × 28
              104 + 56
              160

P = 575       P + P*R*T
R = 0.06      575 + 575 × 0.06 × 9
T = 9         575 + 310.50
              885.50

P = 575       P*(1 + R*T)
R = 0.06      575 × (1 + 0.06 × 9)
T = 9         575 × (1 + 0.54)
              575 × (1.54)
              885.50

P = 300       P/(1 − D*T)
D = 0.08      300/(1 − 0.08 × 5)
T = 5         300/(1 − 0.4)
              300/0.6
              500
```

Although these examples do not completely represent the manner in which the Basic system evaluates expressions, they clearly illustrate the fundamental principles.

Exercises

9.8 Following are algebraic expressions and possible corresponding Basic equivalents. For the incorrect Basic versions, identify the error and write a corrected form.

Algebra	Basic	
a. $2l + 2w$	2L + 2W	$2 * L + 2 * W$
b. $\dfrac{abc}{wx}$	A*B/W*C/X	apply operation from left to right
c. $\dfrac{a + b}{2}$	A + B/2	$(A + B)/2$
d. $(i - j)(i + j)$	(I − J)(I + J)	$(I - J) \times (I + J)$

9.9 If W = 1, A = 6, B = 2, and C = 20, evaluate each of the following expressions.

a. A + B/2   b. A/B + C − W*5

$6 + 2/2$ $6/2 + 20 - 1 \times 5$
7 $23 - 5$
                          18

THE LET STATEMENT   By use of the LET statement we direct the computer to perform desired calculations. For instance, the new inventory balance is calculated by the following:

    22Ø   LET N = O + R − S − L

In algebra, we think of the equal sign ($=$) used in a context such as this as representing an equation. That is, the equal sign has the meaning of equality where N is *equal to* O plus R minus S minus L. In Basic, the equal sign does *not* imply equality in this sense. We must remember that the letters N, O, R, S, and L represent storage areas within the computer into which we place or store data. Then we can understand the idea that the expression to the right of the equal sign (which resembles an expression in algebra) must first be evaluated using the numbers stored in the given areas. Then the result is placed into the storage area reserved for the variable name appearing on the left of the equal sign. These important characteristics are summarized in the following definition.

The LET Statement
General form: *n* LET *Variable* = *Basic expression*

where: *n* is the line number,

the *Basic expression* on the right is evaluated using current values of the indicated variables, and

the result is stored in the *Variable* on the left.

For instance, using the input values of 453, 150, 313, and 2 for O, R, S, and L, respectively, execution of the Basic statement

    220 LET N = O + R − S − L

would proceed as follows.

1. The values for O, R, S, and L would be retrieved from storage and the expression on the right would be evaluated yielding 288.
2. This numeric result would then be placed in the storage area reserved for N (thereby destroying the previous contents).
3. The current values in O, R, S, and L would remain unchanged.

INCREMENTING A QUANTITY   The important distinction between the algebra equation and the Basic LET statement is clearly demonstrated by the second LET statement (statement 230) used in the program of Figure 9.1.

    230 LET C = C + 1

This statement characterizes the difference between the equal sign as used in algebra and in Fortran. In algebra, the equation

$$x = x + 1$$

is never true, regardless of the value assigned to x; it is a contradiction. In Basic, the statement

    C = C + 1

is quite valid and very useful. Remember, the equal sign says, "Evaluate the expression on the right and assign that value to the variable on the left." Initially, the value in C will be 0. Execution of the statement will cause the expression C + 1 to be evaluated as 0 + 1, or 1. Then the result, 1, will be stored back in C, replacing the previous value of 0. Continuing, if we assume that the fourth record has been processed and execution has proceeded to the GO TO statement, the value of C will be 4. Upon executing the loop once more (processing the fifth record), C + 1 will be evaluated as 5, with the result being stored back into C replacing the previous value of 4.

Exercise

9.10 Distinguish between the use of the equal sign in Basic and in algebra.

9.5
OTHER
STATEMENTS

THE GO TO STATEMENT   In the program of Figure 9.1, it is necessary to return to the READ statement after a given set of data has been printed. This is accomplished with the GO TO statement, as used in the program of Figure 9.1 and repeated here:

```
210   READ B,O,R,S,L
        .
        .
        .
250   GO TO 210
```

This statement interrupts the sequential execution of statements and specifies the number of the next statement to be executed; in this case it causes a branch to statement 210. The designated instruction may be anywhere in the program: that is, we can direct the computer to branch back to an earlier statement or to skip ahead to a later statement, whichever is required in the program.

THE END STATEMENT   The last statement in a Basic program must be the END statement. In Figure 9.1 its sole purpose is to indicate to the Basic processor that no more statements follow. We will note that during execution of this program the END statement does not play any role. That is, the READ statement (210) is first executed followed by the two LETs and the PRINT. Then control is returned to the READ by the GO TO statement (250). This loop is repeated until there is no more input data, at which time execution is terminated.

On the other hand, the END can also be used to terminate execution of a program. For instance, Figure 9.1 is modified in Figure 9.4 to process one data record.

```
100   DATA 4451,453,150,313,2
110   READ B,O,R,S,L
120   LET N = O + R − S − L
130   PRINT B,O,N
140   END
```

Fig. 9.4 Using the END to terminate processing.

In this case, the END serves both to signfy no more statements in the program to the Basic processor and to terminate processing after the printing operation.

Exercise

9.11 What would occur in the program of Figure 9.1 if statement 250 were accidentally written as

  a. 25Ø GO TO 22Ø *continuously repeated. Burst*

  b. 25Ø GO TO 24Ø

PROCESSING LOGIC In looking at the program of Figure 9.1, we see what appears to be an infinite loop; that is, there appears to be no logical end to execution. (Of course, we know that execution is automatically terminated when there is no more data.) On the other hand, in Figure 9.4 the sequence is executed just once and execution is terminated by the END statement.

  The flowcharts in Figure 9.5 illustrate the logic of both cases. In Figure 9.5(a), the GO TO causes a continuous loop, with execution being terminated when the data is gone. Since the end-of-data check is performed automatically (by the Basic system) and is not programmed by the user, it is indicated in the flowchart by the broken flowline. In Figure 9.5(b), execution proceeds through to the END; in this case, termination of execution is caused by the END statement (number 140 in Figure 9.4).

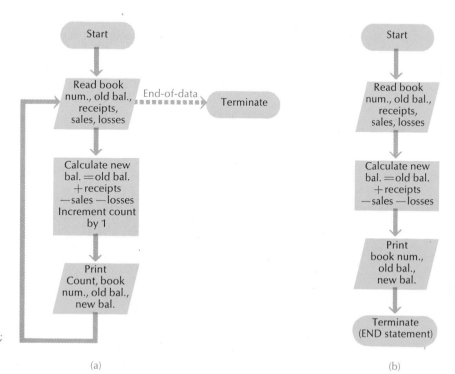

Fig. 9.5 (a) Automatic termination of execution; (b) processing a single record.

(a)   (b)

9.6
THE NATURE
OF BASIC

In the early days of computers, whenever a number of jobs were to be run, each would be placed in the machine and run to completion before the next was loaded. Most modern machines are able to handle two or more programs concurrently with ease through any of several techniques. (This subject is discussed in Chapter 13.) One of these techniques is *timesharing*, in which many users can communicate with the machine concurrently via remote terminals. Although many users might be sharing the computer resources, the high speed of modern machines makes it appear to any given user that no one else is on the machine. One very important feature of timesharing is the ability of the user to program directly into the computer or "converse" with the machine, then have the program stored for later use.

BASIC COMMANDS   Basic programs are made up of *statements* which tell the computer what operations to perform during execution of the program. Control of the timesharing computer system is provided the user through *commands*. In general, a statement has a line number; a command has no line number. For instance, if we are to create a new program, we must type in the command NEW; then we can type the statements which make up the program. Some of the commonly used commands are:

NEW	Typing NEW followed by the name we wish to call the program initializes everything so that we can enter a new program.
RUN	Submits a program to the Basic system for execution.
LIST	Causes the Basic system to list the current program.
SAVE	Causes the current program on which the user is working to be "permanently" saved within the system.
OLD	Allows the user to recall a program which was previously saved so that it may be used as if it were just keyed in.

The normal sequence of operations which most programmers encounter when entering a new program and attempting to debug it is as follows.

1. Key in the command NEW and the program name for a new program.
2. Key in the program.
3. Request execution via the RUN command.
4. Examine the results and/or error messages from the Basic system.
5. Key in corrected program statements. For instance, if A and B were to have been read in but the statement in the program was

    17Ø   READ A,D

then the user would enter a new statement 170 which would be

    17Ø   READ A,B

6. The corrected program would be checked by listing with the LIST command.
7. Request execution of the corrected program via the RUN command.
8. If the program is fully debugged and ready to be saved, then catalog it into the system using the SAVE command.

Exercise

9.12 What is the difference between a Basic command and a Basic statement?

INTERACTION IN BASIC   One of the most important features of Basic is that it allows the user to interact with the computer during execution. This provides the user with such capabilities as responding to previous results and changing the input data and allows the user to "communicate" with the computer under various conditions (for instance, playing games with the computer either for fun or as part of a learning experience). As a simple illustration of this capability, let us consider Example 9.2.

EXAMPLE 9.2

A simple interest calculation is to be performed for any set of values of principal (P), interest rate (r), and time (t) entered from a terminal. Use the formula

$$A = P(1 + rt)$$

The computer output of Figure 9.6 illustrates not only the program but a typical sequence of events which might occur during a "session" with the computer. The printed portions which are not shaded are keyed into the system by the user; everything else was printed out by the computer.

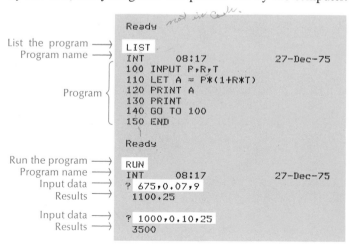

Fig. 9.6   A conversation with the computer.

With the exception of the INPUT statement, all program statements are familiar from previous descriptions. The INPUT statement is used exactly like the READ statement except that data is entered from the terminal at execution time rather than from a DATA statement. Upon encountering the INPUT statement, the computer types a question mark. That is the signal to the user to enter the required fields. In this case, three quantities are required, so they are entered, separated by commas. The computer then continues processing and prints the calculated result on the next line.

Exercise

9.13   What is the difference between the READ statement and the INPUT statement?

PRINTING HEADINGS   We need only glance at the output of Figure 9.6 to realize that interacting to a question mark from the computer might be a bit confusing at times. For instance, it is essential that the input fields be entered in the proper sequence; P, R, then T. If we became confused and entered them in the order R, T, and P, the results would be quite incorrect. To ensure against this mistake, we can program the computer to print simple directions to us, as illustrated by the program and resulting "conversation" of Figure 9.7. As in Figure 9.6, the responses from the computer are shaded, whereas entries made by the user are not. Execution of statement 130

```
130   PRINT "TYPE IN PRINCIPAL, RATE AND TIME";
```

causes the computer to print the information exactly as quoted. In this case, we do not request the computer to print the values of any variables in storage, only the directions to the user which have been enclosed in quotes. Since the message is followed by a semicolon (;), the typewriter does not reposition to a new line but waits to continue any new typing where it finished from the PRINT statement. Thus, the directions from the PRINT statement, the question mark from the INPUT statement, and our typed entries are all on the same line. Once the input quantities are entered, execution continues. Statement 180 prints the input fields together with required descriptions. Figure 9.8 illustrates the action of various components of this output statement. The accumulated amount (A) is printed by statement 210 in much the same way.

Exercise

9.14   In which of the printing areas will A and B be printed for each of the following?
   a. 210   PRINT "A IS"; A, "B IS"; B
   b. 220   PRINT "A IS", A, "B IS", B
   c. 230   PRINT "THE CURRENT VALUE OF A IS", A

```
LIST

INT

100 REM SIMPLE INTEREST CALCULATIONS
110 REM USER SIMPLY FOLLOWS DIRECTIONS
120 REM
130 PRINT "TYPE IN PRINCIPAL, RATE AND TIME";
140 INPUT P,R,T
150 LET A=P*(1+R*T)
160 PRINT
170 PRINT "IF PRINCIPAL, RATE AND TIME ARE"
180 PRINT "PRINC =";P,"RATE =";R,"TIME =";T
190 PRINT
200 PRINT "THEN THE ACCUMULATED AMOUNT IS"
210 PRINT "AMOUNT =";A
220 PRINT
230 PRINT
240 GO TO 130
250 END

READY

RUN

INT

TYPE IN PRINCIPAL, RATE AND TIME?675, 0.07, 9

IF PRINCIPAL, RATE AND TIME ARE
PRINC = 675    RATE = .07    TIME = 9

THEN THE ACCUMULATED AMOUNT IS
AMOUNT = 1100.25


TYPE IN PRINCIPAL, RATE AND TIME?1000, 0.10, 25

IF PRINCIPAL, RATE AND TIME ARE
PRINC = 1000   RATE = .1     TIME = 25

THEN THE ACCUMULATED AMOUNT IS
AMOUNT = 3500
```

Fig. 9.7 Getting directions from the computer.

9.7 ALPHANUMERIC DATA

The handling of alphanumeric data in Basic is every bit as simple as handling numeric data. Corresponding to numeric variables, we can define alphanumeric variables; they are distinguished from numeric variables by using the dollar sign character ($) after the name. For example, the variable names A, B5, and Z6 will be accepted by the Basic system for use in storing numeric quantities. Correspondingly, the variable names A$, B5$, and Z6$ will reserve storage areas for storing alphanumeric data.* An alphanumeric field can be a single

---

*Some versions of Basic allow alphanumeric variable names to consist only of a single letter followed by the dollar sign character. In such systems A$ and P$ are valid, but N6$ and P3$ would not be.

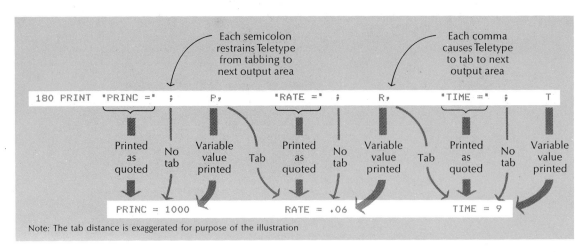

Note: The tab distance is exaggerated for purpose of the illustration

Fig. 9.8 Execution of a print statement.

letter, an ordinary word, or a collection of words. Furthermore, an alphanumeric field may include any of the characters on the keyboard. Following are some example alphanumeric fields.

```
T
HEADING
COMPUTER PROGRAMMING
DATA 25
```

Such a data field is commonly referred to as a *string* or *data string*. Variables such as A$ are similarly referred to as *string variables*. The maximum size of a character string depends upon the particular computer on which the Basic program is run, so the reader should check his/her computer system for this restraint.

As a simple illustration of using a string variable in a program, let us expand Figure 9.1 as follows.

EXAMPLE 9.3

Prepare a program to calculate the number of copies of each book in an inventory, given the following information.

Book identification number
Author
Inventory balance at beginning of month
Copies received during the month
Copies shipped during the month
Copies lost or destroyed during the month

The printed results must include the following:

A line count
Book identification number
Author
Inventory balance at beginning of month
Updated inventory balance

In the program of Figure 9.9 we see the string variable A$ used in the READ and PRINT statements in exactly the same way as the numeric variables.

```
100 REM     EXAMPLE 9.3
110 REM     PROCESSING ALPHANUMERIC DATA
120 REM
130 READ B,A$,0,R,S,L
140 LET N = 0 + R - S - L
150 PRINT B,A$,0,N
160 GO TO 130
170 DATA 4451,JOHNSON,453,150,313,2
180 DATA 4892,ALBERTSON,512,0,186,4
190 DATA 5118,HALL,82,500,160,1
200 DATA 6881,IRWIN,0,200,0,0
210 DATA 7144,MCGRAW,147,180,60,1
220 END
```

Fig. 9.9 Using a string variable—Example 9.3.

9.8 CONDITIONAL BRANCHING

RELATIONAL EXPRESSIONS   The program of Figure 9.1 provides sufficient Basic capabilities to perform a variety of functions. The ability to loop or branch back is a result of the simple GO TO statement, which causes an unconditional transfer of control to a designated statement. Although this unconditional branching capability is important, much of the power of the computer lies in its ability to branch only if a designated condition is satisfied during execution. If a calculated student grade point average falls below a certain level, for instance, then the student's name should be printed on a deficiency list; otherwise, it need not be printed. This type of testing is performed in Basic by use of the IF statement. For example, the following statement will cause a branch to statement 200 whenever a student GPA (called G) is found to be less than 1.8.

IF G $<$ 1.8 THEN 200

The portion of this statement of interest to us at this point is the *relational expression*

G $<$ 1.8

In general, a relational expression involves two arithmetic expressions and a *relational operator*. (For example, G and 1.8 are simple arithmetic expressions and < is a relational operator.) Relational operators available to the Basic programmer are the following.

Symbol	Meaning
>	Greater than
=	Equal to
<	Less than
>=	Greater than or equal to
<=	Less than or equal to
<>	Not equal to

In evaluating a relational expression, the arithmetic expressions are first evaluated and then the indicated comparison is made. The relational expression will be found to be either true or false; the following examples illustrate this.

Relational expression: G < 1.8

If G is	then G < 1.8 is
1.5	true
1.8	false
2.0	false

Relational expression: 25 >= 2*N − 1

If N is	then 2*N − 1 is	so 25 >= 2*N − 1 is
5	9	true
13	25	true
14	27	false

Relational expression: P <> 2*R

If P is	and R is	then 2*R is	so P <> 2*R is
10	− 3	− 6	true
10	5	10	false
10	10	20	true

THE IF STATEMENT   Now let us consider how the relational expression might be used in an IF statement to branch to statement 200 only when the student GPA (G) is less than 1.8; otherwise, execution is to continue to the next sequential statement. The logic of this is illustrated in Figure 9.10(a), and the IF statement to perform the test is shown in Figure 9.10(b). We will note that the IF-THEN statement includes the relational expression

G < 1.8

which is evaluated and found to be true or false. If it is true, then a branch to statement 200 is executed; otherwise, execution continues to the next statement. For instance, consider the following three example values for G:

If G is	then G < 1.8 is	and execution
1.5	true	branches to statement 200
1.8	false	continues to next statement
2.5	false	continues to next statement

T_5^8

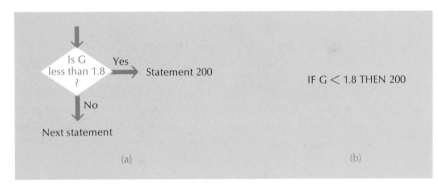

IF G < 1.8 THEN 200

Fig. 9.10 (a) Logic of the IF statement; (b) the IF statement.

(a)   (b)

The general form of the IF is as follows:

The IF statement
General form: *n* IF *Relational expression* THEN *statement number*

where: *n* is the statement number,
Relational expression consists of two arithmetic expressions related by a relational operation, and
Statement number is the statement to which the branch occurs if the relational expression is true; otherwise, execution continues to the next sequential statement.

Exercises

9.15 Consider the following IF statement:
    18Ø   IF 3.2*T7 >= 16 THEN 29Ø
    a. Identify the relational expression. $3.2 * T7 >= 16$
    b. What will occur when

       T7 = −10   F
       T7 =   5   T
       T7 =   20   T

Reprinted by permission of *Creative Computing*.

9.16 Write a sequence of statements to change the variable N to 0 if N is less than 0; otherwise, leave N unchanged. Then print the value for N.

PROGRAMMING USING THE IF   In Chapter 7 we studied the concepts of flowcharting through use of several examples. One of them, Example 7.4, is ideal to illustrate using the IF statement in a program. Let us assume that we work in the programming department of a small company and we have been assigned to write a program for searching the personnel records as described by the following problem statement.

EXAMPLE 9.4

Print a list of all employees who meet both the following requirements (1) and (2).

    1. (a) Has been with the company 25 years or more, or (b) is 65 years of age or older.
    2. Has accumulated more than 120 days of sick leave.

The data input fields for each employee will be

    Employee number
    Name
    Age
    Seniority
    Accumulated sick leave

Although both conditions (1) and (2) must be satisfied, we must note that condition (1) is satisfied by employees meeting either the 25 years seniority requirement or the 65 year age requirement. This is illustrated by the flow-chart of Figure 9.11(a), a minor variation of Figure 7.9, which mirrors the corresponding program in 9.11(b) almost exactly. An inspection of this program shows nothing new; it is merely an application of principles learned in previous sections. Further consideration of this program is left to the reader.

A COMPUTER ASSISTED INSTRUCTION EXAMPLE   To further illustrate conditional branching and the conversational aspect of Basic, let us consider an example program which allows the computer to serve as a tutor for addition of signed numbers.

EXAMPLE 9.5

This tutorial program is to provide drill and practice in addition of signed numbers and is to function as follows:

    1. The computer prints two numbers to be added.
    2. The student types in an answer.
    3. The computer checks the answer and responds that it is either correct or incorrect.
    4. The student is given three chances to obtain the correct answer; after the third try, the computer prints the correct answer.
    5. The process is repeated for another pair of numbers.

T 59

T 59

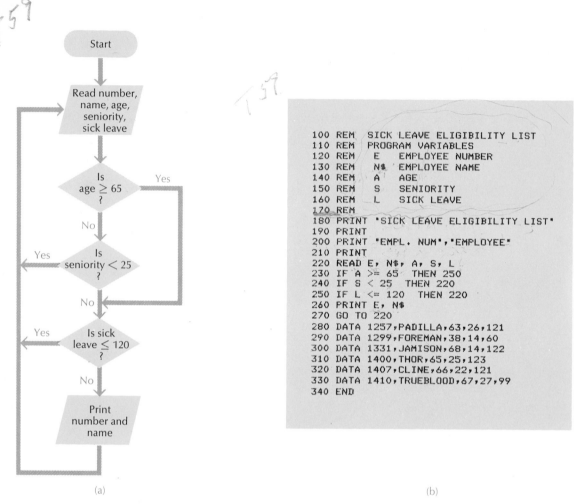

```
100 REM   SICK LEAVE ELIGIBILITY LIST
110 REM   PROGRAM VARIABLES
120 REM   E     EMPLOYEE NUMBER
130 REM   N$    EMPLOYEE NAME
140 REM   A     AGE
150 REM   S     SENIORITY
160 REM   L     SICK LEAVE
170 REM
180 PRINT "SICK LEAVE ELIGIBILITY LIST"
190 PRINT
200 PRINT "EMPL. NUM","EMPLOYEE"
210 PRINT
220 READ E, N$, A, S, L
230 IF A >= 65   THEN 250
240 IF S < 25    THEN 220
250 IF L <= 120   THEN 220
260 PRINT E, N$
270 GO TO 220
280 DATA 1257,PADILLA,63,26,121
290 DATA 1299,FOREMAN,38,14,60
300 DATA 1331,JAMISON,68,14,122
310 DATA 1400,THOR,65,25,123
320 DATA 1407,CLINE,66,22,121
330 DATA 1410,TRUEBLOOD,67,27,99
340 END
```

(a)   (b)

Fig. 9.11   (a) A flowchart for Example 9.4; (b) a program for Example 9.4.

The logic of this problem is illustrated in the flowchart of Figure 9.12, and a program is shown in Figure 9.13. A detailed study of this program is left to the reader.

Exercise

9.17   What would happen in execution of the program in Figure 9.13 if statement 200

    220   LET Z = 0   no more errors
                                    Change

were left out?

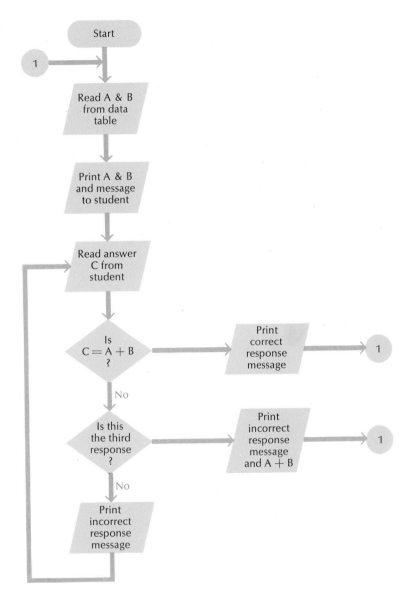

Fig. 9.12 Flowchart for Example 9.5.

FILE PRINCIPLES Considerable emphasis in this book has been placed on the concept of data files and their processing. Examples in this book have used DATA statements or INPUT statements to make the data available to the computer. Both of these methods are impractical for most applications, especially those involving large data files. To satisfy this need, Basic has special provisions for storing data files on magnetic disk or other auxiliary storage devices, completely independent of the program which will process the data. In fact, each

```
100 REM     EXAMPLE 9.5
110 REM     ADDITION OF TWO SIGNED NUMBERS
120 REM     DRILL AND PRACTICE
130 REM
140 PRINT "THIS IS A DRILL AND PRACTICE EXERCISE FOR ADDING SIGNED"
150 PRINT "NUMBERS.  I WILL TYPE OUT TWO SIGNED NUMBERS AND YOU MUST"
160 PRINT "ENTER THE SUM.  IF IT IS CORRECT I WILL TELL YOU AND GIVE"
170 PRINT "YOU TWO MORE NUMBERS.  IF WRONG, YOU CAN TRY AGAIN.  AFTER"
180 PRINT "THREE TRIES I TELL YOU THE CORRECT ANSWER.  HERE WE GO"
190 PRINT
200 PRINT
210 READ A,B
220 LET Z=0
230 PRINT "WHAT IS THE SUM OF "; A; " AND "; B,
240 LET D=A+B
250 INPUT C
260 IF C=D THEN 340
270 LET Z=Z+1
280 IF Z=3 THEN 310
290 PRINT C; " IS NOT RIGHT - TRY AGAIN ",
300 GO TO 250
310 PRINT C; " IS NOT RIGHT.  "; A; " PLUS "; B; " IS "; D
320 PRINT "LET US TRY TWO MORE NUMBERS"
330 GO TO 200
340 PRINT "CORRECT  "; A; " PLUS "; B; " IS "; C
350 PRINT "LET US TRY TWO MORE NUMBERS"
360 GO TO 200
370 DATA 25,37,-49,83,27,82,131,-84,-28,-97,189,77,153,-96,-82,65,-123,56
380 END
```

Fig. 9.13 Interactive program for drill and practice.

program which is stored in the system is itself a file. Thus, the file storage capability allows us to save program files *and* data files. In each case, whenever we must store a file, we simply give it a name (from one to six characters in length), then direct the Basic system to SAVE it. The file will be stored in auxiliary storage and will be available to us by its name.

Thus, a large data file can be keyed into storage by a clerk and saved in much the same way that the same data would be punched into cards. For instance, the book inventory test data used in Figure 9.9 might be entered into the system as the file BOOK by the following.

```
TYPE OLD OR NEW: NEW
FILENAME: BOOK
READY

100   DATA 4451,JOHNSON,453,150,313,2
110   DATA 4892,ALBERTSON,512,0,186,4
120   DATA 5118,HALL,82,500,160,1
130   DATA 6881,IRWIN,0,200,0,0
140   DATA 7144,MCGRAW,147,180,60,1
150   END

SAVE
```

Note that each line is entered just as it was in the program of Figure 9.9.*
Furthermore, each record includes a line number as do statements in a program.
This way, we can easily enter new records into the file or correct existing ones
just as with programs. Reading data from a file into a program is done with a
slight variation of the INPUT statement, with which we have already become
quite familiar.

USING A FILE IN A PROGRAM   In using a file for data input, we must be able
to:

1. Identify the required file from among the many stored in the system.
2. Read data into the program from the file.

Both of these principles are illustrated by the program of Figure 9.14, which
is a modification of Example 9.3 (Figure 9.9). Identification of the data file
to be processed is achieved by the FILES statement

130 FILES BOOK

In general, this statement may name any number of files to be used in the
program. For instance, if we were planning to process the three files INVEN,
CASH, and ERROR we would identify them in a FILES statement as follows:

140 FILES INVEN, CASH, ERROR

Within the program, we would refer to the first file listed (INVEN) as #1,
the second (CASH) as #2, and the third (ERROR) as #3. Since there is only
one file (BOOK) listed in statement 130 of Figure 9.14, it is referred to within

```
100 REM    EXAMPLE 9.3 MODIFIED
110 REM    PROCESSING A DATA FILE
120 REM
130 FILES BOOK
140 INPUT #1, B,A$,O,R,S,L
150 LET N = O + R - S - L
160 PRINT B,A$,O,N
170 GO TO 140
180 END
```

Fig. 9.14 Using data files.

---

*Most versions of Basic have special provisions for entering data files. In some, the word
DATA may be omitted. Others use special system editors in which both the statement number
and the word DATA are omitted.

the program as #1. Identification of the appropriate file during reading is achieved in the INPUT statement as follows.

    14Ø   INPUT #1, B, A, O, R, S, L

The INPUT is immediately followed by the file number from which the data is to be obtained (#1 in this case). Following the file designation we see the list of variables, which is identical to that of statement 130 in Figure 9.9.

Basic also includes the capability to continually monitor the reading of a file for its end and the repositioning of a file so that it may be reread. In addition, files may be written from a program as well as read. However, further treatment of file capabilities is beyond the scope of this book.

9.10
IN RETROSPECT

By comparing the machine language concepts of Chapter 8 with Basic described in this chapter, we can see that Basic is much more "user oriented." The programmer can effectively use the computer with virtually no idea of how it works or of its language. One of many higher-level languages now available, Basic is one of the most commonly used and, in fact, is the most commonly used timesharing language. One of the first considerations for its development was simplicity of use for the person not knowledgeable about computers. Although originally developed for use in an educational environment, its features have been expanded by most computer manufacturers for a variety of operations. As such, it is well adapted to such nonprofessional programmers as engineers, statisticians, economists, and students in a wide variety of disciplines. Recent extensions of the language provide capabilities for business data processing with the result that it is finding acceptance in traditional business areas for some applications.

Due to the wide acceptance of Basic, the American National Standards Institute (ANSI) is currently working on a Basic standard which will serve as an industrywide standard for implementing Basic. It is expected that this standard will be available in the near future.

Answers to Preceding Exercises

9.1 All Basic program statements entries must have line numbers.

9.2 A descriptive remark is indicated by entering REM following the line number.

9.3 All variables in a Basic program contain zero prior to execution.

9.4 B   valid variable name
        Q293   invalid

12.62	valid constant
5D	invalid
D5	valid variable name
3,685.21	invalid
9	valid constant
LOW	invalid
12587	valid constant
Z	valid variable name

9.5 260 DATA 4451,453
262 DATA 15Ø,313
264 DATA 2,4892
268 DATA 512,Ø
27Ø DATA 186,4

9.6

Execution of Read	Values read	
	A	B
First	25	13.3
Second	271	1.287
Third	0	28
Fourth	17.5	53.35

9.7 The value for N2 will begin in printing position 1.

The value for N4 will begin in printing position 16.

The value for N6 will begin in printing position 31.

9.8 a. 2L + 2W should be 2*L + 2*W (asterisk missing).
b. This form is correct—apply the operations from left to right.
c. A + B/2 yields $a + \dfrac{b}{2}$; correct form is (A + B) /2.
d. (I − J) (I + J) should be (I − J)*(I + J); asterisk missing.

9.9 a. 7; b. 18

9.10 In algebra, the equal sign indicates that the quantities on each side of the equal sign are identical. In Basic, it denotes that the expression to the right is to be evaluated and the result stored in the variable to the left.

9.11 a. Only the first record would be read and calculations would be made continuously for the same data set. For the sample input values, the output would be

1	4451	453	288
2	4451	453	288
3	4451	453	288
.	.	.	.
.	.	.	.

Note that the line counter would change.

b. No new calculations would be made, and the first line would be continuously repeated:

1	4451	453	288
1	4451	453	288
1	4451	453	288
.	.	.	.
.	.	.	.

9.12 Basic command: Provides control of the time-sharing computer system; does not have a line number; for example, RUN causes the system to execute a program.

Basic statement: A component of a program will tell the computer what operations to perform in executing a program; must have a line number; for example,

2ØØ READ A,B,C

causes three data values to be read.

9.13 The READ statement causes listed variables of the program to be loaded with data which has already been placed in the computer system (for example, via the DATA statement).

The INPUT statement causes the computer to stop and await data to be entered from a keyboard by an operator.

9.14 a. A IS: first printing area (beginning in position 1).
Value of A: first printing area (immediately following A IS).
B IS: second printing area (beginning in position 16).
Value of B: second printing area (immediately following B IS).
b. A IS: first printing area (beginning in position 1).
Value of A: second printing area (beginning in position 16).
B IS: third printing area (beginning in position 31).
Value of B: fourth printing area (beginning in position 46).
c. THE CURRENT VALUE OF A IS: fills the first printing area and, overlaps into the second.
Value of A: third printing area (beginning in position 31).

9.15   a. 3.2*T7 >= 16

b. If T7 *is*   execution

     − 10   continues to next statement

        5   branches to statement 290

      20   branches to statement 290

9.16   3ØØ   IF N >= Ø THEN 32Ø

31Ø   LET N = Ø

32Ø   PRINT N

9.17   Since Z is the counter for "incorrect answers," failing to set it to 0 would allow the student only three errors during the entire lesson. For instance, three errors for the first pair of numbers would mean no more "retries" for any errors made with exercises after the first.

Additional Exercises

2 pts each

9.18 **Matching.** Match each item 1-8 with the corresponding description a-h.

    1. IF   2. LET   3. DATA

    4. READ   5. GO TO   6. END

    7. REM   8. PRINT

a. Allows the inclusion of descriptive comments.

b. Calculate the perimeter of a rectangle, given the length and width, and store the result in P.

c. Indicate the end of the source program to the system.

d. Transfer control to statement 570.

e. Bring data into the program.

f. Compare the value of F to D in order to determine the action to be taken.

g. Provides data quantities for the program.

h. Provides for output of results.

9.19 **True-False.** Determine whether each of the following is true or false.

a. Variable names in Basic may consist of one letter or one letter and one digit.

b. For each data value to be brought into a program, the programmer must use one READ statement.

c. The statement

    LET A = A − 1

will cause the value of A to be decreased by 1 each time the statement is executed.

d. In writing Basic statements, the user may use blanks to improve readability since,

with few exceptions, the system ignores blanks.

e. In algebra, *lw* means "*l* times *w*"; in Basic, multiplication can also be implied—for instance, LW means "L times W."

f. Some typical Basic commands are LET, READ, and GO TO.

g. All Basic statements and commands must be given line numbers.

h. Constants in Basic must consist of six or fewer digits.

i. Before execution of a program, the Basic system gives all numeric variables an initial value of 0.

j. The GO TO is used for unconditional branching, whereas the IF is used for conditional branching.

9.20 **Multiple Choice.** Determine which answer best completes or answers each of the following statements.

a. The Basic language is best described by (1) requires detailed knowledge of the computer, (2) requires a large computer, (3) an interactive language, (4) designed for batch processing, (5) none of the preceding.

b. Basic variable names (1) may be only one letter, (2) may be chosen by the programmer, (3) are larger than constants, (4) are optional in a program.

c. Which of the following is an incorrect Basic expression?

    (1) A(B + C),   (2) I/J*K/L,

    (3) D6 − D4/7.5,   (4) all are incorrect, (5) all are correct.

d. In the Basic expression $A + 5*B - 4.\emptyset/C$ which operation will be performed first? (1) addition, (2) multiplication, (3) division, (4) subtraction, (5) you cannot tell without knowing values of A, B, and C.

e. An example of an unconditional branching statement is (1) END, (2) GO TO, (3) IF, (4) BRANCH, (5) none of the preceding.

f. A PRINT statement (1) can cause one or more lines to be printed, (2) can only be used after a READ, (3) requires a DATA statement, (4) both 1 and 2, (5) none of the preceding.

g. The END statement (1) indicates no more data, (2) is optional, (3) indicates that there are no more program statements, (4) can be used in place of GO TO, (5) none of the preceding.

h. Control of a Basic system in a timesharing computer is achieved by using Basic (1) statements, (2) directives, (3) commands, (4) RUN statements, (5) control of the system is automatic.

i. An example of a Basic command is (1) LET, (2) DATA, (3) END, (4) both 2 and 3, (5) none of the preceding.

j. The INPUT statement (1) can usually be substituted for the READ, (2) requires a DATA statement, (3) provides interactive capability, (4) is used to print headings.

9.21 Programming Problems

a. Each record in a salesperson work file includes the following:

Salesperson number
Units sold
Commission/unit
Bonus

Write a program to calculate gross pay which is:

Gross pay = units sold
× commission/unit + bonus

Print one line per salesperson as follows:

Salesperson number
Gross pay
Units sold

b. Each customer of a clothing store has an account record with the following information.

Customer number
Old balance
Payments
Other credits
Charges
Service charges

Write a program to calculate the new balance as

New Balance = old balance
− payments − other credits
+ charges + service charges

For each customer print three lines as follows:

First line	Customer number
Second line	Old balance and new balance
Third line	Blank (results from a PRINT with no variable list)

c. Write an interactive program which will calculate compound interest using the formula

$$I = P(1 + r)^t - P$$

where $P =$ principal,
where $r =$ interest rate, and
$t =$ time in years

The user should be required to key in P, r, and t, and the computer should display P, r, t, and I. This can be "dressed up" by printing appropriate instructions and descriptions.

d. Expand Exercise c to allow the user to key in a beginning value and an ending value for t, then calculate I for each value over the range. For instance, if the values were $t = 5$ and $t = 10$, then I would be calculated for $t = 5, 6, 7, 8, 9,$ and 10.

e. The input record of Exercise b has been expanded as follows:

Customer name
Old balance

Payments
Other credits
Charges
Service charges
Credit limit

Calculate the new balance in Exercise *b* and for each customer whose new balance is equal to or greater than the credit limit, print the following:

First line	Customer name
Second line	Old balance, new balance, and credit limit
Third line	Blank

f. Each salesperson has a sales record in the sales file with the following information.

SB Salesperson name
C Total commissions
Q Commission quota
B Bonus

Total pay for each salesperson is to be calculated as:

If total commissions are less than commission quota,
then gross pay = total commissions;
otherwise, gross pay = total commissions + bonus

Print the following for each salesperson:

Salesperson number
Gross pay

g. Each record in a file contains three fields. Write a program to find the largest value of each set of three fields and for each record, print the following:

First line	Original three fields
Second line	Largest field of the three
Third line	Blank

This program can be written either to process previously entered data or, as interactive, to allow the user to enter each of the three fields.

Chapter 10

The Elements of Programming in Fortran

10.1
BASIC CONCEPTS
OF FORTRAN

Every computer programming language must provide the programmer with the means to do input/output operations, data manipulation, calculations, and conditional and unconditional branching. All of these types of operations can be coded in machine language or in an assembly language, but the programmer must write on the detailed instruction level. In a compiler language, as much of the detail as possible is made automatic. One such language, Fortran, is a scientific-mathematical language using a notation that is basically algebraic, with strong capabilities in the area of calculation but somewhat limited in input/output and alphanumeric data manipulation operations. The purpose here is to show programming examples written in Fortran to illustrate the language; although they will be sufficient to provide the reader with the ability to write a few simple programs, this discussion is far from a complete study of Fortran.

A BOOKSTORE INVENTORY   Let us assume that we work for a bookstore with a large stock of books and that keeping a check on the number of each title in stock has become a problem. In the interest of streamlining the inventory record-keeping process, the manager has decided to convert to a computer-aided inventory accounting system. For each title, certain descriptive information such as the book number, inventory balance at beginning of month, copies sold, received, and so on will be punched into a card. An example data card showing these fields is illustrated in Figure 10.1. From this card, we can see that the following relates to book number 4451:

Copies on hand (beginning of month)	453
Copies received during month	150
Copies shipped during month	313
Copies lost and destroyed during month	2

Each card of this type contains information for one book title and would thus be an *Inventory Record*. Consistent with the principles of Chapter 2, the entire collection of records forms the Inventory File.

For this application, we have been directed to write a simple Fortran program to calculate the updated inventory balance for each book title—that is, the number of copies on hand at the end of the month. The procedure is certainly easy enough; we merely carry out the following sequence.

1. Read the old balance, copies received, copies sold, and copies lost and destroyed.
2. Calculate the new balance as
   New balance = old balance
   + received
   − sold
   − lost and destroyed

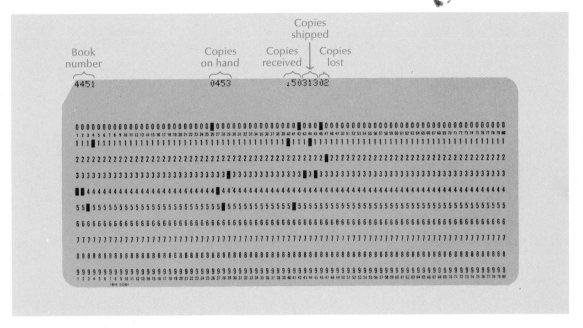

Fig. 10.1 Example data card with punched fields.

3. Print the result.
4. Repeat the sequence for the next data record (book title).

Before we can begin programming this problem, we must know the exact data format of the input cards and the required results from the computer. The following is a formalized problem statement for this program.

EXAMPLE 10.1

A bookstore summarizes the monthly transactions on cards; one card is used for each book title, with the following fields punched:

Field	Card Columns
Book identification number	1–4
Inventory balance at beginning of month	26–29
Copies received during month	40–42
Copies shipped during month	43–45
Copies lost or destroyed during month	46–47

A program is to be written to calculate the updated inventory balance and to print one line for each record (numbering the lines in ascending order) showing the book number, the previous inventory balance, and the updated balance.

We can see that the operations are relatively simple; the sequence involves reading a data card, performing additions and subtractions to update the inventory, then printing a line. Typical printed results from a processing run are shown below as an example of what is required. Note that the first line represents the results for book number 4451, the input card of Figure 10.1.

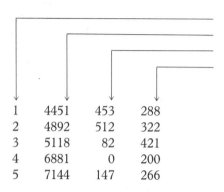

1	4451	453	288
2	4892	512	322
3	5118	82	421
4	6881	0	200
5	7144	147	266

A complete Fortran program, coded on a standard Fortran coding form, is shown in Figure 10.2.

FORTRAN CODING FORM   For convenience, Fortran programs are usually written on special Fortran coding forms which are preprinted to correspond to punching positions on a card. Each line on the form is divided into 80 positions into which one Fortran statement may be printed (punched in a card). Columns 1–5 are used to assign a number to any statement which will be referred to elsewhere in the program; the number can be any positive integer up to 99999. Although a number consisting of fewer than five digits can be recorded anywhere in these five columns, it is considered good practice to right-justify each number—that is, the units digit of each number should be punched in column 5. The Fortran statement itself is written in columns 7–72. If a statement is too long for one line, it may be continued on the next line by placing any character other than 0 or blank in column 6 of that line. Columns 73–80 are provided for the convenience of the programmer; they are usually used for program identification and/or sequence numbering. Let us now begin our study of the Fortran language by considering this example program line by line.

COMMENT CARDS   By placing a C in column 1, that entire line (card) may be used by the programmer for descriptive comments. Although the Comment card is ignored by the compiler, it will still be printed with the program when compiled by the computer. The comments included in this program adequately describe the purpose of the program. The value of using extensive comments in a program cannot be overemphasized. A programmer must often modify or expand an extensive program after completing it and progressing to another

FORTRAN CODING FORM

Program	EXAMPLE 10.1			Punching Instructions			Page	of
Programmer	W. PRICE	Date		Digit	1 2 0	Card Form #	Identification	
				Letter	I Z O			73 80

FORTRAN STATEMENT

```
C      EXAMPLE 10.1
C      PROGRAM TO UPDATE AN INVENTORY.
C      INPUT IS ID NUMBER, INVENTORY BALANCE, RECEIPTS, SHIPMENTS,
C      AND LOSSES. OUTPUT IS TO INCLUDE ID NUMBER, OLD INVENTORY
C      BALANCE AND UPDATED BALANCE.
C
       INTEGER ID,OBAL,REC,SHIP,LOST,COUNT,NBAL
       COUNT = 0
 101   READ(1,31) ID,OBAL,REC,SHIP,LOST
  31   FORMAT(I4,2IX,I4,I0X,I3,I3,I2)
       NBAL = OBAL + REC - SHIP - LOST
       COUNT = COUNT + 1
       WRITE(3,32) COUNT,ID,OBAL,NBAL
  32   FORMAT(IX,3X,I3,3X,I4,3X,I4,3X,I4)
       GO TO 101
       END
```

Fig. 10.2   Program for Example 10.1.

job. Much of a program can be very confusing, even to the programmer who wrote it, unless comments are used liberally. Although the program of Figure 10.2 uses comments only as the first cards, they may be inserted at any point in the program.

FORTRAN STATEMENTS Following the Comment cards is a sequence of Fortran statements which are directives to the computer to carry out the required operations. The similarity to ordinary English and algebra makes the function of this program and of individual statements intuitively apparent. Comparing the statements to what we know of the problem requirements and programming itself, we can surmise the following:

READ(1,31) ID,OBAL, · · ·	Read input record
NBAL = OBAL + REC · · ·	Calculate new balance
WRITE(3,32) COUNT,ID, · · ·	Print results
GO TO 101	Branch to read next record

As we shall see, this program illustrates enough important concepts to provide us with a good background in Fortran for writing some elementary Fortran programs. Points to be discussed relative to Figure 10.2 are the following:

1. Fortran constants and variables
2. Fortran expressions
3. Input and output capabilities
4. The arithmetic assignment statement
5. The transfer statement
6. The END statement
7. Executable and nonexecutable statements

In the following sections of this chapter, we shall study each of these statements and relate them to the basic principles of Fortran.

Exercises

10.1 Name and describe the field areas on the Fortran coding form.

10.2 How is a descriptive comment indicated in a Fortran program?

10.2
CONSTANTS AND VARIABLES

The second and sixth statements, which set the line count to 0 and then increment it, utilize constants and variables in a form similar to that of the algebraic equations. In Fortran, there are several different types of data; the most commonly encountered are *integer* and *real*. Effectively, integer quantities are whole numbers, and real quantities are numbers with a decimal point. The

[handwritten notes in top margin: Names for whole numbers must begin with I J K L M or N, not more than 6 characters. Name for real or decimal number begin with A thru H + O thru Z.]

notion of constants and variables, both real and integer, is basic to the structure of Fortran; the first example program involves only integer quantities.

FORTRAN CONSTANTS   A constant is any numeric quantity which has a fixed value for an entire program. In Fortran, constants are numbers which appear on the coding sheet as such and remain unchanged throughout the program. Thus, in the example program the two integer constants used are 0 and 1 in the statements

    COUNT = 0
    COUNT = COUNT + 1

Although the magnitude of integers varies from computer to computer, virtually all versions of Fortran provide for at least five-digit integers (the System/360 range is approximately $\pm$ 2 billion; most large computer systems allow from 10 to 13 digits). However, in 16-bit word computers such as the IBM 1130 the allowable range is approximately $\pm$ 32000. The following are valid integer constants:

    25386   0 -327

On the other hand, the following are invalid integers for the reasons indicated:

    32.2   Not an integer
    25.0   A decimal point must not be included in an integer
    5,280   A comma is not allowed

As we shall learn in later sections, Fortran has convenient provisions for handling fractional quantities with a decimal point, as well as integer quantities.

FORTRAN VARIABLES   The term *variable* has much the same meaning in Fortran as in algebra; it is a symbolic name given to a quantity that may change in value during execution of a program. Each variable will be assigned by the compiler to some internal storage area into which a number may be stored. In Figure 10.2, we see the following variable names to represent the designated quantities:

Variable	Field
ID	Identification number
OBAL	Old inventory balance
REC	Number received
SHIP	Number shipped
LOST	Number lost
COUNT	Line count
NBAL	New inventory balance

Whereas in algebra variables are usually represented by a single letter, Fortran variable names are not so restricted; they may consist of one to six alphabetic and/or numeric characters (no special characters).* However, the first character in the name must always be a letter. Otherwise, the choice of names is completely at the discretion of the programmer. Numeric values that variablés may assume are the same values that may be assigned to constants.

To summarize these restrictions, the following are examples of valid and invalid variable names:

Valid Variable Names
MAX	P4CON
Y1	ABCD
Z	JKLMN

Invalid Variable Names
6KR	First character is a number
WORK+	Special characters not allowed
DATA356	Exceeds allowable six characters
FAC 1	Blanks cannot be included within the name

THE INTEGER STATEMENT   Every variable in a program must be identified as being used for integer or for real quantities since the internal coding is different for the two. This is accomplished by either of two means: (1) allowing the Fortran system to decide through appropriate choice of the first letter in the name, or (2) explicitly naming each variable in a special identifying statement. Using the first method, the programmer may begin each name with one of the six letters I, J, K, L, M, or N, and Fortran will automatically consider it an integer. The second method involves use of a special capability called the INTEGER statement, the means used in the program of Figure 10.2 and shown here.

```
INTEGER ID,OBAL,REC,SHIP,LOST,COUNT,NBAL
```

Note that the word INTEGER is followed by a list of variables, separated by commas, to be used in the program. The INTEGER statement allows the programmer to select the first letter of the name without restriction. Without the INTEGER statement, the names OBAL, REC, SHIP, and COUNT could not be used for integer quantities. (Since the names ID, LOST, and NBAL begin with one of the six integer letters, they could be omitted from the INTEGER statement.)

---

*In the Fortran systems used on some computers, variable names may consist of no more than five characters.

Exercise

10.3 Identify each of the following as a variable or an integer constant; for those that are invalid, state the reason.

NUMBR	25SAVE	0
WORK 5	P	−25768
276	DATA+3	NETWORK
SIXTY	3,815	47.0

But do you know Fortran?

Copyright by Computerworld, Newton, Mass. 02160

10.3
PERFORMING
CALCULATIONS
IN FORTRAN

ARITHMETIC EXPRESSIONS Fortran includes five basic arithmetic operations: addition, subtraction, multiplication, division, and exponentiation (raising to a power). Examples in this chapter will not deal with exponentiation. Each of these operations is signified by an *operational symbol* as follows:

Addition	+
Subtraction	−
Multiplication	*
Division	/

The reader will note that these symbols are identical to those of ordinary arithmetic, with the exception that an asterisk (*) is used to denote multiplication.

The term *expression* carries much the same meaning in Fortran as in algebra—that is, any collection of constants and variables related by arithmetic operations. The program of Figure 10.2 includes the following two expressions:

```
OBAL + REC − SHIP − LOST
COUNT + 1
```

The reader should note that blanks are included on either side of the addition symbol (+), but are not required. With only a few exceptions, the compiler ignores all blanks in the Fortran program. Thus, the above expressions could be written

```
OBAL+REC−SHIP−LOST
COUNT + 1
```

The following additional examples further illustrate Fortran expressions.

Description		Algebra	Fortran
Perimeter of rectangle		$2l + 2w$	2*LEN + 2*WIDTH
Simple interest amount		$P + Prt$	PRIN + PRIN*RATE*TIME
	or	$P(1 + rt)$	P*(1 + R*T)
Simple discount amount		$\dfrac{P}{1 - dt}$	P/(1 − D*T)

Note the similarity of each Fortran expression to the corresponding algebra expression. In writing expressions, the programmer must keep in mind that each operation is explicitly indicated with an operational symbol. Whereas, in algebra, multiplication is commonly implied (for instance, $2w$ means $2 \times w$), this is never true in Fortran. *An arithmetic operation must always be signified by an operational symbol.* Even parentheses are used in Fortran strictly to group terms and *not* to indicate multiplication (as in algebra).

The rules for evaluating Fortran expressions are much the same as the rules for evaluating algebraic expressions. That is,

1. All expressions within parentheses are evaluated first.
2. Multiplication and divisions are performed next.
3. Additions and subtractions are performed last.

The following examples illustrate this concept.

LEN	= 52	2*LEN + 2*WIDTH
WIDTH	= 28	$2 \times 52 + 2 \times 28$
		$104 + 56$
		160
PRIN	= 500	PRIN + PRIN*RATE*TIME
RATE[†]	= 0.06	$500 + 500*0.06*10$
TIME	= 10	$500 + 300$
		800
P	= 500	P*(1 + R*T)
R	= 0.06	$500 \times (1 + 0.06 \times 10)$
T	= 10	$500 \times (1 + .6)$
		$500 \times (1.6)$
		800
P	= 300	P/(1 − D*T)
D	= 0.08	$300/(1 − 0.08*5)$
T	= 5	$300/(1 − 0.4)$
		$300/0.06$
		500

Although these examples do not completely represent the manner in which the Fortran system evaluates expressions, they clearly illustrate the basic principles.

Exercises

10.4 Following are algebraic expressions and corresponding Fortran equivalents. For the incorrect Fortran versions, identify the error and write a corrected form.

	Algebra	*Fortran*	
a.	$2l + 2w$	2L + 2W	2 * L + 2 * W
b.	$\dfrac{abc}{wx}$	A*B/W*C/X	
c.	$\dfrac{a + b}{2}$	A + B/2	(A + B) / 2
d.	$(i − j)(i + j)$	(I − J)(I + J)	(I − J) * (I + J)

10.5 If WORK = 1, A = 6, B = 2, and C = 20, evaluate each of the following expressions.

a. A + B/2   b. A/B + C − WORK*5

$6 + \frac{2}{2} = 7$ $\frac{6}{2} + 20 − 1 \times 5 = 18$

[†]Although our study at this point is confined to integer quantities, some noninteger (real) quantities are shown in these examples to illustrate expressions.

THE FORTRAN ARITHMETIC STATEMENT   Let us return our attention to the
Fortran expressions in the program of Figure 10.2 as they are used in that
program. For convenience, one of these statements is repeated here:

NBAL = OBAL + REC − SHIP − LOST

In algebra, this is referred to as an *equation*; in Fortran, it is called an *arithmetic
statement*. In algebra, the equal sign (=) has the meaning of equality; that is,
NBAL is equal to OBAL plus REC minus SHIP minus LOST. In Fortran, the
equal sign does *not* imply equality in this sense. It denotes that the expression
on the right is to be evaluated and the resulting number should replace the
current value of the variable on the left. This distinction is of sufficient importance that many programmers refer to this type of statement as an *arithmetic
assignment* statement, an *assignment* statement, or a *replacement* statement,
all of these in the interest of avoiding the confusion implied by the equal sign.
These important characteristics are summarized in the following definition.

Arithmetic Assignment Statement
General form: *Variable = Fortran expression*

where the expression on the right is evaluated using current values of the indicated variables and the result is stored in the variable on the left. For instance,
using the input values of 453, 150, 313, and 2 for OBAL, REC, SHIP, and
LOST, respectively (see Figure 10.1), execution of the machine instructions
resulting from the Fortran statement

NBAL = OBAL + REC − SOLD − LOST

would proceed as follows.
1. The values for OBAL, REC, SHIP, and LOST would be retrieved from
   storage in order to evaluate the expression on the right, yielding 288.
2. This numeric result would then be placed in the storage area reserved
   for NBAL, thereby destroying the previous contents.
3. The current values in OBAL, REC, SHIP, and LOST would remain
   unchanged.

INCREMENTING A QUANTITY   The important distinction between the algebra
equation and the Fortran arithmetic statement is clearly demonstrated by the
two other arithmetic statements used in the program of Figure 10.2.

COUNT = 0
    .
    .
    .
COUNT = COUNT + 1

Since we can never be certain of what is in storage if we do not put it there ourselves, a value of 0 is placed in the variable COUNT. As we can see, this value is later changed in the program by the second statement. This statement characterizes the difference between the equal sign as used in algebra and in Fortran. In algebra, the equation

$$x = x + 1$$

is never true, regardless of the value assigned to x; it is a contradiction. In Fortran, the statement

COUNT = COUNT + 1

is quite valid and very useful. Remember, the equal sign says, "Evaluate the expression on the right and assign that value to the variable on the left." Assuming that the fourth record has been processed and execution has proceeded to the GO TO statement, the value of COUNT will be 4. Upon executing the loop once more (processing the fifth record), COUNT + 1 will be evaluated as 5, with the result being stored in COUNT.

Exercise

10.6 Distinguish between the use of the equal sign in Fortran and in algebra.

10.4
INPUT/OUTPUT
OPERATIONS*

Whenever it is necessary to read information into the computer or to print results out, a pair of statements is required, one to specify the operation and

---

*Users of the WATFOR or WATFIV compilers may wish to omit or simply scan this section because of the simplified I/O capability provided by these compilers. By using special READ and PRINT statements without formatting, I/O operations are greatly simplified for the beginner. However, input fields must be separated from each other by at least one blank column or a comma. The following adjustments to the input format of Example 10.1 would accommodate WATFOR or WATFIV.

Copies shipped during month	44–46
Copies lost or destroyed during month	48–49

Then a comparable WATFOR-WATFIV program would be

```
        INTEGER ID,OBAL,REC,SHIP,LOST,COUNT,NBAL
        COUNT = 0
101     READ,ID,OBAL,REC,SHIP,LOST
        NBAL = OBAL + REC − SHIP − LOST
        COUNT = COUNT + 1
        PRINT,COUNT,ID,OBAL,NBAL
        GO TO 101
        END
```

the variables involved and the other to describe the necessary format. The input and output statements from Figure 10.2 are repeated in Figure 10.3.

Fig. 10.3   Input and output.

```
101   READ(1,31) ID,OBAL,REC,SHIP,LOST
 31   FORMAT(I4,21X,I4,10X,I3,I3,I2)
         .
         .
         .
      WRITE(3,32) COUNT,ID,OBAL,NBAL
 32   FORMAT(1X,3X,I3,3X,I4,3X,I4,3X,I4)
```

The READ and WRITE statements are commonly called *general I/O statements* and statements 31 and 32 are referred to as *format statements.*

THE READ STATEMENT   Data is brought into the computer storage from an external medium such as punched cards by the READ statement. More specifically, the READ statement designates the following:

1. From which input device (such as card reader, console keyboard, or magnetic tape unit) the data is to be read.
2. Which statement in the program describes the input record format (for example, the card format as designated in Example 10.1).
3. The variables into which data is to be read.

These characteristics are illustrated by the following READ statement of Example 10.1, shown here as Figure 10.4. This statement will cause one data card to be read from the card reader (device 1)* storing the first field read from the card into the storage area allocated to ID, the second field to the area allocated for OBAL, the third field into the area allocated for REC, and so on. The fields will be read from card columns as designated in statement 31 (described in the next section). The general definition of the READ statement follows.

The READ statement
General form: READ(i,n) *List*

---

*Technically, this code is called the *data set reference number* and has implications beyond the scope of this presentation. It is extremely important to recognize that the digit 1 is not "universally recognized" as referring to the card reader, although 1 is a commonly used "default" value. For instance, the code 1 is used in IBM 360/370 Disk Operating System, whereas the digit 5 is used under the 360/370 Operating System; the digit 2 is used for the IBM 1130. Before running a program, the reader must obtain the device code used at his/her installation.

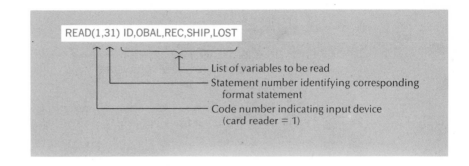

Fig. 10.4 The READ statement.

where: *i* is an unsigned integer constant (or variable) which specifies the input device (see footnote on preceding page).

n is the statement number of the corresponding format statement. *List* is a sequence of variable names, separated by commas, which correspond to the data to be read.

THE WRITE STATEMENT The WRITE statement to print the results, which is repeated in Figure 10.5, is virtually identical to the READ statement. Here the computer is being directed to print the values in storage for the variables COUNT, ID, OBAL, and NBAL on the line printer* according to the format specified in statement number 32 of the program.

The general definition of the WRITE statement follows.

The WRITE Statement
General form: WRITE (*i,n,*) *List*

where: *i* is an unsigned integer constant (or variable) which specifies the output device (see footnote to this section).

n is the statement number of the corresponding format statement. *List* is the sequence of variable names, separated by commas, whose values are to be conveyed to the appropriate output device.

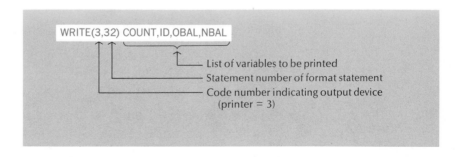

Fig. 10.5 The WRITE statement.

---

*As with the card reader, the user must take care to substitute the code used at her/his installation for the printer in place of the code 3 used in this book.

Exercises

10.7 Describe the meaning of each part of the following statements.
a. READ(1,226) J,KFIELD,LWORK
b. WRITE(3,17) IN,LOOK

10.8 What special consideration must the programmer give to writing input/output statements in switching from one computer installation to another?

THE FORMAT STATEMENT The problem definition for Example 10.1 specifies the input fields to be located as follows:

Field	Card Columns
Identification number (ID)	1–4
Old inventory balance (OBAL)	26–29
Receipts (REC)	40–42
Shipments (SHIP)	43–45
Losses (LOST)	46–47

Positioning of fields on an input record is clearly somewhat arbitrary; for instance, the identification number could as well have been placed in columns 77–80. Once field locations have been chosen for a given application, however, they must be carefully adhered to and their positions described in the program. This is the purpose of the FORMAT statement. The FORMAT statement, which is always used in conjunction with an input or output statement, is commonly referred to as a *nonexecutable* statement because it does not describe a function to be performed. As such, its placement in the sequence of statements is at the discretion of the programmer.

Included within the parentheses of the FORMAT statement

    31 FORMAT (I4,21X,I4,10X,I3,I3,I2)

is a series of *field descriptors* indicating the nature of the data fields. Here we see the integer and skip descriptors which are summarized as follows.

General Form	Description	Examples
Iw	An integer field of w digits	I4 indicates a 4-digit field I1 indicates a 1-digit field
wX	Skip the next w positions of the record	4X indicates skipping next 4 positions 25X indicates skipping next 25 positions

The reader will note that the field width number (indicated by w in the general form) *follows* the integer code I but *precedes* the skip code X. The relationship between the input card format and the FORMAT statement is illustrated as follows:

Field	Card Columns	Format Descriptor
Book identification number	1-4	I4
Unused columns	5-25	21X
Balance at beginning of month	26-29	I4
Unused columns	30-39	10X
Copies received during month	40-42	I3
Copies shipped during month	43-45	I3
Copies lost or destroyed during month	46-47	I2

The relationship between the input statement, the FORMAT statement, and the data record is illustrated in Figure 10.6.

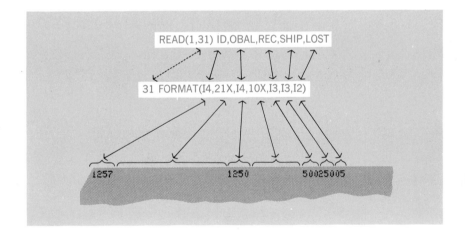

Fig. 10.6   The input format.

FORMATTING FOR OUTPUT   These principles of formatting for input also apply to output; integer quantities are printed according to the I descriptor, and spacing between output fields is designated with the X descriptor. Each time a WRITE statement is executed, one line of output will be printed according to the data list in the WRITE statement and the designations in the FORMAT statement. Care must be taken by the programmer in planning the output format. Sufficient space must be provided between fields to give a neat, easily read report. Field width for quantities calculated in the program must be large enough for the expected results. The relationship between the WRITE statement, the FORMAT statement, and the printed line is shown in Figure 10.7. Referring to the sample output of Figure 10.7, we see that whenever an output field consists of fewer digits than provided by the field width, the quantity will be positioned to the right of the field (right-justified): for instance, refer to the results printed for COUNT, OBAL, and NBAL.

Another point of importance relates to the programmer's ability to control positioning of the printer. This is accomplished through a special carriage control character which is included as the first "position" by the FORMAT statement but is never printed. In Figure 10.7 this is taken care of by the 1X descriptor, which should be provided in each program written from this chapter. Details of printer carriage control is a topic which is beyond the scope of this book.

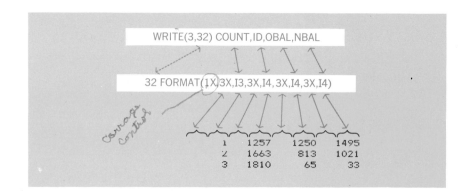

Fig. 10.7   The output format.

Exercises

10.9   Designate the card columns from which each variable will be read by the following statement:

```
READ(1,225) A,MAX,AMNT,DATA
225   FORMAT(3X,I4,I4,7X,I5,1X,I4)
```

10.10.   Designate the print positions in which each of the variables in the following statement will be printed.

```
WRITE (3,15) OUTP,J,LAM
15   FORMAT(2X,I6,2X,I5,5X,I4)
```

10.5
OTHER
STATEMENTS

UNCONDITIONAL GO TO STATEMENT   In the program of Figure 10.2, it is necessary to return to the READ statement after a given set of data has been printed. This is accomplished with the GO TO statement, as used in the program of Figure 10.2 and repeated here:

```
101    READ(1,31) ID,OBAL,REC,SHIP,LOST
         .
         .
         .
       GO TO 101
```

This statement interrupts the sequential execution of statements and specifies the number of the next statement to be executed; in this case it causes a branch to statement 101. The designated instruction may be anywhere in the program.

THE END STATEMENT   The last statement in the program is the END statement. With the exception of the INTEGER and the FORMAT statements, each of the preceding statements in the program represents a directive to the computer to carry out some operation; for example, read from a card, perform arithmetic operations, and so on. Thus, they are commonly called *executable statements*. On the other hand, the sole purpose of the END statement is to signal the compiler that the last card of the Fortran source program has been processed and that the compiling operation is completed. Where each of the executable statements will result in equivalent machine language instructions, the END card has no such counterpart. It merely signals the end of the source program. Similarly, the INTEGER statement conveys information to the compiler regarding the nature of variables to be used in the program, and in itself, does not cause any operation to be carried out. Thus, these are commonly referred to as *nonexecutable* statements.

10.6
CONDITIONAL
BRANCHING

THE ARITHMETIC IF STATEMENT   The program of Figure 10.2 provides sufficient Fortran capabilities to perform a variety of functions. The ability to loop or branch back is a result of the simple GO TO statement that causes an unconditional transfer of control to a designated statement. Although this unconditional branching capability is important, much of the power of the computer lies in its ability to branch only if a designated condition is satisfied during execution. If a calculated student grade point average falls below a certain level, for example, then the student's name should be printed on a deficiency list; otherwise, it need not be printed. This type of testing is performed in Fortran by use of the IF statement. (There are two forms of the IF: the arithmetic IF, described here, and the logical IF.) The ability to evaluate an expression and branch to different statement numbers depending upon whether the result is negative, zero, or positive is illustrated by the following example of an arithmetic IF.

Evaluate this expression for test

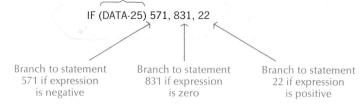

IF (DATA-25) 571, 831, 22

Branch to statement	Branch to statement	Branch to statement
571 if expression	831 if expression	22 if expression
is negative	is zero	is positive

Execution of this statement for three example values of DATA will be as follows:

If DATA is	then (DATA-25) is	and branch to statement
3	− 22 (negative)	571
25	0 (zero)	831
38	13 (positive)	22

The expression to be evaluated in the IF statement may be as complicated as needed, or relatively simple, as in the example, or even a single variable, as in the following example.

IF(NBAL) 391,391,14

Various values of NBAL yield the following results:

If NBAL is	then branch to statement
− 22 (negative)	391
0 (zero)	391
345 (positive)	14

In this case, note that both the negative and zero conditions cause transfer to statement 391; that is quite valid.

Exercise

10.11 Consider the following IF statement

IF(6*DATA-FIELD) 25,13,114

What will be the value of the IF expression and to which statement number will the branch take place when:

    a. DATA = 1   FIELD = 10

    b. DATA = 125   FIELD = −75

    c. DATA = 20   FIELD = 120

INVENTORY CONTROL WITH THE IF STATEMENT   In the program of Example 10.1 the updated inventory is printed for each book title. As an illustration of the IF statement, let us consider a modification to this problem in which information for each book is printed only if the updated inventory falls below a predesignated inventory level.

Example 10.2

A bookstore summarizes the monthly transaction on cards; one card is used for each book title with the following fields punched:

Field	Card Columns
Book identification number	1–4
Inventory balance at beginning of month	26–29
Copies received during month	40–42
Copies shipped during month	43–45
Copies lost or destroyed during month	46–47
Minimum inventory level	61–64

A program is to be written to calculate the updated inventory balance and print the following information for each book with an updated balance which is less than the minimum inventory level.

Field	Print Position
Book identification number	4–7
Minimum inventory level	12–15
Updated inventory balance	18–21

The last card in the data deck will be followed by a "trailer" card with zero punched for the ID number (as illustrated). Terminate processing upon detecting this card.

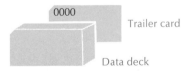

0000   Trailer card

Data deck

Alternate paths of logical flow in a programming problem can be readily illustrated in flowchart form, as shown in Figure 10.8. Here we see that each record is checked immediately to determine if it is a data record. If not, processing is terminated; if so, the updated inventory balance is calculated. This balance is in turn compared to the minimum allowable balance to determine whether or not it should be printed. With the aid of the flowchart, the program of Figure 10.9 is relatively easy to follow. As each record is read, the ID is

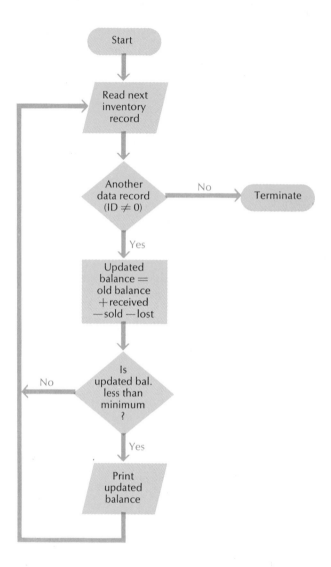

Fig. 10.8 Flowchart for Example 10.2.

compared to zero. Upon detecting a zero (or negative) value, which signals that all of the data has been processed, control is passed to statement 230 (STOP) which terminates execution of the program. However, if the card read is a data record, the new inventory balance is calculated (statement 210), then compared to the minimum allowable balance by the second IF statement. The tested expression

$$NBAL - MIN$$

will cause the following to occur.

```
C   EXAMPLE 10.2    INVENTORY UPDATE AND CHECK
C   CALCULATE UPDATED INVENTORY LEVEL FROM OLD INVENTORY
C   AND TRANSACTIONS.  PRINT UPDATED LEVEL FOR ONLY THOSE
C   ITEMS BELOW MINIMUM INVENTORY LEVEL.
C
        INTEGER ID,OBAL,REC,SHIP,LOST,NBAL,MIN
   200  READ(1,30) ID,OBAL,REC,SHIP,LOST,MIN
        IF(ID) 230,230,210
   210  NBAL = OBAL + REC - SHIP - LOST
        IF(NBAL-MIN) 220,200,200
   220  WRITE(3,40) ID,MIN,NBAL
        GO TO 200
   230  STOP
    30  FORMAT(I4,21X,I4,10X,I3,I3,I2,13X,I4)
    40  FORMAT(1X,3X,I4,4X,I4,2X,I4)
        END
```

Fig. 10.9   Program for Example 10.2.

Condition	Branch Statement	Result
NBAL less than MIN	220	Print the result
NBAL equal to MIN	200	Read next record
NBAL greater than MIN	200	Read next record

Further consideration of this program is left to the reader.

Exercise

10.12 What change would be required if it were necessary to print all items where the new balance was equal to or less than the minimum balance?

10.7 FLOATING POINT CAPABILITIES OF FORTRAN

REAL QUANTITIES   In the descriptions relating to Examples 10.1 and 10.2, all numeric quantities are referred to as *integers*. Although whole number values are useful for a variety of applications, they are very cumbersome in dealing with fractional quantities. For instance, a student grade point average might be 2.56, or the average score of a set of exams might be 81.4. One of the powerful features of Fortran and other mathematically oriented languages is their ability to accommodate decimal point positioning automatically. Within the computer, such quantities are effectively stored in a scientific notation format, as, for instance,

$$186,000 = .186 \times 10^6$$
$$0.0005732 = .5732 \times 10^{-3}$$

In Fortran, these are referred to as *real* quantities (as described in an earlier section); the terminology *floating point* is also commonly used. However, the programmer simply sees real quantities in the program or on the output as numbers written with a decimal point. All decimal positioning and alignment during execution of the program is automatically handled by the system. As programmers, we shall write real quantities in the following form:

16.537   − 2.501   3.1416   0.000012487   53670.

Although the number of significant digits and the magnitude of real quantities vary from computer to computer, up to seven or eight significant digits and exponents of approximately ± 75 are commonly encountered.

NAMING VARIABLES   The program of Figure 10.1 includes an INTEGER statement which identifies each variable to be used in the program as an integer variable. Similarly, other variables can be *typed* as real with the REAL statement. For example, consider the following pair of statements:

```
INTEGER ACT,MAX,OKAY
REAL WORK,NEG,KON
```

Here the variables ACT, MAX, and OKAY are identified as integer, whereas WORK, NEG, and KON are identified as real. Designating the *mode* of a variable through the INTEGER or REAL statement is termed *explicit typing*.

Any variable not explicitly named will be typed according to the first letter of its name; the letters, I, J, K, L, M, and N indicate an integer variable, and all others represent reals. For example, the following variables are *implicitly* typed according to the first letter of their names.

Real	Integer
DATA	JDATA
WORK	IWORK
A257	M257
AMAX	MAX
CON25	KON25

Both integer and real variables and constants may be used in a given program, but it is considered good practice to avoid mixing the two modes in a given arithmetic statement. (Such mixing of modes is illegal in earlier versions of Fortran.)

Exercises

10.13 Distinguish between a real quantity and an integer quantity in Fortran.

10.14 Identify each of the following as an integer or a real variable or constant (assume implicit typing).

QUANT	LIMIT	0
POINT	0.06	0.0
256	MIN	OKAY

INPUT AND OUTPUT Where the I data descriptor is used for input and output of integer quantities, the F data descriptor is used for real data. For instance, consider the data requirements of Figure 10.10.

Field	Columns	Format
Student number	2–6	xxxxx
Cumulative units	11–14	xxxx
Cumulative points	15–18	xxxx
GPA	26–28	xxx

Note: xxx indicates a 3-digit number with an understood decimal between the first and second digits. For example, 321 represents 3.21.

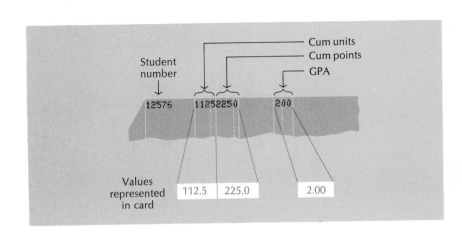

Fig. 10.10 Input quantities.

The following READ and FORMAT statement will cause this card to be read according to the prescribed format.

        READ(1,47) ID,UNITS,PTS,GPA
    47   FORMAT(1X,I5,4X,F4.1,F4.1,7X,F3.2)

Note the use of the F specification; for instance, the F4.1 designation represents

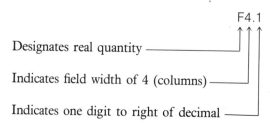

Designates real quantity ——————————⌐
Indicates field width of 4 (columns) ——⌐
Indicates one digit to right of decimal ——⌐

The decimal point is seldom punched in input data since the format specification designates its positioning. However, since output documents are read by people, the decimal point is normally printed, thus requiring an additional printing position. Output of the preceding data would appear as shown in Figure 10.11.

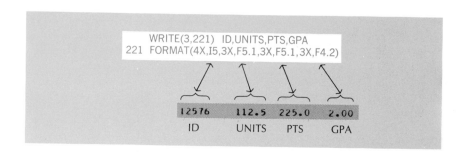

Fig. 10.11 Output of real data.

Exercise

10.15 Referring to the following statements, designate which columns each field will be read from and whether it is real or integer; if real, specify the format in the xxx form.

        READ(1,44) A,WORK,OKAY,LIMIT
    44   FORMAT(F4.1,F5.3,6X,F3.0,14X,I5)

10.8
INPUT/OUTPUT
OF
ALPHANUMERIC
DATA

The manipulation of alphanumeric data in Fortran is, at best, a clumsy operation. For instance, the simple operation of reading alphabetic information from a card, rearranging the format, and printing it involves an inconvenient sequence of steps which are beyond the scope of this brief introduction. However, Fortran does include convenient provisions for printing headings through use of the Hollerith or H specification. For instance, let us assume that we wish to print short titles together with our output, as illustrated in Figure 10.12. The Hollerith specification, which has the following general form

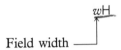

Field width

causes the w characters immediately following the H to be printed on the output as punched in the FORMAT statement.

Descriptive information of this type may be printed on separate lines to serve as headings or on each output line together with the data (as done in Figure 10.12). In Figure 10.13(a), additional output statements have been added to the program of Figure 10.9; typical printed results are shown in Figure 10.13(b). Note that careful planning is required to obtain the proper alignment between various headings and the data itself. The blank lines, as we can see, are obtained by printing with no message in the FORMAT statement. Although other methods are commonly used for spacing, this is adequate for the simplified presentation of this book.

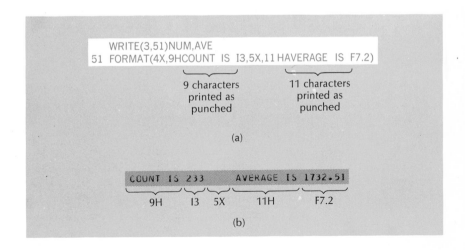

Fig. 10.12 Printing headings.

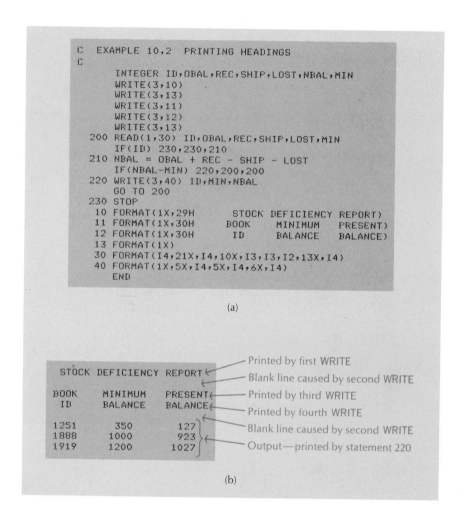

```
C   EXAMPLE 10.2  PRINTING HEADINGS
C
        INTEGER ID,OBAL,REC,SHIP,LOST,NBAL,MIN
        WRITE(3,10)
        WRITE(3,13)
        WRITE(3,11)
        WRITE(3,12)
        WRITE(3,13)
200 READ(1,30) ID,OBAL,REC,SHIP,LOST,MIN
        IF(ID) 230,230,210
210 NBAL = OBAL + REC - SHIP - LOST
        IF(NBAL-MIN) 220,200,200
220 WRITE(3,40) ID,MIN,NBAL
        GO TO 200
230 STOP
 10 FORMAT(1X,29H         STOCK DEFICIENCY REPORT)
 11 FORMAT(1X,30H     BOOK     MINIMUM     PRESENT)
 12 FORMAT(1X,30H      ID      BALANCE     BALANCE)
 13 FORMAT(1X)
 30 FORMAT(I4,21X,I4,10X,I3,I3,I2,13X,I4)
 40 FORMAT(1X,5X,I4,5X,I4,6X,I4)
        END
```

(a)

```
    STOCK DEFICIENCY REPORT ←────── Printed by first WRITE
                            ←────── Blank line caused by second WRITE
    BOOK     MINIMUM     PRESENT ←── Printed by third WRITE
     ID      BALANCE     BALANCE ←── Printed by fourth WRITE
                            ←────── Blank line caused by second WRITE
    1251       350         127 ┐
    1888      1000         923 ├←── Output—printed by statement 220
    1919      1200        1027 ┘
```

(b)

Fig. 10.13 (a) Printing Hollerith fields; (b) computer output.

10.9 OTHER FORTRAN PRINCIPLES

SUBPROGRAMS In programming, situations are commonly encountered where it is necessary to perform a particular operation a number of times. For example, we might have a program in which it is necessary to find the square roots of several quantities or to determine the largest number in each of several sets of numbers. Although it would be possible to program a sequence of statements to perform these operations, it could become a cumbersome process if the operations were required several times in a program. As do most programming languages, Fortran provides a means for using special prewritten subprograms in the main program. Fortran subprograms fall in two broad categories: the *subroutine* subprogram and the *function* subprogram. Most systems include a large number of both types as part of the *system library*. In this way, they are readily available to the Fortran user. For instance, the standard *library function* to determine the square root of a number is available in all standard Fortran systems. Its use is illustrated by the following two examples.

```
ROOT = SQRT(AMOUNT)
SAVE = BASE + 3.0*SQRT(PROD + 5.0)
```

In the first, the square root of AMOUNT will be determined and placed in ROOT. In the second, the square root of PROD + 5.0 will be multiplied by 3.0; the product will be added to BASE and the sum placed in SAVE. As an illustration, consider the following example values.

```
BASE = 10.5
PROD = 20.0
SAVE = 10.5 + 3.0*SQRT(20.0 + 5.0)
     = 10.5 + 3.0*5.0
     = 25.5
```

Additionally, convenient facilities are provided for programmers to write their own subprograms, compile them (independent of a main program), and catalog them into the system library, thus making them readily available.

THE DO STATEMENT   The concept of program loops has been emphasized in previous programming chapters. Generally speaking, we can say that a problem must involve a certain degree of repetition before it can be considered a practical computer application. Control of program loops in Fortran may be achieved using a counter and an IF statement to check against an upper limit. However, the process is considerably simplified by the DO statement, which automatically performs the counting and testing operations. For instance, let us assume that the book inventory summary (Example 10.1) must be done in groups of 20 input records; that is, 20 records must be processed, certain other calculations performed, and then the next 20 must be processed. The program segment of Figure 10.14 includes a DO statement to control the loop; program logic is illustrated in the flowchart in which the shaded blocks represent operations performed by the DO statement. This statement, which is a typical DO, causes all statements down through (and including) 98 to be executed repeatedly under the control of the counter JCNT. The variable JCNT is to have the initial value of 1 and is to be incremented (by 1) until the last value 20 has been reached. That is

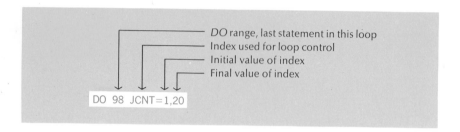

SUBSCRIPTED VARIABLES AND ARRAYS   In mathematics, it is common practice to name a set of variables by the use of subscripts. For instance, assume that we have examination scores for 16 students. Rather than naming these data points $a, b, c, \ldots, p$ (which could be cumbersome), we might call them $a_1, a_2, a_3, \ldots, a_{16}$. Thus, in referring to the seventh point, we can speak of a_7 rather than g, which would take a moment to figure out. Furthermore, we can speak of the data set a_i, consisting of 16 elements. Virtually the same notion carries over to Fortran, where the programmer can define an array A consisting of *elements* or *subscripted variables* A(1), A(2), A(3), $\ldots$, A(16).

To define an array of subscripted variables, the program must designate the array name and the number of elements it contains in the special DIMENSION statement. Then the resulting subscripted variables can be used in exactly the same way as simple variables. Following is a simple sequence illustrating these principles:

```
      DIMENSION WORK(100)
      TOTAL = 0.0
      DO 63 J = 1,25
      READ(1,31) WORK(J)
  63  TOTAL = TOTAL + WORK(J)
```

The DIMENSION statement defines the array as consisting of 100 elements; the sequence which follows it causes data values to be read into WORK(1) through WORK(25) and to be summed in TOTAL.

10.10
IN RETROSPECT

By comparing the machine language concepts of Chapter 8 with Fortran as described in this chapter, we can see that Fortran is much more "user oriented." The programmer can effectively utilize the computer with virtually no concept

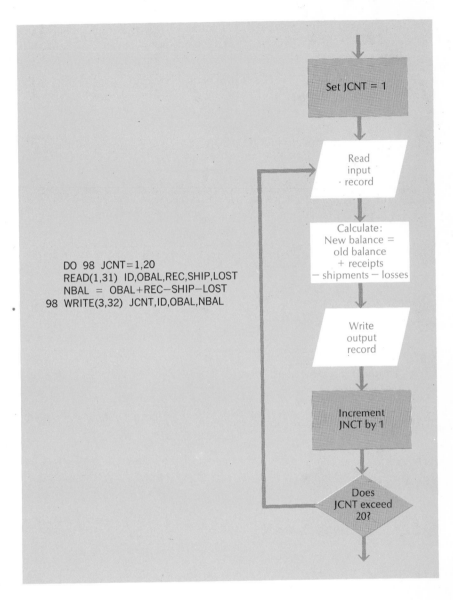

```
    DO 98  JCNT=1,20
       READ(1,31) ID,OBAL,REC,SHIP,LOST
       NBAL = OBAL+REC−SHIP−LOST
  98 WRITE(3,32) JCNT,ID,OBAL,NBAL
```

Fig. 10.14   The DO loop.

of the computer or of its language. Of the many higher-level languages now available, Fortran is the most commonly used. This is due to a combination of factors. To begin with, it was the first machine-independent, user-oriented language to be developed and made available. Furthermore, it is one of the simplest of the commonly used higher-level languages. As such, it was and still is well adapted to such nonprofessional programmers as engineers, statisticians, and students in a wide variety of disciplines. The language includes powerful computational features only touched on in this chapter and many others which have not been covered. Although Fortran is sometimes used in business data processing (usually with a small system that does not support another higher-level language) it is not well suited for such applications. In particular, manipulation of alphanumeric data and data file management are relatively clumsy operations using Fortran. However, the language is well suited to the general area of computational types of jobs for which it was designed.

Answers to Preceding Exercises

10.1   The fields on a Fortran coding form are

Positions	Field	Remarks
1–5	Statement number	For statement identification
6	Continuation	To indicate continuation from previous line
7–72	Fortran statement	For the Fortran statement itself
73–80	Identification	For user information only

10.2   The use of a C in column 1 indicates a comment card.

10.3

NUMBR	valid variable (even with incorrect spelling)
WORK 5	invalid variable, blanks cannot be included in name
276	valid integer constant
SIXTY	valid variable
25SAVE	invalid variable; first character must be a letter
P	valid variable
DATA+3	invalid variable, no special characters allowed
3,815	invalid constant, no punctuation allowed
0	valid integer constant
−25768	valid integer constant
NETWORK	invalid variable, exceeds allowable six characters
47.0	invalid integer constant, no decimal point allowed

10.4   a. 2L + 2W should be 2*L + 2*W (asterisk missing).

b. This form is correct—apply the operations from left to right.

c. A + B/2 yields $a + \dfrac{b}{2}$; correct form is (A + B) /2.

d. (I − J)(I + J) should be (I − J)*(I + J); asterisk missing.

10.5   a. 7;   b. 18

10.6   In algebra, the equal sign indicates that the quantities on each side of the equal sign are identical. In Fortran, it denotes that the expression to the right is to be evaluated and the result stored in the variable to the left.

10.7   a. READ(1,226) J,KFIELD,LWORK

1   code indicating from which device the input is to be obtained

226   number of the FORMAT statement which describes the input record

J, KFIELD and LWORK
variables in storage into which the three fields from the input record are to be stored

b. WRITE(3,17) IN,LOOK

3   code indicating the output device to be used

17   number of the FORMAT statement which describes the desired output format

IN, LOOK   variables in storage whose values are to be printed

10.8 Each input or output device in a given computer installation is assigned a device code. Since these codes are not industrywide standards, the programmer must be certain of using the code standards of the given installation.

10.9

Columns	Field
1–3	Skipped
4–7	A
8–11	MAX
12–18	Skipped
19–23	AMNT
24	Skipped
25–28	DATA
29–80	Ignored

10.10

Position	Field
1	Blank (first 1X is for carriage control)
2–7	OUTP
8–9	Blank
10–14	J
15–19	Blank
20–23	LAM
24–	Remainder of line blank

10.11 a. − 4; branch to statement 25; b. 825; branch to statement 114; c. 0; branch to statement 13.

10.12 The IF statement

IF(NBAL − MIN) 220,200,200

would be changed to

IF(NBAL − MIN) 220,220,200

10.13 An integer is a whole number quantity; a real is a quantity with a decimal point.

10.14

QUANT	real variable
POINT	real variable
256	integer constant
LIMIT	integer variable
0.06	real constant
MIN	integer variable
0	integer constant
0.0	real constant
OKAY	real variable

10.15

Field	Type	Columns	Format
A	Real	1–4	xxxx
WORK	Real	5–9	xxxxx
OKAY	Real	16–18	xxx
LIMIT	Integer	33–37	xxxxx

Additional Exercises

10.16 Matching. Match each of the Fortran statements in 1–8 with the corresponding operation in a–h.

1. IF
2. END
3. WRITE
4. arithmetic statement
5. GO TO
6. READ
7. INTEGER
8. FORMAT

a. Define the positioning of fields on a data card.

b. Calculate the perimeter of a rectangle, given the length and width, and store the result in PERIM.

c. Indicate the end of the source deck to the compiler.

d. Transfer control to statement 57.

e. Bring data into storage from cards.

f. Compare the value of FIELD to DATA in order to determine the action to be taken.

g. Define WORK and ABLE as integer variables.

h. Print a heading on a page.

10.17 True-False. Determine whether each of the following is true or false.

a. If the letter C is placed in column 1 of a Fortran program card, then that entire card may be used for descriptive comments and will be ignored by the compiler.

b. The following are all valid Fortran integer constants: 37, −658, 0, and 25.0.

c. The following are all valid Fortran variable names: ID, VARIABLE, AMOUNT, and OKAY.

d. In writing Fortran statements, programmers may use blanks at their discretion to improve readability, since the compiler ignores the blank character.

e. The Fortran arithmetic statement

$$J = J + 2$$

would cause the value of J to be increased by 2 each time the statement is executed.

f. The following FORMAT statement, if used in conjunction with a READ statement, implies that two fields are to be read, the first from columns 2-6 and the second from columns 10-13:

FORMAT (1X,I5,4X,I4)

g. The FORMAT statement is commonly termed a nonexecutable statement, and as such it may be placed anywhere in the program.

h. Statements in a Fortran program are executed one after the other until a transfer statement such as a GO TO is encountered.

i. The purpose of the END statement is to indicate that the program should be ended after all the data cards have been read and processed by the program.

j. In the statement

IF(J − 25) 13,128,27

execution will branch to statement 27 if the value of J exceeds 25.

10.18 Multiple Choice. Determine which answer best completes or answers each of the following statements.

a. Which of the following is a valid variable name? (1) C, (2) DATA06, (3) A-WORK, (4) FORMULA, (5) none of the preceding.

b. In the Fortran expression X/Y*Z, (1) X is divided by the product of Y and Z, (2) X is divided by Y and this quotient is divided by Z, (3) X is divided by Y and this quotient is multiplied by Z, (4) the order of operations depends on the values of X, Y, and Z, (5) none of the preceding.

c. Which of the following is not a valid Fortran expression? (1) X/Y*Z, (2) WORK +FIELD/2.0, (3) A/(−B)*5.0, (4) 25.0+ WORK/−2.0, (5) all of the preceding are valid.

d. Parentheses, when used in a Fortran expression, (1) alter the normal sequence of operations in evaluating the expression, (2) designate quantities which are not to be used in evaluating the expression, (3) designate the format of the data to be operated upon, (4) parentheses should not be used in Fortran expressions.

e. Which of the following is not an executable statement? (1) END, (2) GO TO, (3) WRITE, (4) all of the preceding (5) none of the preceding, (6) both 1 and 2.

f. Which of the FORMAT statements would be invalid for use with the following WRITE statement, assuming explicit typing of all variables?

WRITE(3,44) ABLE,INT,WORK,P

(1) 44 FORMAT(5X,F6.1,4X,I4,4X,F5.2, 4X,F4.1)

(2) 44 FORMAT(2X,F9.1,I8,F10.2,F10.1)

(3) 44 FORMAT(6X,F5.1,3X,F6.0,5X, F8.2,3X,F6.1)

(4) none of the preceding is invalid,

(5) all of the preceding are invalid.

g. In the Fortran expression

$$A+5.0*B-5.0/C$$

which operation will be performed first? (1) the addition, (2) the multiplication, (3) the division, (4) the multiplication and division will be performed concurrently, (5) it is impossible to predict without knowing the values of A, B, and C.

h. An example of an unconditional branching statement is (1) GO TO, (2) END, (3) BRANCH, (4) IF, (5) none of the preceding.

i. In the statement

$$IF(2.0*F-12.0)\ 5,13,19$$

if the value of F is 4.0, then control is transferred to statement (1) 4, (2) 5, (3) 13, (4) 19, (5) none of the preceding.

j. An example of a conditional transfer statement is (1) IF, (2) GO TO, (3) RETURN, (4) all of the preceding, (5) both 1 and 2.

10.19 Programming Problems. Prepare a flow-chart and write a Fortran program for the following.

a. Each record in a salesperson data file includes the following integer quantities.

Field	Card Columns
Salesperson number	1-5
Units sold	6-7
Commission/unit	8-10
Bonus	12-14

Write a program to calculate gross pay which is

Gross pay = units sold × commission/unit
          + bonus

Print one line per salesperson as follows:

Field	Print Positions
Salesperson number	4-8
Gross pay	13-16
Units sold	19-20

b. A teacher has grade examinations information punched into cards as the following integer quantities:

Field	Card Columns
Student number	1-5
First hour exam grade	31-33
Second hour exam grade	34-36
Third hour exam grade	37-39
Final exam grade	40-42

Three quantities are to be calculated:

Hour exam total = first hour exam grade
                + second hour exam grade
                + third hour exam grade

Total points = hour exam total
             + 2 × final exam grade

Average grade = $\dfrac{\text{total points}}{5}$

For each student, print the following

Field	Print Positions
Student number	2-6
Hour exam total	11-13
Total points	16-18
Average grade	23-25

c. Each card in a data set includes the following information for calculating simple interest.

Field	Card Columns	Format
Principal (P)	16–20	xxxxx
Interest rate (i)	21–22	xx
Number of years (n)	23–24	xx

The accumulated amount (A) may be calculated using the formula

$$A = P + inP$$

Write a program to calculate P and print the following:

Field	Print Positions	Format
Principal (P)	3–8	xxxxx.
Interest rate (i)	11–13	.xx
Number of years (n)	16–17	xx
Accumulated amount (A)	20–27	xxxxx.xx

d. Each customer of a clothing store has an account record with the following information.

Field	Card Columns	Format
Customer number	1–5	xxxxx
Old balance	43–47	xxxxx
Payments	48–52	xxxxx
Charges	54–58	xxxxx
Credit limit	59–61	xxx

Calculate the new balance as

New balance = old balance + charges − payments

For each customer whose new balance exceeds the credit limit, print the following.

Field	Print Positions	Format
Customer number	1–5	
Old balance	11–16	xxx.xx
New balance	19–25	xxxx.xx
Credit limit	28–31	xxx.

e. Each salesperson has a sales record in a sales data file with the following information.

Field	Card Columns	Format
Salesperson number	1–5	xxxxx
Total commissions	25–29	xxxxx
Commission quota	62–64	xxx
Bonus	65–67	xxx

Total pay for each salesperson is to be calculated as:
if total commissions are less than commission quota

Gross pay = total commissions

otherwise

Gross pay = total commissions + bonus

For each salesperson, print

Field	Print Positions	Format
Salesperson number	3–7	xxxxx
Total commission	11–16	xxx.xx
Gross pay	20–26	xxxx.xx

f. Each record in a file contains three integer fields located in columns 71–73, 74–76, and 77–79. For each record, find the largest of the three fields and print:

Field	Print Positions
First field	2–4
Second field	8–10
Third field	14–16
Largest of the three	21–23

Chapter 11

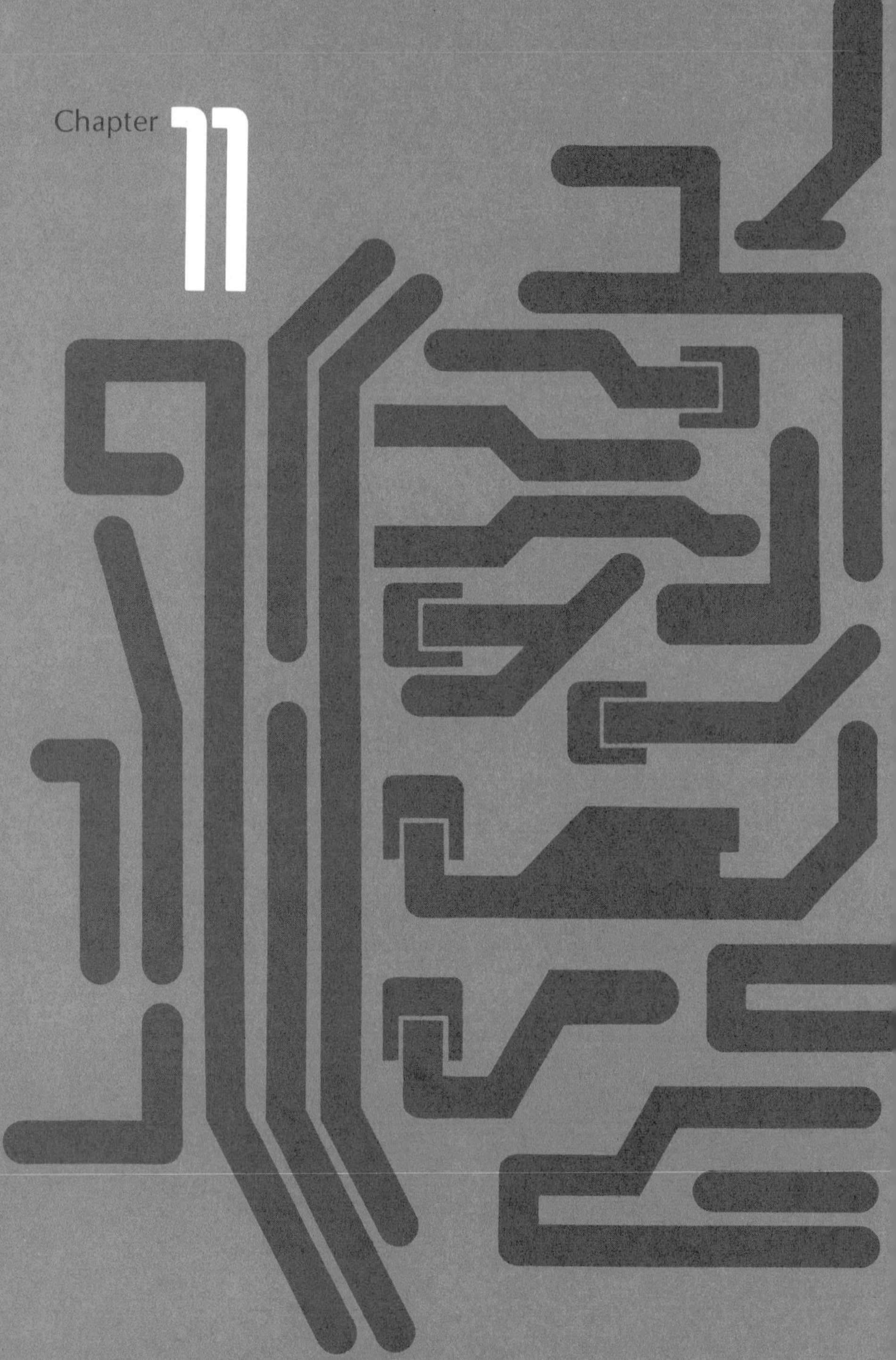

The Elements of Programming in Cobol

11.1
COBOL
LANGUAGE
ELEMENTS

THE NATURE OF COBOL   The Cobol language, like Fortran, is actually a simplified user-oriented shorthand for giving directions to the computer. Technically speaking, Cobol is termed a *procedure-oriented language.* Where Fortran is designed for math-science applications, Cobol is oriented to business procedures. (The word *Cobol* is derived from COmmon Business Oriented Language.) The language is derived from English; in fact, a Cobol program looks very much like ordinary English. Although Cobol is somewhat more complex than Fortran and is more oriented toward the professional programmer, the computer user can prepare programs by simply learning basic rules of the language without knowing extensive details of the computer being used. The following are typical Cobol statements:

SUBTRACT WITHDRAWALS FROM OLD-BALANCE GIVING
    NEW-BALANCE.
IF NEW-BALANCE IS NEGATIVE, GO TO OVERDRAWN-ROUTINE.

Here a new balance is calculated and then checked to determine if it is negative. As we can see, both of these statements are relatively meaningful, even to a casual reader. Although a Cobol program reads like English, Cobol programs cannot be composed simply by writing descriptive English sentences. Indeed, the rules for writing programs are relatively strict, and the user must take care in properly implementing them. Broadly speaking, the Cobol language is made up of the following six elements.

1. Reserved words
2. Programmer-supplied names
3. Symbols
4. Literals
5. Level numbers
6. Pictures

These are shown in the sample Cobol program entry of Figure 11.1. The role played by each element in constructing a program is illustrated by the example programs of this chapter.

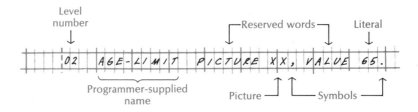

Fig. 11.1 Cobol elements.

A BOOKSTORE INVENTORY Let us assume that we work for a bookstore with a large stock of books and the manager desires a monthly report on all books in stock. The report is to include such information as the number of copies on hand, the number sold, and so on. To automate this process, a decision has been made to record the necessary data regarding book sales in a punched card form. Each card contains vital data, such as author, title, copies sold, copies received, and so on. An example data card showing these fields is illustrated in Figure 11.2. From this card, we can see that the following relates to the book *Beginning Algebra:*

Copies on hand (beginning of month)	453
Copies sold during month	313
Copies received during month	150

Each card of this type contains information for one book title and would thus be an *inventory record.* Consistent with the principles of Chapter 2, the entire collection of records form the inventory file. This record will be used in two of the programming examples of this chapter; in the first example, a very simple listing of the data from the input record will be generated. In the second example, performing arithmetic operations and conditional branching will be illustrated.

Fig. 11.2 Example data card with punched fields.

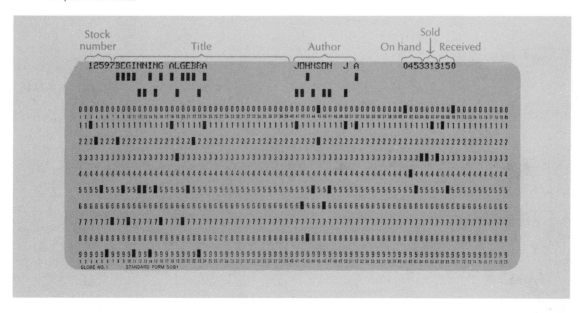

EXAMPLE 11.1

The weekly report to be printed by the computer must contain the following information for each book in stock.

Field	Print Positions
Stock number	5–9
Author	13–24
Book title	26–58
Number of copies sold during week	64–66
Number of copies received during week	69–71
Number of copies on hand (beginning of week)	76–79

This information is to be obtained from the data cards illustrated in Figure 11.2. One line is to be printed for each card (book) in the data set. Each card in the book inventory file includes the following information:

Field	Card Columns
Stock number	3–7
Book title	8–40
Author	41–52
Number of copies on hand (beginning of week)	61–64
Number of copies sold during week	65–67
Number of copies received during week	68–70

PROBLEM CHARACTERISTICS   The reader will note that in this example there will be no calculations; it will only be necessary to read the data into the computer's storage, rearrange the fields to the desired format, and print the line.

Whenever a data record is read into the computer's storage, it is read exactly as recorded in the input record. Thus, an 80-column card is read into 80 consecutive storage positions within the computer's storage. One of the tasks of the programmer is to define this input area and to break it down to the component fields corresponding to those of the card. Similarly, the programmer must define a second storage area corresponding to the printed line desired. Then the data may be written from this line to the printer. The task of "rearranging" the data, as described in preceding paragraphs, simply consists of moving each field from the input area to the corresponding portion of the input area.

This overall process is illustrated in Figure 11.3. The reader will note that the card data is read into storage in the exact format of the card. It is then moved to a second storage area which has been set up to correspond exactly

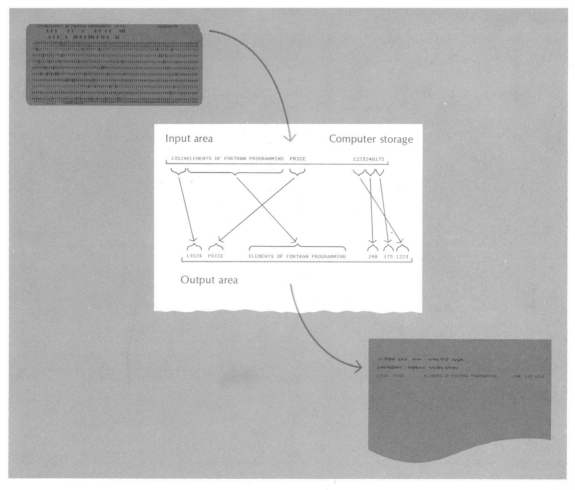

Fig. 11.3 The Read-Move-Write sequence.

to the desired format of the printed line. Printing then consists of duplicating the output storage area onto the printed page. The emphasis in this first example will be in defining the input and output areas and moving the data from the input area to the output area.

For convenience, Cobol programs are usually written on special Cobol coding forms which are preprinted to correspond to punching positions on a card; Figure 11.4 shows the solution to Example 11.1 on three such forms. Each line on the form is divided into 80 positions into which one Cobol statement may be printed (punched in a card). Columns 1-6 are used to sequence number the Cobol statements. The standard convention is to use columns 1-3 for the line number and 4-6 for the page number. However, these are for the purpose of documentation only. Columns 73-80 are also provided for the convenience of the programmer; they are usually used for program identification. Columns 8-72 are used for the Cobol statements to be entered into the

COBOL PROGRAM SHEET

System			Punching Instructions						Sheet	of
Program		Digit	0 1 2				Card Form #	*	Identification	
Programmer		Date	Letter	Ō I Z					73 80	

SEQUENCE (PAGE) (SERIAL)	CONT	A	B														
1 3	4 6	7	8	12	16	20	24	28	32	36	40	44	48	52	56	60	64	68	72

```
001 010    IDENTIFICATION DIVISION
001 020    PROGRAM-ID.
001 030        EXAMPLE.
001 040
001 050    ENVIRONMENT DIVISION.
001 060    CONFIGURATION SECTION.
001 070        SOURCE-COMPUTER. IBM-370-135.
001 080        OBJECT-COMPUTER. IBM-370-135.
001 090    INPUT-OUTPUT SECTION.
001 100    FILE-CONTROL.
001 110        SELECT BOOK-FILE ASSIGN TO SYS006-UR-2501-S.
001 120        SELECT REPORT-FILE ASSIGN TO SYS005-UR-1403-S.
001 130            RESERVE NO ALTERNATE AREA.
001 140
001 150    DATA DIVISION.
001 160    FILE SECTION.
001 170    FD  BOOK-FILE    LABEL RECORDS ARE OMITTED.
001 180    01  BOOK-INFO.
001 190        02  FILLER          PICTURE XX.
001 200        02  STOCKNUM-IN     PICTURE 9(5).
```

SEQUENCE (PAGE) (SERIAL)	CONT	A	B														
1 3	4 6	7	8	12	16	20	24	28	32	36	40	44	48	52	56	60	64	68	72

```
002 010        02  TITLE-IN        PICTURE X(33).
002 020        02  AUTHOR-IN       PICTURE X(12).
002 030        02  FILLER          PICTURE X(8).
002 040        02  ONHAND-IN       PICTURE 9999.
002 050        02  SOLD-IN         PICTURE 999.
002 060        02  RECEIVED-IN     PICTURE 999.
002 070        02  FILLER          PICTURE X(10)
002 080    FD  REPORT-FILE LABEL RECORDS ARE OMITTED.
002 090    01  OUTPUT-LINE.
002 100        02  FILLER          PICTURE X(4).
002 110        02  STOCKNUM-OUT    PICTURE 9(5).
002 120        02  FILLER          PICTURE X(3).
002 130        02  AUTHOR-OUT      PICTURE X(12).
002 140        02  FILLER          PICTURE X.
002 150        02  TITLE-OUT       PICTURE X(33).
002 160        02  FILLER          PICTURE X(5).
002 170        02  SOLD-OUT        PICTURE 999.
002 180        02  FILLER          PICTURE XX.
002 190        02  RECEIVED-OUT    PICTURE 999.
002 200        02  FILLER          PICTURE XXXX.
```

Fig. 11.4 A complete Cobol program.

SEQUENCE																		

```
003010        02  ONHAND-OUT         PICTURE 9999.
003020
003030  PROCEDURE DIVISION.
003040  START-OUT.
003050        OPEN INPUT BOOK-FILE.
003060        OPEN OUTPUT REPORT-FILE.
003070        MOVE SPACES TO OUTPUT-LINE.
003080  READ-A-CARD.
003090        READ BOOK-FILE,
003100        AT END CLOSE BOOK-FILE, REPORT-FILE, STOP RUN.
003110        MOVE STOCKNUM-IN TO STOCKNUM-OUT.
003120        MOVE TITLE-IN TO TITLE-OUT.
003130        MOVE AUTHOR-IN TO AUTHOR-OUT.
003140        MOVE ONHAND-IN TO ONHAND-OUT.
003150        MOVE SOLD-IN TO SOLD-OUT.
003160        MOVE RECEIVED-IN TO RECEIVED-OUT.
003170        WRITE OUTPUT-LINE.
003180        GO TO READ-A-CARD.
```

Fig. 11.4   (Cont.)

computer. Of great importance is that column 8 is marked A and column 12 is marked B. The A marks the first position of the *A-area*, which consists of columns 8–11; similarly, the B marks the first position of the *B-area*, which includes columns 12–72. As we shall learn, certain types of Cobol entries must begin in the A-area and others in the B-area. Column 7 is used for purposes which we shall not consider.

Referring to the program, we see that it consists of four *divisions;* all Cobol programs must include these four basic components. The *Data Division* is the portion of the program in which the input and output areas illustrated in Figure 11.3 are defined. The *Procedure Division* contains actual directives to the machine describing which operations are to be carried out. This structure of a Cobol program is shown in Figure 11.4. Each of the four Cobol divisions (components) is clearly identified.

Line	Division
001010	IDENTIFICATION DIVISION.
001050	ENVIRONMENT DIVISION.
001150	DATA DIVISION.
003030	PROCEDURE DIVISION.

Let us first consider the Data Division, which serves the purpose of reserving the required storage positions for the input and output areas and of defining the individual fields within each record area.

11.2
THE DATA
DIVISION

Whenever we write a program to process data, we must describe in great detail all of the characteristics of that data set. In doing so, we must give each data set (*data file*), each basic unit of information (the data record itself), and each field of each record a Cobol name. Furthermore, we must define in detail the card columns or printer positions allocated to each field. This is all done in the *File Section* of the Data Division.

THE FILE DESCRIPTION (FD)   Referring to the program of Figure 11.4, we see two file descriptions, one defining the input card file beginning line 001170 (named BOOK-FILE) and the other defining the output printer file beginning line 002080 (named REPORT-FILE).

Input data cards

Printed report

File name:
BOOK-FILE

File name:
REPORT-FILE

Each file used in a program must be given a name (selected by the programmer) and defined as done in Figure 11.4. (A program involving information to be read from and written to magnetic tape or disk might involve several files, each requiring a file description.)

In addition to defining the record name, the FD must include a clause defining the nature of the label information. This refers to processing using magnetic tape or disk and has no meaning when using cards or the printer; hence the clause LABEL RECORDS ARE OMITTED. Additional clauses are commonly included with the FD but consideration of these is beyond the scope of this book.

LEVEL NUMBERS   In programming, we commonly refer to *data levels*. For instance, a record can be broken down into fields; in some cases, a given field can be broken down into component parts or "subfields." For instance, a six-position date field could be broken down to the three two-position fields—month, day, and year. In Cobol, *level numbers* are used to indicate the hierarchy, where the level number 01 is always used to identify a record name and numbers 02 through 49 to identify fields or subfields within the record. For instance, in the program of Figure 11.4, the input record is defined as shown in Figure 11.5(a). The record name BOOK-INFO is identified by the level number 01 and the fields which comprise this record by the level number 02. This is illustrated schematically in Figure 11.5(b).

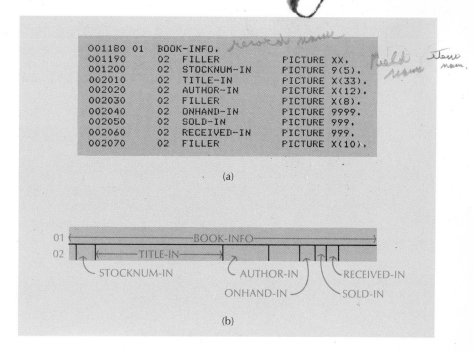

(a)

(b)

01
02

Fig. 11.5   Level numbers.

THE INPUT RECORD DESCRIPTION   Let us compare the record description from lines 001190–002070 of Figure 11.4 to the input card format described in the problem definition.

Field	Card Columns	Field Width	Cobol Record	Description
Not used	1–2	2	FILLER	PICTURE XX.
Stock number	3–7	5	STOCKNUM-IN	PICTURE 9(5).
Book title	8–40	33	TITLE-IN	PICTURE X(33).
Author	41–52	12	AUTHOR-IN	PICTURE X(12).
Not used	53–60	8	FILLER	PICTURE X(8).
Copies on hand	61–64	4	ONHAND-IN	PICTURE 9999.
Copies sold	65–67	3	SOLD-IN	PICTURE 999.
Copies received	68–70	3	RECEIVED-IN	PICTURE 999.
Not used	71–80	10	FILLER	PICTURE X(10).

The correspondence of names is readily apparent; for instance, STOCKNUM-IN corresponds to stock number, SOLD-IN corresponds to copies sold, and so on. Furthermore, note that in each instance where columns are skipped (not used) the Cobol word FILLER is used to so indicate. Another glance at this table and we see that the PICTURE description apparently corresponds to the field width entry which derives from the assigned card columns. For example, columns 1 and 2 are not used so the FILLER has a PICTURE of XX (two Xs); the copies on hand field, which is numeric, has a width of four positions and ONHAND-IN has a PICTURE of 9999 (four 9s); the book title field, which is alphabetic, has a width of 33 positions and TITLE-IN has a PICTURE of X(33)— indicating 33 Xs. In other words, each field name is defined together with a PICTURE indicating the field width through the use of the X or the 9 character. Numeric fields are defined with 9s and alphanumeric fields with Xs. The length of the field is implied by the number of 9s or Xs by either of the following methods:

- A series of Xs or 9s equal in number to the field width. For example, a 3-position field is indicated by XXX (alphanumeric) or 999 (numeric).
- An X or 9 followed by the field width enclosed in parentheses. For example, a 24-position alphanumeric field is indicated by X(24) and a 7-position numeric field by 9(7).

In Cobol, data elements are commonly referred to as *items*; more specifically, they can be classified as either *group items* or *elementary items*. A group item is one which is subdivided into smaller items; an elementary item is one which is not further subdivided. Therefore, the record BOOK-INFO is a group item and the fields STOCKNUM-IN, TITLE-IN, and so on are elementary items. [Figure 11.5(b) illustrates this concept.]

By the rules of Cobol, only elementary items may have PICTURES. This is illustrated in the record description of Figure 11.5(a), where we see that the record name (BOOK-INFO) does not have a PICTURE associated with it, but each of the fields defined as part of that record do.

THE OUTPUT RECORD DESCRIPTION   The preceding descriptions of the input record apply equally well to the output record. The reader will note that in the problem definition, placement of each field is clearly defined by print position on the output page. Computer printers are calibrated and designed with a fixed number of printing positions (120 and 132 are common). Results to be printed must be arranged in storage exactly corresponding to the desired output format. Each FILLER and each data-name specifying an output field includes a PICTURE which corresponds to the output format description.

Exercises

11.1   What are the four divisions of a Cobol program?

11.2   Each card in a data deck is punched with the following:

Field	Card Columns
Employee name	2–23
Social Security number	24–32
Occupation code	41–45
Sex	51
Year of first employment	52–53
Card code	80

Write a record description for this card format.

11.3 WORDS AND NAMES IN COBOL

The choice of words used in the program of Figure 11.4 goes a long way in making the program easy to follow. For instance, it is rather apparent that STOCKNUM-IN refers to the stock number and AUTHOR-IN to the author. Even the word FILLER seems to be consistent with the notion of unused positions in the record. Furthermore, a Cobol statement such as

SUBTRACT TAXES FROM GROSS–PAY GIVING NET–PAY

does not require a Cobol expert to figure out what it means. When preparing a program, the user must take great care in the choice of words, since what is acceptable in English may not be acceptable in Cobol. In general, words used in Cobol can be grouped into two broad categories: *reserved words* and *programmer-selected names*.

RESERVED WORDS   In defining an input or output record in the Data Division, positions not used are indicated to the Cobol system by the word FILLER. This is a special word defined by the designers of the Cobol language meaning that one or more positions in a record are to be skipped. Special words such as FILLER are commonly referred to as *reserved words*, of which there are approximately 400 in Cobol. (A list of reserved words may be found in the table at the end of this chapter.) Simply stated, a reserved word is a word which has a special meaning to the Cobol system and must be used only in the proper context. The following are a few selected examples of reserved words and minor variations that are not reserved words.

Reserved Words	Not Reserved Words
COBOL	COBOLX
DATA	DATA-IN
END-OF-PAGE	END-OF PAGE
PICTURE	DATA-PICTURE
ZERO	ZEROW

PROGRAMMER-SELECTED NAMES   From our study of the Data Division we see that the Cobol programmer must name things. For instance, the file, the record, and each field comprising the record (all of which are found in the Data Division) must be given unique names. *Programmer-selected names* which we shall study in this chapter fall in four categories: data-names, record-names, file-names and paragraph-names. The choice of names is strictly up to the programmer (within certain limitations). Names should be selected which are meaningful to the programmer and thus serve as good documentation, but they *can* simply be a meaningless collection of letters. However, programmer-supplied names must conform to the following rules:

1. Names may contain letters (A–Z), digits (0–9), or hyphens (-). No other characters, *including the blank*, are allowed.
2. A name may be from 1 to 30 characters in length.
3. The hyphen cannot be used as the first or the last character in the name.
4. Each name must include at least one letter. (An exception to this is the paragraph-name, which is discussed in a later section of this chapter).
5. A programmer-selected name must not be a Cobol-reserved word.

Following are some examples of valid and invalid data-names.

Valid Names	Invalid Names	Reason
OKAY	REPORT	Reserved word
X-REPORT	5973-82	At least one letter required
WORK-FIELD	GROSS PAY	Should not be a blank between GROSS and PAY
157INVOICE	INVOICE-	Must not end with a hyphen
A-941138	TAX-%	Special characters (%) not allowed

Exercise

11.3 Identify each of the following as a reserved word, a valid data-name, or an invalid data-name. If invalid, give the reason.

a. HOLD   e. MAXIMUM DIFFERENCE
b. LIMITX   f. REPORT # 7
c. 123456   g. LINE
d. RECORD-FIELD   h. 5457-A-122

11.4

THE IDENTIFICATION AND ENVIRONMENT DIVISIONS

IDENTIFICATION DIVISION   The Identification Division from Example 11.1 consists of the following three lines.

```
001010   IDENTIFICATION DIVISION.
001020   PROGRAM-ID.
001030        EXAMPLE.
```

Although a number of entries are permitted in this division, the only one required is the PROGRAM-ID. The program identification (program name) chosen for this program is EXAMPLE; it may be any name of eight or fewer characters selected by the programmer, subject to the other limitations for programmer-selected names. Note the use of periods; they are essential, as shown in this example.

ENVIRONMENT DIVISION   The Environment Division of the Cobol program is used to describe particular characteristics of the computer on which the program is to be run. Following is the Environmental Division from Example 11.1.

```
001050    ENVIRONMENT DIVISION.
001060    CONFIGURATION SECTION.          computer ident
001070        SOURCE COMPUTER. IBM-370-135.
001080        OBJECT COMPUTER. IBM-370-135.
001090    INPUT-OUTPUT SECTION.            I/o device
001100    FILE-CONTROL.
001110        SELECT BOOK-FILE ASSIGN TO SYS006-UR-2501-S.
001120        SELECT REPORT-FILE ASSIGN TO SYS005-UR-1403-S.
001130            RESERVE NO ALTERNATE AREA.
```

As we can see, the Environment Division consists of two sections: the Configuration Section and the Input-Output Section. The Configuration Section (which may be omitted in some Cobol versions) indicates the type of computer on which the program will be processed (Source-Computer) and run (Object-Computer). In most instances, these two are identical, as in the example program which was tested on an IBM 370, Model 135. If this section is required on the system used by the reader, then the appropriate code should be obtained from the computer installation.

The Input-Output Section serves the purpose of describing the input and output devices to be used with the program. Modern digital computers commonly are equipped with several input and output devices (for instance, a computer might have two printers). Consequently, it is the responsibility of the user to designate which of the physical devices are to be used. This is the purpose of the SELECT statement; in the first one, BOOK-FILE is assigned to the particular card reader which will be designated as SYS006-UR-2501-S. Although Cobol is designed to be manufacturer independent (for instance, a given Cobol program written for an IBM computer should run on a Honeywell or any other computer which implements Cobol), the Environment Division is the one component which will vary from one computer to another. The reader should refer to the manufacturer's manuals or to the instructor to determine the exact codes to use. The same applies to the second SELECT statement which relates the output file REPORT-FILE to SYS005-UR-1403-S. Note that in both cases, the file name used in the SELECT statement is the same as the file name defined in the FD of the Data Division.

The additional clause RESERVE NO ALTERNATE AREA is included with the SELECT statement for the printer file to avoid a potential problem relating to the manner in which the computer actually does input and output operations. A detailed discussion of this is beyond the scope of this book.

Exercises

11.4   Name the required entries in the Identification Division.

11.5   In which division is the SELECT clause found?

11.5
THE
PROCEDURE
DIVISION

COBOL COMMANDS   Input and output data formats are defined in the Data Division, as we have seen; directions to the computer to operate on that data are found in the Procedure Division. The Procedure Division from Figure 11.4 is repeated here as Figure 11.6.

```
START-OUT.
    OPEN INPUT BOOK-FILE.
    OPEN OUTPUT REPORT-FILE.
    MOVE SPACES TO OUTPUT-LINE.
READ-A-CARD.
    READ BOOK-FILE,
        AT END CLOSE BOOK-FILE, REPORT-FILE, STOP RUN.
    MOVE STOCKNUM-IN TO STOCKNUM-OUT.
    MOVE TITLE-IN TO TITLE-OUT.
    MOVE AUTHOR-IN TO AUTHOR-OUT.
    MOVE ONHAND-IN TO ONHAND-OUT.
    MOVE SOLD-IN TO SOLD-OUT.
    MOVE RECEIVED-IN TO RECEIVED-OUT.
    WRITE OUTPUT-LINE.
    GO TO READ-A-CARD.
```

Fig. 11.6 A Procedure Division.

The following are some important points which we should note about these commands in the Procedure Division:

1. Each statement starts with a verb—a word that says to do something. In fact, statements in the Procedure Division are sometimes called *commands* since they command the computer to do something.
2. Each statement, or command, ends with a period in exactly the way we end a sentence in ordinary English.
3. Each statement includes data-names which have been defined previously in the Data Division. They are *not* names which are made up in the Procedure Division.

Each of the Cobol commands we study will exhibit these characteristics. In the interest of simplifying this introduction to Cobol, most of the forms presented will not illustrate all of the options available to the programmer. For the purpose of defining statement forms, the following standards will be used:

1. Reserved words used to form the statement will be printed in capital letters and underscored. Although some statement forms allow optional use of certain words, no such distinction will be made.
2. Names to be supplied by the programmer will be indicated in lowercase by the words *data-name, record-name,* or *file-name*. When two or more data-names are required in a statement, they will be indicated as *data-name*-1, *data-name*-2, and so on.

THE MOVE STATEMENT   The general form of the MOVE statement is:

MOVE *data-name*-1 TO *data-name*-2.

For example: MOVE AUTHOR-IN TO AUTHOR-OUT.

Basically, this statement says

MOVE the contents of the field defined by the programmer as AUTHOR-IN in the Data Division TO the field which has been defined as AUTHOR-OUT in the Data Division.

In this case, the "transmitting field" (AUTHOR-IN) is defined in the input record, and the "receiving field" (AUTHOR-OUT) is defined in the output record. For instance, let us consider an example of what might be in storage before and after execution of a MOVE statement.

Storage contents before execution of the MOVE statement

| J | O | V | A | N | O | V | I | C | H | | | | | | W | I | N | T | E | R | H | A | L | T | E | R |

AUTHOR-IN   AUTHOR-OUT

Storage contents after execution of the MOVE statement

| J | O | V | A | N | O | V | I | C | H | | | | | | J | O | V | A | N | O | V | I | C | H | | |

AUTHOR-IN   AUTHOR-OUT

The reader will note that

1. The contents of the transmitting field are unchanged, but the original contents of the receiving field have been destroyed.

2. The transmitting field consists of 12 characters: 10 letters and 2 blanks. All 12 characters are moved to the receiving field.

This discussion of the MOVE statement has been limited to fields of equal length. How fields are handled if the fields are different lengths is beyond the scope of this book.

Exercise

11.6   In studying the MOVE statement, a student encounters a problem. He considers two 10-position fields, AUTO-IN and AUTO-OUT, with contents as follows.

F	O	R	D						

AUTO-IN

C	H	E	V	R	O	L	E	T	

AUTO-OUT

Upon executing the statement MOVE AUTO-IN TO AUTO-OUT, he maintains that the word FORD, consisting of only four letters, will leave the last five letters of CHEVROLET with the following result.

F	O	R	D						

AUTO-IN

F	O	R	D	R	O	L	E	T	

AUTO-OUT

Comment on this.

INITIALIZING THE OUTPUT LINE   Preceding portions of this chapter describe how record descriptions in the Data Division cause areas to be set up within storage which correspond exactly to the respective record descriptions. It is of utmost importance to recognize that the areas are only reserved and that nothing is placed in these storage positions by the Cobol system. The reading of a data card under control of the program or the moving of data from one part of storage to another causes information to be placed into the record areas. Initially, all of these areas contain whatever was left over from the previous program—commonly referred to as "garbage." The entire 80 positions of garbage in the input area are replaced by the first data record brought in by the READ statement. Similarly, garbage in each of the output fields is replaced by fields moved from the input record. However, areas of the output record defined in FILLER will continue to contain garbage which will appear as such when the output line is printed. To avoid this problem, the output record is cleared to blank spaces by the statement

     MOVE SPACES TO OUTPUT-LINE.

The word SPACES is a Cobol-reserved word called a *figurative constant.* It is a special code to the Cobol system indicating that one or more spaces (blanks)

are to be provided. In this case, the entire output record area is cleared to blanks.

PREPARING DATA FILES FOR USE   Needless to say, we cannot do much data movement of any great value without the ability to get information into the machine and results out. The Data Division in the example program defines areas which can be used for bringing data into storage and for printing results out. However, any Cobol program which reads or writes files must first get the files ready before any reading or writing can take place. This includes telling the computer whether data will be read from the file (Input File) or written to a file (Output File) as well as performing other "housekeeping" operations. The OPEN statements from lines 003050 and 003060 of Figure 11.4 (repeated below) perform these functions.

```
003050              OPEN INPUT BOOK-FILE.
003060              OPEN OUTPUT REPORT-FILE.
```

Note that the word OPEN is followed by either the word INPUT or the word OUTPUT, indicating whether the file will be used for input or for output. This is followed by the file-name as defined in the Data Division.

Before terminating processing, we must tell the computer that we are all finished with each file which has been opened. This is done with the CLOSE statement. In the program of Figure 11.4, the CLOSE is made part of another statement (the READ statement) in order to be concise. This is an option available to the Cobol programmer. In any case, the CLOSE statement in line 003100 of Figure 11.4 is repeated here.

```
. . . CLOSE BOOK-FILE, REPORT-FILE, . . .
```

When opening files, we must tell the computer whether they are input or output. When closing files, we simply name the files; we do *not* indicate input or output.

Exercise

11.7   What is the purpose of the OPEN statement?

THE READ STATEMENT   As we can see by inspection of Figure 11.4, the READ statement involves more than simply reading data.

```
READ BOOK-FILE,
     AT END CLOSE BOOK-FILE, REPORT-FILE, STOP RUN.
```

Needless to say, READ causes the computer to read the next record from the file, named BOOK-FILE. Thus, if the seventh card has already been read, execution of the READ will bring the eighth card into the computer input area. Now what happens when the last record has been read and the computer attempts to read again? The answer to this relates to standard techniques used with most modern computers. The last data record in every input data file is always followed by an end-of-file record with a special code recorded in it.

End-of-file record

Data file

Whenever a READ is executed, the computer performs a special check for the end-of-file code before giving the card to the program. Upon detection of the end-of-file, execution is not allowed to continue but is given to the AT END portion of the input statement. This corresponds to the portion of the flowchart shown in Figure 11.7. Note that upon detecting the end-of-file record, the Cobol statements following AT END are executed. This consists of a command to close the files and a second command to terminate processing (STOP RUN). We might refer to this as a "compound" statement since it consists of more than one Cobol command.

The general form of the READ statement is

<u>READ</u> *file-name* <u>AT</u> <u>END</u> *Cobol-statement.*

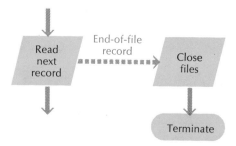

Fig. 11.7   The End-Of-File process.

Exercise

11.8   A data set used in the program of Figure 11.4 consists of 20 records. What will occur when the READ statement is executed the twenty-first time? Or will it be executed 21 times? *yes It will read end-of-file record*

THE WRITE STATEMENT   To write a record, we simply say WRITE and name the output record:

003170   WRITE OUTPUT-LINE.

The general form is

WRITE *record-name.*

Now we must take great care in reading and writing; notice that to read we must designate the file-name, but to write we designate the record-name. Here is the reason: When we read a record, we do not know what kind of a record we are going to get, so we simply say, "Give me the next record from that file." When we WRITE a record, however, we know exactly what kind of a record we are going to write, so we specify the record name.

Exercise

11.9 When reading and writing, which must the programmer tell the computer to read or write, the file-name or the record-name?

TRANSFER OF CONTROL AND PARAGRAPH-NAMES   From our knowledge of this problem, we know that upon writing a line we would like the computer to go back and read another record. It is not possible to simply tell the computer to "return to the beginning," or to "go back to the READ statement," (there may be several) or to "do it again." The particular form used in Cobol is the GO TO statement. In order to use the GO TO statement, we must label the "go to" point in the program. In Cobol, *paragraph-names* are provided for this purpose (although this is not the only reason for their existence). Paragraph-names, like data-names, are selected by the programmer and are formed according to the same rules for forming data-names.

Use of the paragraph-name and the GO TO statement in Example 11.1 is shown below:

```
READ-A-CARD.
     READ BOOK-FILE,
     .
     .
     .
     GO TO READ-A-CARD.
```

Note that the paragraph-name, which is followed by a period, precedes the statement to which the branching is to occur. The transfer of control is accomplished by using the paragraph-name in the GO TO statement.

The general form of the GO TO is

GO TO *paragraph-name.*

11.6
OTHER DETAILS

A- AND B-AREA ENTRIES   As we have learned, each Cobol program must contain four divisions: Identification, Environment, Data, and Procedure. Furthermore, divisions may be divided into sections. For instance, the Environment Division in Figure 11.4 includes the Configuration Section and the Input-Output Section. Paragraph-names described for use in the Procedure Division further subdivide the program into paragraphs. So, generally speaking, we have division names (for instance, Data Division), section names (for instance, File Section), and paragraph names (selected by the programmer). These, the FD (indicating file descriptions) and the 01 (indicating a record name in the Data Division) must all be coded beginning in the A-area. All other entries are considered Cobol statements and must begin in the B-area.

FORMATTING AND THE USE OF PUNCTUATION   The use of periods as illustrated in the example program is extremely important. All division, section, and paragraph names *must* be followed by a period. All statements as well must be followed by a period. If a statement is too long to be entered on one line (it extends beyond column 72), then it may continue in the B-area of the next card. For instance, consider the SELECT statement from Figure 11.4.

```
SELECT REPORT-FILE ASSIGN TO SYS-005-UR-1403-S
       RESERVE NO ALTERNATE AREA.
```

The RESERVE NO ALTERNATE AREA clause, which is too long to fit on the same line as the SELECT, is written beginning column 16. (A common practice for good documentation is to indent four positions.) The Cobol system recognizes the end of a statement only by the period after AREA. The comma, as used here and elsewhere in the program, is ignored by the Cobol system and is used solely as an aid to the user to make the program more readable.

Exercise

11.10   Designate whether each of the following begins in the A-Area or the B-Area.
  a. MOVE WORK-IN TO OUTPUT-WORK.   *B*
  b. FILE SECTION.   *A*
  c. OPEN INPUT READER-FILE.   *B*
  d. Paragraph-name.   *A*
  e. PROCEDURE DIVISION.   *A*
  f. Sequence numbers.

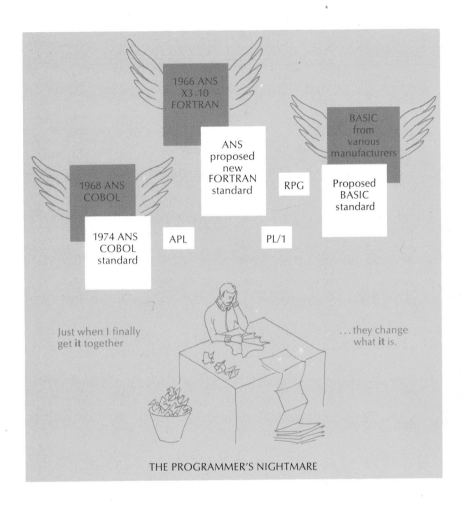

1966 ANS
X3.10
FORTRAN

ANS
proposed
new
FORTRAN
standard

BASIC
from
various
manufacturers

RPG

Proposed
BASIC
standard

1968 ANS
COBOL

1974 ANS
COBOL
standard

APL

PL/1

Just when I finally
get **it** together

...they change
what **it** is.

THE PROGRAMMER'S NIGHTMARE

11.7

UPDATING AN
INVENTORY

PROBLEM DEFINITION Reading data into storage and rearranging it for the purpose of printing a report is a highly commendable task, but most data processing applications involve some form of calculation. For instance, the book inventory of Example 11.1 involves the number of copies on hand at the beginning of the week, the number of copies sold, and the number received during the week. Needless to say, the bookstore manager is going to be interested in this data, but the main purpose of keeping inventory records is to insure that sufficient copies are on hand. Let us consider Example 11.2, which is written to calculate the updated number of copies on hand, then check to insure that it does not fall below a predetermined level.

EXAMPLE 11.2

This is an expansion of Example 11.1; input data format is as follows:

Field	Card Columns
Stock number	3–7
Book title	8–40
Author	41–52
Copies on hand (beginning of week)	61–64
Copies sold during week	65–67
Copies received during week	68–70
Minimum allowable inventory balance	71–74

Compute the updated copies on hand as

Updated copies on hand = beginning copies on hand
+ copies received
− copies sold

For only those titles where the updated copies on hand are equal to or less than the minimum allowable inventory balance, print the following.

Field	Print Positions
Line count	4–6
Stock number	11–15
Author	19–30
Book title	32–64
Updated copies on hand	70–73
Minimum allowable inventory balance	78–81

A PROGRAM–EXAMPLE 11.2 In this program, it will be necessary to print *only* if the newly calculated inventory balance does not exceed the minimum allowable balance. Otherwise, processing is to continue to the next input record. The logic of this problem is illustrated by the flowchart of Figure 11.8, which clearly shows the necessary sequence of operations.

The additional operations which will be performed for this problem beyond those performed for Example 11.1 include the following.

1. Arithmetic operations must be performed to calculate the new inventory balance.
2. The new balance must be compared to a minimum allowable balance and printed only upon a designated condition.
3. The printout is to include a line count.

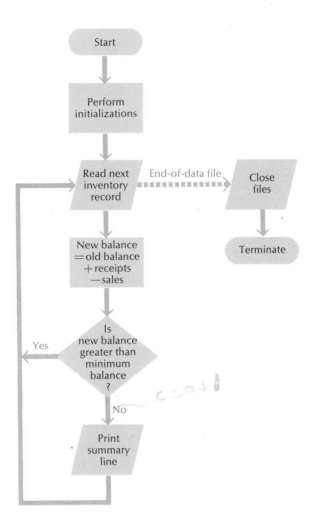

Fig. 11.8 Flowchart for
Example 11.2.

4. Leading 0s on numeric quantities will be replaced with blanks on the printed output.

Since the Identification and Environment Divisions are identical for Examples 11.1 and 11.2, Figure 11.9 includes only the Data and Procedure Divisions for this example. Although many of the statements in Figure 11.9 are identical to those of Figure 11.4, those that are different and that will be the topic of the following descriptions include the following:

1. Edit fields for improving the appearance of printed output (lines 00212, 002200, and 003020).
2. The Working-Storage Section (lines 003030-003050) in which arithmetic work areas are defined.

```
001150 DATA DIVISION.
001160 FILE SECTION.
001170 FD  BOOK-FILE    LABEL RECORDS ARE OMITTED.
001180 01  BOOK-INFO.
001190     02  FILLER          PIC XX.
001200     02  STOCKNUM-IN     PIC 9(5).
002010     02  TITLE-IN        PIC X(33).
002020     02  AUTHOR-IN       PIC X(12).
002030     02  FILLER          PIC X(8).
002040     02  ONHAND-IN       PIC 9999.
002050     02  SOLD-IN         PIC 999.
002060     02  RECEIVED-IN     PIC 999.
002070     02  MIN-BALANCE-IN  PIC 9999.
002080     02  FILLER          PIC X(6).
002090 FD  REPORT-FILE   LABEL RECORDS ARE OMITTED.
002100 01  OUTPUT-LINE.
002110     02  FILLER          PIC XXX.
002120     02  LINECNT-OUT     PIC ZZ9.
002130     02  FILLER          PIC XXXX.
002140     02  STOCKNUM-OUT    PIC 9999.
002150     02  FILLER          PIC XXX.
002160     02  AUTHOR-OUT      PIC X(12).
002170     02  FILLER          PIC X.
002180     02  TITLE-OUT       PIC X(33).
002190     02  FILLER          PIC X(5).
002200     02  UPDATED-BAL-OUT PIC ZZZ9.
003010     02  FILLER          PIC XXXX.
003020     02  MIN-BALANCE-OUT PIC ZZZ9.
003030 WORKING-STORAGE SECTION.
003040 77  LINECNT-W           PIC 999.
003050 77  UPDATED-BAL-W       PIC 9(4).
003060 PROCEDURE DIVISION.
003070 INITIALIZE.
003080     OPEN INPUT BOOK-FILE.  OPEN OUTPUT REPORT-FILE.
003090     MOVE SPACES TO OUTPUT-LINE.
003100     MOVE 0 TO LINECNT-W.
003110 PROCESS-LOOP.
003120     READ BOOK-FILE, AT END GO TO FINISH-UP.
003130     MOVE ONHAND-IN TO UPDATED-BAL-W.
003140     ADD RECEIVED-IN TO UPDATED-BAL-W.
003150     SUBTRACT SOLD-IN FROM UPDATED-BAL-W.
003160     IF UPDATED-BAL-W IS GREATER THAN MIN-BALANCE-IN,
003170         GO TO PROCESS-LOOP.
003180     MOVE UPDATED-BAL-W TO UPDATED-BAL-OUT.
003190     ADD 1 TO LINECNT-W.
004010     MOVE LINECNT-W TO LINECNT-OUT.
004020     MOVE STOCKNUM-IN TO STOCKNUM-OUT.
004030     MOVE TITLE-IN TO TITLE-OUT.
004040     MOVE AUTHOR-IN TO AUTHOR-OUT.
004050     MOVE MIN-BALANCE-IN TO MIN-BALANCE-OUT.
004060     WRITE OUTPUT-LINE.
004070     GO TO PROCESS-LOOP.
004080 FINISH-UP.
004090     CLOSE BOOK-FILE, REPORT-FILE.
004100     STOP RUN.
```

Fig. 11.9 Program for Example 11.2.

3. The arithmetic commands (lines 003140, 003150, and 003190) for updating the inventory and performing the line count.
4. Conditional branching capabilities represented by the IF statement (lines 003160 and 003170).

11.8
ADDITIONAL
DATA DIVISION
ENTRIES

THE EDIT SYMBOL   A very important function in preparing reports by computer is the process of *editing*, that is, placing decimal points and commas in numeric fields, replacing leadings 0s by blanks, and so on. The editing function is controlled by definition of the receiving field in the Data Division. The simple editing function performed in this program consists of replacing leading 0s in numeric fields by blanks. This is called *zero suppression*. For example, it is usually more convenient to have a column of numbers printed as shown on the right rather than with unnecessary 0s as shown on the left.

```
10578          10578
00692            692
01875           1875
90000          90000
00000              0
```

Cobol provides this capability in an easy-to-use fashion through the zero-suppress Z descriptor. Like the 9, each Z descriptor defines one position in the receiving field to which data may be moved. Thus, the picture clauses*

PIC   99999   PIC   ZZZZ9

are equivalent except that the first will always print five digits, including leading 0s (as in the left-hand column above), but the second will suppress leading 0s (as in the right-hand column). Of particular importance are two points: first, only nonsignificant (meaningless) 0s to the left are replaced by blanks and, second, only leading 0s which are moved into storage defined by the Z are suppressed. In the last example, the quantity 00000 is edited by a field defined as ZZZZ9. Therefore, the final 0 is left unchanged. Edit fields defined in the Data Division are commonly called *numeric edited items*.

The actual editing itself automatically occurs whenever an elementary item defined as a numeric field is moved to a report item. For instance, the statement

MOVE MIN-BALANCE-IN TO MIN-BALANCE-OUT.

causes the field read from columns 71–74 of the input record to be moved to the output area defined as MIN-BALANCE-OUT *and* causes the leading 0s to be automatically suppressed, as designated by the Z descriptor.

Exercise

11.11   Write an output record definition for the following.

---

*Note that the word PIC is used in place of PICTURE. This is an acceptable abbreviation since PIC is defined in Cobol as being equivalent to PICTURE. We might consider this as a minor concession to every Cobol programmer who has suffered from "writer's cramp."

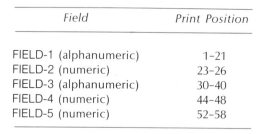

Field	Print Position
FIELD-1 (alphanumeric)	1–21
FIELD-2 (numeric)	23–26
FIELD-3 (alphanumeric)	30–40
FIELD-4 (numeric)	44–48
FIELD-5 (numeric)	52–58

All positions of FIELD-2 must be zero-suppressed, FIELD-4 must not be zero-suppressed, and FIELD-5 must be zero-suppressed except for the last digit.

THE WORKING-STORAGE SECTION   In general, the Data Division consists of two sections: the File Section used in the preceding example programs and the *Working-Storage Section*. As we have learned, each input and output record is defined in the File Section. Generally speaking, the Working-Storage Section contains all other records and/or fields which are required for the processing of data. This includes intermediate work areas for arithmetic calculations as required in Example 11.2. Although the Working-Storage Section may define records as well as individual fields, our attention will focus only on individual fields or *independent items*, as they are commonly called. Following is the Working-Storage Section from Figure 11.2.

```
WORKING-STORAGE SECTION.
      77   LINECNT-W        PIC 999.
      77   UPDATED-BAL-W   PIC 9(4).
```

Whereas fields in the File Section are defined with level numbers in the range 02–49, all independent items in the Working-Storage Section are defined by the specially assigned level number 77, as illustrated here. Note that the 77-level indicator is coded in the A-area. Because these are data fields, names for independent items are programmer-selected and must conform to the rules for choosing data-names. Like fields defined in the File Section, each independent item must include a Picture Clause defining the nature of the field (alphanumeric or numeric) and the length.

11.9
ARITHMETIC
OPERATIONS

ADDITION   The operation of updating involves adding receipts to the old balance, then subtracting sales. The addition operation is set up and carried out by the following pair of statements from Figure 11.9.

```
003130        MOVE ONHAND-IN TO UPDATED-BAL-W.
003140        ADD RECEIVED-IN TO UPDATED-BAL-W.
```

Here the old balance is moved to the arithmetic work area UPDATED-BAL-W which has been defined in the Working-Storage Section. Then the receipts (RECEIVED-IN) field is added. To illustrate how this pair of statements will function, let us assume that the values for ONHAND-IN and RECEIVED-IN, which have just been read from a card, are 477 and 125, respectively. Then the following example illustrates what happens within the computer when these operations are carried out. (The value of 981 stored in UPDATED-BAL-W is simply a result of a previous calculation and has no meaning at this point; in this sense, it would be termed "garbage.")

Storage contents:	ONHAND-IN	RECEIVED-IN	UPDATED-BAL-W
Initial values	477	125	981
After MOVE ONHAND-IN TO UPDATED-BAL-W	477	125	477
After ADD RECEIVED-IN TO UPDATED-BAL-W	477	125	602

The reader will note that the addition operation occurs in exactly the way that the English wording tends to imply. The first field is added to the second, with the sum replacing the original contents of the second field.

The statements

```
003100       MOVE 0 TO LINECNT-W.
```

and

```
003190       ADD 1 TO LINECNT-W.
```

serve the purpose of providing the line counter for the printed output. They also illustrate the use of constants, or so-called *numeric literals,* in a program. In the MOVE statement, a value of zero (0) will be placed in the field LINECNT-W during the initial portion of the program. A value of one (1) will be added to LINECNT-W by the ADD statement each time a line is to be printed. Thus, we can either add another field from storage or a fixed value to a field in storage. These two forms of the ADD statement may be generalized as follows.

$$\underline{\text{ADD}} \left\{ \begin{array}{c} \textit{data-name-1} \\ \text{or} \\ \textit{literal} \end{array} \right\} \underline{\text{TO}} \ \textit{data-name-2}.$$

When performing arithmetic operations, we must take care to ensure that all fields being used are numeric: that is, they have been defined in the Data Division with 9s. It is *not* possible to involve alphanumeric fields or edit fields in arithmetic operations.

literal is a constant

Exercise

11.12   Assume that the contents of the following fields are as indicated:

PAY   450
BONUS   200

What will be the value in RESULT after execution of each of the following?
a. ADD PAY TO BONUS.
   MOVE BONUS TO RESULT.   *6 50*
b. MOVE PAY TO RESULT.
   ADD BONUS TO RESULT.   *·650*
c. MOVE BONUS TO RESULT.
   ADD 100 TO PAY.
   ADD PAY TO RESULT.   *750*
d. MOVE 0 TO BONUS.
   ADD BONUS TO RESULT.   *no change in Result*

SUBTRACTION   The operation of subtraction in Cobol is very similar to that of addition. This is illustrated by the following subtract instruction from the program of Figure 11.9:

003150   SUBTRACT SOLD-IN FROM UPDATED-BAL-W.

Here the quantity in SOLD-IN will be subtracted from the value in UPDATED-BAL-W with the result replacing the original contents of UPDATED-BAL-W. Since the old inventory balance had been moved to UPDATED-BAL-W and then the receipts added, subtraction of the quantity sold yields the updated inventory balance in UPDATED-BAL-W.

This form of the Subtraction instruction can be generalized as follows.

$$\underline{SUBTRACT} \left\{ \begin{array}{c} \textit{data-name-1} \\ \text{or} \\ \textit{literal} \end{array} \right\} \underline{FROM}\ \textit{data-name-2}.$$

MULTIPLICATION AND DIVISION   The arithmetic operations of multiplication and division are also similar to addition. That is, two fields are involved with the result replacing the second field, for example:

MULTIPLY DISCOUNT BY CHARGE.
MULTIPLY 25 BY QUANTITY.
DIVIDE COUNT INTO POINTS.
DIVIDE 20 INTO TOTAL-VAL.

Execution of each will take place exactly as the English wording implies; the result for each of the four will replace the previous value in CHARGE,

QUANTITY, POINTS, and TOTAL-VAL, respectively. The generalized form of these commands are as follows.

$$\underline{\text{MULTIPLY}} \left\{ \begin{array}{c} \textit{data-name-1} \\ \textit{or} \\ \textit{literal} \end{array} \right\} \underline{\text{BY}} \; \textit{data-name-2.}$$

$$\underline{\text{DIVIDE}} \left\{ \begin{array}{c} \textit{data-name-1} \\ \textit{or} \\ \textit{literal} \end{array} \right\} \underline{\text{INTO}} \; \textit{data-name-2.}$$

Exercise

11.13 What value will be stored in EXERCISE after execution of each of the following sequence of statements?

    a. MOVE 25 TO DATA-A.
       MOVE 200 TO DATA-B.
       ADD DATA-A TO DATA-B.
       SUBTRACT 50 FROM DATA-B.
       MOVE DATA-B TO EXERCISE.
    b. MOVE 500 TO EXERCISE.
       DIVIDE 5 INTO EXERCISE.
       MOVE EXERCISE TO HOLD-A.
       MULTIPLY 6 BY EXERCISE.
       SUBTRACT 50 FROM EXERCISE.
       SUBTRACT HOLD-A FROM EXERCISE.

**11.10
CONDITIONAL
BRANCHING**

THE IF STATEMENT The GO TO statement provides *unconditional* branching capability to the programmer. On the other hand, the IF statement can be used to provide *conditional* branching capabilities; that is, selected operations will be done only if a certain condition is satisfied. In Figure 11.9, the IF statement (repeated here) is used to determine if the updated inventory balance is greater than the minimum allowable balance.

```
003160      IF UPDATED-BAL-W IS GREATER THAN MIN-BALANCE-IN,
003170         GO TO PROCESS-LOOP.
```

This statement consists of two basic parts: the *relational test*

    UPDATED-BAL-W IS GREATER THAN MIN-BALANCE-IN

which may be either true or false, followed by the Cobol command

    GO TO PROCESS-LOOP.

If the test condition is true, the command is carried out; if the test condition is false, the command is ignored and execution continues to the next line.

The relational test can be used to determine if a given quantity in a program is less than, equal to, or greater than any other quantity through use of the following relational operators.

```
IS GREATER THAN
IS EQUAL TO
IS LESS THAN
IS NOT GREATER THAN
IS NOT EQUAL TO
IS NOT LESS THAN
```

relational operators

The general form of the relational test is

$$\left\{ \begin{array}{c} data\text{-}name\text{-}1 \\ or \\ literal \end{array} \right\} relational\ operator \left\{ \begin{array}{c} data\text{-}name\text{-}2 \\ or \\ literal \end{array} \right\}$$

Following are examples of relational tests which may be used in an IF statement.

```
DEDUCTION IS LESS THAN MAX-ALLOWED
HOURS-WORKED IS GREATER THAN 40
CARD-CODE IS NOT EQUAL TO 9
```

Any of these relational tests may be included within an IF statement which has the form

IF *Relational test,*   *Cobol imperative statement.*

In general, if the test condition is true, then the Cobol imperative statement is executed; if it is false, then the imperative statement is ignored.

EXAMPLES OF THE IF STATEMENT   Basic characteristics of the IF statement are best illustrated by a few examples.

EXAMPLE 11.3

If the amount withheld for Social Security is equal to or greater than the maximum allowable amount, then branch to a sequence named CHECK-OUT. *Solution*

```
IF SOC-SEC IS NOT LESS THAN MAX-SOC-SEC,
    GO TO CHECK-OUT.
```

EXAMPLE 11.4

The data file STUDENT-FILE is to be processed and the names of all students who meet the following conditions are to be printed from F-S-LINE.

1. Foreign student, indicated by F-CODE value of 20.
2. Senior, indicated by LEVEL-CODE value 4.
3. Full time student, indicated by UNITS equal to or greater than 12.

Solution

```
READ-LOOP.
        READ STUDENT-FILE, AT END · · ·
        IF F-CODE IS NOT EQUAL TO 20
            GO TO READ-LOOP.
        IF LEVEL-CODE IS NOT EQUAL TO 4
            GO TO READ-LOOP.
        IF UNITS IS LESS THAN 12
            GO TO READ-LOOP.
                .
                .
                .
        · Appropriate MOVE statements
                .
                .

        WRITE F-S-LINE.
        GO TO READ-LOOP.
```

EXAMPLE 11.5

If the value in AGE is greater than 21, then add 1 to A-COUNT and move A-COUNT to A-SAVE; otherwise, leave A-COUNT unchanged. Then move NAME-IN to NAME-OUT.

Solution

```
        IF AGE IS GREATER THAN 21
            ADD 1 TO A-COUNT,
            MOVE A-COUNT TO A-SAVE.
        MOVE NAME-IN TO NAME-OUT.
```

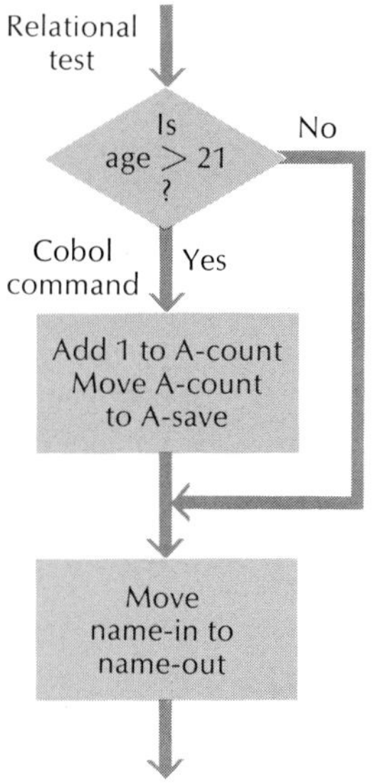

In this case, Cobol commands form a single compound command which will be executed only if the tested condition is true. A flowchart segment is shown in Figure 11.10.

Fig. 11.10

Exercise

11.14 Write Cobol statements to perform each of the following operations.
  a. If ERROR-CODE is 5, then branch to CHECK.

b. If J-LEVEL is equal to or exceeds 15, then increase I-COUNT by 1 and
      branch to CONT.
   c. Calculate COMMISSION given SALES, QUOTA, RATE-A, and RATE-B
      as follows:

     if SALES exceeds QUOTA
        COMMISSION = SALES × RATE-A
     if SALES does not exceed QUOTA
        COMMISSION = SALES × RATE-B

11.11 DATA INVOLVING DECIMAL POINTS

PROBLEM DEFINITION   One exceptionally important characteristic of most modern programming languages is the automatic positioning of decimal points. Within the computer, the Cobol system not only "remembers" where the decimal point belongs but also properly positions it with each arithmetic operation. To illustrate use of the decimal point, let us consider a simplification of the bookstore inventory which involves the book price.

EXAMPLE 11.6

Each record of bookstore inventory system includes the following

Field	Card Columns	Format
Stock number	1–5	
Inventory balance	6–9	xxxx
Unit cost	10–13	xxxx*

Compute the inventory value as

$$\text{Inventory value} = \text{inventory balance} \times \text{unit cost}$$

Output should be

Field	Print Positions	Format
Stock number	6–10	
Inventory balance	15–18	
Inventory value	23–31	xx,xxx.xx†

---

*This form xxxx indicates a four-digit field with an understood decimal point between the second and third digits. For instance, the quantity punched as 1573 would actually represent 15.73.

†The form xx,xxx.xx indicates a seven-digit field with appropriate "punctuation," for instance, 31,506.28. Note that this will occupy nine positions.

```
001160 DATA DIVISION.
001170 FILE SECTION.
001180 FD  BOOK-FILE   LABEL RECORDS ARE OMITTED.
001190 01  COST-RECORD.
001200     02  STOCKNUM-IN     PIC 9(5).
002010     02  BALANCE-IN      PIC 9(4).
002020     02  UNIT-COST       PIC 99V99.
002030     02  FILLER          PIC X(67).
002040 FD  LINE-FILE   LABEL RECORDS ARE OMITTED.
001050 01  LINE-RECORD.
002060     02  FILLER          PIC X(5).
002070     02  STOCKNUM-OUT    PIC 9(5).
002080     02  FILLER          PIC XXXX.
002090     02  BALANCE-OUT     PIC ZZZ9.
002100     02  FILLER          PIC XXXX.
002110     02  VALUE-OUT       PIC ZZ,ZZ9.99.
002120 WORKING-STORAGE SECTION.
002130 77  VALUE-WORK          PIC 99999V99.
002140 PROCEDURE DIVISION.
002150 OPEN-FILES.
002160     OPEN INPUT BOOK-FILE, OPEN OUTPUT LINE-FILE.
002170     MOVE SPACES TO LINE-RECORD.
002180 PROCESS-LOOP.
002190     READ BOOK-FILE, AT END CLOSE BOOK-FILE,
002200               CLOSE LINE-FILE, STOP RUN.
003010     MOVE STOCKNUM-IN TO STOCKNUM-OUT.
003020     MOVE BALANCE-IN TO BALANCE-OUT.
003030     MOVE UNIT-COST TO VALUE-WORK.
003040     MULTIPLY BALANCE-IN BY VALUE-WORK.
003050     MOVE VALUE-WORK TO VALUE-OUT.
003060     WRITE LINE-RECORD.
003070     GO TO PROCESS-LOOP.
```

Fig. 11.11 Program for Example 11.6.

The Data and Procedure Divisions of Figure 11.11 illustrate input and output of data fields with decimal points.

DECIMAL POINT POSITIONING ON INPUT Whenever numeric fields involving decimal points are punched into cards or recorded on magnetic tape or disk, the decimal point itself is seldom recorded. Thus, the quantity $13.85 would normally be punched in four adjacent columns as 1385. Needless to say, the program must give some indication regarding actual placement of the point. This is accomplished in Cobol by means of the PICTURE clause which defines the input fields. For instance, the unit cost is defined in Figure 11.11 by the statement.

002020   02 UNIT-COST   PIC 99V99.

Here the unit cost is defined as a four-digit field (indicated by four 9s) with an understood decimal point between the second and third digits (as indicated by the V). If the quantity 1762 is read into UNIT-COST, it will be interpreted by the computer as 17.62, as indicated by the PICTURE.

Other examples are

Picture	Punched-In Card	Interpreted As
PIC 99V99	0008	00.08
PIC V999	315	.315
PIC 9(5)V99	1234567	12345.67
PIC 9(4)V9(3)	1234567	1234.567

EDITING OUTPUT QUANTITIES   While input data cards are read by machine, reports generated by the computer are designed for people to read (not for machines), and appropriate punctuation can make printed matter much easier for us to comprehend. Thus, a quantity stored in the machine as 157283 with an understood decimal between the digits 2 and 8 might be printed as

1,572.83

It is important to recognize that the commas and decimal point each occupy one printing position, so this field requires a total of eight positions on the printed page. Placement of the decimal point and comma are controlled through the PICTURE in the Output Record description. For instance, the following statement from Figure 11.11 defines the inventory value.

002110   02   VALUE-OUT   PIC ZZ,ZZ9.99.

Following are simple values in storage and printed results.

VALUE-OUT

Storage Contents	Printed Output
2157340	21,573.40
0800023	8,000.23
0076080	760.80
0000705	7.05
0000085	0.85

Note that zero suppression automatically includes the comma when the digit immediately preceding it is suppressed.

Exercises

11.15 Following are data pictures and corresponding fields punched in cards. What will be stored for each example?

Picture	Punched-In Card	
99V9	125	12.5
V999	014	.014
9999V9	28001	2800.1
9(4)V9(3)	9876543	9876.543
9(3)V9(4)	9876543	987.6543

11.16 Following are selected fields in storage. How will each of these be printed according to the Picture Z,ZZ9.99?

128376 1,283.76

2513 25.13

47721 477.21

53 0.53

15882 15,882.

Answers to Preceding Exercises

11.1 IDENTIFICATION DIVISION
ENVIRONMENT DIVISION
DATA DIVISION
PROCEDURE DIVISION

11.2 01 INPUT-RECORD.

02	FILLER	PICTURE X.
02	EM-NAME	PICTURE X(22).
02	SS-NUMBER	PICTURE X(9).
02	FILLER	PICTURE X(8).
02	OCCUPATION	PICTURE X(5).
02	FILLER	PICTURE X(5).
02	SEX	PICTURE X.
02	EMPLOY-YEAR	PICTURE XX.
02	FILLER	PICTURE X(26).
02	CARD-CODE	PICTURE X.

11.3
a. HOLD valid data-name.
b. LIMITX valid data-name.
c. 123456 invalid data-name; does not include any letters.
d. RECORD-FIELD valid data-name.
e. MAXIMUM DIFFERENCE invalid data-name; must not include a blank.
f. REPORT # 7 invalid data-name; no special characters other than the hyphen allowed,

g. LINE reserved word.
h. 5457-A-122 valid data-name.

11.4 The only required entry in Identification Division is the PROGRAM-ID.

11.5 The SELECT clause is found in the Environment Division.

11.6 The student is incorrect because the name FORD, when stored as a 10-position field in storage, consists of exactly 10 characters: 4 letters and 6 blanks. The result will be

11.7 To inform the computer whether each file is input or output and to direct the computer to make them ready for processing.

11.8 The READ statement will be executed the twenty-first time and will detect the end-of-file record. This will cause execution of the AT END clause in the READ statement.

11.9 The READ statement must designate the file-name; the WRITE statement must designate the record-name of the record to be written.

11.10 a. B-Area; b. A-Area; c. B-Area; d. A-Area; . e. A-Area; f. neither; sequence numbers are punched in columns 1–6.

.11.11
```
01  EXERCISE-11.
    12  FIELD-1  PIC X(21).  ·
    12  FILLER   PIC X.
    12  FIELD-2  PIC ZZZZ.  or  PIC Z(4).
    12  FILLER   PIC XXX.
    12  FIELD-3  PIC X(11).        .
    12  FILLER   PIC XXX.
    12  FIELD-4  PIC 9(5).
    12  FILLER   PIC XXX.
    12  FIELD-5  PIC ZZZZZZ9.  or  PIC Z(6)9.
```

11.12 a. 650; b. 650; c. 750; d. whatever was in RESULT prior to execution will remain unchanged.

11.13 a. -175; b. 450.

11.14
a. IF ERROR-CODE IS EQUAL TO 5
   GO TO CHECK.
b. IF J-LEVEL IS NOT LESS THAN 15,
   ADD 1 to I-COUNT,
   GO TO CONT.
c. IF SALES IS GREATER THAN QUOTA,
   MOVE RATE-A TO COMMISSION,
   GO TO NEXT.
   MOVE RATE-B TO COMMISSION.
   NEXT.
   MULTIPLY SALES BY COMMISSION.

11.15 12.5
.014
2800.1
9876.543
987.6543

11.16 1,283.76
25.13
477.21
0.53
15.88

Additional Exercises

11.17 Matching. Match each of the Cobol commands 1–8 with the corresponding description a–h.

1. IF   2. MULTIPLY
3. READ   4. ADD
5. OPEN   6. STOP RUN
7. MOVE   8. GO TO

a. Bring a record into storage from a designated file.

b. Compute the sum of A and B.

c. Execution of the program is to be terminated.

d. Make a data file ready for use in the program.

e. Make an unconditional branch to ERROR-ROUT.

f. The data in WORKA must be saved in an area named HOLDAREA.

g. Determine if the hours worked exceeds forty.

h. Calculate overtime pay as base pay times 1.5.

11.18 True-False. Determine whether each of the following is true or false.

a. The words MOVE, EQUAL, and SECTION are examples of Cobol reserved words; these are words which have been assigned special meaning for use in writing Cobol programs.

b. The Identification Division of a program is considered machine dependent and must be rewritten if the program is run on different computers; however, the other three divisions are machine independent.

c. The Cobol coding form consists of two areas or margins: the A-margin is for program statements and the B-margin for descriptive comments.

d. The primary purpose of the Identification Division is to provide the program with a name.

e. The basic characteristics of a file are defined in the Data Division.

f. The term *item* in Cobol refers, broadly speaking, to what we call a field in data processing in general.

g. A group item is composed of elementary items; in turn, elementary items may be composed of independent items.

h. Elementary items which make up a group item always have level numbers that are higher than the group item level number.

i. Editing, such as including a dollar sign and decimal point, is commonly done with the numeric edited item.

j. In the sequence

    IF DATA EQUAL TO 30.0,
       MOVE DATA TO WORK.
    ADD DATA TO SUM.

when DATA is not equal to 30, it will be added to SUM. However, if DATA is equal to 30, it will be moved to WORK but not added to SUM.

11.19 Multiple Choice. Determine which answer best completes or answers each of the following.

a. One of the following is not a criterion for selecting programmer-supplied names: (1) may contain no special characters, (2) must not exceed 30 characters in length, (3) no spaces allowed within the name, (4) must contain at least one letter, (5) all of the above are criteria for selecting names.

b. The level number 01 is (1) reserved for input files only, (2) reserved for output files only, (3) used to define independent items, (4) used to designate a record.

c. Which of the Cobol divisions is optional and may be omitted from a Cobol program? (1) Identification, (2) Environment, (3) Data, (4) Procedure, (5) all four divisions must be included.

d. A portion of a Cobol program which includes information about the computer

on which the program is to be run (and is therefore machine dependent) is the (1) Description Section, (2) Select Clause, (3) File Section, (4) Environment Division.

e. An end-of-file sequence would be found in the (1) File Section of the Data Division, (2) Environment Division, (3) Procedure Division, (4) data set to be operated upon by the program.

f. The record description entry PICTURE 99V99 designates (1) a four-position field with an implied decimal point between the second and third digits, (2) a four-digit field with a decimal point punched between the second and third digits, (3) a four-position constant value of 99.99, (4) the maximum value which an input field can assume.

g. A numeric edited item must (1) be defined in the Working-Storage Section, (2) always be an independent item, (3) be an elementary item, (4) never be defined in an output record.

h. The level number 01 defining a record (1) must be placed in the A-area, (2) must be placed in the B-area, (3) can be used only once in a program, (4) none of the preceding, (5) both 1 and 3.

i. One type of test which can be performed with the IF statement is the (1) relational test, (2) overflow test, (3) end-of-file test, (4) sequencing test.

j. If BF = 25.0 and CF = 30.0, the values of BF and CF after execution of the following statement will be

    IF CF NOT GREATER THAN BF,
       ADD BF TO CF.
    ADD 20.0 TO BF.

(1) BF = 25.0, CF = 30.0, (2) BF = 45.0, CF = 30.0, (3) BF = 25.0, CF = 55.0, (4) BF = 55.0, CF = 30.0, (5) none of the preceding.

11.20 The following is an input (card) record description found in the Data Division of a program.

List the card columns each field will occupy on the card according to this description.

			Card Columns
01 CREDIT-CARD.	*Record.*		
02 NAME.	*field group view.*		*1 – 20*
03 INIT1	PICTURE X. *elem item*		*1*
03 INIT2	PICTURE X.		*2*
03 LNAME	PICTURE X(18)		*3 – 20*
02 NUMBER	PICTURE 9(5).		*21 – 25*
02 ADDRESS	PICTURE X(20).		*26 – 45*
02 TRANS	PICTURE 9(5).		*46 – 50*
02 DATE. *group item*			
03 MONTH	PICTURE 99. *elem item*		*51, 52*
03 YEAR	PICTURE 99.		*53, 54*
02 ITEM	PICTURE X(26).		*55, 80*

11.21 Programming Problems. Prepare a flowchart and write a Cobol program for each of the following.

a. An employer keeps an Employee Information File; each record in the file includes:

Field	Card Columns
Social Security number	1–9
Name	10–34
Job title	35–44
Job code	51

This information is to be printed, one card per line, according to the following format.

Field	Print Positions
Name	Beginning 1
Social Security number	Beginning 30
Job title	Beginning 45
Job code	57

The Social Security number should be broken into three parts, each separated by a blank; for instance, 555123456 should be printed as 555 12 3456.

b. The particular file of Exercise *a* includes annual summary information for special pay computations with the following additional information recorded in each record.

Field	Card Columns
Unused vacation (days)	55–56
Compensatory time (days)	57–58
Unauthorized leave (days)	59–60

At the end of each year, employees are paid for their compensation days, which are determined as follows.

Number of compensation days
= unused vacation
+ 2 × compensatory time
− unauthorized leave

Output is to be as in Problem (a) with the addition of the following field.

Field	Print Positions
Compensation days	Beginning 61

c. Following are three further modifications of Problem (b).
  (1) Print only those employees whose number of compensation days is greater than 21.
  (2) Print only those employees whose number of compensation days is between 14 and 21 (inclusive).
  (3) In calculating number of compensation days, multiply compensatory time by 2 only for the first five days, then count the remainder on a one-for-one basis, for example:

Compensatory Time	Calculations
3	2 × 3 = 6
5	2 × 5 = 10
8	2 × 5 + 3 = 13

Also, do not subtract out unauthorized leave unless it exceeds 3 days.

d. Each record in an Employee Pay File includes the following.

Field	Card Columns	Format
Employee number	1–5	
Employee name	6–26	
Hours worked	41–43	XXX
Pay rate	44–47	XXXX

Write a program to calculate gross pay as

$$\text{Gross pay} = \text{hours worked} \times \text{pay rate}$$

Print the input fields and the gross pay; do your own output format planning.

e. Following are two variations on Problem (d).
  (1) In calculating gross pay, all hours worked in excess of 40 must be paid at time and a half rate (multiply the pay rate by 1.5).
  (2) At the end of the report, print the totals (for all employees) for hours worked and gross pay.

Table 11.1 ANSI COBOL-RESERVED WORDS

ACCEPT	CLOCK-UNITS	DAY	ERROR
ACCESS	CLOSE	DE	ESI
ACTUAL	COBOL	DECIMAL-POINT	EVERY
ADD	CODE	DECLARATIVES	EXAMINE
ADDRESS	CODE-SET	DELETE	EXCEPTION
ADVANCING	COLLATING	DELIMITED	EXIT
ALSO	COLUMN	DELIMITER	EXTEND
AFTER	COMMA	DEPENDING	FD
ALL	COMMUNICATION	DEPTH	FILE
ALPHABETIC	COMP	DESCENDING	FILE-CONTROL
ALTER	COMP-1	DESTINATION	FILE-LIMIT
ALTERNATE	COMP-2	DETAIL	FILE-LIMITS
AND	COMP-3	DISABLE	FILLER
ARE	COMPUTATIONAL	DISPLAY	FINAL
AREA	COMPUTATIONAL-1	DISPLAY-n	FIRST
AREAS	COMPUTATIONAL-2	DIVIDE	FOOTING
ASCENDING	COMPUTATIONAL-3	DIVISION	FOR
ASSIGN	COMPUTE	DOWN	FROM
AT	CONFIGURATION	DUPLICATES	GENERATE
AUTHOR	CONSOLE	DYNAMIC	GIVING
BEFORE	CONTAINS	EGI	GO
BEGINNING	CONTROL	ELSE	GOBACK
BLANK	CONTROLS	EMI	GREATER
BLOCK	COPY	ENABLE	GROUP
BY	CORR	END	HEADING
CALL	CORRESPONDING	END-OF-PAGE	HIGH-VALUE
CANCEL	COUNT	ENDING	HIGH-VALUES
CD	CURRENCY	ENTER	I-O
CF	DATA	ENVIRONMENT	I-O-CONTROL
CH	DATE	EOP	IDENTIFICATION
CHARACTER	DATE-COMPILED	EQUAL	IF
CHARACTERS	DATE-WRITTEN	EQUALS	IN

Table 11.1 (Cont.)

INDEX	NOT	RELEASE	START
INDEXED	NOTE	REMAINDER	STATUS
INDICATE	NUMBER	REMARKS	STOP
INITIAL	NUMERIC	REMOVAL	STRING
INITIATE	OBJECT-COMPUTER	RENAMES	SUB-QUEUE-1
INPUT	OCCURS	REPLACING	SUB-QUEUE-2
INPUT-OUTPUT	OF	REPORT	SUB-QUEUE-3
INSPECT	OFF	REPORTING	SUBTRACT
INSTALLATION	OMITTED	REPORTS	SUM
INTO	ON	RERUN	SUPPRESS
INVALID	OPEN	RESERVE	SYNC
IS	OPTIONAL	RESET	SYNCHRONIZED
JUST	OR	RETURN	TABLE
JUSTIFIED	ORGANIZATION	REVERSED	TALLY
KEY	OUTPUT	REWIND	TALLYING
KEYS	PAGE	REWRITE	TERMINAL
LABEL	PAGE-COUNTER	RF	TERMINATE
LABEL-RETURN	PERFORM	RH	TEXT
LAST	PF	RIGHT	THAN
LEADING	PH	ROUNDED	THROUGH
LEAVE	PIC	RUN	THRU
LEFT	PICTURE	SAME	TIME
LENGTH	PLUS	SD	TIMES
LESS	POINTER	SEARCH	TO
LIMIT	POSITION	SECTION	TOP
LIMITS	POSITIVE	SECURITY	TRACE
LINAGE	PRINTING	SEEK	TRAILING
LINAGE-COUNTER	PROCEDURE	SEGMENT	TYPE
LINE	PROCEDURES	SEGMENT-LINK	UNIT
LINE-COUNTER	PROCEED	SELECT	UNSTRING
LINES	PROCESSING	SEND	UNTIL
LINKAGE	PROGRAM	SENTENCE	UP
LOCK	PROGRAM-ID	SEPARATE	UPON
LOW-VALUE	QUEUE	SEQUENCE	USAGE
LOW-VALUES	QUOTE	SEQUENTIAL	USE
MEMORY	QUOTES	SET	USING
MERGE	RANDOM	SIGN	VALUE
MESSAGE	RD	SIZE	VALUES
MODE	READ	SORT	VARYING
MODULES	RECEIVE	SORT-MERGE	WHEN
MOVE	RECORD	SOURCE	WITH
MULTIPLE	RECORDING	SOURCE-COMPUTER	WORDS
MULTIPLY	RECORDS	SPACE	WORKING-STORAGE
NATIVE	REDEFINES	SPACES	WRITE
NEGATIVE	REEL	SPECIAL-NAMES	ZERO
NEXT	REFERENCES	STANDARD	ZEROES
NO	RELATIVE	STANDARD-1	ZEROS

Chapter

12

Concepts and Applications of Magnetic Tape and Disk

12.1
PRINCIPLES OF MAGNETIC TAPE

THE TAPE   From the generalized description of the computer in Chapter 4, we learned that magnetic tape is commonly used with modern computers to serve the needs of both large capacity storage and high-speed input/output. Recall that a typical tape system, as a storage device, can retain approximately 250,000 fully punched cards on one 2400-foot reel of half-inch tape. This amounts to 125 full boxes of cards (one box contains 2000 cards and measures approximately $8 \times 15 \times 3\frac{1}{2}$ inches). If these were placed one on top of the other, they would form a stack almost 37 feet high. As an input/output medium, the speed of magnetic tape is also staggering when compared to cards. A very fast card reader will read cards at the rate of 2000 cards per minute; a typical tape unit will read data from a magnetic tape at a rate equivalent to 25,000 cards per minute. These characteristics are indeed impressive when compared to cards. For a better insight into magnetic tape principles, let us consider the basic means for storing and retrieving information tape.

The magnetic tape used in computers is virtually identical to that used in the common home tape recorder; it is made by coating one side of a plastic tape with a material which can be magnetized (Figure 12.1). Although the most commonly used size is one half inch in width and 2400 feet in length, reels are sometimes used with both shorter and longer lengths. Also, some systems are designed to process wider tapes. The tape itself is wound on reels $10\frac{1}{2}$ inches in diameter, as illustrated in Figure 12.2.

INFORMATION STORAGE ON TAPE   Although the tape consists of a uniform magnetic surface one half inch by 2400 feet, it is effectively divided into lengthwise strips termed *tracks* or *channels* for data coding. A *seven-track* system uses the seven-bit BCD coding; the EBCDIC code used with the IBM 360/370 uses *nine-track* tape (eight tracks for EBCDIC coding and one for parity). Figure 12.3 illustrates BCD coding on a section of seven-track tape. As we can see, the tape coding uses even parity as opposed to the odd parity used in core storage of most computers. We can see that the tape concept of storing infor-

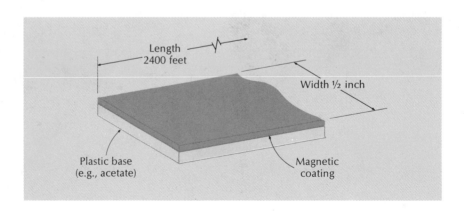

Fig. 12.1 Section of magnetic tape.

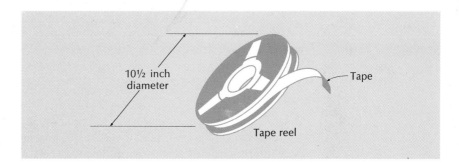

Fig. 12.2 Magnetic tape reel.

mation is similar to that of storing information on cards. That is, the tape is logically divided into six tracks (plus one for parity) corresponding to the twelve rows of the card. Similarly, one character is stored in a single vertical position, often termed a *frame*, in much the same manner that the card is divided into columns. However, an important difference, which we shall consider in detail in a later section, is that respective frames cannot be addressed as can the columns of a card. Where data is stored indelibly on a card by punched holes, it is recorded on the magnetic tape surface by magnetized spots. The short vertical marks in Figure 12.3 represent magnetized spots on the tape which are equivalent to punches in the card or 1-bits in core storage. The unmarked positions represent spots on the tape which are not magnetized and are equivalent to no-punches in the card or 0-bits in core storage.

As emphasized in earlier sections, one of the advantages of magnetic tape is its ability to store large quantities of data. This is due to the high data *density* on the medium. For instance, 800 and 1600 frames per inch (termed *bits per inch* or *bpi*) are commonly used. Special *hypertape* systems are also available with a density of 6250 bpi. This phenomenal packing makes it possible to store the contents of 78 fully punched cards on a 1-inch segment of tape, or an entire box of 2000 cards on a piece of tape which is slightly more than 2 feet in length.

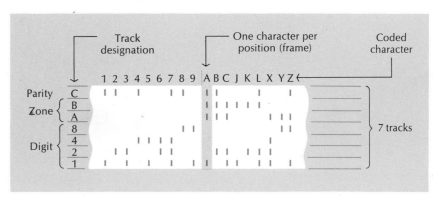

Fig. 12.3 Information storage on magnetic tape.

The tape density used with a given computer depends upon the particular model of tape drive. Needless to say, the higher the density, the greater the cost of the tape drive.

TAPE DRIVE UNITS   The tape drive units used on computers (Figure 12.4) function in much the same manner as home tape recorders. That is, tape is wound from one reel to another, passing through a reading/writing device where it can be read repeatedly without destroying the information stored. New information can be rewritten, thus replacing the previously stored data, and the tape can be rewound and backspaced. Some tape drives are even designed to allow the tape to be read backwards. With the high-speed starts and stops (a common tape speed is 112.5 inches per second), it is physically impossible to start and stop the relatively heavy tape reels instantaneously. To compensate for this, the tape is looped through special *vacuum columns* which control a smooth and steady movement of the tape through the reading and writing devices. The principle of a vacuum-operated magnetic tape drive

Fig. 12.4   Magnetic tape drive. (Courtesy Honeywell Information Systems)

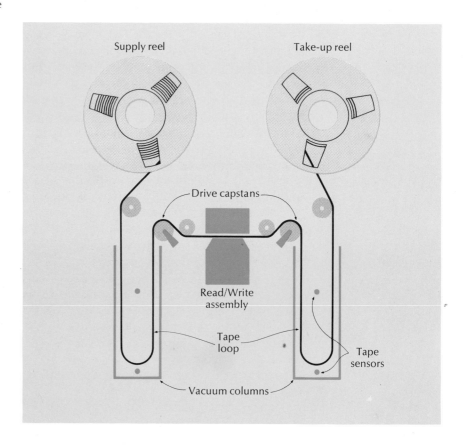

Fig. 12.5   Schematic of magnetic tape drive.

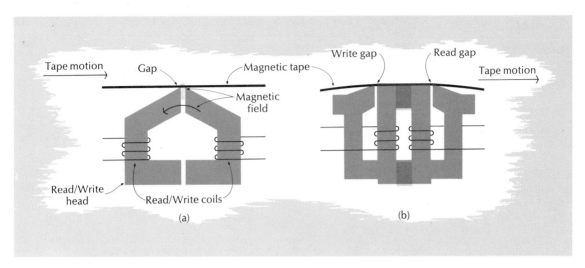

Fig. 12.6 (a) One-gap read/write head; (b) two-gap read/write head.

is illustrated in Figure 12.5. Special sensing devices in the vacuum columns control feeding of the tape into and out of the columns from the reels. Movement of the tape across the read/write mechanism is controlled by the drive capstans, which are only required to work against the slight inertia of the few feet of tape within the columns. This makes it possible to bring the tape from a complete stop to full speed (for example, 112.5 inches per second) in a few milliseconds, where one millisecond is $\frac{1}{1000}$ second.

The read/write assembly is designed with a set of special read/write mechanisms, one for each channel of the tape. Typical single-gap and double-gap read/write heads are illustrated in Figure 12.6. As the tape is transported across the head for a writing operation, electrical current in the coils is changed to correspond to the data to be encoded. This affects the magnetic field within the head which, in turn, produces the proper magnetic encoding across the gap and onto the tape. With the single gap, the same gap is used for both reading and writing; with the double gap, the dual head feature allows reading to take place at one gap and writing at the other. Most tape units use the double-gap feature due to its error checking capability. That is, data written at the write gap can immediately be read at the read gap and compared to the original information in storage to insure that the writing operation was not in error.

A wide variety of both seven- and nine-channel tape units is available to the computer user (present emphasis is on nine-track units, which are generally replacing the older seven-track systems). These vary in terms of both density and reading speed. Figure 12.7 is a summary of operating characteristics for typical magnetic tape drives currently in use. Speed at which data can be read or written by a tape unit is called the *data rate* and is commonly measured in frames per second. Referring to Figure 12.7, we see that the data rate is simply the density times the tape speed. To appreciate the high data rates associated with magnetic tape, the reader might consider that at a rate of 100,000 characters per second this entire book could be read by a tape drive in approximately 15 seconds.

Exercises

12.1 If an entire reel of tape is used for storage of data, how many fully punched cards could be stored on a 2400-foot reel? Use a density of 1600 frames per inch.

12.2 A hypothetical tape drive has the ability to operate at either of the two densities 700 and 1400 frames per inch. With a tape speed of 100 inches per second, what would be the data rates at each of the two densities?

RECORDS ON TAPE   When using cards, the record length is always 80 characters, since even blank columns are read. With magnetic tape, this restriction is removed; records may be any size. They can be less than 80 characters, but more often they are made as large as the available storage will permit, which may be 5000 characters or even more.

Large records save time because of fewer starts and stops of the tape, and they make more efficient use of the tape itself. When the tape is written, the tape motion stops between every record, and a $\frac{3}{4}$-inch gap of unrecorded tape is left between records (for high-density nine-channel tapes, this gap is $\frac{6}{10}$ inch). These spaces are commonly called *interblock gaps*. If the records are short, such as the 80 characters of a card, the amount of tape used for gaps far exceeds the amount of tape used for information. With 80-character records, tape

Unit		Number of tracks	Tape density (frames/in.)	Tape speed (in./sec)	Data rate (frames or characters/sec)
IBM 2401	Model 1	7	800	37.5	30,000
		7	200	37.5	7,500
	Model 3	7	800	112.5	90,000
			556	112.5	62,500
	Model 4	9	1600	37.5	60,000
	Model 6	9	1600	112.5	180,000
IBM 3420	Model 3	9	1600	75	120,000
	Model 7	9	1600	200	320,000
	Model 8	9	6250	200	1,250,000
Honey-well	MTH 502	9	800	75	60,000
		9	1600	75	120,000
	MTH 505	9	800	125	100,000
		9	1600	125	200,000

Fig. 12.7 Tape unit characteristics.

recorded at 556 characters per inch with a $\frac{3}{4}$-inch gap is approximately $\frac{1}{6}$ information and $\frac{5}{6}$ gap; at 1600 characters per inch with a $\frac{6}{10}$ inch gap, it is approximately $\frac{1}{12}$ information and $\frac{11}{12}$ gap. By using long records, the portion lost by interblock gaps becomes negligible.

The advantages of long records can be gained for short records by a technique called *blocking*. For example, ten 80-character records might be placed end-to-end in core storage and written as one 800-character record. It is then said to have a *blocking factor* of 10. The space-saving advantage of blocking is graphically illustrated in Figure 12.8, where single record blocks in 12.8(a) can be compared to ten-record blocks in 12.8(b).

Whenever the tape is read, an entire 800-character block is brought into storage. Since the program usually processes one record at a time, special programming techniques must be utilized to access each record from the block (this function is commonly referred to as *deblocking*). For modern computers, this is done automatically through special input/output programs which are furnished by the manufacturer (such *system software* is discussed extensively in Chapter 13). The advantages gained from blocking, through increased tape capacity and speed, far outweigh the disadvantage of the additional program instructions required.

DATA ORGANIZATION ON TAPE   The previous example of blocked records illustrates one of the four basic means used in the System/360 tape system for blocking of information to be stored on magnetic tape. In the example, each block consists of a fixed number of records (10) and each record of a fixed number of characters (80). This is referred to as a *fixed-fixed* format. In some applications it is desirable to vary the record length from record to record, or the number of records in a block or both. For instance, the length of a student record might vary depending upon the number of courses in which the student is enrolled. That is, if the student is carrying several courses, the record would be relatively long to contain all of the course information; if just one course,

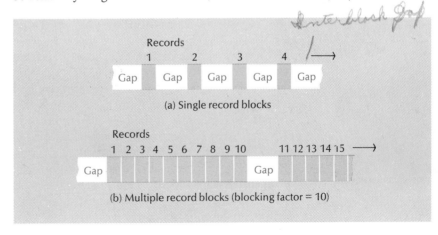

(a) Single record blocks

(b) Multiple record blocks (blocking factor = 10)

Fig. 12.8 Blocking records on tape.

the record would be shorter. On the other hand, with variable block sizes we might be working with an inventory system where each block consists of one record for each assembly of an electrical system plus individual records for each subassembly constituting the main assembly. If the number of subassemblies varies from 1 to 30, then the number of records in a block would vary from 2 to 31.

These needs give rise to the other three blocking formats; *fixed* blocking factor–*variable* record length, *variable* blocking factor–*fixed* record length, and *variable* blocking factor–*variable* record length. As we might expect, working with such formats is somewhat more involved than working with the simpler fixed-fixed format. However, much of the task is handled automatically by the standardized system software.

Exercises

12.3 This section stated: "With 80-character unblocked records, tape recorded at 556 characters per inch with a $\frac{3}{4}$ inch gap contains approximately $\frac{1}{6}$ information and $\frac{5}{6}$ gap." Verify this statement.

12.4 Using a blocking factor of 10 (Figure 12.8), a density of 556, and a gap of $\frac{3}{4}$ inch, what will be the ratio of information to gap as described in Exercise 12.3?

12.2
MAGNETIC TAPE
PROCESSING

SEQUENTIAL NATURE OF MAGNETIC TAPE   A computer system using magnetic tape as the primary input/output and auxiliary storage medium is commonly referred to as a *tape system*. A typical system, equipped with eight tape drives, is shown in Figure 12.9. With the capability of card input and multiple tape drives, a tape system can easily perform all of the functions, and many more, of the unit record system (Chapter 2) far more efficiently and quickly. Supplementing tape drives as auxiliary storage devices, most modern tape systems include at least one random access auxiliary device, such as magnetic drum or disk, to increase further the overall system versatility. (Magnetic disk is described in Section 12.3 of this chapter.)

Probably one of the most commonly encountered systems in data processing is the company payroll system. This is a typical batch operation in which transactions (hours worked and other data) are accumulated over a period of time and then processed in a single *batch*. In its basic form, a payroll system involves the processing of two files: the Employee Master File, which includes each employee's pay rate and other fixed information, and a Detail or Transaction File which includes information such as hours worked for each employee. Due to the sequential nature of magnetic tape, data in both files must be organized and processed sequentially. For example, both the Master File and the Detail File might be arranged in ascending sequence based on the employee number. Then corresponding records from each file would be read and processed to produce the pay checks and the updated Master File. If we

Fig. 12.9 A modern computer system equipped with magnetic tape and disk. (Courtesy of Honeywell Information Systems)

recall from Chapter 2, the customer account example used to illustrate the unit record system involved the basic data processing operations of sorting, merging, updating, and report generation. Precisely the same steps are involved in performing the operation on a tape-oriented computer.*

All tape processing of any significance involves two or more magnetic tape drives. To illustrate, let us consider a vast simplification of calculating the pay for the employees of a company. (The sequence of steps involved in performing this operation on unit record equipment is illustrated in the flowchart of Figure 2.18.) We will assume that we have at our disposal three tape drives that we shall refer to as units 1, 2, and 3. The sequence of events in updating the Employee Master File and calculating pay might proceed as follows:

1. Read and load the time cards (transaction records) to drive 1 (computer operator action required).
2. Sort the Transaction File with sorted file remaining on drive 1 (sorting itself requires several drives).

---

*The reader should *not* take this to imply that a magnetic tape computer system is a high-speed equivalent of a unit record system. A tape system has most of the capabilities of a card system and many more. When tape-oriented computers were first introduced, a serious error made by some installations was to adapt their unit record systems and procedures almost directly to the tape-oriented computer without taking advantage of the added power provided by magnetic tape. A conversion from a unit record to a tape computer calls for redesigning virtually the entire data handling and processing system.

3. Mount the Employee Master File on drive 2 (computer operator action).
4. Read a Master Record from drive 2 and all corresponding transaction records. from drive 1.
5. Update the Master Record.
6. Write updated Master Record to new Master File on drive 3.
7. Print a paycheck for this employee.
8. Return to step 4 and repeat this operation until all records are processed.

In other words, a Master File and a Transaction File are merged and processed, producing an updated Master File, just as with the unit record system.

A serious disadvantage of magnetic tape processing relates to the fact that the entire Master File must be processed and written on the updated tape, regardless of whether or not transaction records exist for each master. If, during each transaction period, virtually every Master Record has corresponding Transaction Records, this is no problem. However, if there have been transactions for a very small percentage of the master records, the entire Master File must still be read and written on the new master tape. For a large file, this can be a relatively inefficient operation and is a drawback of sequential processing as required with magnetic tape files.

The batch processing sequence is repeated each processing period as illustrated in Figure 12.10, where two processing cycles are illustrated. The output of each cycle serves as the input for the next cycle. In this illustration

Fig. 12.10 Updating a tape file.

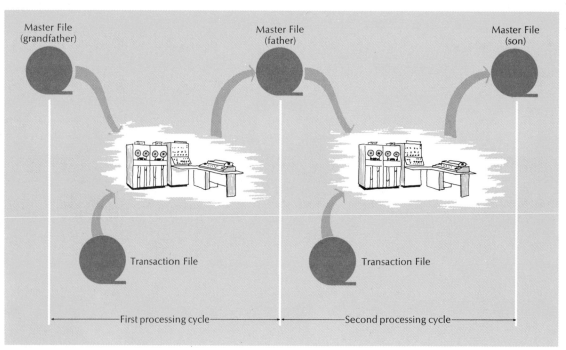

Master File (grandfather)

Master File (father)

Master File (son)

Transaction File

Transaction File

First processing cycle

Second processing cycle

we see the most recently updated Master File and the two outdated Master Files from previous runs. (Note that these are termed the "son," the "father," and the "grandfather.") It is common practice to save not only the most recently updated Master File (son), but also the one from the preceding update run (father). In the event the son file is inadvertently destroyed, or erroneous results occurred during the run, it is possible to fall back on the father file and the corresponding Transaction File to make a rerun, thus producing a new copy of the son file. Such back-up provisions are an important part of system design.

Exercise

12.5 What is meant by the statement, "Magnetic tape files require sequential processing"?

A TYPICAL TAPE APPLICATION   The abbreviated payroll example of the preceding section represents the briefest of introductions to processing on a tape-oriented computer. Let us now consider this application in more detail to gain an insight into some of the many operations involved in a typical data processing operation.

EXAMPLE 12.1

One of the primary data processing applications for a company is its Payroll/Personnel File, which includes one data record for each employee. Each record in the file is 1000 positions long; information stored in the record is classified in one of the following four categories.

1. Permanent data (does not change)
   For example: Social Security number
                birthdate
2. Semipermanent data (does not change during a normal processing cycle but may be modified or changed by special control records)
   For example: employee's home address
                number of dependents
                job-related education and training
                pay rate or salary
3. Cumulative payroll data (ordinarily changes during each payroll processing cycle)
   For example: year-to-date earnings and deductions
                quarter-to-date earnings and deductions
                accumulated sick leave
4. Current payroll data (calculated for each appropriate pay period)
   For example: gross pay
                deductions (taxes, credit union, and so on)
                net pay
                paycheck number

A payroll computation is far more complex than it first appears. For example, some employees are paid a fixed salary once per month; others, twice per month. Still other employees are paid on an hourly basis once per week, which may or may not involve overtime. Furthermore, control and audit files and reports must be prepared, and checks to local, state, and federal agencies as well as credit unions must be printed. Indeed, payroll processing involves an extremely complex system. For our consideration of such a system, many of the system flowchart symbols described in Chapter 2 will be used; additionally, the illustrated two symbols represent data stored on magnetic tape and magnetic disk, respectively.

Magnetic tape

Magnetic disk

The story of the payroll system is told in Figure 12.11. The reader will note that the control file is stored on magnetic disk. This file contains needed information which is used throughout several of the steps of processing. It includes such information as the type of payroll being run (for example, hourly employees payable weekly or salaried employees payable monthly), the type of quarterly or annual reports to be run, and so on. For a detailed description of the cycle, the reader is referred to Figure 12.11 (which extends to pages 386 and 387). The reader should note that many steps have been omitted for the sake of simplicity, such as audit steps, account balancing, preparation of numerous reports, and issuance of checks to various agencies. However, these omissions do not detract from the basic concepts involved.

12.3
MAGNETIC DISK
STORAGE

THE NEED FOR DIRECT ACCESS   As we have learned, the utility of the digital computer is greatly enhanced through magnetic tape. With a tape system, vast quantities of data can be handled easily and with great speed. However, tape is seriously limited for many applications by being a nonaddressable medium. For this reason, all data must be stored sequentially, and processing must be done in that sequence. Let us consider an application where a file consisting of 5000 records involves daily transactions relating to 200 of them. If this

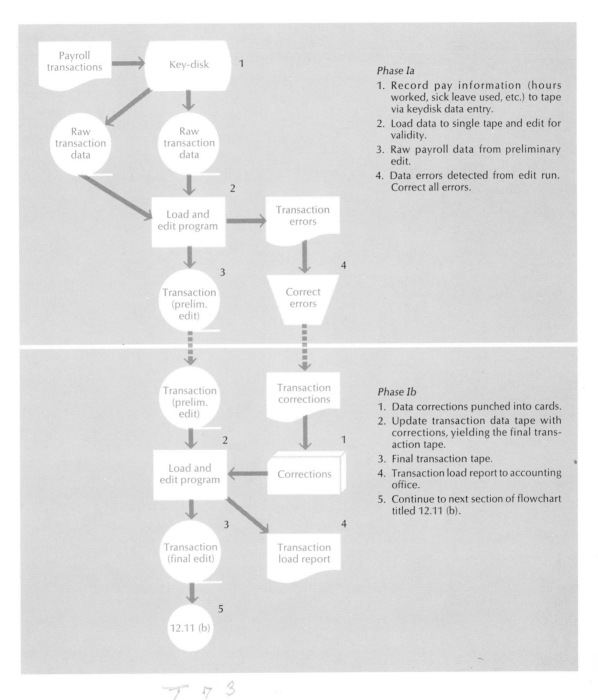

Phase Ia

1. Record pay information (hours worked, sick leave used, etc.) to tape via keydisk data entry.
2. Load data to single tape and edit for validity.
3. Raw payroll data from preliminary edit.
4. Data errors detected from edit run. Correct all errors.

Phase Ib

1. Data corrections punched into cards.
2. Update transaction data tape with corrections, yielding the final transaction tape.
3. Final transaction tape.
4. Transaction load report to accounting office.
5. Continue to next section of flowchart titled 12.11 (b).

Fig. 12.11(a) Processing a Payroll File.

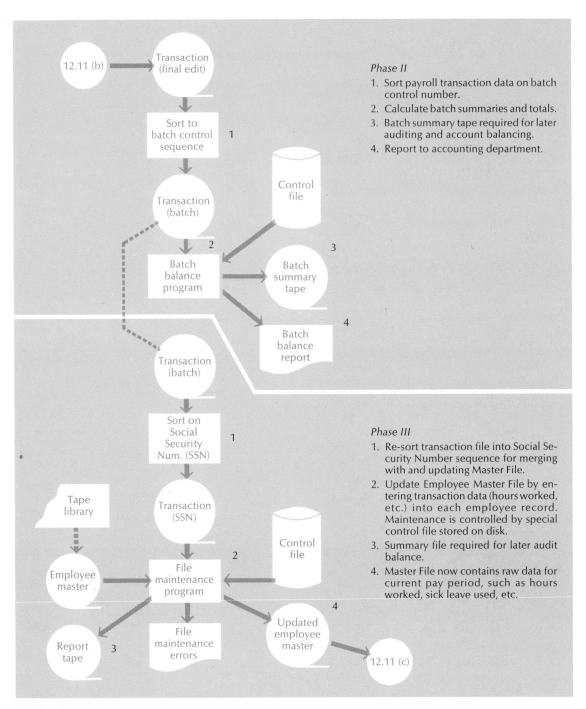

Phase II

1. Sort payroll transaction data on batch control number.
2. Calculate batch summaries and totals.
3. Batch summary tape required for later auditing and account balancing.
4. Report to accounting department.

Phase III

1. Re-sort transaction file into Social Security Number sequence for merging with and updating Master File.
2. Update Employee Master File by entering transaction data (hours worked, etc.) into each employee record. Maintenance is controlled by special control file stored on disk.
3. Summary file required for later audit balance.
4. Master File now contains raw data for current pay period, such as hours worked, sick leave used, etc.

Fig. 12.11(b) Processing a Payroll File (cont.).

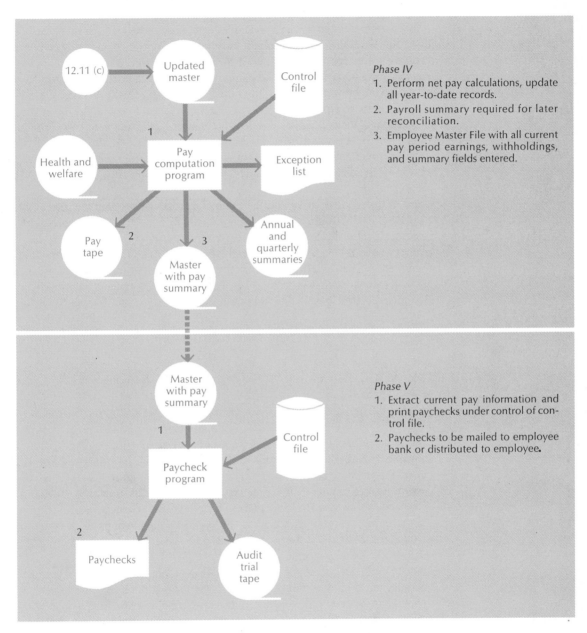

Phase IV
1. Perform net pay calculations, update all year-to-date records.
2. Payroll summary required for later reconciliation.
3. Employee Master File with all current pay period earnings, withholdings, and summary fields entered.

Phase V
1. Extract current pay information and print paychecks under control of control file.
2. Paychecks to be mailed to employee bank or distributed to employee.

Fig. 12.11(c) Processing a Payroll File (cont.).

file must be processed daily, then only 4 percent of the entire file requires updating. However, due to the sequential nature of tape, the entire file of 5000 records must be read and rewritten (on another tape) in order to update the 200. This is clearly an inefficient process. To further complicate matters, in many applications it is simply not possible to accumulate a batch and process it at predefined intervals. For example, in an airline reservation system, a request for a seat on a particular flight must be handled immediately; the customer can hardly be expected to wait until the next batch is processed. This involves *random processing*, in which the computer system is capable of accessing any given record just as quickly as any other. (Obviously, this is not possible with tape since, in an alphabetic sequence, Anderson would be located much more quickly than Vance.) As we learned in Chapter 4, the *magnetic disk* provides *random* or *direct access* capabilities. Magnetic drums and the data cell also provide direct access capability, but these will not be described in this book. However, the direct access principles that we shall study are applicable to these devices.

A magnetic disk drive and the removable disk pack (commonly used with the IBM 360/370) are shown in Figure 12.12. The disk pack consists of a stack of metal disks coated with a magnetic material capable of storing information in much the same way as magnetic tape. When the pack is in operation (mounted on the drive), it rotates continuously at a high speed. The surfaces are read from and written on by a special movable read/write mechanism which is similar in principle to the read/write heads of a magnetic tape drive.

Exercise

12.6 What is the principal difference between batch (sequential) processing and random processing?

THE MAGNETIC DISK CONCEPT   The number of disks used in a particular disk pack and drive depends upon the model of drive. For instance, the unit shown in Figure 12.12(a) involves six disks mounted on a single spindle with ten of the twelve surfaces used for recording data (Figure 12.13). The discussion in this chapter will center on a ten-surface disk unit (the IBM 2316 disk pack). However, the principles are directly applicable to larger-capacity units commonly in use. Although the IBM 3340 unit shown in Figure 12.12(b) involves some slightly different principles than those described in the following sections, the basic concepts still apply.

Although each disk surface is effectively a continuous sheet of magnetic material, the design of the drive is such that the surface is considered to be divided into 200 concentric strips. These strips, commonly referred to as *tracks*, are illustrated in Figure 12.14. Each track can be thought of as a flattened, circular section of magnetic tape, with a capacity of 3625 bytes. (Remember from Chapter 6 that the byte is the standard eight-bit storage unit used in the 360/370.) With 200 tracks per surface and 10 surfaces per pack, we can see that the total storage capacity of one disk pack is approximately 7 million bytes. However, as we shall learn, the actual amount of data which can be stored on a pack is somewhat less because of techniques used in recording it.

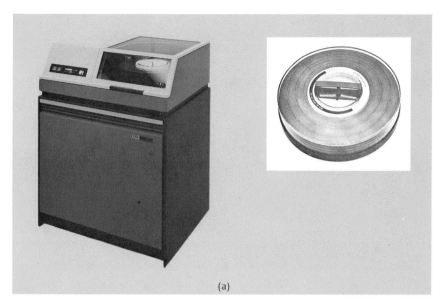

(a)

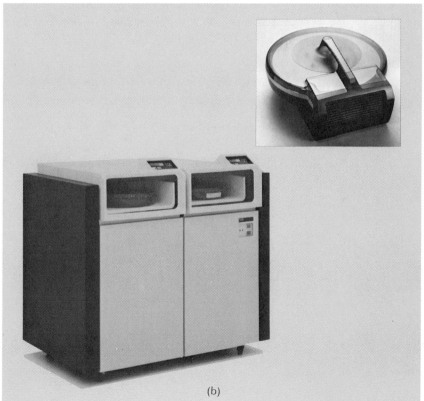

(b)

Fig. 12.12 (a) Magnetic disk pack and drive (Courtesy IBM Corporation); (b) Data module (Courtesy BASF Systems); 3340 drive (Courtesy IBM Corporation)

26,000 bit 16 750 Pru.

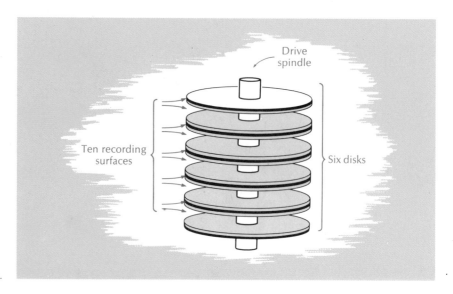

Fig. 12.13 Recording surfaces on a disk pack.

The preceding sections on magnetic tape emphasized that tape is a non-addressable storage medium; that is, data records are stored one after the other with no means for referring to them by location. Let us consider the techniques whereby records on disk are, in fact, addressable. Figure 12.15 is a cutaway schematic of track arrangements on disk pack. We can imagine that for each track on one of the 10 recording surfaces, there are exactly 9 other tracks (on the other surfaces) which have exactly the same diameter. Thus, if we were

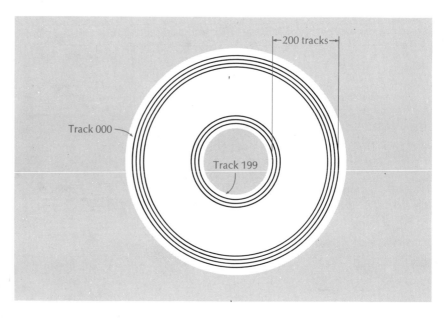

Fig. 12.14 Track layout on a disk surface.

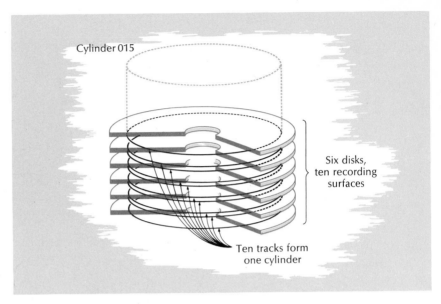

Ten tracks form
one cylinder

Fig. 12.15 The cylinder concept.

to look down on a transparent disk pack, we could consider 10 tracks in a group, one directly above the other. Such a grouping of tracks is commonly referred to as a *cylinder*; since each surface consists of 200 tracks, we can see that the pack consists of 200 concentric cylinders. To transfer data to or from the disk surfaces (which rotate at a speed of 2400 revolutions per minute) some type of mechanism is required. This consists of a group of *access arms* which are capable of moving, in a group, in and out between the recording surfaces of the pack. Figure 12.16 illustrates the access mechanism position in which the read/write heads are positioned over the tracks which make up cylinder 015.

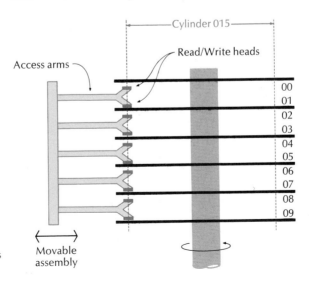

Fig. 12.16 The access mechanism.

Exercise

12.7   How many bytes are in one cylinder of an IBM 2316 disk pack (used on the 2311 disk drive)? How many are in the entire pack?

DISK ADDRESSING   In other words, each of the 10 read/write heads is positioned over one of the 10 tracks comprising a cylinder. In this manner, data from each of the tracks in the cylinder is accessible without moving the mechanism. This provides us with an insight into the nature of disk addressing; that is, cylinders are numbered from 000 through 199, and tracks within each cylinder are numbered from 00 through 09. (Two-digit track addresses are used for compatibility with larger disk packs consisting of twenty surfaces with the track number range 00–19.) Thus, any given track can be addressed by designating the cylinder number and the read/write head number (effectively the track number). For instance, we might have a particular record stored on cylinder 015, track 04.

Unlike core storage, it is not possible to address individual characters or even fields on disks. Information is addressed as records, which may be blocked or unblocked as with magnetic tape. As with tape, the record length may be set at the discretion of the programmer. (However, a record may not exceed the capacity of a track which, for the IBM 2316 pack, is 3625 bytes.) In preparing an application for a disk system, the programmer must decide on the record size and blocking factor which will, in turn determine how many records occupy one track. Figure 12.17 is a schematic of a track in which five 651-byte records are stored. Each record is preceded by a small address record which contains the address of the record following. For example, in Figure 12.17 we see the address 015045 as consisting of the cylinder number, the track number within that cylinder and the record number within the track. Since there are five records per track, they are numbered 1 through 5. It is through the use of these addresses that it is possible to address any desired record on the disk. Note that records are separated by gaps, somewhat analogous to the interblock gap in magnetic tape.

Since the address records and the gaps occupy a portion of the track, it is impossible to store a full 3625 bytes of data on a track when more than one record per track is stored. For instance, in this example, simple arithmetic shows us that five 651-byte records give us only 3255 bytes of data, substantially less than the maximum of 3625. As we might expect, the amount of data decreases with the number of records per track because of the increased number of address records and gaps required. For example, if the record size were 80 bytes (the size of the punched card), then the track capacity would be 25 records for a total data capacity per track of 2000 bytes. As with magnetic tapes, blocking of records increases overall capacity; representative figures are summarized below.

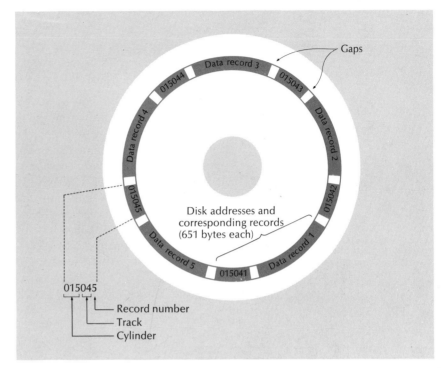

Fig. 12.17 Records on a track.

Record Size (Bytes)	Record/Track	Data (Bytes)
3625	1	3625
651	5	3255
80	25	2000
800*	4	3200

*80-byte records with blocking factor of 10.

THE DATA MODULE   Figure 12.12(b) shows the IBM 3340 disk drive and the corresponding *data module* which is rapidly replacing many conventional disk drives. The data module differs from the conventional disk packs in that the disk surfaces and the access mechanisms are sealed within the module container itself. Furthermore, *two* read/write heads for each recording surface are mounted on each access arm. One of them reads the inner portion of the surface and the other reads the outer portion, with a resulting increase in speed for overall data handling. Two models are available, one with three recording surfaces (capacity of 35 million bytes) and the other with six recording surfaces (capacity of 70 million bytes).

Exercise

12.8 What does the disk address 151093 tell you about the placement of a data record?

TIMING   In determining the amount of time required to access a record from disk storage, three factors must be considered: *access mechanism motion*, *rotational delay*, and *data transfer*. The time required to position the access mechanism to the desired cylinder is termed the *access motion time*. Obviously, if the read/write heads are already positioned over the desired track, this time is 0. As we might expect, the access motion time depends on how far the mechanism must be moved. For instance, if the mechanism is at cylinder 020 and it must be moved to cylinder 080, then it will travel 60 cylinders. Typical access motion times are shown below.

Number of Cylinders Traveled	Time (msec)
1	25
60	71
200	135

Since the pack is rotating at 2400 revolutions per minute, any given position on the surfaces passes the read/write heads every 25 milliseconds (0.025 second). If, after positioning the access mechanism over the desired track, the selected record has just passed, then the *rotational delay* will be a full revolution or 25 milliseconds. If, on the other hand, the desired record has just come under the read/write head, the rotational delay is 0. For timing calculations, an average of $12\frac{1}{2}$ or 13 milliseconds is used.

The *data transfer* time is the time required to transfer data between the disk unit and core storage. For a given disk drive, this is a function of the record size. For instance, the data transfer rate of the IBM 2311 is 156,000 bytes per second. The data transfer times for example record sizes are as follows:

Record Size (Bytes)	Data Transfer Time (msec)
3625	23
651	4
80	0.5

READING AND WRITING ON DISK   For a programming application, the time required to read a record from a disk can be determined by simply adding the access mechanism time, the rotational delay (an average of 12.5 milliseconds is commonly used) and the data transfer time. From this, the total time to read an entire file can easily be determined.

As the reader might expect, writing a disk record involves basically the same considerations as reading. However, in the interest of insuring accuracy, the newly written record is usually read back and compared to the original information in storage for verification. The sequence of steps in writing a record is as follows:

1. Assemble the record in core storage.
2. Write the record from storage onto disk.
3. After one complete disk rotation, read the record and compare it to the original version in storage.
4. If there are no discrepancies, then continue processing; if there are any errors, then institute error recovery procedures.

In performing timing calculations when writing, the normal time components for reading must be increased by the additional rotational delay and data transfer time for the *read-back check* operation. This amounts to approximately the time required for one complete rotation, or about 25 milliseconds. The following example illustrates timing calculations.

EXAMPLE 12.2

How much time is required to read, update, and rewrite an Employee Record (assuming the updating operations themselves require a negligible amount of time)? Using the following conditions:

Record size: 800 bytes
Access mechanism motion: 50 cylinders (average)
                         70 milliseconds

Read

Access mechanism motion	70 ms	
Rotational delay	13	
Data transfer	5	
		88 ms

Write

Access mechanism motion	0	
Rotational delay and		
data transfer	25	
		25 ms

Read-Back Check

Access mechanism motion	0	
Rotational delay and data transfer	25	
		25 ms
Total time required per record		138 ms

This total time of 138 milliseconds (slightly more than $\frac{1}{10}$ second) might at first appear insignificant. However, if an entire file consisting of 8000 records were to be updated in this manner, the total time required would be approximately 18 minutes. Through careful design of the file, it might be possible to reduce this time to only a few minutes (depending upon the application itself); similarly, through thoughtless file design, the time could be doubled or worse. The subject of file organization is the next topic to be covered.

Exercises

12.9   What is meant by access motion time, rotational delay, and data transfer time?

12.10   Determine the time required to (a) read a record, and (b) write a record, under the following conditions. (Consider the two operations independent of each other.)

Record size: 651 bytes
Access mechanism motion: 50 cylinders

12.4
BASIC PRINCIPLES OF FILE ORGANIZATION

As we have learned, tape files must be organized and processed sequentially due to the nonaddressability of magnetic tape. With the addressing and direct access characteristics of the magnetic disk, considerably more latitude is introduced. In selecting an efficient method of organization, two primary factors (familiar from our unit record studies) must be considered: volatility and activity.

Volatility refers to the frequency with which records are added to and deleted from the file. A static file is one which has a low percentage of additions and deletions; a volatile file is one with a high rate of additions and deletions. *Activity* is an indication of the percentage of records processed during a run. A payroll application in which virtually all employee records are processed in a given run would be a very high-activity file. An airline reservation system where each record is processed as it is received would be a low-activity file since only one record is processed on each run. However, the actual number of transactions would be large because of the frequency of use of the file.

A FILE ILLUSTRATION—SEQUENTIAL ORGANIZATION   To illustrate features of different methods for organizing direct access files, let us assume that we have the following situation.

EXAMPLE 12.3

Equipment Inventory File
Record size: 1000 bytes.

File size: Nine records identified by part identification numbers*
Part identification numbers: 122, 204, 269,
                                          320, 359, 366
                                          441, 523, 622
Record per track: 3
Disk storage allocated: As many tracks as required on cylinder 026.

With these conditions, we can see that the nine records would require three
2311 tracks (three records per track). Thus, we shall allocate tracks 00, 01,
and 02 of cylinder 026. Recalling the disk-addressing techniques illustrated
in Figure 12.17 (cylinder number, track number, and record number), we
could store the records as follows:

Record	Disk Address
122	026001
204	026002
269	026003
320	026011
359	026012
366	026013
441	026021
523	026022
622	026023

Sequential processing of this file would be carried out by processing the
sorted Inventory Transaction Records against the corresponding Master Records. This operation is much the same as a corresponding tape updating run.
In contrast to tape, the disk records can be processed *in-place*. Because of the
addressability of disk, processing of a record would proceed as follows:

1. Read a Master Record from disk into storage.
2. Read corresponding Transaction cards and update the Master Record.
3. Write the updated Master Record onto disk *over the old* Master Record.

In contrast to tape, it is *not* necessary to write the entire file onto a new tape.
This update in-place characteristic of the disk is an important feature of disk
processing.

Since the records are stored in sequence, the amount of access mechanism
movement would be minimized even for a very large file occupying many
cylinders. However, random processing would be slow, because file searching
procedures would be required. That is, to locate a selected record, it would

---

*This file is limited to nine records strictly for purposes of illustration; in practice, such
a file could easily consist of several thousand or more records.

be necessary to read and check each record, beginning with the first one, until the desired record is found. For instance, if this example file consisted of 6000 records (which would occupy a full 2311 pack), and the desired record happened to be the last one in the file, a complete search would require almost $3\frac{1}{2}$ minutes. This is a substantial amount of time for a busy system.

RANDOM ORGANIZATION   Each record within the file is identifiable by its part identification number, which is commonly referred to as the *record key* or simply *key*. Thus, the identifying key for records of the Customer Master-Balance File in Chapter 2 would be customer number, and the key for records in an Employee Master File might be the employee's Social Security number. As we know, a sequential file is arranged in sequence on the identifying key. In contrast, a random file is arranged through use of some type of relationship between the record key and the disk address of that record. Usually this means that records within the file are distributed nonsequentially. To illustrate random organization, we will consider further the abbreviated nine-record file of Example 12.3

The following technique, to be used for determining disk addresses, has been contrived for purposes of illustration and should not be construed as a standard technique. Let us assume that we intend to allocate the four tracks 00, 01, 02, and 03 for this file (in contrast to the three required for sequential organization). Furthermore, let us assume that, through statistical studies, we have found the following relationship between the record key and the disk address.

$$\frac{\text{Record key}}{4} \rightarrow \text{quotient \& remainder}$$

Track number = remainder (values of 0, 1, 2, or 3)

$$\frac{\text{Record key}}{3} \rightarrow \text{quotient \& remainder}$$

Record number = remainder + 1 (values of 1, 2, or 3)

For example, consider record 122:

for track number $\frac{122}{4}$ = 30; remainder of 2
for record number $\frac{122}{3}$ = 40; remainder of 2
Track number = 2
Record number = 2 + 1 = 3

therefore,

Disk address = 026023

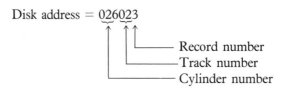

Similar calculations for each of the nine record keys produce the following disk address assignments:

Disk Address	Record
026001	204
026002	(no record)
026003	320
026011	441
026012	(no record)
026013	269
026021	366
026022	622
026023	122
026031	(no record)
026032	523
026033	359

The reader will note that this randomizing technique does not fully utilize the disk area provided. That is, disk locations 026002, 026012, and 026031 do not contain records. This is a problem common to randomizing techniques, and one with which the system designer must live. Usually the unused space is kept below 20 percent of the allocated disk area. Another problem which must be considered is the possibility of two record keys which produce the same address. For example, if the file included a tenth record numbered 680, the computed disk address would be 026003, which is already assigned to record 320. Two or more records that yield the same address are referred to as *synonyms* and are usually stored in a specially reserved *overflow* section of the file. In any randomizing technique, it is important to minimize the number of *overflow records* (synonyms) because of the increased time required to find them. Obviously, the occurrence of synonyms complicates the programming.

Direct inquiry processing can be readily handled with a random file as the following sequence illustrates.

1. The key of the desired record is entered into the computer.
2. The program, using a predefined randomizing technique, calculates the disk address.
3. The program directs the disk drive to read the required record. No searching is necessary since the address is known.

Again using an example file of 6000 records, the maximum time required to access a given record would be approximately 170 milliseconds.

In most random access applications, it is occasionally necessary to perform certain processing runs sequentially. For instance, with an inventory system which uses direct inquiry terminals, it might be necessary to run periodic reports in a part identification number sequence for the entire file. For large files, the time required for access arm motion can be substantial. For instance, if the first three records are arranged as shown in Figure 12.18, the access mechanism motion would be across the entire 200 cylinders in moving from record 1 to record 2 and then back across 100 cylinders from record 2 to record 3.

Exercises

12.11 What is meant by "random processing?"

12.12 What is the principal problem in performing random processing on a sequentially ordered file?

12.13 What is the principal problem in performing sequential processing on a randomly ordered file?

INDEXING A FILE   The advantages of a sequentially ordered file for sequential processing and of a randomly ordered file for direct processing can be combined through a technique called *indexing*. This effectively consists of maintaining the file sequentially but keeping a directory or an *index* to the file. For

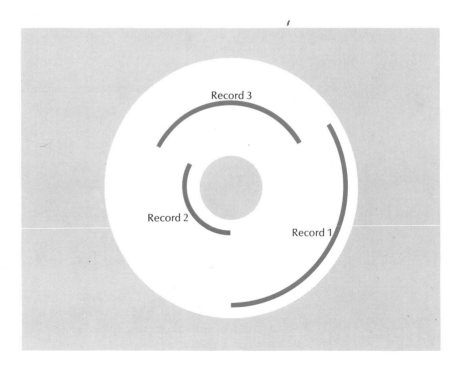

Fig. 12.18   Records on a disk.

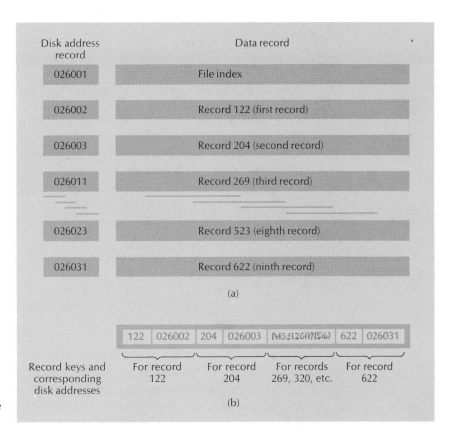

Disk address record	Data record
026001	File index
026002	Record 122 (first record)
026003	Record 204 (second record)
026011	Record 269 (third record)
026023	Record 523 (eighth record)
026031	Record 622 (ninth record)

(a)

| 122 | 026002 | 204 | 026003 | (M53120i171SiL) | 622 | 026031 |

Record keys and corresponding disk addresses — For record 122 — For record 204 — For records 269, 320, etc. — For record 622

(b)

Fig. 12.19 (a) A data file with an index; (b) the file index record.

instance, the file of Example 12.3 would be stored sequentially as illustrated in Figure 12.19(a). Note that the first record of the file consists of an index to the file. As illustrated in 12.19(b), this record contains the record key and the corresponding disk address for each record in the file. Random processing of the file is accomplished as follows:

1. The key of the desired record is entered into the computer.
2. The file index record is read into core storage from the disk.
3. The program searches the index for the desired key and corresponding disk address.
4. The program directs the disk drive to read the required record. No searching is necessary since the address is now known.

Sequential processing of the file can obviously be accomplished with all the simplicity of the purely sequential file. Thus we can see that a sequentially organized file with an index (commonly referred to as an *indexed sequential file*) can offer the advantages of both the sequential and the random files.

IBM SYSTEM/360 AND 370 FILE ORGANIZATION   The IBM System/360 and 370 sequential, random, and indexed sequential methods of file organization are similar in basic principle to the three types of file organization described in the preceding chapters. As we might expect, the actual implementation of these techniques into a software system involves many details which we have not considered. For instance, the addition of records to an indexed sequential or a random file after the file has been built involves rather complex techniques. Fortunately, most of the work in file management is taken care of by the 360/370 Input/Output Control System (IOCS) software which is part of the software furnished with the complete 360/370 software package. Chapter 13 includes a brief description of IOCS.

Exercise

12.14   What is an indexed sequential file?

12.5 DATABASE SYSTEMS

HANDLING MULTIPLE FILES   What is a database? We might anticipate from the word that the Employee Master Payroll File used to illustrate sequential processing in Section 12.2 represents a database. It clearly serves as the organized collection of all data relative to a particular application and could thus be considered as the data base from which payroll processing is performed. However, the term *database* is now used in a much broader and more comprehensive sense. To appreciate this, let us contrast a "conventional" data processing system, consisting of one or more separate files for each application, with a database system in which a single large collection of data serves all applications. For the sake of simplicity, the following example is greatly simplified and is limited to the processing of three files. However, it serves to illustrate the concepts at hand with a minimum of confusion.

EXAMPLE 12.4

Prime Research Corporation carries on a number of research projects at its main office and several branch sites. The data processing department for Prime has developed several systems for performing normal accounting and report generation functions. Among the many files in the system are the following.

1. Department File—sample record contents:
   a. Department description and function
   b. Budget information
   c. Projects in progress
   d. Names of employees in the department
2. Project File—sample record contents:
   a. Project description
   b. Financial data

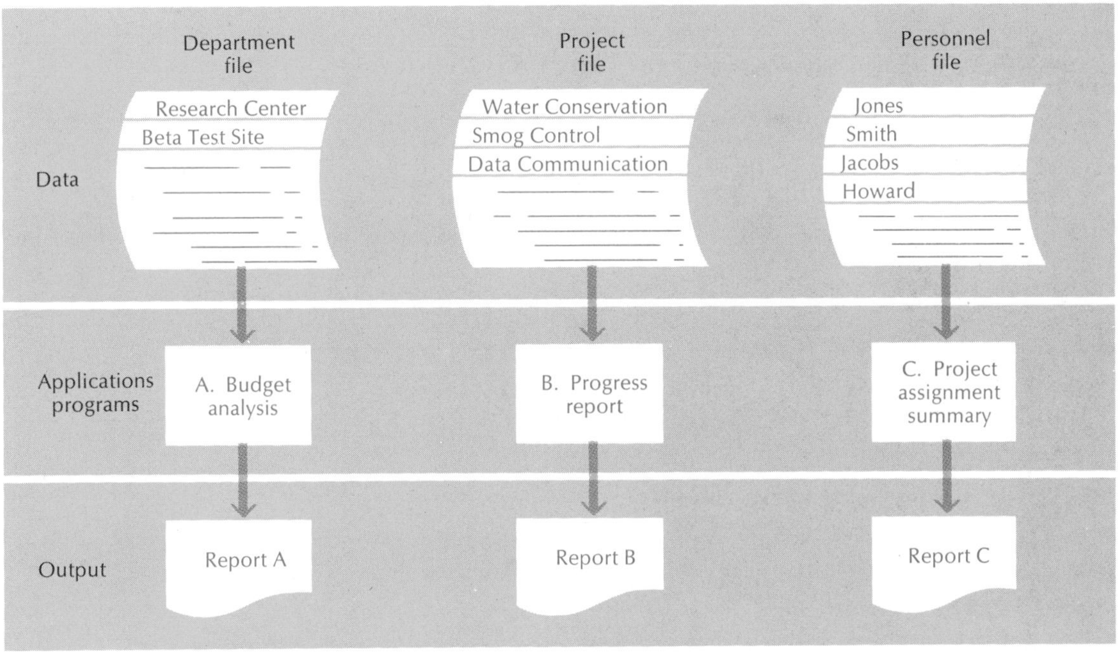

Fig. 12.20 Conventional processing.

c. Names of departments participating
d. Personnel assigned to the project

3. Personnel File—sample record contents:
   a. Personnel and professional data
   b. Payroll information
   c. Department to which assigned
   d. Project(s) to which assigned

Associated with each of these three files is a set of programs for preparing required reports as illustrated in Figure 12.20.* Here we see that each file is processed virtually independently of the other files and each will include its own set of processing programs (such as program C in Figure 12.20) for processing that file. On the other hand, if we reread the example statement carefully, we will see that each file includes some information contained in other files. For instance, each record of the Department File includes the names of all employees assigned to that department. This is illustrated in Figure 12.21.

This duplication, although undesirable, is usually necessary for most processing applications. The amount of duplication depends upon the application. For instance, a project progress report might require the names of all employees

*Here the symbol 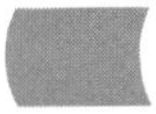 is used to represent an online file. These may represent files on individual tape units; or one or more files might be on a single disk drive.

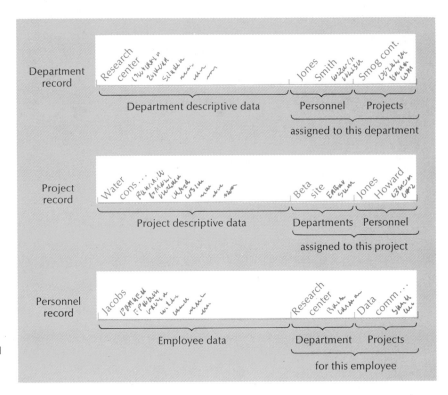

Fig. 12.21 Typical record contents with cross-referencing fields.

working on each project (which would be stored in the Project File) but would probably not require employee payroll information (which would not be stored in the Project File).

This method of file processing was used on virtually all early computers and, indeed, is still commonly used today. However, for most modern processing needs, this type of system has a number of shortcomings, two of which are:

1. Redundancy of data between files represents wasted storage, wasted processing time in updating all copies, and introduces the problem of inconsistency. If the same "fact" is stored in several files, wasted storage will obviously result (this could be critical in a disk system). Furthermore, if that "fact" changes (for example, a woman marries and changes her last name), then all of the files containing that fact must be updated. The latter point leads to the problem of inconsistency. If one of the files is inadvertently not updated correctly, then the same entries in the different files will be different (inconsistent).

2. The data stored in the various files cannot easily be shared. This is perhaps the key issue; data in one system tends to be isolated from data

in other systems. Thus, processing which requires data from both systems can be clumsy and in many cases extremely inefficient. For instance, extraction of the required data from multiple files might require that special programs be written specifically for this task, as illustrated in Figure 12.22. Although this may appear to be a simple procedure, it is often quite impractical even though the final output might be important.

THE CONCEPT OF A DATABASE   Now let us consider once again the question, "What is a *database*?" by looking at the characteristics of a database.

- It is a single collection of all data used by a data processing installation (for example, a combination of all the files used by Prime Research).
- It is organized and structured in other than ordinary multiple file form.
- Its organization permits access to any or all data quantities by all applications with equal ease.
- Its organization allows duplication to be minimized, if not eliminated entirely.

To achieve these characteristics, it is necessary to use some type of random access storage device, such as magnetic disk or drum. These provide the necessary capabilities for random addressing (described in Section 12.4) required by a database system. The subject of database theory and the many different techniques is far beyond the scope of this book. To illustrate the elementary notions of how a database works, let us consider a grossly simplified version of a database for Prime Research Corporation. In Figure 12.23, the original three files are collected in a single large online "file" or database. Although the original files retain much of their identity, they are now interrelated by system pointers

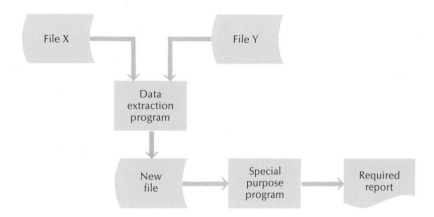

Fig. 12.22 Manipulating multiple files.

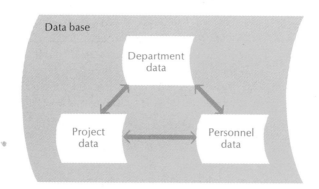

Fig. 12.23 Database concept of related files.

which allow easy processing of data within two or more of the files. Conceptually, the easiest way of achieving these pointers is by the record addressing capabilities which random access storage provide the programmer. For instance, the Water Conservation Record in the Project File shown in Figure 12.24 includes all of the necessary information on that project. It also includes two address areas: first contains the disk address of each department record relating to this project, and the second contains the disk record address for each employee working on the project. With this data organization, information in the Department or Personnel files is readily available when processing the Project File. For instance, preparation of a report involving project expenditures and the salaries of assigned employees can easily be prepared.

Needless to say, this is a very simplified representation of a database. Obviously, this simplified version can quickly become complex merely by adding three or four more files to the base, each with a complete set of pointers to each of the others. In general, the maintenance and processing of database systems is an entire topic within itself.

Exercise

12.15   This exercise refers to the example Project Records in Figures 12.21 and 12.24. In serving as a pointer to relate two files, how does the employee name information in Figure 12.21 differ conceptually from the storage address information in Figure 12.24?

DATABASE MANAGEMENT   It should be apparent that a full-scale integrated file system structure can be extremely large and complex. So much so, in fact, that database systems and associated software are normally supplied by the computer manufacturer or by an independent software company. These are often referred to as *database management systems* and consist of three basic components.

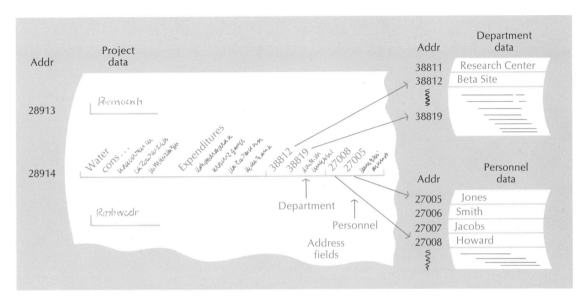

Fig. 12.24 Pointers in a
database system.

1. The database itself (as described in the preceding section).
2. A data description language which defines the structure and format of data in the database, the relationship among units of data, and the methods used to access the data.
3. A data manipulation language, which is effectively the database system "programming language." It provides the capability to retrieve information and to add, delete, and modify data.

A simplified schematic representation of these components is shown in Figure 12.25.

Database management systems, used in conjunction with terminals, provide a powerful tool. The business manager or school administrator can make decisions based on a comprehensive summary of all the data available. However, the very device which broadens the use of database systems also contributes a serious problem: security and privacy. That is, if a comprehensive database is accessible by terminal, what is to prevent unauthorized individuals from gaining access to "sensitive" or private information? Because of this, extensive security techniques have evolved to protect files, including use of multiple secret passwords, limiting a given user to only that portion of the database needed for the given application, and so on. In spite of these and other problems, it is obvious that extensive use of database systems is the wave of the future.

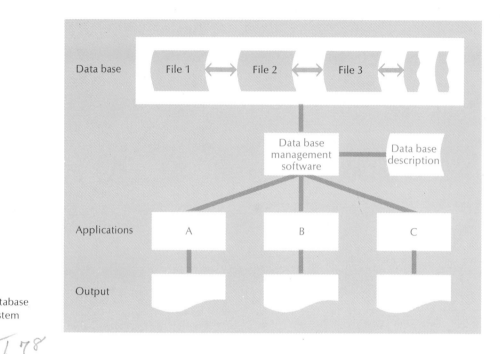

Fig. 12.25 A database management system representation.

12.6
EVALUATION OF
TAPE AND DISK

DISK—VERSATILITY The direct access characteristics of the magnetic disk allow for either sequential or random processing. With disk, it is practical to process transactions as they occur rather than waiting to accumulate a batch. A record may be read, updated, and rewritten on the disk without disturbing the remainder of the file. (With tape, the entire file must be read, the selected records updated, and a new file written.)

TAPE—COST As we can see in referring to Figure 12.26, the capacities of both disk and tape have increased significantly over a relatively short period of time. To the delight of users, unit cost of storing data has correspondingly decreased at a rapid rate. We can see that both the capacity and cost for storage of data are roughly equal for the newer tape and disk drives. However, if huge quantities of data are to be stored offline, then the bottom line becomes significant —that is, the cost of the storage mediums themselves. We can see that the cost of an IBM 3340 data module is approximately 10 times that of a reel of tape. For certain types of applications, large quantities of information must be retained. For example, maintaining records for a large insurance company might involve a thousand or more reels of tape. The cost of disk packs would be too high to consider using a disk system.

As the experienced systems planner knows, certain applications obviously require direct access devices such as disk, whereas others are obvious tape

	Model Drive					
	IBM 1311 Disk	IBM 2314 Disk	IBM 3330 Disk	IBM 3340 Disk	IBM 3420 Model 7 Tape	IBM 3420 Model 8 Tape
Year introduced	1964	1967	1970	1973	1970	1973
*Approx. monthly rental	$1900	$3300	$5000	$2600	$3000	$4300
*Storage capacity (millions of bytes)	9	108	400	280	180	720
Approx. cost per million bytes	$210	$31	$13	$9	$17	$6
Cost of pack (or tape)	$300	$525	$1000	$2200	$25	$25

*Figures based on four drives and required controller.

Fig. 12.26 Disk and tape
unit comparison.

system applications. Still others require a degree of judgment and common sense in making the determination.

Answers to Preceding Exercises

12.1 In practice, data on tapes is separated by gaps (discussed in the section following Exercise 12.1). However, assuming no gaps, but simply a continuous string of data, would give the following capacity:

$$\frac{2400 \times 12 \times 1600}{80} = 576,000 \text{ cards}$$

12.2 70,000 and 140,000 frames per second, respectively.

12.3 Each record requires one gap.

$$\text{Record} + \text{gap} = \frac{80}{556} + 0.75 = 0.144 + 0.75$$
$$\simeq 0.9 \text{ inch}$$

$$\text{Record} \qquad \frac{0.144}{0.9} \simeq \frac{1}{6}$$

$$\text{Gap} \qquad \frac{0.75}{0.9} = \frac{5}{6}$$

12.4 $10 \text{ records} + \text{gap} = \frac{80}{556} \times 10 + 0.75$
$$= 1.44 + 0.75$$
$$\simeq 2.2$$

$$\text{Record} \qquad \frac{1.44}{2.2} \simeq \frac{2}{3}$$

$$\text{Gap} \qquad \frac{0.75}{2.2} \simeq \frac{1}{3}$$

12.5 Processing magnetic tape involves reading from one end of the tape to the other; it is impossible to read a record from the center of a tape without reading and checking all records preceding it. Thus, the only practical means to process data on tape is to store it in some type of sequence, then process it from the first record through the last (sequentially).

12.6 In batch (sequential) processing, transactions are accumulated and run in batches periodically; in random processing, transactions are run as they occur (in random sequence). Batch and random processing are common to tape and disk systems, respectively.

12.7 Cylinder capacity: 36,250 bytes; disk capacity: 7,250,000 bytes.

12.8 The record is the third record on track 09 of cylinder 151.

12.9 *Access motion time*—the time required for the read/write heads to be moved and positioned over the desired track.
      Rotational delay—the time required in waiting for the disk to rotate into position so that the desired record is under the read/write head.
      Data transfer time—the time required to transfer the data between disk and storage.

12.10 a. Reading

Access mechanism time	70 ms
Rotational delay	13
Data transfer	4
Total	87 ms

    b. Writing

Access mechanism time	70 ms
Rotational delay	13
Data transfer	4
Read-back check	25
Total	112 ms

12.11 Random processing is the processing of transactions on demand, as opposed to collecting them in batches and running them periodically.

12.12 The principal problem in performing random processing on a sequentially ordered file is that the file must be searched by reading and inspecting each record until the desired record is found. For a large file, the time required can be prohibitive.

12.13 The principal problem in performing sequential processing on a randomly ordered file is that considerable access mechanism motion may be required for a large file due to the random locations of the records. Overall processing can be slowed significantly for a large file.

12.14 An indexed sequential file is a sequentially ordered file which may be processed as a sequential file or as a random file by use of an index. The index is simply a table containing each record key and the corresponding disk address for that record.

12.15 The list of employee names in the Project Record of Figure 12.21 merely represents a duplicated entry from the Personnel File. It does *not* serve as a pointer into the Personnel File in order to integrate it with the Project File. On the other hand, the list of disk addresses in the Project Record is not the employee information but a set of addresses identifying where to find the entire record for each employee associated with the particular project.

Additional Exercises

12.16 Matching. Match each item 1–8 with the corresponding description a–h.

    1. random file   2. density
    3. frame   4. overflow record
    5. blocking   6. database
    7. magnetic tape   8. data rate

    a. Improves efficiency of data storage on disk or tape.
    b. Indicative of tape capacity.
    c. The speed with which information can be read from disk or tape.
    d. Has the capacity for storing one character.
    e. Produced as a result of an address synonym.

    f. A sequential processing medium.
    g. Poorly suited to sequential processing.
    h. Requires use of random access storage devices.

12.17 True-False. Determine whether each of the following is true or false.

    a. Magnetic tape used with present computers is very much like the tape used in ordinary home tape recorders.
    b. Generally speaking, the data rate depends on the tape density and the tape speed; the lower the density and the higher the speed, the higher will be the data rate.

c. A blocking factor of 12 means that 12 consecutive blocks of tape are required for each data record.

d. One serious disadvantage of tape for many types of applications is that records on a tape must be processed sequentially.

e. Records stored on magnetic tape are classified as nonaddressable, whereas records on magnetic disk are addressable.

f. For practical use, the effective storage capacity of a disk is usually reduced by special address records and by gaps.

g. Writing a disk file involves the same factors from the point of view of timing as reading a file; thus, the time required to write a file will always be the same as the time required to read it.

h. Sequential processing techniques for processing a sequential disk file are identical to those for processing a tape file.

i. One disadvantage of random file organization is that extra storage is required, since most randomizing techniques are not capable of utilizing 100 percent of the disk area provided.

j. Database management systems require that the computer be equipped with either magnetic tape or disk.

12.18 Multiple Choice. Determine which answer best completes or answers each of the following statements.

a. One character of information is stored on magnetic tape in a single (1) column, (2) frame, (3) storage position, (4) unit.

b. The magnetic tape channel is equivalent to the punched card (1) row, (2) column, (3) field, (4) track.

c. The data rate of a tape drive is dependent upon the (1) tape speed, (2) tape width, (3) tape density, (4) both 1 and 3, (5) none of the preceding.

d. Perhaps the principal characteristic of magnetic tape relates to its (1) sequential processing nature, (2) use of the BCD code, (3) magnetic properties, (4) low price.

e. When only a few records of a tape file are to be updated, (1) only those records to be processed are read and updated, (2) the job is usually done with cards, (3) the entire file must be read and rewritten on a new tape, (4) it is not possible to update only a few records of a file.

f. Random processing (1) is accumulating transactions for a predetermined amount of time, then processing them without sorting, (2) is impractical with magnetic disk systems, (3) can be performed with disk files but not with tape files, (4) is practical only with very large files.

g. The principal advantage of magnetic disk over tape is its (1) versatility, (2) much higher data transfer rate, (3) convenience for sequential processing, (4) all of the preceding.

h. For timing calculations, the time required to read a record is generally different than that for writing a record because (1) each record that is read must be reread to insure accuracy, (2) the reading process is simply slower than the writing process, (3) the writing process is simply slower than the reading process, (4) each record that is written is commonly reread to insure accuracy.

i. The concept of in-place processing refers to (1) the ability to process a record on disk by rewriting the updated record over the original record, (2) the ability, through the use of several tape drives, to process a tape file completely without mounting new tapes, (3) the processing of a Master-Detail File in one operation, (4) none of the preceding.

j. A database management system requires (1) all data to be combined into a single large file, (2) both tape and disk units, (3) a very large computer, (4) both 1 and 3, (5) none of the preceding.

12.19 Other Problems.

a. A data file has the following characteristics:

Record size: 400 bytes
File size: 40,000 records

This file is to be stored on magnetic tape using the IBM 3420 Model 3 tape drive. In addition to the characteristics summarized in Figure 12.7, the 3420 has an interblock gap of 0.6 inch and a start/stop time of 0.008 second. (The start/stop time is the time required to set the tape in motion from an interblock gap before reading can begin, plus the time required to stop the tape at the next gap after the block has been read.)

Answer the following questions for blocking factors of 1, 10, and 100.

(1) How many bytes will each block consist of? (This will correspond to the number of storage bytes required to read a block.)

(2) How many feet of tape are required to store the file?

(3) How many minutes will be required to read the entire file?

5. In Exercise 12.19(a), note that the amount of tape required and the reading time decrease with increased block size. Then why not increase the block size to 1000 or more? Discuss factors which you feel would determine the block size for a given application.

6. The IBM 3340 disk system has a capacity of 8368 bytes per track if the data on the track consists of one full record (block). As we have learned, the effective data capacity is reduced with an increasing number of records per track. Thus, by using a carefully planned blocking factor, the disk capacity can be most efficiently

used. The following table summarizes the number of blocks that can be stored on one track as a function of the block size.

Blocks/Track	Maximum Bytes/Block	Blocks/Track	Maximum Bytes/Block
1	8,368	10	686
2	4,100	11	608
3	2,678	12	544
4	1,966	13	489
5	1,540	14	442
6	1,255	15	402
7	1,052	16	366
8	899	17	335
9	781	18	307

For instance, using unblocked records of 350 bytes, it would be possible to store 16 blocks (records) per track (see the corresponding shaded portion of the table). However, if the records were blocked 2 per block (700 bytes/block), it would be possible to store 9 blocks, or 18 records, per track (as shown in the corresponding shaded portion of the table).

Using the table, compile another table for the number of 500 byte records that may be stored on one track, using various blocking factors ranging from one to the maximum allowable. Repeat this process using a record size of 300 bytes but assume that the largest allowable block size is 2500 bytes.

1. Bits = $10 \times 400 = 4000$

2. Block length = $\frac{4000}{1600} = 2.5$ rec.

   $\frac{.6\ \text{in each}}{3.1\ \text{per record}}$

   $\frac{40,000 \times 3 in}{12} = 1033.33\ ft.$

3. $\frac{400 \times 40,000}{120000} = 133.3\ \text{sec to read total record}$

   copy $4000 \times .008\ \frac{32\ \text{sec}}{115.9} \div 60 = 2.75\ \text{min. or 2 min. 45 sec.}$

Chapter

13

System
Software

THE NEED FOR OPERATING SYSTEMS   First-generation and many second-generation computers required considerable attention from the operator. That is, in running a series of jobs, the operator would ready the computer, load one job (deck of cards constituting the program of instructions), and start the computer executing the program. If error conditions occurred which stopped the program, the machine would frequently remain idle while the operator investigated the problem. Furthermore, after the program was completed, the computer would often be idle during preparation for the next job. Overall, the machine would be waiting for operator action a significant portion of the time. With the vastly improved computing speeds and capabilities of newer computers, and the increased demand for computer use, this primitive type of manual control became totally impractical. Special supervisory types of programs quickly came into being for the purpose of providing automatic or semiautomatic control over many of the machine functions. These programs improved computer utilization and relieved the operator of many mundane activities. We now know these types of systems as *operating systems*. In a nutshell, an operating system is a set of programs, resident in the computer system, designed to maximize the amount of work the computer system can do.

High computing speed, large storage capacities, and sophisticated input/output capabilities are three of the many hardware features of present-day computers, including the IBM 360 and 370. However, to most users, programming systems or *software* (including diverse languages and operating systems) supplied by the manufacturer are just as important. For, in general, these systems relieve the user of extensive, detailed programming and operational responsibilities, allowing for much more efficient utilization of the computer. Since third-generation computers were designed specifically to work with operating systems, their machine capabilities are used much more efficiently than those of earlier computer systems.

To gain an insight to the capabilities of operating systems, let us consider a sequence of three jobs which the operator of a card-oriented computer must perform to begin the morning's work.

Job 1:   Run a master-detail job named "UPDATE"; both the program and master deck are punched in cards and stored in a card filing cabinet. The output is an updated Master and a printed report.

Job 2:   Translate a Cobol program into machine language, yielding a machine language program and a computer listing of the program. (This operation, termed *compiling*, is described extensively in Chapter 7.) Run the machine language program using special test data for a test run; the output is the printed test result.

Job 3:   Translate a Fortran program into machine language. The output is to be a computer listing and the machine language program punched into cards for later use.

This sequence of operations is illustrated in Figure 13.1. In Job 1 [Figure 13.1(a)], the operator must obtain the UPDATE program and the master deck from the card file, then sort and merge the master and transaction decks in preparing for the runs. Next he/she readies the computer, runs the job, and, upon completion, returns the updated Master (and the program) to the file cabinet. In progressing to Job 2, the computer would likely be idle for a few minutes. As we see in Figure 13.1(b), Job 2 consists of two steps. First, the operator must use the special language translator program to convert the program from the Cobol language to machine language (see Chapter 7). Then he/she must prepare the machine language program (output of the translation phase) together with the data set for the test run, which constitutes step 2. Between steps 1 and 2 there will again be a period of a few minutes when the computer will be idle. Upon completing Job 2, the operator will progress to Job 3, involving another translation and considerable card handling.

Of prime significance here is the inefficiency of the overall operation. Because of the large number of tasks required of the operator, we might term this a "stop-and-go" environment, in which the computer does a considerable amount of waiting. Although we might not think that a few minutes of idle computer time here and there is overly significant, consider an installation which processes 30 jobs per eight-hour day (this is *not* a large number). If there is an average three-minute computer idle period between each job, the computer will be idle for approximately one and a half hours per eight-hour shift. Viewed in this light, we are speaking of a significant amount of time. One of the objectives of an operating system is to utilize the computer more efficiently and to minimize such lost time.

USING AN OPERATING SYSTEM   With the extensive use of magnetic tape, and especially of direct access devices such as magnetic disk, the utilization of operating systems has become commonplace. The key to an operating system is the *Supervisor* program (sometimes called a *Monitor* or an *Executive program*). The Supervisor remains in storage at all times and maintains control, directly or indirectly, while the computer is in use (see Figure 13.2). In addition, an operating system consists of other special *Control* programs, *Systems Service* programs and *Processing* programs. Through the use of *system libraries*, these are integrated into the comprehensive operating system which may be controlled by the user through special *Job Control commands*. (All of these topics will be discussed in more detail in the following sections.)

The overall nature of the operating system in general and the Supervisor in particular is illustrated in the schematic representation of Figure 13.3. As an illustration of how such an operating system fits into our scheme of things, let us consider the previous three jobs illustrated in Figure 13.1. For this example, we will assume that the following conditions exist:

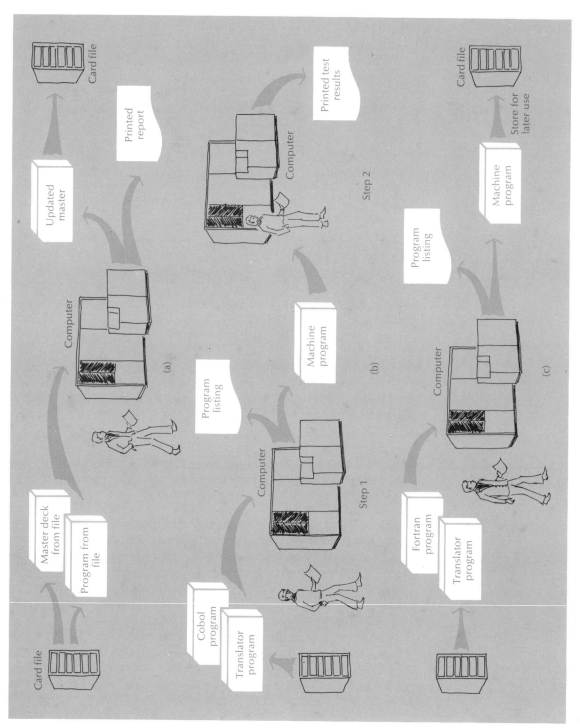

Fig. 13.1   Running jobs with a card system: (a) first job; (b) second job—with two steps; (c) third job.

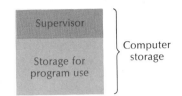

Fig. 13.2 The Supervisor in storage.

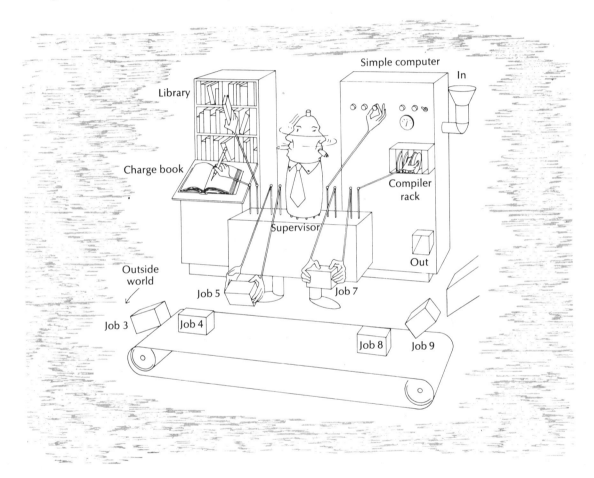

Fig. 13.3 Animated representation of an operating system. (From J. K. Rice and J. R. Rice, *Introduction to Computer Science*; copyright 1969 by Holt, Rinehart and Winston. Used by permission.)

- The jobs are to be run on a disk system.
- The UPDATE program, the UPDATE Master File, the Cobol and Fortran translators, and the data set for Job 2 are all stored on disk.

Figure 13.4 represents a *job stream* for the IBM 360/370 *Disk Operating System* (*DOS*) to perform these operations. The following descriptions provide a bird's-eye explanation of the designated 16 components in Figure 13.4.

1. Job card—designates that a new job (to be named J1) follows.
2. Execute UPDATE card—directs the Supervisor to bring the UPDATE program from disk and begin execution. The program will obtain the Master File from disk by means of Job Control cards not illustrated.
3. The Transaction Data deck—required for updating the Master File.
4. End-of-Job card—special coding /& to signal the end of this job.
5. Job card—designates that a new job follows (J2).
6. Execute COBOL card—directs the supervisor to bring the Cobol translator into storage and to translate the Cobol program which follows.
7. The Cobol program—to be translated to machine language and temporarily stored on disk.
8. Execute Linkage Editor program—directs the computer to prepare the preceding program for loading into storage.
9. Execute card—causes the program to be loaded into storage, and control of the computer to be given to that program. The program will obtain its data from disk.
10. End-of-Job card—signals end of job J2.
11. Job card—designates that a new job follows (J3).
12. Cataloging card—indicates to the system that this program, upon translation, is to be permanently saved in the system library (on disk).
13. Execute FORTRAN card—directs the Supervisor to bring the Fortran translator into storage and to translate the Fortran program which follows.
14. The Fortran program—to be translated to machine language.
15. Execute Linkage Editor program—directs the computer to catalog the previously translated program into disk storage for future use.
16. End-of-Job card—signals end of job J3.

These represent the more pertinent Job Control commands; each job stream will also include commands describing data files to be processed and needed information. Although these Job Control commands relate specifically to the IBM DOS Job Control Language (JCL), they are similar in principle to those of most other operating systems. However, for many operating systems, the JCL is more concise, and considerably more of the bookkeeping functions are handled by the operating system. We will note that many of the operations carried out by the operator of the card system are now handled automatically by the computer's operating system. This is illustrated graphically by comparing Figure 13.5 with the card system representation of Figure 13.1. Through use of the Job Control cards, which are prepared prior to the run, jobs may be stacked and entered into the computer as one large deck. Assuming that no error conditions occur requiring operator attention, the computer will automatically proceed from one job to the next until they are all completed. The operating system frees the operator from many of the

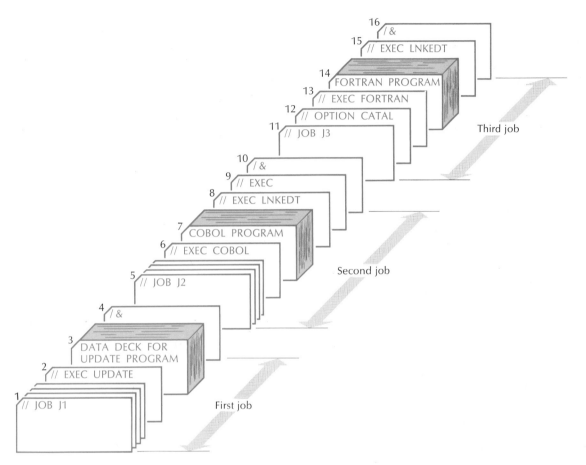

16 /&
15 // EXEC LNKEDT
14 FORTRAN PROGRAM
13 // EXEC FORTRAN
12 // OPTION CATAL
11 // JOB J3
Third job

10 /&
9 // EXEC
8 // EXEC LNKEDT
7 COBOL PROGRAM
6 // EXEC COBOL
5 // JOB J2
Second job

4 /&
3 DATA DECK FOR UPDATE PROGRAM
2 // EXEC UPDATE
1 // JOB J1
First job

Fig. 13.4 Typical IBM 360/370 DOS job stream.

clerical jobs, thus providing more time to plan and direct the overall operation of the system.

OPERATING SYSTEMS FOR THE IBM 360 AND 370   Operating systems first came into broad use with medium and large-scale second-generation computers. By today's standards, the capabilities of these systems were relatively primitive. With the introduction of the System/360 in 1964, IBM also introduced three software systems: *Basic Programming Support (BPS)*, *Basic Operating System (BOS)*, and *Operating System*/360 (*OS*/360 or simply *OS*). In fact, a significant characteristic of third-generation computers is that most of them are equipped with operating systems. The Basic Programming Support is a set of card-oriented programs providing the most basic of utility software needs. (The BPS is not an operating system as described in this chapter.) The Basic Operating System was designed for the small end of the 360 series. The much

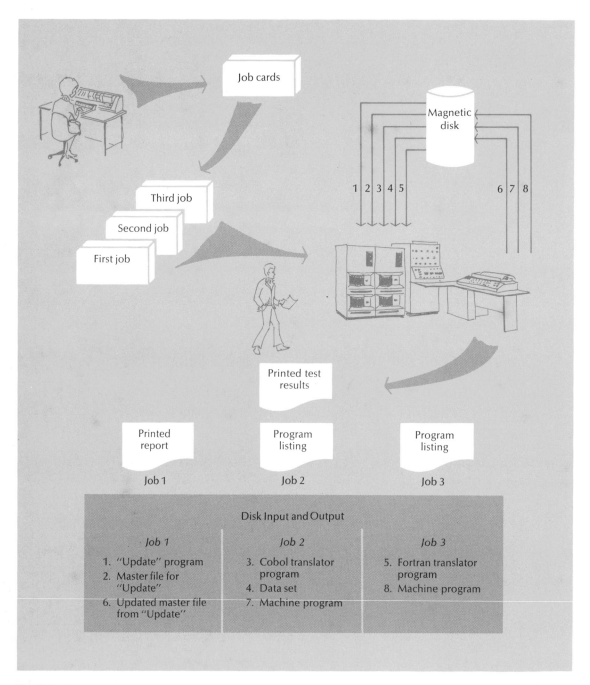

Fig. 13.5 Running jobs with an operating system.

larger and more powerful Operating System was designed for the larger and higher-speed machines in the 360 line. (The BOS requires a storage capacity of at least 8000 bytes; OS requires at least 65,000 bytes but is usually used with 131,000 bytes or more.) Since many computer installations required a more powerful system than BOS but did not have the capacity for OS, two additional systems were introduced in 1966: the *Disk Operating System (DOS)* and the *Tape Operating System (TOS)*, both requiring 16,000 bytes of storage. DOS and OS, both designed around the random access capabilities of disk storage, are the most widely used 360 operating systems; the following specific descriptions of an operating system will refer to DOS.

The 1970 announcement of the System/370 included both DOS and OS, with a special feature to simplify the transition for the user from DOS to the more powerful and complex OS. Since that time, a number of variations to the operating systems have been introduced, both by IBM and by other companies. One such operating system involves the so-called *virtual storage* concept (DOS-VS and OS-VS). With a virtual storage system, each user has the illusion that his/her portion of storage is far greater than it actually is. For instance, let us assume that a user has 40K bytes of internal storage but the program is 100K bytes in length. The program would be compiled as a 100K byte program and stored on disk. To begin execution, the first 40K bytes of the program would be brought into storage. That portion of the program would remain in storage until execution was to continue to a segment of the program not in storage. At that time, the operating system would automatically "swap" the required section of program into internal storage and continue execution.

Exercises

13.1 What is an "operating system?"

13.2 In the job stream of Figure 13.4, do you think it would make any difference if the stack were changed so that job J2 would be run first and job J1 next? Explain your answer.

13.3 Can you conceive of a situation where the operating system might require that a given job be run before another?

13.2 COMPONENTS OF THE DISK OPERATING SYSTEM

THE SYSTEM LIBRARY Fundamental to the notion of an operating system is the *system library* which is stored on the *system residence* device (for DOS, this is a magnetic disk). As illustrated in Figure 13.6, the system library includes three components: the *core image* library, the *relocatable* library, and the *source statement* library. All programs in the core image library have been completely edited and are ready to be loaded directly into storage for execution. As we see in Figure 13.6, the Supervisor itself is stored in the core image

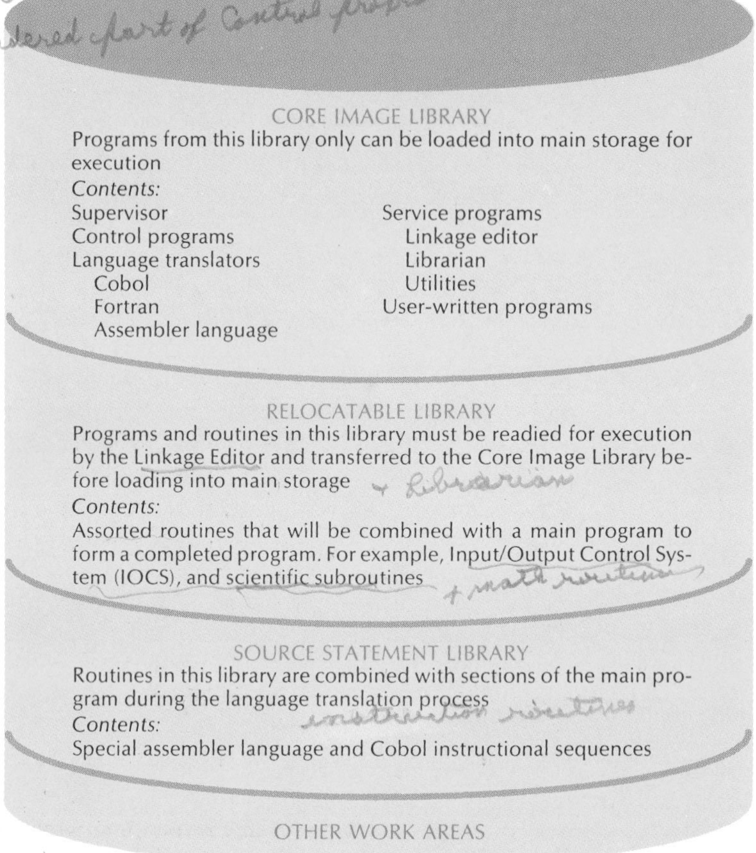

Operating System [handwritten annotation]

Supervisor Programs must be loaded from System Library, but may be considered part of Control program [handwritten annotations]

Control programs [handwritten annotation]

Systems Service Programs Librarian [handwritten annotation]

Processing Programs Compiler user programs [handwritten annotation]

CORE IMAGE LIBRARY
Programs from this library only can be loaded into main storage for execution
Contents:

Supervisor	Service programs
Control programs	Linkage editor
Language translators	Librarian
Cobol	Utilities
Fortran	User-written programs
Assembler language	

RELOCATABLE LIBRARY
Programs and routines in this library must be readied for execution by the Linkage Editor and transferred to the Core Image Library before loading into main storage *+ Librarian* [handwritten annotation]
Contents:
Assorted routines that will be combined with a main program to form a completed program. For example, Input/Output Control System (IOCS), and scientific subroutines *+ math routines* [handwritten annotation]

SOURCE STATEMENT LIBRARY
Routines in this library are combined with sections of the main program during the language translation process *instruction routines* [handwritten annotation]
Contents:
Special assembler language and Cobol instructional sequences

OTHER WORK AREAS

Fig. 13.6 DOS system residence disk.

Job Control Commands are by user [handwritten annotation]

library, together with language translation and system service types of programs. In addition, each computer installation will store most of their commonly used programs in this library. Thus, programs such as Payroll, Inventory Accounting, Grade Reporting, and so on are available for nearly instantaneous use simply by preparing and reading in the proper job control cards. (For example, see the job stream for the first job in Figure 13.4.)

When a user prepares a program, whether it be in assembler language, Cobol, or Fortran, he/she includes instructions or statements directing the computer to perform the desired operations. From the program logic point of view, the program is usually complete. However, the machine language equivalent of the program (after translation) does not contain all of the necessary components. For instance, directing the computer to read a card or a disk record is a simple one-line task in writing the program. However, special *subprograms* or *subroutines* must be provided to perform these complex internal operations. (Input and output are handled by the Input/Output Control System, IOCS, discussed in a later section of this chapter.) Similarly, in using Fortran, a programmer can designate that a square root must be taken simply by writing the code letters SQRT. A special subroutine must be made available to perform this function. These and many other routines are stored in the *relocatable library*. Any of them are available to the Linkage Editor program for combining with the user written portion of the program to form the complete program. With the assignment of storage addresses for various components of the program, the Linkage Editor can then place it in the core image library.

The *source statement* library contains certain commonly used sequences of instructions for both the assembly language and Cobol. By using predefined code names, users can cause sets of instructions to be included in their programs from this library. This both simplifies and speeds up the overall programming task.

Associated with each library is a directory of all programs in that library. For each program or subroutine in any of the libraries, a unique descriptive entry is made in the corresponding directory with the name of the program or subroutine and other information necessary for its use.

Exercise

13.4 Name and briefly describe the DOS libraries.

CONTROL PROGRAMS   An earlier section of this chapter describes the operating system as consisting of three types of programs: *Control programs, System Service programs,* and *Processing programs.* The Control programs form the framework of the Disk Operating System; they prepare and control execution of all other programs. Through the combination of hardware features and DOS software characteristics, the Supervisor remains in storage at all times and performs the job of overall operation management (as illustrated in Figure 13.3). Processing time is divided between the Supervisor and the program (or programs) being executed.

The *Job Control* program is loaded into storage by the Supervisor whenever it is needed. It processes the job control cards and prepares the system for execution of other programs as required. (Job Control cards are characterized in Figure 13.4 by the // in columns 1 and 2.) The third component of the Control program set is the *Initial Program Loader (IPL).* Its primary function is to load the Supervisor into main storage when system operation is first initiated. The functions of these programs are illustrated in Figure 13.7, which also shows storage allocation and job-to-job transition for a portion of the job stream from Figure 13.4.

Fig. 13.7 Storage allocation during job-to-job transition.

SYSTEM SERVICE PROGRAMS   The System Service programs, which include the *Linkage Editor* and the *Librarian,* perform the general function of maintaining the system. The machine language results of translating any Cobol, Fortran, or assembly language program are in what is termed a *relocatable format.* That is, specific storage addresses have not yet been assigned. In order to load them into storage, these addresses must be defined, and various subroutines required by each program must be integrated with the program. This capacity of the Linkage Editor facilitates the ability to prepare programs and program segments (subroutines) that may be placed anywhere in storage with only minor editing prior to loading. As we shall see later in this chapter, *relocatability* (the ability to locate a program anywhere in storage) makes the important technique of *multiprogramming* feasible (multiprogramming is also described in a later section of this chapter).

The *librarian* consists of a set of programs that maintains and reorganizes the library. Through the librarian, the user can catalog new programs or subroutines to the libraries or delete programs which are no longer required. There is a separate set of library programs for each of the libraries: core image, relocatable, and source statement.

PROCESSING PROGRAMS   The processing programs include all user-written programs (Problem programs) such as Payroll, Inventory Control, Production Control and Customer Billing. In addition, standard IBM-supplied programs include Language Compilers, Sort/Merge, and Utilities. The most commonly used compilers are Cobol, Fortran, Report Program Generator, PL/1, and the assembly language. The Sort/Merge package is a standard set of programs for performing the sorting and merging operations (on tape or disk). The Utilities comprise a set of programs to simplify such operations as copying the contents of a disk pack onto tape.

Exercise

13.5   Match the type of program a–g with the corresponding function 1–7.
   1. Job Control   2. Problem program
   3. Supervisor   4. Initial Program Loader
   5. Linkage Editor   6. Language Translator
   7. Librarian

   a. Performs the data processing job.
   b. Maintains the disk libraries.
   c. Identifies the job to be done.
   d. Converts programs such as Cobol to machine language.
   e. Loads the Supervisor into storage.
   f. Loads a Problem program from the library into storage.
   g. Prepares programs for loading into storage.

APPLICATIONS PACKAGES   In addition to the standard operating systems provided with third-generation computers, most manufacturers make available special applications packages. These include complete sets of programs for a wide variety of applications, ranging from typesetting and composition to inventory control to comprehensive database management systems.

Applications systems and programs are by no means limited to computer manufacturers; indeed, within recent years the growth of so-called *software companies* has become an important factor in the computer industry. These companies (and in some cases even private individuals) offer for sale or lease a wide variety of programs and systems, from automated letter writing systems to ultra-high-speed language translators. They will range in cost from a few hundred dollars purchase price to several thousand dollars per month lease price. Some are sold on a "you're-on-your-own" basis, but most are carefully documented and fully supported by the producing firm. The software descriptions of Figure 13.8 are typical of those to be found in computer magazines and newspapers. We might note that these four cover a wide range of applications. Although "Shorthand Cobol," "Biorhythms," and "Automatic Flowcharter for

Fig. 13.8 Advertised software. [(a) and (b) Reprinted with permission of Datamation®, Copyright 1976 by Technical Publishing Company, Greenwich, Connecticut 06830; (c) Reprinted from *Computer Decisions,* June 1976, Haden Publishing Company; (d) Reprinted from *Computer Decisions,* November, 1975, page 73, copyright 1975, Haden Publishing Company.]

"Shorthand" Cobol

SHORTHAN is just what its name suggests, a shorthand way of entering COBOL source statements. It is not a precompiler, but rather a means of reducing the COBOL coding effort required by using easy to remember abbreviations which, in turn, automatically generate COBOL source code. This eliminates the need for monotonous and redundant aspects of COBOL coding. Abbreviations are usually determined from the first letter of each expanded word. For example, LABEL RECORDS ARE STANDARD would be coded on a keypunch form as LRAS and expanded accordingly. The purchase price is a one-time charge of $500 plus travel expenses associated with the installation. A training session, documentation, and warranty are included in the price. A 30-day trial period is offered. C. W. JACKSON & ASSOCIATES, INC., Tampa, Fla.

(a)

Automatic flowcharter for Cobol programs

FLOBOL is an automatic flowcharter for *Cobol* source programs. The flowchart produced provides a complete flowline throughout the program. *FLOBOL* is written in ANSI Standard *Cobol* and will flow chart *Cobol* programs including most vendor extensions. Program price is $480. **Cosmic,** Suite 112, Barrow, University of Georgia, Athens, GA 30602. (404) 542-3265.

(c)

Biorhythms

This service bureau is offering charts of individuals' biorhythms, personal compatibility charts, and the programs themselves for other IBM 5100 users. The biorhythms, physical, emotional, and creative cycles thought to influence everyone, are calculated simply by supplying birthdates. The charge is $1.25, $1.50 per month for the compatibility charts. The APL version of the program used to calculate the rhythms is priced at $345 for the BASIC version and $275 for the APL version. A 32K system is required. BAM DATA SERVICE, Binghamton, N.Y.

(b)

RPG II patient billing system for IBM System/3 and 32

The *Patient Billing and Accounts Receivable (PBAR) System* is a complete insurance reporting and receivable system available in *RPG II* for the *IBM* System/3 or 32. *PBAR* is a complete system for use by the medical group or clinic as an in-house system or for use by service firms servicing doctors. It features a comprehensive family/patient master file with information on up to nine dependents as well as insurance company data and financial data. *PBAR* can establish installment payment plans and levy a finance charge for the patient accounts. It is provided in *RPG II* for a 16k system with a minimum of 5 million bytes of disk. Price is $9,600. **Occidental Computer Systems, Inc.,** 10202 Riverside Dr., N. Hollywood, CA 91602. (213) 763-5144.

(d)

Cobol Programs" are relatively inexpensive, the RPG billing system is somewhat more costly. (A large, extensive system might lease for as much as $10,000 per month.) In many cases, the software furnished by independent vendors is superior in performance to that furnished by the manufacturer.

On one hand, the computer user should not consider such software packages to be a cure-all for all programming ills. On the other, such systems, when adequately tailored to meet the specific needs of a given user, can justify their costs many times over.

13.3 INPUT/OUTPUT PROGRAMMING

BASIC CONCEPTS OF OVERLAPPING OPERATIONS With the extremely high speed of modern computers, it is easy to overlook the notion of efficiency. However, one of the significant inefficiencies of computer systems relates to the fact that certain components of the system may be idly waiting for another component to complete its function. For instance, let us consider the simple process of reading a record, performing processing operations, and printing the results, as illustrated in the representation of Figure 13.9. Assuming that input, processing, and output require equal amounts of time, we see that a record is read during one time interval and then the input device remains idle during the next two intervals (processing and output). In fact, each of the three system components is idle two thirds of the time while waiting for the third to complete its operation. This handicap was overcome in second-generation card systems by the use of input/output storage *buffers,* through which the card reader and line printer are capable of performing certain functions independent of the CPU. For instance, the reading of a card by a *fully buffered* card reader involves two steps: (1) the card is physically transported through the reader and read into a special 80-position buffer storage area within the card reader—this operation is independent of the CPU—and (2) the card image is transferred from the buffer storage to CPU storage upon request from the CPU. Upon completion of the transfer to the CPU, the card reader automatically reads the next card into its buffer. Similarly, the line printer may be

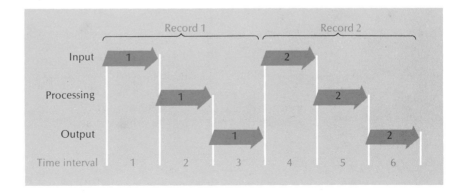

Fig. 13.9 Simple processing.

buffered. Execution in the CPU of a write instruction causes the buffer to be loaded with the output line and initiates the printing operation. Execution continues to the next instruction in the program as the printer simultaneously performs its printing operation. As a result, reading of a record by the card reader, processing by the CPU, and printing results by the printer all take place concurrently. Thus, buffering provides the capability for *overlapped processing* as illustrated in Figure 13.10. Here we can see, for instance, that during time interval 4, record 4 is being read into the buffer by the card reader, record 3 is being processed, and record 2 is being printed from the buffer of the line printer. For this ideal case, the overall time required to process a large file would be reduced to slightly more than one third the time required with nonoverlapped processing of Figure 13.9. (The reader must recognize that these are ideal illustrations and represent greater improvements than are actually encountered in practice.)

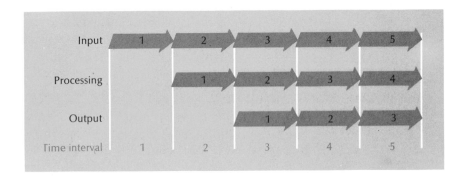

Fig. 13.10   Overlapped processing.

Exercise

13.6 a. If each time interval in Figures 13.9 and 13.10 represents $\frac{1}{10}$ second, compute the time required to process ten records for both nonoverlapped and overlapped processing.
    b. Repeat part (a) using a 1000-record file.

DATA CHANNELS   Although buffers within I/O (input/output) devices are adequate for fixed record length devices such as the card reader and the line printer, they are impractical for magnetic disk and tape units, where the record length is determined by the programmer. (Also, some commonly used card readers for third-generation computers are unbuffered.) Considering an unbuffered tape system, the processing would be nonoverlapped as illustrated in Figure 13.9, except that the CPU would be controlling the input and the output

Buffers are storage locations
Channel are subcomputers

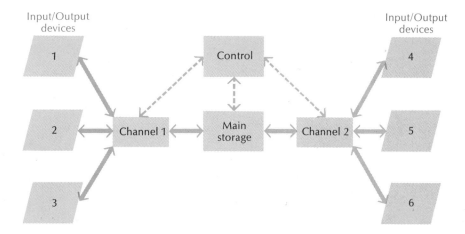

Fig. 13.11 Computer system with channels.

operations. Because of the high speed of the CPU relative to the tape drive, the CPU would be transferring data approximately 10 percent of the time, and waiting for the drive to read the next byte of data approximately 90 percent of the time. This problem is overcome by utilizing special hardware devices which can control the input/output operations relatively independent of the CPU. These so-called *channels* are effectively "subcomputers" which can perform their specialized I/O functions at the direction of the CPU. The relationship of these channels to the computer system is illustrated in Figure 13.11. If we assume, for example, that I/O devices 1 and 4 are an unbuffered card reader and a tape drive, respectively, then the control unit can initiate reading via channel 1 and writing via channel 2, and continue processing while the channels perform the I/O operations. However, without versatility of buffers built into the I/O devices, the programmer must provide equivalent buffers within main storage.

INTERNAL STORAGE BUFFERS In considering the buffered card systems, we saw that two 80-position buffer areas were available for reading the card images: one in the card reader itself and the other in storage. Similarly, using channels to control input/output operations and to achieve overlapped processing, two separate areas must be provided for each input or output device. This becomes apparent if we remember that the channel is reading a new record into storage while the CPU is processing the previous one. The use of alternate buffer areas is illustrated in Figure 13.12(a), where record 3 is read into input buffer 1, record 2 is processed from input buffer 2, with the results placed in output buffer 1, and output record 1 is written from output buffer 2. Upon completing that cycle, the CPU begins processing record 3 from input buffer 1 into output buffer 2; input of record 4 is then switched to input buffer 2 and output of record 2 is accomplished from output buffer 1. This is illustrated in Figure 13.12(b).

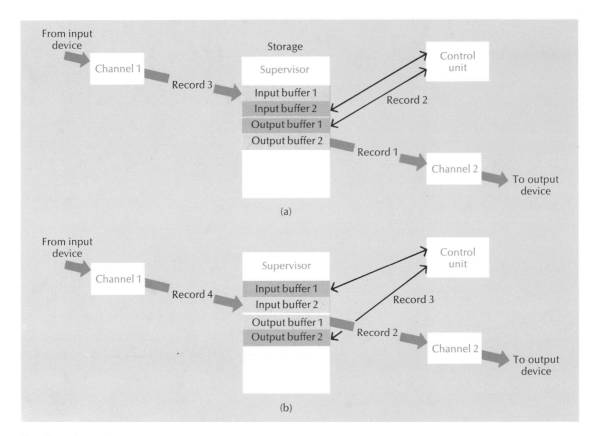

Fig. 13.12 Input/output buffers in storage.

As the reader might suspect, the improved efficiency of overlapped processing through use of channels is not "free." First of all, the channels themselves represent an additional cost to the computer system. In addition, the use of multiple I/O areas requires extra programming considerations since it is now necessary to switch back and forth between buffer areas. The input/output programs themselves can occupy a significant amount of storage and require CPU time in carrying out their operations. This can mean additional cost because of greater storage requirements for a given machine. However, these additional equipment and programming expenses are usually justified by the increased throughput capacity of the computer system.

INPUT/OUTPUT CONTROL SYSTEM When one considers the notion of blocking and unblocking records and of switching between alternate I/O areas, it would appear that programmers have their hands full simply programming the input/output operations. However, this task is significantly simplified by the use of extensive input and output subroutines which automatically perform most of the drudgery. In the IBM 360/370 systems, these are referred to collectively as the *Input/Output Control System*, or simply *IOCS*. In brief, IOCS is a set of subroutines which perform all the functions necessary to locate and access a logical record for processing. The IOCS subroutines perform the following functions:

- Block and deblock records.
- Switch between I/O areas when two areas are specified by the programmer.
- Handle conditions occurring when the end of a file is reached during processing.
- Check and write special descriptive records required for tape and disk processing (termed *label* records).
- Handle error conditions occurring during input/output operations.

For instance, if a file consists of blocked records, and a block has been read into storage, IOCS makes each record in succession available to the program (as required by the program) until the end of the block is reached. When the last record in the block has been processed, IOCS automatically reads the next block into storage.

From the programmer's point of view, the overall input/output operation is considerably simplified. It is only necessary to define the general nature of the file and its characteristics at the beginning of the program; after that, the programmer can be relatively unaware of the operations going on within the CPU. He/she simply directs the computer to READ (or GET) an input record or to WRITE (or PUT) an output record and IOCS handles the details.

Again, as we might expect, the user must pay a price in storage required by IOCS and in execution time required by the routines. However, this price is more than balanced by the more efficient utilization of the computer and the programmer's time.

Exercises

13.7 What is a channel?

13.8 Why must two buffer areas be used with a channel for overlapped processing?

13.9 What is IOCS and what function does it serve?

13.4 MULTI-PROGRAMMING

HARDWARE FEATURES   As we have learned, the use of an operating system can increase the total amount of useful work (*throughput*) of a computer system. Through use of channels and overlapped processing techniques, each component of the system is more fully utilized. Another means for further increasing the usage of the CPU is through *multiprogramming*. With the storage-resident

Supervisor concept, we have been introduced to the notion of having two programs in storage at the same time: the Supervisor for overall system control and the problem program for performing the data processing function. In multiprogramming, this concept is carried one step further by placing two or more problem programs in storage and executing them concurrently. Although two or more programs may reside in storage simultaneously, the computer is capable of executing only one instruction at a time. Thus, at any given time, only *one* of the programs has control of the computer and is executing instructions. Simultaneous execution of two programs with one CPU is impossible. Basic to multiprogramming and many of the concepts we have studied are several hardware features including *storage protection, program interrupt,* and *program status preservation.*

We can readily appreciate the need for restricting a program in one portion of storage from changing information or instructions of a program in another portion of storage. For example, in Figure 13.13, we would not want program 1 to inadvertently destroy something in the completely independent program 2 or in the Supervisor. In a multiprogramming environment, this is prevented by the *storage protection* ability, a combination hardware and software system which prevents one program from addressing beyond the limits of its own allocated storage area.

The *program interrupt* feature is a combination of hardware and software whereby execution of a program may be interrupted under certain types of conditions and returned to the Supervisor. The Supervisor may, in turn transfer control to another program in storage. However, in order to accomplish this without destroying the various register contents of the first program, all of this information must be saved and then restored when the control is ultimately returned to the first program. This is known as *program status preservation* (in the System/360 and 370, the collective contents of the functional registers are referred to as the *Program Status Word* or *PSW*).

Exercise

13.10   What is "multiprogramming?"

2 or more programs in storage at same time

Fig. 13.13   Storage
protection.

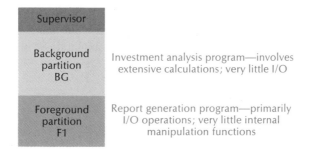

Investment analysis program—involves extensive calculations; very little I/O

Report generation program—primarily I/O operations; very little internal manipulation functions

Fig. 13.14 Fixed partitions.

BASIC PRINCIPLES OF MULTIPROGRAMMING One of the simpler means of multiprogramming is to divide the storage into fixed sized *partitions*, as was done in 360 DOS when it was first introduced. Under this system, the user could assign three partitions (the amount of storage assigned to each being at the discretion of the user) as follows:*

- *Foreground 1* partition (F1)–the F1 partition has highest priority for program execution.
- *Foreground 2* partition (F2)–the F2 partition has second priority for program execution.
- *Background* partition (BG)–the BG partition has lowest priority for program execution.

To gain an insight to the notion of priority and how multiprogramming works, let us consider the example illustrated by Figure 13.14.

Important characteristics of the Report Generation program in Figure 13.14 are its extensive input/output requirements and its minimal CPU needs. Even with the concept of overlapped processing, the CPU will remain idle for significant periods of time, as shown in Figure 13.15. (A program of this

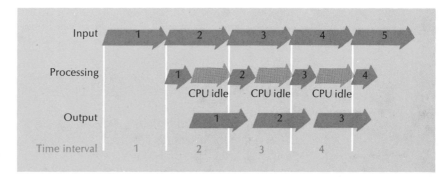

Fig. 13.15 Input/output–bound processing.

---

*Current versions of DOS support five partitions. Although the numbers have changed, the concept remains the same.

type is said to be *I/O-bound*.) On the other hand, the I/O requirements of the Investment Analysis program are negligible, being almost entirely *processing-bound*. The idea in this multiprogramming example is to execute the analysis program during the "CPU idle" periods of the report program; this is accomplished as follows. (Refer to Figure 13.15 for the *time interval* references.)

Time Interval	Action Taken
3	1. The F1 program (Report Generator), having control of the computer, initiates input cycle 3.
	2. Processing cycle 2 is carried out by the F1 program.
	3. Upon completion of processing cycle 2, output cycle 2 is begun.
	4. Then control is returned to the Supervisor (since the CPU is idle) which, in turn, gives control to the lower-priority program in BG.
	5. Execution of the BG program (Investment Analysis) proceeds.
4	6. Completion of input cycle 3 causes the BG program to be interrupted (all register contents are saved) and control returned to F1 via the Supervisor.
	7. Steps 1 through 4 of time interval 3 are repeated for the next set of cycles (input cycle 4, processing cycle 3, and output cycle 3).
	8. The register contents and system status are restored to their values when the BG program was interrupted in step 6. Execution of the BG program then proceeds.

Ideally, this process will utilize the complete computer resource to the fullest possible extent.

Where the IBM 360/370 DOS partitions are fixed in size, more powerful operating systems, available from most manufacturers of large computers, are not so restricted. In fact, job scheduling is an important activity of the Supervisor, which allocates storage to the fullest possible extent. Complete and ready-to-go jobs are "lined up" in auxiliary storage waiting to be loaded into main storage and executed. (An ordered sequence of objects awaiting service is commonly called a *queue*.) A large computer, utilizing *dynamically allocated* partitions, may have several programs in storage simultaneously. As each is completed, the next program is selected from the queue and placed in storage. By designating a program to be high priority, it can be placed at the front of the queue. If the priority is sufficiently high, some operating systems will even temporarily remove lower-priority programs from storage to make room. Upon completion of the high-priority job, the other programs are returned.

Although these functions sound highly efficient, they are not without their problems. Indeed, the process of juggling programs, determining priority, allocating time intervals, and so on can require a significant amount of CPU time, the very quantity the system is attempting to optimize. This "nonproductive time" is commonly referred to as *overhead*, and must be minimized to take full advantage of the operating system.

Exercises

I/O Bound programs given high priority
CPU " " low priority

13.11 In the multiprogramming example illustrated by Figure 13.14, what would be the consequence of assigning the I/O-bound Report Generator program to the lower-priority partition, and the Investment Analysis program to the higher-priority partition?

13.12 Distinguish between "fixed partitions" and "dynamically allocated partitions."

uses storage as needed

13.5
ONLINE SYSTEMS AND TIMESHARING

ONLINE SYSTEMS In many applications, it is important that a number of users be able to communicate directly with the computer and receive rapid response to inquiries. This is made possible by the modern digital computer with large storage capabilities, powerful operating systems, and multiprogramming. For instance, in a banking application, tellers require immediate access to customer account information; in an airline reservation system, a ticket salesman requires immediate information regarding space availability; in a college environment, a counselor requires entrance examination scores for a student in the office. Through the use of typewriter and video display terminals connected to the computer either directly or via telephone lines, such information stored in the system can be instantly available. A typical multiprogramming system to achieve this is illustrated in Figure 13.16. In this schematic, the CPU will normally be processing the lower-priority payroll application. However, upon request from a terminal for student information, the Payroll program will be interrupted and control given to the Student Information program. Upon satisfying the inquiry, control would be returned to the Payroll program.

Although online processing is commonly handled on a multiprogramming basis, in some applications the computer is dedicated solely to the online processing. This is frequently encountered with special-purpose process control computers, in which the computer is used to control an industrial process such as petroleum refining, an electrical distribution system, or a machine tool operation.

Exercise

13.13 What would be the consequence of giving the Student Information program in Figure 13.16 second priority and the Payroll program first?

inquiry delay

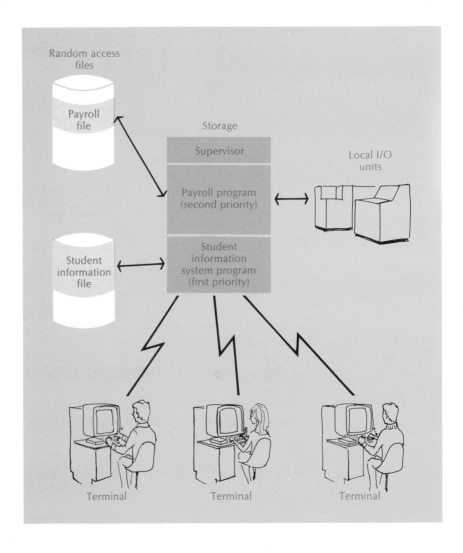

Fig. 13.16 Online
processing.

TIMESHARING   The term *timesharing* was introduced in 1959 in a paper by
British mathematician Christopher Strachey. Since then, much development,
publicity, time, and money have been devoted to the concept. The term has
been applied broadly to include any system where the components are used on
a shared basis (based on such a broad usage, multiprogramming and online
processing would be classified as timesharing). "Timesharing," like much of
the jargon in the computer field, has been so grossly overused and misunder-
stood that it no longer has a strict and conventionally accepted definition.
However, rigorously speaking, timesharing refers to the allocation of computer
resources *in a time-dependent* fashion to several programs simultaneously in

storage. The principal notion of a timesharing system is to provide a large number of users direct access to the computer for problem solving. The user thus has the ability to "converse" directly with the computer for problem solving (hence the terms *conversational* or *interactive* computing). In multi-programming, the principal consideration is to maximize utilization of the computer, but in timesharing it is, in a sense, to maximize efficiency of each computer user and keep him/her busy. Figure 13.17 illustrates the notion of a timeshared system. Each user has his/her own communications terminal, portion of storage, and auxiliary storage. In contrast to multiprogramming, where programs are executed on a priority basis, in timesharing the CPU time is divided among the users on a scheduled basis. Each program will be allocated its "slice" of the CPU time (commonly measured in milliseconds) based on some predetermined scheduling basis, beginning with the first program and proceeding through the last. Upon completing the cycle, it is begun again so that an individual user scarcely realizes that someone else is also using the

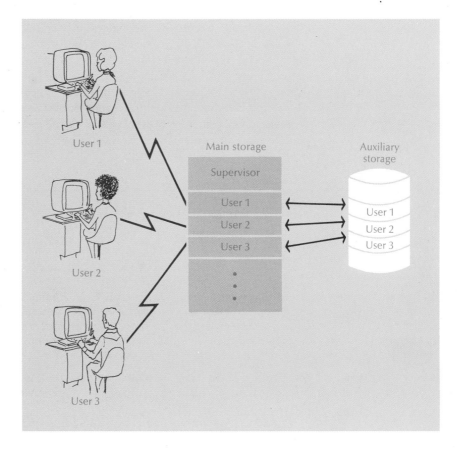

Fig. 13.17 Timesharing environment.

computer. Basic characteristics of timesharing are summarized and contrasted with multiprogramming in Table 13.1.

Table 13.1   COMPARISON OF TIMESHARING AND MULTIPROGRAMMING

Timesharing	Multiprogramming
• Users share CPU time on a scheduled basis	• Users share CPU time on a demand basis
• Prime objective: keep user busy (maximize response)	• Prime objective: keep computer busy (maximize throughput)
• Man-machine interaction is emphasized	• Minimal man-machine interaction
• Rapid response time is of primary importance	• Response time is not a consideration (usually slow)
• Response generally implies partial completion of computing requirements	• Response implies completion of computing requirements

The capabilities described in this chapter for modern computers and software sound quite impressive; indeed, they are. On the other hand, most of the principles described in this chapter represent developments over the past 10–15 years. At first, sophisticated concepts such as operating systems, multiprogramming, and timesharing were implemented on only the larger and more sophisticated computers. Now, with the continually increasing power and decreasing cost of minicomputers, very powerful software is available with virtually every computer that is currently marketed. Significant and exciting advances can be expected in these fields over the next several years.

Exercise

13.14   What is the difference between multiprogramming and timesharing?

Answers to Preceding Exercises

13.1   An operating system is a set of programs, resident in the computer system, designed to maximize the amount of work the computer can do. For a more detailed discussion, see the section preceding this exercise.

13.2   It would make no difference, since the two programs are independent of each other; see Exercise 13.3 for an instance in which they are not.

13.3   Referring to the job stream of Figure 13.4, assume that program UPDATE does not update a

Master File as illustrated, but rather reads in a set of raw data, performs initial calculations on it, then stores it on disk. If this is to be the data for job J2, then J2 cannot be run until J1 has successfully completed its task.

13.4   The three DOS libraries are core image, relocatable, and source statement. For descriptions, see Section 13.2.

13.5   a. 2; b. 7; c. 1; d. 6; e. 4; f. 3; g. 5.

13.6 a. nonoverlapped processing—3.0 seconds; overlapped processing—1.2 seconds. b. nonoverlapped processing—5 minutes; overlapped processing—1 minute, 40.2 seconds.

13.7 A channel is a device capable of handling input/output operations independent of the CPU.

13.8 Considering the input operation, if only one input area were used, the channel would have to wait until the CPU was finished processing a record before it could read the next one. Otherwise, the first record would be destroyed before processing were complete.

13.9 The Input/Output Control System (IOCS) is a set of subroutines to perform the detailed operations necessary to locate and access a logical record for processing. For a more complete description, see the section preceding this exercise.

13.10 Multiprogramming is the technique whereby two or more programs reside in storage simultaneously and are executed concurrently in order to utilize the computer resource more fully.

13.11 The Investment Analysis program is CPU-bound since it involves very little I/O and much computation. If it is given first priority, very little "CPU idle" time will be available for the Report Generator program. Effectively, the Report Generator program would have to wait until the Analysis program has been completed. Generally speaking, I/O-bound programs are given high priority and CPU-bound programs are given low priority.

13.12 In a system operating with fixed partitions, the partition size and number of partitions is predetermined and is not variable during operation of the system. Thus, programs designated to run in a given partition are limited to the size of that partition. With a dynamically allocated system, the operating system provides the amount of storage required for each program; the only limitation on the number of programs in storage is the available storage itself.

13.13 The online component must have top priority or else the response time will be degraded. This is inconsistent with the entire notion of a rapid-response online system. No problem is encountered if the payroll calculation is delayed slightly, but great inconvenience can result if the remote inquiry is not handled immediately.

13.14 See Table 13.1.

Additional Exercises

13.15 **Matching.** Match each item 1–8 with the corresponding description a–h.

1. timesharing	2. buffer
3. system library	4. supervisor
5. channel	6. operating system
7. multiprogramming	8. overlapped processing

a. Involves sharing a computer on a priority basis.

b. A capability resulting from the use of I/O buffer areas.

c. A set of programs designed to maximize the amount of work done by a computer.

d. Used for temporary storage of data during input or output operations.

e. Directs input and output operations.

f. Remains in storage at all times.

g. Involves sharing a computer on a time-scheduled basis.

h. Used for storage of programs and subroutines.

13.16 **True-False.** Determine whether each of the following is true or false.

a. The term "software" refers to programs to be used with the computer.

b. An operating system is a set of programs designed primarily to replace computer operators.

c. In most operating systems, control of the computer is under the supervisor until a user's program is to be run; then the Supervisor is replaced in storage by the program, and control is given to the program.

d. Overlapped processing involves having several programs in storage, all executing at the same time.

e. If the time required to handle a record of a given card file is equally divided between input, processing, and output, the time to process the entire file with a fully buffered system would be approximately one third that required with an unbuffered system.

f. A channel is designed to perform input and output relatively independently of the CPU.

g. In a multiprogramming environment, the program with the heaviest computation load would be assigned to the highest-priority partition to insure that the processing gets done.

h. Multiprogramming involves high-speed processing by a computer of many programs, one after the other.

i. The principal philosophy of multiprogramming system is to keep the computer as busy as possible.

j. In a timesharing system, users can communicate directly with the computer via terminals, but in multiprogramming systems, they cannot.

13.17   Multiple Choice. Determine which answer best completes or answers each of the following statements.

a. Relating to third-generation computers, the word "supervisor" usually refers to (1) the person in charge of a computer installation, (2) the operating system, (3) the system libraries, (4) a program which remains in storage and directs operation of the computer.

b. The purpose of Job Control commands is to (1) provide directions to the Supervisor in carrying out a series of operations, (2) provide directions to the computer in carrying out a series of operations, (3) be used in writing computer programs, (4) control the number of jobs to be run.

c. The three libraries of IBM 360 DOS are (1) system, users, and general, (2) reserved, public, and overflow, (3) relocatable, source

statement, and core image, (4) system, source statement, and core image.

d. Two types of processing programs are (1) user-written programs and Job Control, (2) Utilities and Supervisor, (3) Utilities and user-written programs, (4) Initial Program Loader and user-written programs.

e. Overlapped processing involves (1) two or more user-written programs in storage at the same time, (2) performing input or output operations concurrently with processing, (3) using buffered card readers, (4) all of the preceding, (5) both 1 and 2 of the preceding.

f. Storage protection refers to (1) preventing one program in storage from working on data of another program, (2) the storage, offline, of permanent data files, (3) protection measure used to store magnetic disk and tapes, (4) the program status word.

g. Partitioning refers to (1) dividing the storage of a computer into two or more segments, (2) scheduling program time, (3) the use of input/output buffers, (4) the Input/Output Control system (IOCS).

h. In a multiprogramming environment, a program which is heavily processing bound should be assigned (1) high priority, (2) low priority, (3) exclusive use of the computer, (4) whatever priority is available.

i. An application in which the computer is used to control an industrial process (such as a machine tool operation) is said to be (1) offline, (2) direct inquiry, (3) buffered operation, (4) online.

j. The principal advantage of multiprogramming over timesharing is (1) time is scheduled on a priority basis, (2) the computer is most fully occupied, (3) a greater number of programs can be handled at one time, (4) since multiprogramming and timesharing have completely different objectives, such a comparison is unrealistic.

13.18   Additional Problems

a. Summarize the basic features of the operating system used by your computer installation.

b. Obtain information on one or more software packages available from the manufacturer of your computer or from a private software firm. Summarize the nature of the package and its basic features with regard to functions performed, main and auxiliary storage required, cost, and so on. Brief summaries of available software and names of software companies may be found in trade magazines such as *Datamation* (Technical Publishing Company) and *Data Processing* (North American Publishing Company).

c. As described in the text, the use of alternate input/output storage buffers improves the overall efficiency of the system through overlapped processing. However, this is at the expense of special I/O routines requiring additional storage and execution time. Since overlapped processing is achieved through the use of internal buffers within card readers and line printers, give your opinion as to why such buffers are not used with magnetic disk and tape units.

d. A college computer center is set up to operate under the System/360 DOS with three partitions (F1, F2, and BG). The computer is to be used concurrently for instruction and administration with requirements for three partitions as follows:

- Administrative processing—roughly an equal balance between processing and I/O.
- Instructional control system—handles all instructional input and output, and job scheduling; primarily I/O.
- Instructional processing—language translation and program execution; primarily internal processing.

Assign these to the respective partitions and justify your answer.

Chapter

14

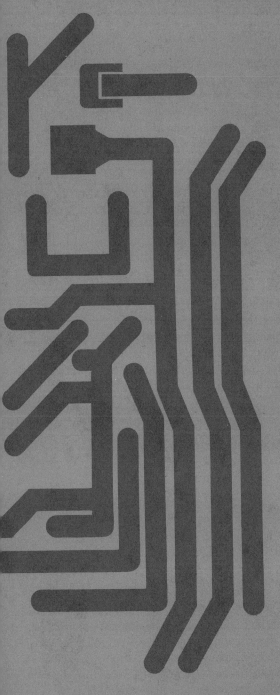

The Evolution of a Data Processing System

In previous chapters we have studied many aspects of data processing, including various types of hardware, the concept of system software, programming languages, and computer applications. Furthermore, in Chapter 2 we considered various processing steps and the overall cycle of a typical data processing system through a case study of a hardware wholesale company. We will now turn our attention to integrating many of these concepts while gaining an insight to the management and use of a computer system via another case study.

14.1
CASE STUDY
DEFINITION

INTRODUCTION TO THE XYZ CONTRACTING COMPANY   Located in a large metropolitan area, the firm of Xiezopolski, Yamagiwa, Zboyovsky, and Associates (commonly termed XYZ for obvious reasons) is a building contracting company capable of contracting for anything ranging from an individual home to condominiums to an office building. The firm employs approximately 250 people in the main office and a branch office. The staff includes a small engineering section, the clerical and accounting department, and a large field section. The company had its founding in 1955 by Mr. Yamagiwa, who began as a small-home remodeling contractor. Although much of the company's phenomenal growth was carefully planned and directed, the computer and data processing needs were somewhat neglected along the way.

By 1971, the following major application areas involved the use of services and computer time from firms specializing in such applications.

1. Payroll
2. Accounts payable
3. Accounts receivable
4. Project progress analysis
5. Engineering analysis

The downturn in the economy as a whole and the construction business in particular which occurred in the early 1970s was a prime factor which forced the management of XYZ to reassess their computer needs. A very brief investigation revealed glaring inefficiencies in the existing uncoordinated system.

BUSINESS ACCOUNTING FUNCTIONS   During the early years of XYZ, most of the ordinary business bookkeeping operations were performed manually or with the aid of a basic accounting machine. However, by the time the company reached the size of 100 employees, the existing semiautomated payroll system became overburdened. After consideration investigation, the business manager recommended that XYZ contract with Business Accounts Service Bureau to take over accounts payable and accounts receivable as well as payroll. Business Accounts was a local independent company (possessing a medium-size computer) with "a computer and associated services for hire." Although Business Accounts was quite willing to prepare a computerized system tailored specifically to the needs of XYZ, the management of XYZ felt that it would be far more economical to use the standard payroll and accounts payable and receivable services already available. This required some minor modifications to the information network of XYZ so that the raw data to be processed was in a form compatible with the Business Accounts standards. Once the system was implemented, a courier service would deliver a record of the XYZ daily activities to Business Accounts at the end of each day. At prescheduled times throughout the month, appropriate processing runs were made and the results returned to XYZ. For instance, hourly rate construction workers were paid weekly, clerical employees were paid twice per month, and salaried employees were paid once per month. Checks for each category of employee were run by Business Accounts and delivered as scheduled. For an agreed-upon monthly fee, the complete service was provided to XYZ. This solution to these data processing needs was an ideal one for XYZ for a number of reasons, the two foremost being:

1. The volume of processing was too great to be handled by the semi-automated methods used previously, but not enough to justify acquisition of a computer.
2. The XYZ management was relatively nonknowledgeable about computers and was fearful of "ending up in the computer business" when their expertise was in the contracting business.

However, XYZ found it necessary to establish a data clerk position to coordinate activities between XYZ and Business Accounts. The overall process is illustrated in Figure 14.1. This system served the needs of XYZ adequately and, in fact, management was quite pleased with the simplicity of the operation. On the other hand, the complaint was sometimes voiced that this method of servicing data processing needs forced XYZ to conform to the Business Accounts methods and was not really tailored specifically to the needs of XYZ. After less than two years of operation, XYZ hired an experienced programmer as a general data processing coordinator to serve as an advisor in such areas as system design and activity coordination and to perform a limited amount of programming.

PROJECT PROGRESS ANALYSIS   As the construction business became more competitive and building costs spiraled upward, the management of XYZ became increasingly aware of the need for continually monitoring the progress of each project. It finally got to the point where the manually maintained progress charts and reports simply could not supply sufficient and timely reports required by the firm. To satisfy this need, XYZ contracted with a small service bureau which specialized in this particular field. The task of tailoring the available services to the needs of XYZ and coordinating the overall process was assigned to the newly hired data processing coordinator.

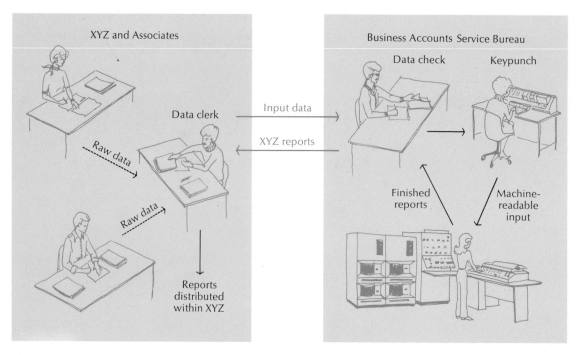

Fig. 14.1   Using a service bureau.

ENGINEERING ANALYSIS   As the complexity and size of construction jobs performed by XYZ increased, the engineering staff encountered a continually expanding need for computing services. Although most of the extensive engineering work requiring computer analysis was farmed out to another firm, XYZ entered into a contract with a timesharing service via a CRT terminal located in the main office of XYZ.

THE EXISTING SYSTEM   By 1971, therefore, the computing and data processing needs of XYZ were handled as follows.

1. Business data processing (payroll, accounts payable, and accounts receivable): performed by Business Accounts Service Bureau.
2. Project progress analysis: performed by a second service bureau.
3. Engineering analysis: the bulk of computer analysis performed by an engineering firm; some analysis performed locally by terminal and computer time purchased from a timesharing service.

Staffing within XYZ to handle these needs consisted of the data processing coordinator and the data clerk. Their places in the firm are illustrated by the organizational chart of Figure 14.2. The manner in which the data processing

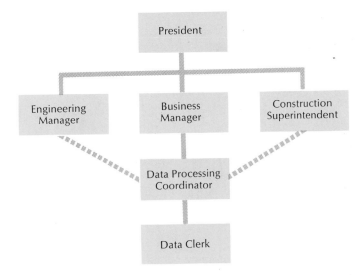

Fig. 14.2 Organizational chart for XYZ.

services evolved (with the lack of any overall planning) saw the data processing coordinator reporting to the business manager.

As time progressed and the demand for computer services increased, a number of problems became apparent.

- Whenever work loads increased, business data processing needs were given first priority, thus creating friction with other departments.
- The activities were fragmented; XYZ was obtaining computer services from four separate companies.
- The timeliness of many reports began to lag.
- Management desired a more extensive and timely project progress analysis.
- The engineering staff felt that more in-house analysis should be done using interactive terminals.
- And so on.

Exercise

14.1 In your opinion, what should be the principal factor in deciding whether to use a service bureau or to install a computer to satisfy data processing needs of a company?

14.2
A LONG-RANGE
FEASIBILITY STUDY

PRELIMINARY STUDY Before proceeding further, the president of XYZ decided to hire a data processing consultant to assist in a study and to provide computer expertise which the firm sorely lacked. The first action of the consultant was to recommend that a study team be set up, consisting of the following individuals in addition to himself.

1. Business manager
2. Engineering manager
3. Construction superintendent
4. Data processing coordinator

The consultant emphasized the importance of a preliminary study which was supported at the highest levels of the company. The purpose of this study was severalfold:

1. To summarize all of the current computer-related activities.
2. To determine what data processing improvements are actually needed.
3. To determine if projected improvements appeared to be practical and economically justifiable.
4. To make a preliminary recommendation about further action to be taken.

A 45-day period of time was allocated for each team member to scrutinize his/her area of responsibility and, with the assistance of subordinates, draw up a "wish list" of potential computer applications. These summaries were then brought together and presented at a work session of the study team. Each application was discussed, argued, and subjected to the following questions:

- Is the information required to generate the desired reports available or could it be made available?
- Will the output really be used or will it merely receive lip service?
- Does the desired report or function appear to be economical?
- Does the desired report or function appear to be practical; will it fit into the system?

The preliminary study findings presented to the president indicated that the computer services currently being provided by service bureaus together with several new applications of primary importance should justify the acquisition of a computer system. Some of the points the consultant emphasized were:

1. The need for increased data handling capacity and handling speed was imperative.
2. Acquisition of a computer would not reduce computer and data processing costs but would increase them. However, over the long term, the cost increase would be more than offset by increased productivity in a number of areas.
3. A detailed study should be performed to set a realistic time schedule and determine the type of equipment which would best suit the needs of XYZ. The notion of getting "super equipment," merely because everyone else was, must be avoided at all costs.

4. A crash program would lead to nothing but trouble; a carefully planned, realistic schedule must be determined. The overall project, consisting of preliminary planning through final acquisition of the computer and transferring existing applications to that system would require at least 18 months.

Exercise

14.2   In your opinion, what are the principal advantages and disadvantages of a committee such as that formed for the data processing study?

DETAILED STUDY AND ANALYSIS   Following approval of the president, the study team was commissioned to perform a more detailed study to include firm recommendations and a time schedule. This detailed study was considered in two phases: phase 1 was a detailed analysis of the information needs of XYZ, and phase 2 was a determination of the hardware, software, and personnel required. The first step of phase 1 involved identifying and documenting the basic objectives of the study. At first consideration, this might appear to be trivial, since the objective is obviously to study the company's computer and data processing needs. However, consider that a detailed study may take anywhere from a few weeks to several months, that it will involve a substantial amount of valuable time of the company's employees, and, finally, that the action taken will significantly affect the company for years to come. Then it becomes imperative that study objectives and a time scale be carefully determined. Basic objectives include items such as the following.

- Document all aspects of each current computer and data processing application.
- Cost analyze the current operation.
- Project computer and data processing needs for the next three to five years.
- Perform cost analysis on future needs.
- Summarize all benefits of a new system. From a dollar-and-cents point of view, some of these will be tangible. For instance, reducing the cost of providing timesharing services to the engineering department can be easily measured. Other benefits, such as improving customer service, may be very intangible.
- Prepare a preliminary specification for acquisition of a computer.
- Analyze personnel and software needs.

In the case of XYZ, three months were scheduled for this phase of the study. In performing it, each department manager delegated to his/her key personnel specific studies to be carried out. Weekly department meetings were scheduled to hash and rehash all phases of the initial findings. (The purchasing agent suggested that special "combat pay" should be provided for these Friday morning sessions.) The president of XYZ had emphasized that no domains should be considered sacred and that everyone should attempt to be completely objective in viewing what would best serve the company.

At the end of the three-month period, phase 1 of the study was completed These findings strongly suggested the following.

1. That acquisition of a small computer with online capabilities was not only feasible but was economically advisable.
2. That the following business data processing applications be ready when the computer is acquired:
   a. The batch processing payroll system, with only minor modifications to its existing form.
   b. A completely new online accounts payable and accounts receivable system.
3. That a comprehensive project scheduling system be prepared for implementation upon computer acquisition. This substantial project was to be a joint operation with three other construction companies.
4. That existing engineering applications be converted for the new computer.
5. That phase 2 of the detailed study and analysis begin immediately, with ultimate acquisition of the computer scheduled for 18 months.

With this detailed confirmation of the preliminary study findings, the management of XYZ approved the overall findings of the study team and directed that the plan be implemented. Phase 2 of the analysis, which was concerned primarily with the selection of a computer, staffing, and analysis of software requirements, is the topic of the next section.

Exercise

14.3 What factors must be considered in determining whether or not a particular application is suitable for computerizing?

14.3
PLANNING
FOR A NEW
INSTALLATION

ACQUISITION TIME SCHEDULE In preparing a time schedule, the consultant had emphasized the importance of allowing sufficient time for each step. He pointed out that the majority of new installations do not meet their timetables because of unrealistic assessments of how long given tasks will take. It is imperative to recognize that day-to-day business activities must continue concurrently with the planning, preparation, and installation of the new system. With this in mind, the study team adopted the acquisition schedule shown in Figure 14.3. Each of the five general activities shown in 14.3 was further broken down into a more detailed schedule. To ensure that the schedule was met and

	Mar	Apr	May	June	July	Aug	Sept	Oct	Nov	Dec	Jan	Feb	Mar	Apr	May	June	July	Aug
Preparations of specifications and selection of a vendor	▓	▓	▓	▓	▓	▓	▓											
Systems definition and analysis						▓	▓	▓	▓	▓	▓	▓						
Personnel training									▓	▓	▓	▓						
Programming and program modification											▓	▓	▓	▓	▓	▓	▓	▓
Installation and testing																		▓

Fig. 14.3 Overall acquisition time schedule.

to alert the management to any schedule slippage, monthly progress reports were required by each department manager.

To the neophyte, this schedule might appear to provide more than adequate time. However, the experienced professional in data processing will recognize that, in general, a complete system conversion will nominally require from 12 to 30 months, depending upon the size and complexity of the installation.

SELECTION OF A COMPUTER SYSTEM   The first step in selecting a computer was to prepare a *bid specification* for prospective vendors. The bid spec included both broad and detailed data processing needs, such as the following.

Hardware

- The CPU shall include 6 timesharing terminal ports with capability for expansion to 16.
- Removable disk storage capability with an online capacity of at least 50 million 8-bit bytes.
- One-line printer with the following minimum capabilities:
  1. 600 lines/minute alphanumeric printing speed.
  2. 132-print-position line.
  3. 64-character printing unit.

Software

- Programming languages: The vendor may make recommendations regarding programming languages. However, minimum requirements are:
  1. For business data processing: Cobol or RPG II.
  2. For online programming: Basic, or interactive Fortran or APL.

- Languages must conform to ANSI standards or, where appropriate, to detailed definitions in Section VI of this specification.
- The operating system shall have the capability for simultaneously serving as:
    1. A timesharing system supporting interactive computing from terminals.
    2. A batch processing system accepting programs from any input device for a queued batch processing operation.
- The disk storage file structure shall be standarized so that files created through one language can be processed by programs in any of the other languages without format conversion.

Other Requirements

- The vendor must provide six person-weeks of education and training on the proposed system for XYZ employees.
- The vendor must make available to XYZ test time on a computer similar to the one proposed. This is to allow for program preparation and testing prior to delivery of the computer.

Also included as part of the bid specification was the schedule shown in Figure 14.4.

Upon completion of the specification, it was made available to computer manufacturers on June 1, 1973. During the two months which followed, conferences were arranged with various vendors to clarify points of the specification and to provide insight into the needs of XYZ and Associates. Upon receipt of all proposals, the XYZ management evaluated them in light of the XYZ needs and requirements. The three most qualified were invited to run special benchmark programs which had been included in the bid specification. These programs, prepared by the consultant, were designed to represent the typical workload which might be anticipated on the XYZ machine. Results of these benchmark runs were to be used in the final evaluation process to determine the proposal which best fit the needs. The overall selection process is illustrated in Figure 14.5.

Exercise

14.4 The manager of a business approached a computer manufacturer and said, "Our present second-generation computer system is overloaded; we would like to install a third-generation computer in four months." Comment on this statement.

FINANCING COMPUTER EQUIPMENT   During the analysis and selection period, one of the many important factors facing the study team related to how the equipment should be financed. Three methods are commonly available: a rental arrangement with the computer manufacturer, a long-term lease with the manufacturer or a third-party leasing company, and outright purchase.

Activity	Start	Finish	Action by	
			XYZ	Vendor
Issue bid specification to vendors	6/01/73		x	
Vendor confers with XYZ officials as required	6/15/73	8/01/73	x	x
Proposals due from vendors	8/01/73			x
Evaluation of proposals	8/01/73	9/01/73	x	
Announce top three bidders	9/01/73		x	
Run benchmark tests	9/01/73	9/15/73	x	x
Final evaluation	9/15/73	10/01/73	x	
Award contract	10/01/73		x	
Personnel training	11/01/73	2/01/74	x	x
Prepare and test software on vendor's computer	1/01/74	8/15/74	x	x
Installation and testing	7/26/74	9/01/74	x	x
Acceptance of equipment	9/01/74		x	

Fig. 14.4 Computer acquisition schedule.

YOU WANT IT WHEN ?

Original copy provided courtesy of Vi Keily, Allergon Pharmaceuticals; prepared by IA and E Company, Buena Park, Calif.

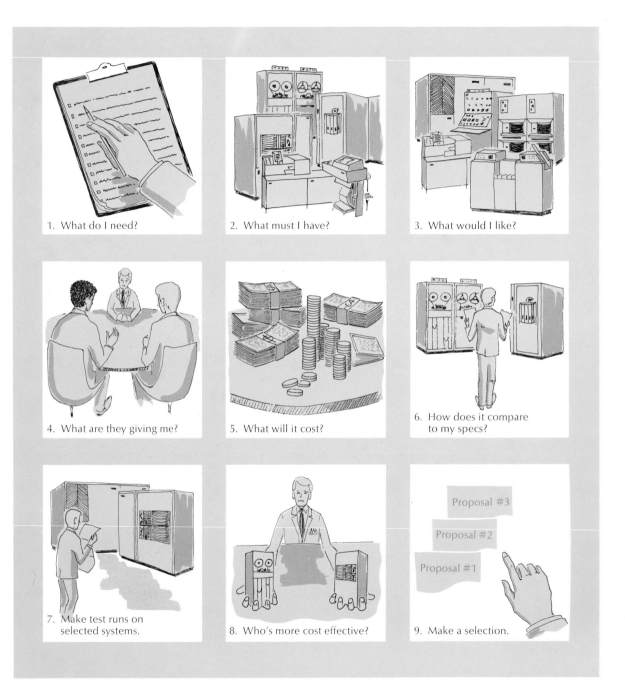

1. What do I need?

2. What must I have?

3. What would I like?

4. What are they giving me?

5. What will it cost?

6. How does it compare to my specs?

7. Make test runs on selected systems.

8. Who's more cost effective?

9. Make a selection.

Fig. 14.5 Steps in the selection of a system.

Rental. Over the years, IBM has stressed the advantages of renting a computer—from IBM, of course. (During the early days of the industry, IBM machines were not for sale, only for rent.) Even today the majority of IBM machines, as well as those of many other large computer manufacturers, are rented. For a fixed monthly rate, the manufacturer provides the computer, required maintenance of the machine, certain basic software, and a limited amount of staff education and training.* The principal advantages of renting include the features that the user can avoid obsolescence, since the rental agreement can be cancelled (usually on a 60–90 day notice), the responsibility for all maintenance rests with the manufacturer, and a large capital outlay is not required. On the other hand, over a period of several years renting becomes more expensive.

Leasing. A large variety of leasing agreements can be made with so-called *third-party* leasing companies or with the manufacturer. Typically, a leasing company will arrange to purchase the computer desired by a user, then lease it to the user for an extended period of time, usually ranging between three and five years. A disadvantage of this type of agreement is that it tends to lock a user into a given system for a set period of time, although this is usually not a problem with careful planning. The primary advantage is cost savings, which can be significant over a long period of time. Many installations find it to their advantage to lease from a third-party leasing company. Far too often, the decision is made to stay with a manufacturer rental arrangement because of the "parent company security blanket" psychology.

Purchase. Although computer rental is the most common procedure, more and more companies are purchasing computers. A number of reasons account for this fact. First, computers now being manufactured are far more reliable and have a significantly longer useful life than those of ten years ago. Second, the cost of a computer with a given computational power has declined rapidly with the evolution of the modern computer. And third, a large number of small companies have emerged in the minicomputer field, making available small but powerful computers. In many cases, their capital base is insufficient to support large-scale rentals, so their machines are available only through purchase. The principal advantage of purchase relates to the cost savings over a long period of time. Figure 14.6 illustrates typical costs for these three methods for a computer with a purchase price of $200,000. The ongoing cost associated with purchase reflects maintenance charges which will typically be

---

*Prior to 1970, the cost of extensive system support and all software was included, or "bundled," into a single price. The effect of this was to retard the growth of independent service and software firms. With pressure from the Justice Department and pending antitrust lawsuits from other companies, IBM "unbundled." The prices for IBM and most other equipment, software, and services are now separated.

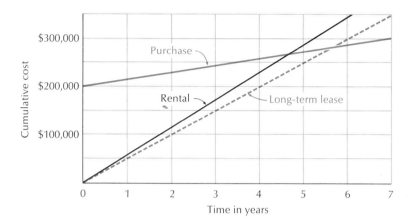

Fig. 14.6 Comparative
computer costs for rental,
lease, and purchase.

$11,000–15,000 per year for a $200,000 computer. Not illustrated by the graph is the fact that the user owns the computer in the purchase arrangement. The relatively high residual value of modern computing equipment can make this a significant economics factor.

The primary advantages and disadvantages of these three basic methods for financing computers are summarized in Figure 14.7. In addition to the methods described, there are other variations, including long-term lease from the manufacturer. Also, most users tend to overlook the availability (for purchase or lease) of used early third-generation computer equipment. Too often, the user becomes locked into the "latest and most powerful" syndrome and overlooks the fact that older equipment can adequately perform the job at a significantly lower cost. A number of both hardware and software enhancements to older third-generation equipment are available which greatly improve the machines' capabilities. The accompanying portion of an article from *Computerworld* describes such a case. Here an IBM 370 is replaced with an older IBM 360 using both software and hardware provided by another company.

DOWNGRADE TO 360 SAVES INSURANCE FIRM $8,000/MO

By Mal Stiefel

LOS ANGELES—Mission Equities Corp., a local insurance company, is saving $8,000 a month since it switched from an all-IBM 370/135 system to a 360/65 with more core and Itel Corp. disk drives and tape drives.

The configuration operates under Itel's Release 30 of DOS/VS, which allows the user to hook 370 peripherals to a 360.

The move was made last October, after Mission Equities decided against using IBM's DL1 data base management system in its planned premium and claims system.

IBM told the firm additional hardware would be needed to support DL1 on the 370/135—512K of core, four to six more 3440 disk drives and four more 3420 tape drives.

At that time, the installation included 192K of core, four 3440s and four 3420s, in addition to a 1403 printer and a 3525 card reader/punch. The system operated under DOS/VS and Power.

IBM also suggested an upgrade to a 370/158 as an alternative to beefing up the 135.

Both proposals were rejected by Mission Equities management, not only because of the costs, but because they felt DL1 wasn't yet widely used, and "most pioneers have a lot of arrows in them," according to a company spokesman, Richard Mittleman.

The system, purchased outright from Itel, carries 1M byte of core on the 360/65, eight Itel 7330 disk drives, seven 9-track Itel 7420 tape drives and one 7-track 7420. IBM took back its old disk and tape drives, and Itel bought the 370/135 from Mission Equities. The company also got rid of a 360/30 that had been leased from Computer Investors Group at the same time.

Exercise

14.5 Describe the commonly used methods for financing computers.

	Advantages	*Disadvantages*
Rental	1. Danger of obsolescence reduced 2. No large capital outlay required 3. All responsibility rests with the manufacturer (a single contact)	1. Most expensive in long run 2. Rental costs may increase periodically
Lease	1. Significant cost savings over rental 2. No large capital outlay required 3. Lease costs remain fixed over life of contract	1. User is committed for a long time period which reduces flexibility
Purchase	1. For the long range, generally the least expensive method 2. Tax advantages can be accrued by the owner	1. Large capital outlay required 2. Less flexibility to meet changing needs 3. Danger of obsolescence

Fig. 14.7 Comparison of computer acquisition methods.

STAFFING THE DATA PROCESSING DEPARTMENT One of the most common pitfalls encountered by many businesses when installing or expanding a computer center is to underestimate the staff required. Computers do not perform all of the wonders we have studied without the aid of people. (We have already learned that programming can be a slow and painstaking task.) Typically, between one half and two thirds of the total cost of operating a computer center will be for staffing (salaries), with the remainder being the cost of the computer. In fact, the preliminary study findings of XYZ and Associates cautioned that computer costs would increase with the acquisition of a computer system. This predicted increase was due in part to increased staffing requirements.

The staffing recommendation of the XYZ study team included the following five positions.

1. **Data processing supervisor.** Shall be responsible for supervision of the computer center. Will coordinate and schedule computer activities and job assignments for the programming staff. In view of the relatively small size of the department, will perform system studies for all new applications.

2. **Programmer, business.** Shall report to the supervisor and be responsible for all business data processing programming required. Shall function as a liaison to software companies performing contract programming for XYZ.

3. **Programmer, general.** Shall report to the supervisor and be responsible for all programming not of a business data processing nature. Shall provide assistance to engineering department as well as act as a liaison to software companies performing contract programming for XYZ.

4. **Computer operator.** Shall be responsible for operation of the computer system, including loading of programs, monitoring results, dispatching reports to appropriate departments, and maintaining system libraries.

5. **Data entry clerk.** Shall enter source data and programs into the system via key-driven data entry devices.

The existing computer and data processing operation at XYZ included a programmer-coordinator assisted by a data clerk. As noted earlier in this Chapter, the programmer-coordinator reported to the business manager (Figure 14.2), which created somewhat of a problem within XYZ. That is, the business manager had his own area of responsibility and was not always completely objective about the relative importance of various computing needs within the entire company. In fact, the engineering manager felt that the business manager "didn't give a damn" about anything but the accounting functions. The point was argued that the computer and data processing operation services all areas of the company and should not be under control of one of the users of those services.

Recognizing this as an extremely important point, the consultant pointed out to the president that companies with the more successful computer installations were marked by the following qualities:

1. An aggressive and alert management totally committed to the use of data processing.
2. The computer manager reporting directly to the chief executive of the business.
3. Clearly defined lines of authority and responsibility relating to all aspects of the computer operation.
4. Constant coordination and communication between the data processing center and the users.

In fact, in perusing a management magazine, the president took special note of a survey of computer installations (Figure 14.8) which illustrated the importance of having the computer manager reporting directly to the chief executive.

Another sobering fact was that only 34 percent of the companies surveyed termed their data processing operation as successful, that is, as actually justifying its cost (many experts term this figure closer to 15–20 percent). Determined to have the most effective and efficient operation possible, the president placed the data processing department directly under his office as illustrated by the organizational chart of Figure 14.9.

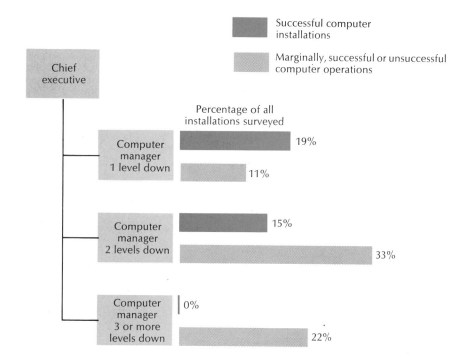

Fig. 14.8 Organization level of the computer manager.

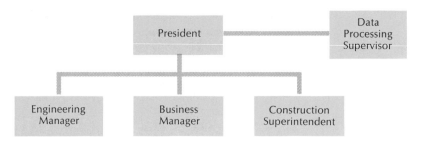

Fig. 14.9 Organization structure of XYZ and Associates.

Exercises

14.6 Assume that you are the manager of a business which is in serious need of upgrading its data processing operation. Your data processing manager approaches you with the proposal: "We can upgrade our operation by replacing our existing Model X computer costing $60,000/year with a new Model Z computer costing $89,000/year. The increased cost for upgrading our system would only be $29,000/year." What would your reaction be?

14.7 The president established the data processing supervisor position as reporting directly to him rather than to a subordinate office. Discuss this action relative to the previous XYZ system.

14.4
THE
CONVERSION
PROCESS

SYSTEMS DEFINITION AND ANALYSIS   At this point, we have seen the word *system* used in a number of ways: a computer system (hardware), an operating system (software), and a data processing system (procedures). In planning for the new computer, the XYZ management was very much aware of the importance of thoroughly analyzing all aspects of their systems and procedures. The overall processing systems had, to a large extent, simply evolved with the growth of the company; very little long-range planning had ever taken place in any of the accounting areas. For instance, when the need for an improved payroll system arose, a brief evaluation was made, resulting in the use of a service bureau. Little attention was given to how the payroll system was to interface with other accounting systems in the company; also, modifications to the XYZ clerical procedures were kept to a minimum in order to simplify the conversion. Generally speaking, most organizations see the growth of their data processing systems lagging behind the corresponding growth of the organization. Reorganization of an existing data processing system rarely occurs until serious problems come to the attention of management.

Unfortunately, a common solution is to "beef up" the existing system (which itself may be inadequate) with more hardware and/or personnel. The management of XYZ and their consultant recognized the importance of starting from scratch. The setting up of a new system meant far more than writing a series of programs and getting a new computer. The systems analysis must go back to the basic processing functions performed, including: (a) what accounting methods are used, (b) what types of files are maintained, and (c) what type of reports are generated. Internal procedures designed for a manual record-keeping system or a semiautomated one will probably be poorly suited to an automated one. The goal of the study team must be to evaluate all aspects of the company, beginning with management goals and methods of accomplishment. The end result must be a detailed plan for implementing the changes and modifications necessary to fill the needs of the organization. In the case of a total system, the implications can be quite significant from a number of points of view, including cost and disruption of ongoing activities. Normally, the plan involves a building block approach in which the basis for the system is laid and components are implemented piece by piece over a period of time.

This was the avenue taken by XYZ: to adjust their basic accounting and clerical methods toward a database management system. Then the first systems to be brought on line were to be payroll, accounts payable, and accounts receivable. Once the computer was installed and these applications were up, work on a series of other applications (beginning with an online inventory control system) was to commence. Thus, transition to a modern computerized information system could proceed with a minimum interruption of ongoing activities.

STAFFING TRAINING AND ORIENTATION   People, like objects, seem to suffer from the physical phenomenon called *inertia*. With people, changes tend to bring on stress, especially when the changes might be interpreted as threatening job security. For instance, the accounting clerk might find that many of the tasks required of his/her position will be done by the new computer—alas, no more job. However, on closer consideration, the clerk, rather than being replaced by a machine, will find that much of the dull, boring work is to be eliminated and replaced with more challenging tasks using the clerk's accounting expertise. It is vitally necessary to orient each employee to his or her place in the new system and how it will influence the job requirements. For some employees who have a minimum interface with data processing, a brief orientation session will be adequate. For others whose jobs will be substantially changed or even eliminated, a considerable amount of company-sponsored training and/or retraining might be required.

To insure that the new data processing operation is recognized as a tool to provide better services and not as a device to put people out of work, the DP supervisor implemented a series of "training and exposure" classes for XYZ employees. Two sections of three two-hour training sessions were held describing the overall operation of the system, the roles played, and the services provided for each of the various departments. These sessions were eagerly attended by most of the staff, many of whom devoted several evenings to further study. In general, the overall program dispelled many false notions and dissolved a number of negative attitudes (although several employees

---

LEARNING TO COPE WITH DEFEAT IS HARDEST DP SKILL

By Miles Benson

One skill they don't teach in computing courses is how to cope with failure.

Once failure has been officially proclaimed, there's still a world out there to be dealt with . . . the people who are concerned about going down with the ship, the people who paid for the ship in the first place and the people who are still waiting for the ship to come in.

Some folks just seem to know intuitively how to do a job right. Some of the people in this story were that kind of people. When this project had fallen on its face, these people picked themselves up, dusted themselves off and began thinking about the uncomfortable tasks still ahead: getting a corporate decision on how to admit to the failure which had occurred, and carrying out that corporate decision.

To these people, there was only one way to do this particular job right.

Heavy Strategy

But picture the strategy sessions leading up to that corporate decision. Imagine the factions at work, each with its own way of decommitting the failed project.

"Let's convince them we cancelled out in their best interest," says one.

"Let's make it all seem like it wasn't important in the first place," says another.

"Let's just hit them with a snowstorm so dense they'll never realize until later what really happened," says still another.

"Why not tell the truth?" comes a voice from the back. "Why not just admit that we screwed up, that we tried to do something we didn't really know how to do and that we learned that we still don't know how?"

A gasp goes through the assembled crowd. Use honesty as a tactic? Lie down and let the users walk all over us? Our competitors will laugh us out of the marketplace. We may be sued. Can't we at least *try* to make it look like we knew what we were doing? . . .

---

remained highly suspicious). At the completion of the orientation, *most* members of the clerical staff were looking forward to installation of the new system with very positive attitudes regarding "being involved."

Staff training at XYZ was not limited to the non-DP employees of the company. With the exception of the computer operator (hired four months before installation of the computer), none of the programming staff had experience on the computer selected by XYZ. As do most computer manufacturers, the one selected by XYZ provided training classes at their educational facility. The following staff members were scheduled for classes at the manufacturer's site as follows:

1. Data processing supervisor
   a. Introduction to the operating system (1 week)
   b. File design and structure (1 week)
2. Programmer, Business
   a. Introduction to the operating system (1 week)
   b. File design and structure (1 week)
   c. Database considerations (3 days)

3. Programmer, General
   a. Introduction to the operating system (1 week)
   b. File design and structure (1 week)
   c. Interactive programming (1 week)

During the scheduled classes, each employee was relieved of all job responsibilities in order to concentrate on the coursework. By spreading this training over three months, ongoing needs of the company could continue to be handled.

Exercise

14.8 The importance of programmer education and training when a new system is to be installed is obvious. However, why bother with classes for clerical staff who will not be directly involved in the data processing operation?

PROGRAM PREPARATION   Contrary to the arguments often proposed by representatives of computer manufacturers, the experienced data processing professional will usually insist that "there is no such thing as an easy conversion." Generally speaking, this tends to be true, although the task can be considerably simplified by careful planning. In an ideal situation, all programs would be written, tested, and running prior to installation of the new computer. However, this is seldom practical. If we refer to the time schedule of Figure 14.3, we see that approximately seven months are scheduled for programming. For normal month-to-month programming needs, the programming staff of XYZ was considered adequate. However, the task of bringing in a new computer and all associated programming systems is monumental in size and one requiring several person-years of programming effort. One commonly used solution to this dilemma is the use of outside assistance; the approach of XYZ involved the following:

- The purchase from a software company of a database management system for the business data processing needs. Applications programs for payroll processing and accounts payable and receivable to be prepared by the software company through the coordination of the XYZ programming staff.
- Obtaining contract programming services to prepare a job analysis and scheduling program. This system was developed and used with three other construction companies that had the same need.
- Reprogramming by the engineering staff, assisted by one of the programmers of several basic programs used by the engineering department.

The notion of adapting prewritten software can often pay huge dividends. In many cases, the cost of "reinventing the wheel" is far more expensive (and often impractical) than simply purchasing from someone who has already completed the job. As described in Chapter 13, a wide variety of excellent applications packages are available from a myriad of software vendors. Similarly, the use of contract programming services can also fill an important need. Many software-oriented companies will provide contract programming in a variety of ways ranging from "a programmer by the day, week, or month" to contracting at a fixed price for systems analysis and programming a predefined application.

With the combined effort of service companies and their own programming staff, XYZ devoted the seven-and-a-half-month period of January into August (Figure 14.3) for the initial programming activities. Since XYZ owned no computer, the computer manufacturer had agreed to provide XYZ extensive test time on a computer with a configuration similar to that of the one ordered by XYZ. Thus it was possible to carry on programming, debugging, and testing operations prior to installation of the new computer. By August, all of the scheduled programs were reasonably ready for operation, although some compromises were necessary due to the tight time schedule.

Exercise

14.9   What is "test time," and what is its importance in a system conversion?

INSTALLATION AND TESTING   Installing a computing system is somewhat more complex than installing a television, which merely requires plugging it in. Actually, the installation process must begin with site preparation months before actual delivery. It is the responsibility of the vendor to advise the customer of the power and air conditioning requirements and other environmental conditions. For instance, Figure 14.10 is typical of the needs of a small computer system. From information such as this, necessary electrical circuits and air conditioning can be planned and installed. Site preparation always takes longer than expected and should not be ignored until the last minute. There is nothing quite as embarrassing and frustrating as no place to plug in a newly arrived computer. If teleprocessing is to be involved, then delivery of equipment from other vendors must be carefully coordinated. Even the simple matter of telephone lines requires planning ahead, since installation of special telephone circuits can require up to a month.

Prior to delivery of the computer, the customer will have supplied the vendor with a room configuration plan. With delivery of the hardware, the vendor can proceed to install the system. Since most computer systems are

Site power requirements

	Device	Circuits Required		
		Number	Type	Circuit Size
1.	CPU	1	208 V, 3 phase	30 amp
2.	Memory cabinet	1	208 V, 3 phase	30 amp
3.	Disk drive	1	208 V, 3 phase	20 amp
4.	Disk controller	1	115 V, 1 phase	30 amp
5.	Peripheral devices	3	115 V, 1 phase	15 amp
6.	Utility circuits	2	115 V, 1 phase	15 amp

Recommended for future expansion

		Number	Type	Circuit Size
		1	208 V, 3 phase	30 amp
		2	115 V, 1 phase	30 amp
		2	115 V, 1 phase	15 amp

Power Dissipation

1.	CPU	1725 watts
2.	Memory cabinet	900 watts
3.	Disk drive	1100 watts
4.	Disk controller	450 watts
5.	Peripheral devices	1500 watts

Environment

65–75°F temperature
40–60% relative humidity

Fig. 14.10 Site requirements for XYZ and Associates.

delivered as several components (with the exception of small units) a considerable amount of interconnection and testing is usually necessary. When all connections have been complete, the service engineer will run special diagnostic routines to ensure that all connections have been properly made and that all components are functioning properly. At this point, a vendor's systems specialist will generate an operating system (this process is called a *sys-gen*) which is tailored to the particular installation. The entire process of installation through generation will require a week or more on a small system. In many cases, the customer will require that the benchmark programs or other typical workload conditions be run prior to acceptance of the computer. In some cases, formal acceptance (and thus payment) are postponed until the computer has operated in a normal environment for a set period of time (often 30 days) with a failure rate and downtime not to exceed precisely defined limits.

If everything has gone according to plan, the applications programs should be ready to be put on the new computer when control is passed from the vendor to the customer. In the case of XYZ, the systems were ready, and incorporating them into the new system was begun immediately. As was anticipated, a number of minor problems arose in finally bringing everything together on the new system. However, these were overcome and the system was operational in less than three weeks, marking the end of a successful installation and the beginning of a new and substantial task.

Answers to Preceding Exercises

14.1 Cost. If a relatively low level of service is required, then a service bureau will probably be most economical. However, as data processing needs increase, it becomes more economical at some point to provide the needed capabilities in-house.

14.2 A carefully selected committee can serve a valuable function in improving data processing services. Through the committee, each user can explain his needs and gain an understanding of and appreciation for those of other users. However, care must be taken to avoid petty arguing within the committee, thus reducing it to a "debating society." Furthermore, the committee's role must be recognized as advisory, with final decisions made by the data processing director or company president.

14.3 a. Is the required input data available? b. Will the output be used? c. Is it economical? d. Is it practical?

14.4 The process of ordering a new computer and performing a conversion cannot be handled in the same manner as buying a new car. Feasibility studies, often requiring several weeks of effort, should be made even before a computer manufacturer is contacted. The overall task of computer selection, system design, program conversion and preparation, and system installation and testing will require from 12 to 30 months, depending upon the system's complexity.

14.5 The three commonly used means for financing computers are: renting from the manufacturer, leasing from a third-party leasing company, and purchase (including lease-purchase). For advantages of each, see descriptions preceding this exercise.

14.6 The cost of the computer itself would be increased by $29,000 per year, but we must recall that computer costs generally average about 30–50 percent of the total data processing costs. Thus, to fully utilize the new system, an increase of approximately $40,000 annually in personnel and other costs should be anticipated.

14.7 In most installations, the data processing operation serves a wide variety of users and affects virtually all areas of a business. Thus, it is generally unrealistic to have the department administered by one of the users, as was the case at XYZ. It is necessary that top-level direction and coordination be provided for the data processing operation to serve all users in the best way. As we recall, the engineering manager complained that his work was not adequately handled. It is this situation which the president wished to avoid.

14.8 Although members of the clerical staff are not directly involved in the data processing operation, they form an integral and important portion of the overall data gathering, processing, and using network. As such, they can more efficiently perform their functions within the company if they have a basic knowledge of the data processing system. Furthermore, employees are less prone to feel "threatened" by the computer if they are aware of how it is to be used.

14.9 When a computer is ordered, the manufacturer usually provides "test time" on a comparable computer system which the user can utilize to prepare and test programs for conversion to the new system. Thus, a major portion of the programming conversion and testing can take place prior to delivery of the new computer.

Appendices

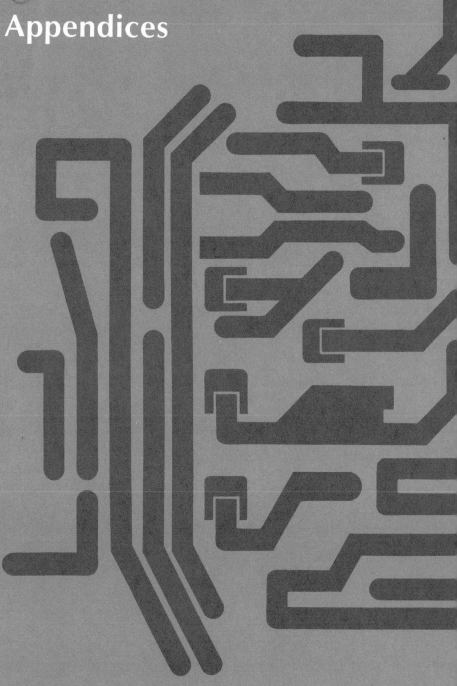

Appendix I

Using the Card Punch

FEATURES OF THE CARD PUNCH

MACHINE COMPONENTS

Although most computer installations employ trained card punch operators, the programmer frequently finds it convenient to have a knowledge of the card punch for preparing a few cards or to make some changes to an existing deck. (In any case, at most schools the student is usually his/her own card punch operator.) The most commonly encountered card punch machines are the IBM Model 26 and the IBM Model 29. The older Model 26 was by far the most commonly used card punch prior to introduction of third-generation computers in 1964. At that time, the Model 29 was made available for use with the IBM System/360. In basic principle, the two machines are essentially the same. They both operate in a serial punching fashion, have punching and reading stations to facilitate reproducing fields from one card to another, and have keyboards similar to that of a typewriter. In Figure I.1(a) we see the Model 26, and in I.1(b) the Model 29; operation components of the two machines are numbered as follows:

1. Main line switch
2. Keyboard
3. Function control switches
4. Card hopper
5. Card stacker
6. Punching station
7. Reading station
8. Backspace key
9. Program unit
10. Program unit control lever

THE KEYBOARD

The keyboards of the two machines are diagrammed in Figure I.2, where we see both the character-punching keys and special functional keys for control of machine operations. (The functional keys are shaded in the diagrams.) The functional keys that will be referred to in this appendix are:

1. NUMERIC (*numeric shift key*)   This key is depressed when a numeric or special character (on the upper portion of the key) is to be punched.
2. FEED   Depression of the FEED key causes one card to be fed from the hopper into the card bed.
3. REG (*register key*)   Depression of the REG key causes a card to be registered at the punching station for punching or one at the reading station for reading. This key is normally used when the keypunch is under manual control.
4. REL (*release key*)   Whenever the REL key is depressed, the cards at the reading and the punching stations are each moved up one station; a new card may be registered at the punching station depending upon the setting of the functional switches.
5. DUP (*duplicate key*)   Depression of the DUP key causes all or part of the information in the card at the reading station to be duplicated into corresponding columns of the card at the punching station.
6. SKIP   Under program control, depression of this key (located to the immediate left of the REG key) causes the card to be advanced to the next field as defined by the program card.

As we can see by referring to Figure I.2, the keyboards of the Model 26 and Model 29 are very similar; the letters and digits are positioned identically on the two. The significant difference relates to the special characters; we will

Fig. I.1   (a) IBM Model 26 key-driven card punch; (b) IBM Model 29 key-driven card punch.

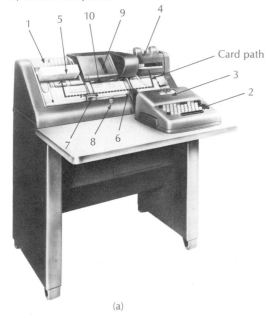

(a)

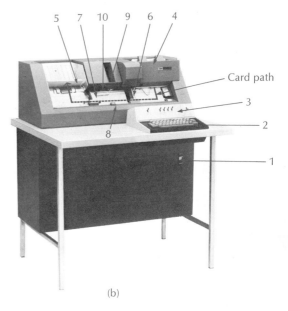

(b)

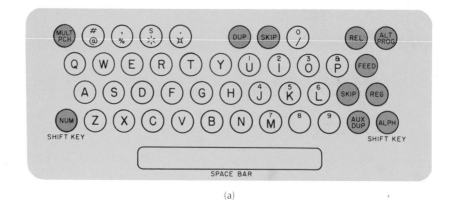

(a)

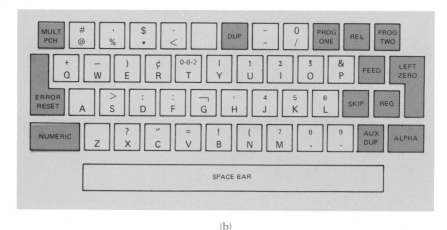

(b)

Fig. I.2 (a) Keyboard for IBM Model 26 card punch; (b) keyboard for IBM Model 29 card punch.

note that the Model 29 keyboard includes a large number of special characters not found on the Model 26. These allow the user to take full advantage of third generation computer characteristics not found in second generation computers.

FUNCTIONAL CONTROL SWITCHES

At the top of the keyboards in Figure I.1 we see the *functional control switches* which are used to control automatic operations of the machine; detailed views of these switches are shown in Figure I.3. The functional switches that a casual card punch user will be inclined to use are:

1. PRINT   When this switch is turned on, the card punch automatically prints the character punched along the top of the card, directly above the column in which punching occurs.

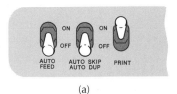

(a)

Fig. I.3 (a) Functional control switches for IBM Model 26 card punch; (b) functional control switches for IBM Model 26 card punch.

(b)

2. AUTO FEED (*automatic feed*)   If this switch is turned on, upon completing the punching of a card, each card in the feed path is automatically moved up one station and a new card from the card hopper is registered at the punch station.

3. AUTO SKIP DUP (*automatic skip and automatic duplication*)   When the card punch is used under automatic control of the program unit, turning this switch on permits automatic field skipping and duplication to take place where programmed.

4. CLEAR (*Model 29 only*)   Depressing this switch causes all cards in the feed path to be cleared into the card stacker.

THE CONTROL UNIT

To facilitate use of the card punch, a special program control unit can be used to provide operations of automatic field duplication and skipping as required in a given application. The control unit and drum with a control card are shown in Figure I.4. The reader will note the special column indication which designates the next card column to be punched during the punching operation. Shown in Figure I.5 is a program drum on which is mounted a special prepunched program card (reflecting field layouts on the cards to be punched).

The program unit is engaged or disengaged by the program control lever (see Figure I.1). Depression of this lever down to the right disengages the program unit; depression down to the left engages it, as illustrated in Figure I.6.

I.2   OPERATING INSTRUCTIONS

The card punch, much like a typewriter, is operated by depressing the appropriate key to record the desired character. The purpose of these brief descriptions is to provide the reader with the basic notions required to use the card

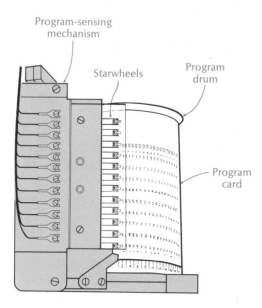

Program-sensing
mechanism

Starwheels

Program
drum

Program
card

Fig. I.4   A program unit.

punch. As we shall see, the descriptions in this appendix are applicable to both the Model 26 and Model 29. These operating instructions consist of three separate descriptions: (1) normal punching without program control, (2) single card and duplication procedures, and (3) punching with program control.

PUNCHING WITHOUT PROGRAM CONTROL

If more than one or two cards are to be punched (such as a computer program or a data set), then the automatic card feeding capabilities should be used. In reading the following descriptions, the reader may find it useful to refer to preceding illustrations for the machine components being described.

Readying the machine

1. Turn on the main line switch (the Model 26 requires approximately 30 seconds to warm up).
2. Insert blank cards in the card hopper.
3. Turn the AUTO FEED and the PRINT switches to the on position.
4. Ensure that the program unit is disengaged by depressing the program control switch (toggle) down to the right.

Procedures

1. Depress the FEED key twice to feed the two blank cards; the first will be registered at the ready position.

Fig. I.5   Program drum.

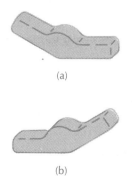

Fig. I.6 (a) Disengaging the program unit; (b) engaging the program unit.

2. Punch the card as required. The machine will be in the alphabetic mode; if digits or special characters are to be punched, then depress the NUMERIC key.
3. If the last field to be punched ends in column 80, each card in the feed path will be advanced one station with a new card being registered at the punching station; if the last field does not end in column 80, this action is initiated by depressing the REL key.
4. After the last card has been punched, the cards are cleared in the Model 29 from the feed path by depressing the CLEAR switch and in the Model 26 by removing the remaining blank cards from the hopper, then depressing the REL key three times.

SINGLE CARD PUNCHING AND CARD DUPLICATION

Readying the machine

1. Turn on the main line switch.
2. Turn the AUTO FEED switch off and the PRINT switch on.
3. Insure that the program unit is disengaged by depressing the program control switch down to the right.

Procedures—single card punching

1. Manually insert the card at the punch station as shown in Figure I.7.
2. Depress the REG key.
3. Punch the card as required.
4. If column 80 is not the last column to be punched, then depress the REL key when punching is completed.
5. To remove the card from the feed path on the Model 29, depress the CLEAR switch; on the Model 26, depress the following keys in the sequence indicated: REG, REL, REG, REL.

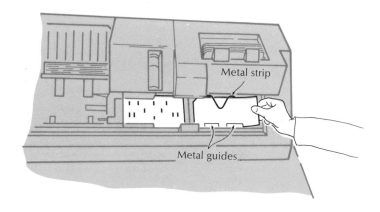

Metal strip

Metal guides

Fig. I.7 Manually inserting a card at the punch station.

Procedures—single card duplication or correction

1. Manually insert a blank card at the punch station, as shown in Figure I.7, and the card to be duplicated at the read station, as shown in Figure I.8.
2. Reproduce all required fields by depressing the DUP key; fields not to be reproduced are skipped by using the space bar. The column indicator must be used as a guide if fields are to be omitted.
3. If one or more columns are to be corrected, then stop the duplication at that field, punch in the corrected information, and then continue the duplication procedure.
4. If column 80 is not the last column to be punched, then depress the REL key when punching or duplication is completed.
5. To remove the cards from the feed path on the Model 29, depress the CLEAR switch; on the Model 26, depress the following keys in the sequence indicated: REG, REL, REG, REL.

PUNCHING WITH PROGRAM CONTROL

The average beginning student generally tends to be reluctant to use the program control feature of the card punch; this is unfortunate, since use of the control unit generally results in fewer errors and speeds up the punching operation. The primary control functions are achieved by punching the control card to indicate field definition, numeric or alphabetic shifting, fields to be skipped, and so on, using the code punches summarized in the following table.

Punch (Code)	Function Required
blank	Indicates beginning of a field to be punched
11 (−)	Indicates beginning of a field to be skipped
0	Indicates beginning of a field to be duplicated
12 (&)	Signifies the remaining positions of the field defined by the blank, 11, or 0 codes
1	Used in combination with the above punches to designate alphabetic fields; otherwise, the card punch will be in numeric shift

Program drum cards which can be used in punching (a) Cobol programs and (b) Fortran programs, are shown in Figure I.9. Punching cards under program control is done as follows:

Readying the machine

1. Turn on the main line switch.
2. Turn on the AUTO FEED, AUTO SKIP DUP, and PRINT switches.

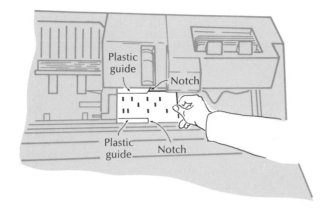

Fig. I.8 Manually inserting a card at the read station.

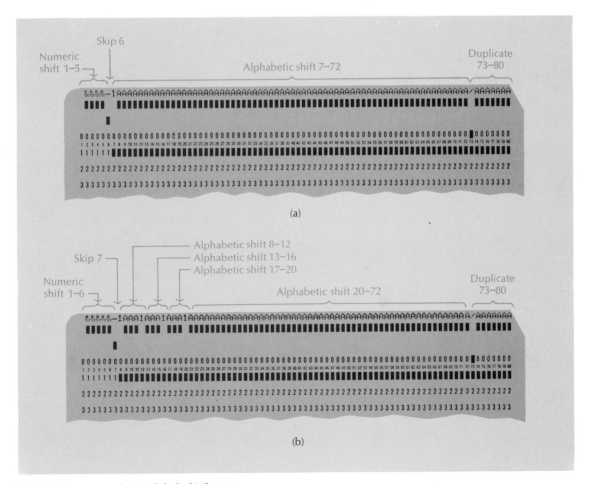

Fig. I.9 Program cards: (a) Cobol; (b) Fortran.

3. Punch one card with any fields to be duplicated into all cards. For example, in punching a Fortran program, this would be in columns 73–80.
4. Insure that the program unit is disengaged by depressing the program control lever down to the right. Then remove the drum, mount the program card on the drum, and insert the drum in the program unit. Engage the unit by depressing the program lever down to the left.

Procedures

1. Insert the blank cards, preceded by the card with the field to be duplicated, if any, into the card hopper.
2. Depress the FEED key twice; if automatic duplication is to be performed and the blank cards are preceded by a card with the field to be duplicated, then also depress the REL key.
3. Punch each card as required. If nothing is to be punched in a given field (for instance, no statement number in a Fortran program), that field may be skipped by depressing the SKIP key.
4. After the last card has been punched, the cards are cleared from the feed path by disengaging the control unit and then clearing as described for nonprogram control operation.

Appendix II

Glossary of Terms

ABSOLUTE ADDRESS An address that is permanently assigned by the machine designer to a storage location.

ABSOLUTE CODING Coding that uses machine instructions with absolute addresses and can be executed by the computer without prior translation.

ACCESS TIME The time interval between the instant at which data is called for from a storage device and the instant delivery begins.

ACCUMULATOR A register in which the result of an arithmetic or logic operation is formed.

ADDRESS An identification, as represented by a name, label or number for a location in storage.

ALGOL ALGOrithmic Language. A language primarily used to express computer programs by computational algorithms.

ALPHANUMERIC Pertaining to a character set that contains letters, digits, and usually other special characters such as the comma, dollar sign, and plus sign.

ARITHMETIC UNIT The unit of a computing system that contains the circuits that perform arithmetic operations; it is one of the components of the central processing unit (CPU) of the computer.

ASSEMBLE To convert or translate a computer program from a symbolic language to a machine language by substituting absolute operation codes for symbolic operation codes and absolute addresses for symbolic addresses.

ASSEMBLER A computer program which performs the task of assembling a symbolic program to machine language.

AUXILIARY OPERATION An offline operation performed by equipment not under control of the central processing unit.

AUXILIARY STORAGE A storage that supplements the main storage of a computer. Magnetic disk and tape are commonly encountered auxiliary storage mediums.

BACKGROUND PROCESSING The automatic execution of lower-priority computer programs when higher-priority programs are not using the system resources. Contrasts with foreground processing.

BATCH PROCESSING A technique in which information items to be processed are collected and processed in groups (batches) for efficient operation. Magnetic tape processing usually involves batching.

BCD　*See* Binary-coded decimal notation.

BINARY　Pertaining to a characteristic or property involving a choice or condition in which there are two possibilities. Pertains specifically to the number representation system with a radix or base of two using the digits 0 and 1.

BINARY-CODED DECIMAL NOTATION　Positional notation in which the individual decimal digits expressing a number in decimal notation are each represented by a binary numeral; e.g., the number twenty-three is represented by 0010 0011 in the 8-4-2-1 type of binary-coded decimal notation. Abbreviated BCD.

BINARY DIGIT　In binary notation, either of the digits 0 or 1.

BIT　A binary digit.

BLOCK　A collection of contiguous records recorded as a unit. Blocks are separated by interblock gaps, and each block may contain one or more records.

BLOCK LENGTH　A measure of the size of a block, usually specified in units such as records, words, computer words, or characters.

BUG　A mistake or malfunction in a program or a computer system.

BYTE　A sequence of adjacent binary digits operated upon as a unit and usually shorter than a computer word; as used with the IBM 360/370, a byte consists of eight bits.

CARD COLUMN　A single line of punch positions parallel to the short edge of a $3\frac{1}{4} \times 7\frac{3}{8}$ inch punched card; each column is capable of storing one character of information.

CARD ROW　A single line of punch positions parallel to the long edge of a $3\frac{1}{4} \times 7\frac{3}{8}$ inch punched card.

CARRIAGE CONTROL TAPE　A tape that is punched with information to control line feeding of a printing device.

CENTRAL PROCESSING UNIT　A unit of a computer that includes the main storage and the circuits controlling interpretation and execution of instructions. Synonymous with the main frame. Abbreviated CPU.

CHECK BIT　A binary check digit, e.g., a parity bit.

CLOSED SUBROUTINE　A subroutine that can be stored at one place and can be linked to one or more calling routines. Contrast with open subroutine.

COBOL　COmmon Business Oriented Language; a business data processing language.

COLLATE　To merge two (or more) sequenced data sets to produce a resulting data set which reflects the sequencing of the original sets.

COLLATING SEQUENCE　An ordering assigned to the characters of a character set to be used for sequencing purposes. The commonly encountered collating sequence involves the special characters, the letters, and the digits, in that order.

COLLATOR   A device to collate, merge, or match sets of punched cards or other documents.

COLUMN   A vertical arrangement of characters or other expressions; *see also* Card column.

COMPILE   To convert or translate a program from a procedure- or problem-oriented language (for example, Fortran, Cobol, or RPG) to an absolute or machine language form. Usually a single-source statement yields more than one machine instruction.

COMPILER   A computer program that performs the compiling operation.

CONSOLE   That part of a computer used for communication between the operator or maintenance engineer and the computer.

CONTROL PANEL   A perforated board into which wires or plugs are manually inserted to control the operation of a machine.

CORE   *See* Magnetic core.

CPU   *See* Central Processing Unit.

DATA   A representation of facts or concepts in a formalized manner suitable for communication, interpretation, or processing by humans or by automatic means.

DATA BASE   A collection of data files integrated and organized into a single comprehensive file system, which is arranged to minimize duplication of data and to provide convenient access information within that system to satisfy a wide variety of user needs.

DATA BASE MANAGEMENT SYSTEM   The software used for management and retrieval of the data stored in a data base.

DEBUG   To detect, locate, and remove mistakes from a program or malfunctions from a computer.

DENSITY   The number of useful storage positions per unit of length or area; for example, a common recording density for magnetic tape is 800 frames per inch of tape.

DIAGNOSTIC   A statement printed by an assembler or compiler indicating errors detected in the source program.

DIRECT ACCESS   Pertaining to a storage device in which the access time is effectively independent of the location of the data. Synonymous with random access.

DISK   *See* Magnetic disk.

DISPLACEMENT   The difference between the base address and the actual machine language address.

DOCUMENT   A medium and the data record on it for human use, e.g., a report sheet, a book; any record that has permanence and that can be read by man or machine.

DOCUMENTATION   The process of preparing descriptions concerning the preparation, use, and general description of a computer program, procedure or system.

DUMP   To print the contents of all or part of the computer's storage.

EAM   *See* Electrical Accounting Machine.

EBCDIC   An eight-bit code used for data representation in the IBM 360/370 and several other commonly-used computers.

EDIT   To modify the form or format of the data; e.g., to insert or delete characters such as commas, decimal points, and dollar signs.

EDP   *See* Electronic Data Processing.

EFFECTIVE ADDRESS   The actual address as determined by summing the base address and the displacement.

ELECTRICAL ACCOUNTING MACHINE   Pertaining to data processing equipment that is predominantly electromechanical, such as a keypunch, mechanical sorter, collator, or tabulator. Abbreviated EAM.

ELECTRONIC DATA PROCESSING   Pertaining to data processing equipment that is predominantly electronic, such as an electronic digital computer. Abbreviated EDP.

ELEVEN-PUNCH   A punch in the second row from the top on a Hollerith punched card. Synonymous with x-punch.

EMULATE   To imitate one system with another, so that the imitating system accepts the same data, executes the same programs, and achieves the same results as the imitated system.

FIELD   In a record, a specified area used for a particular category of data; for example, a group of card columns used to represent a student file number.

FILE   A collection of related records treated as a unit. For example, the entire set of student master data records make up the Student Master File.

FILE LAYOUT   The arrangement and structure of data in a file, including the sequence and size of its components.

FILE MAINTENANCE   The activity of keeping a file up to date by adding, changing, or deleting data.

FIXED WORD LENGTH   Pertaining to the property that all words (fields) in a machine contain the same number of characters or bits. Contrasts with variable field length.

FLOWCHART   A graphical representation for the definition, analysis, or solution of a problem, in which symbols are used to represent operations, data, flow, equipment, and so on.

FLOWCHART SYMBOL   A symbol used to represent operations, data, flow, or equipment on a flowchart.

FLOWLINE   On a flowchart, a line representing a connecting path between flowchart symbols.

FOREGROUND PROCESSING The automatic execution of the computer programs that have been designed to preempt the use of the computing facilities. Contrast with background processing.

FORMAT The arrangement of data in a record.

FORTRAN FORmula TRANslating system; a language primarily used to express computer programs by arithmetic formulas.

HEADER CARD A card that contains information related to the data in cards that follow.

HEXADECIMAL Pertaining to the number system with a base of 16.

HOLLERITH Pertaining to a particular type of code or punched card utilizing 12 rows per column and usually 80 columns per card.

IMMEDIATE ADDRESS Pertaining to an instruction in which an address part contains the value of an operand rather than its address.

INDEX REGISTER A register whose content may be added to or subtracted from the operand address prior to or during the execution of a computer instruction.

INDIRECT ADDRESS An address that specifies a storage location that contains either a direct address or another indirect address. Synonymous with multilevel address.

INPUT The source data entered into a data processing system.

INPUT AREA An area of storage reserved for input.

INPUT DEVICE A device used to bring information into a computer or other data processing devices: for instance, the card reader.

INPUT/OUTPUT Pertaining to either input or output, or both. Abbreviated I/O.

INPUT/OUTPUT CONTROL SYSTEM A set of routines for handling the many detailed aspects of input and output operations. Commonly abbreviated IOCS.

INSTRUCTION A group of coded characters which define an operation to be carried out and the data or data locations involved in the operations.

INSTRUCTION COUNTER A counter that indicates the location of the next computer instruction to be interpreted.

INSTRUCTION REGISTER A register that stores an instruction for execution.

INTERBLOCK GAP *See* Interrecord gap.

INTERNAL STORAGE Addressable storage directly controlled by the central processing unit of a digital computer.

INTERPRETER A machine which reads data already punched into a card and prints on the card.

INTERRECORD GAP A blank space between records (blocks) on a magnetic tape; same as interblock gap.

I/O   *See* Input/output.

IOCS   *See* Input/output control system.

JOB   A specified group of tasks prescribed as a unit of work for a computer.

JOB CONTROL STATEMENT   A statement in a job that is used in identifying the job or describing its requirements to the operating system.

K   When referring to storage capacity, two to the tenth power; (2^{10}); 1024 in decimal notation.

KEY   A field within a data record to identify the record or to control its use.

KEYPUNCH   A keyboard-actuated device that punches holes in a card to represent data.

LABEL   One or more characters used to identify a statement, an instruction, or a data field in a computer program.

LEFT-JUSTIFY   To adjust the printing positions of characters on a page so that the left margin of the page is aligned.

LIBRARY   A collection of files or programs.

LIBRARY ROUTINE   A proven routine that is maintained in a program library.

LINE PRINTER   A device that prints all characters of a line as a unit.

LINKAGE   In programming, coding that connects two separately coded routines.

LOGICAL RECORD   A collection of fields independent of their physical environment. Portions of the same logical record may be located in different physical records, or several logical records may form one physical record.

LOOP   A sequence of instructions that is executed repeatedly until a terminal condition occurs.

MACHINE ADDRESS   Same as absolute address.

MACHINE INSTRUCTION   An instruction that a machine can recognize and execute.

MACHINE LANGUAGE   A language that is used directly by a machine, thus requiring no translation.

MACRO INSTRUCTION   An instruction in a source language that is equivalent to a specified sequence of machine instructions.

MAGNETIC CORE   A small donut-shaped piece of magnetic material capable of storing one binary digit.

MAGNETIC DISK   A flat, circular plate with a magnetic surface on which data can be stored by selective magnetization of portions of the flat surface.

MAGNETIC DRUM   A cylinder with a magnetic surface on which data can be stored by magnetization of portions of the surface.

MAGNETIC TAPE   A tape with a magnetic surface on which data can be stored by magnetization of portions of the surface.

MARK SENSING   The electrical sensing of manually recorded pencil marks on a nonconductive surface.

MASS STORAGE DEVICE   A device having a large storage capacity, for example, magnetic disk, magnetic drum.

MASTER FILE   A file that is either relatively permanent or that is treated as an authority in a particular job.

MEMORY   Same as storage.

MERGE   To combine items from two or more similarly ordered sets into one set that is arranged in the same order.

MICROSECOND   One millionth (0.000001 or 10^{-6}) of a second; commonly abbreviated μs or μsec.

MILLISECOND   One thousandth (0.001 or 10^{-3}) of a second; commonly abbreviated ms or msec.

MULTIPROCESSING   Pertaining to the simultaneous execution of two or more computer programs or sequences of instructions by a computer network.

MULTIPROGRAMMING   Pertaining to the concurrent execution of two or more programs by a computer.

NANOSECOND   One billionth (0.000000001 or 10^{-9}) of a second; commonly abbreviated as ns or nsec.

OBJECT PROGRAM   A fully compiled or assembled program that is ready to be loaded into the computer.

OCTAL   Pertaining to the number representation system with a base of eight.

OFFLINE STORAGE   Storage not under control of the central processing unit.

ONLINE   Pertaining to equipment or devices under control of the central processing unit; also, pertaining to a user's ability to interact with a computer.

ONLINE STORAGE   Storage under control of the central processing unit; usually pertains to mass storage devices such as magnetic tape and disk.

OPEN SUBROUTINE   A subroutine that is inserted into a program at each place it is used. Contrast with close subroutine.

OPERAND   A unit of data to be operated upon.

OPERATING SYSTEM   Software that controls the execution of computer programs and that may provide scheduling, debugging, input/output control accounting, compilation, storage assignment, data management, and related services.

OPERATION CODE   The portion of an instruction which indicates the operation to be performed.

OUTPUT   The finished results of processing by a system.

PARITY BIT   A binary digit added to a group of bits to make the count of all on-bits odd or even as designed into the machine.

PARITY CHECK   A check that tests whether the number of 1s (or 0s) in an array of binary digits is odd or even.

PERIPHERAL EQUIPMENT   In a data processing system, any unit of equipment, distinct from the central processing unit, which may provide the system with outside communication.

PLUGBOARD   *See* Control panel.

PROBLEM-ORIENTED LANGUAGE   A programming language designed for the convenient expression of a given class of problems; for example, RPG.

PROCEDURE-ORIENTED LANGUAGE   A programming language designed for the convenient expression of procedures used in the solution of a wide class of problems; for example, Fortran and Cobol.

PROCESS   A systematic sequence of operations to produce a specified result.

PROGRAMMING LANGUAGE   A language used to prepare computer programs.

PUNCHED CARD   A card punched with a pattern of holes to represent data.

RANDOM ACCESS   Same as direct access.

REAL TIME   Pertaining to the performance of a computation during the actual time that the related physical process takes place, so that results of the computation can be used in guiding the physical process.

RECORD   A collection of related fields of data, treated as a unit; for example, the Customer Master-Balance Record. A complete set of such records forms a file.

RECORD LENGTH   A measure of the size of a record, usually specified in units such as words or characters.

REGISTER   A device capable of storing a specified amount of data, such as one word.

RELATIVE ADDRESS   The number that specifies the difference between the absolute address and the base address. Synonymous with displacement.

RELOCATE   In computer programming, to move a routine from one portion of storage to another and to adjust the necessary address references so that the routine, in its new location, can be executed.

REPORT PROGRAM GENERATOR   A language designed with built-in logic to produce report writing programs given input and output descriptions. Abbreviated RPG.

RIGHT-JUSTIFY   To adjust the printing positions of characters on a page so that the right margin of the page is aligned.

ROUTINE   A set of instructions which is prepared to perform a common type of function for general use.

SEQUENCE   An ordering or arrangement of items according to a specified set of rules.

SEQUENTIAL   Pertaining to the occurrence of events in time sequence (one after the other), with little or no overlap of events.

SERIAL   Pertaining to the sequential or consecutive occurrence of two or more related activities in a single device.

SERIAL ACCESS   Pertaining to the process of obtaining data from or placing data into storage, where the access time is dependent upon the location of the data most recently obtained or placed in storage. Magnetic tape is a typical serial access medium.

SIGN BIT   A binary digit occupying the sign position.

SINGLE-ADDRESS   Pertaining to an instruction format containing one address part. Synonymous with one-address.

SOFTWARE   A set of computer programs, procedures, and possibly associated documentation concerned with the operation of a data processing system; for example, compilers, library routines, manuals, circuit diagrams. Contrasts with hardware.

SORT   To arrange records into a predetermined sequence.

SORTER   A machine which performs a sorting function; for example, the IBM 83 sorter.

SOURCE DOCUMENT   The original document (usually manually prepared) from which information is entered into a system.

SOURCE LANGUAGE   The language from which a statement is translated; for example, assembly language or Cobol.

SOURCE PROGRAM   A computer program written in a source language such as assembly language or Cobol. Contrasts with object program.

SPECIAL CHARACTER   A graphic character that is neither a letter, a digit, nor a space character; for example, the dollar sign and comma.

STORAGE   Pertaining to a device into which data can be entered, in which it can be held, and from which it can be retrieved at a later time; loosely, any device that can store data. Synonymous with memory.

STORAGE CAPACITY   A measure of the amount of data that can be contained in a storage device.

STORED PROGRAM COMPUTER   A computer controlled by internally stored instructions that can store, and in some cases alter instructions as though they were data and that can subsequently execute these instructions.

SUBROUTINE   A routine that can be part of another routine or program.

SUMMARIZE   To condense a set of data into a more concise form through simple arithmetic operations.

SYMBOLIC ADDRESS   An address expressed in symbols convenient to the computer programmer.

SYSTEM   A collection of methods, procedures, or techniques united by regulated interaction to form an organized whole. An organized collection of men, machines, and/or methods required to accomplish a set of specific functions.

ro

TABULATING EQUIPMENT   Data processing machines which use punched cards for processing of data; for example, the accounting machine, the sorter, the collator, and so on.

TELECOMMUNICATIONS   Pertaining to the transmission of data over long distances through telephone facilities.

THREE-ADDRESS   Pertaining to an instruction format containing three address parts.

THROUGHPUT   The total amount of useful processing carried out by a data processing system in a given time; effectively, an indication of the system efficiency.

TIMESHARE   The use of a device for two or more interleaved purposes; for example, the use of one computer by two or more users through terminals.

TRANSACTION FILE   A file containing relatively transient data to be processed in combination with a Master File. For example, in a payroll application, a Transaction File indicating hours worked might be processed with a Master File containing employee name and rate of pay. Synonymous with Detail File.

TRANSLATE   To transform statements from one language to another without significantly changing the meaning.

TWELVE-PUNCH   A punch in the top row of a Hollerith punched card. Synonymous with y-punch.

TWO-ADDRESS   Pertaining to an instruction format containing two address parts.

VARIABLE   A quantity that can assume any of a given set of values.

VARIABLE FIELD LENGTH   Pertaining to the property that fields within a machine may have a variable number of characters. Contrast with fixed word length.

VARIABLE-LENGTH RECORD   Pertaining to a file in which the records are not uniform in length.

VERIFY   To determine whether a data recording operation has been accomplished accurately; to check the results of keypunching.

WORD   A character string or a bit string considered as an entity; for example, the 32-bit IBM 360/370 word.

WORD LENGTH   A measure of the size of a word, usually specified in units such as characters or binary digits.

x-PUNCH   Same as 11-punch.

y-PUNCH   Same as 12-punch.

ZERO SUPPRESSION   The elimination of nonsignificant zeros in a numeral.

ZONE PUNCH   A punch in the 11, 12, or 0 row of a punched card.

Appendix III

Machine Language Simulator

Programs written in the machine language of Chapter 8 can be run on any computer equipped with Fortran through use of the simulator program listed in Figure III.2. Program instructions must be punched one per card according to the following format:

Columns	Field
1–2	Storage address into which the instruction is to be loaded
4–7	Instruction
8–80	Descriptive

For any instruction card without an address punched in columns 1 and 2, that instruction will be loaded into storage immediately following the instruction on the preceding card.

Within the simulator program, the end-of-file is signalled by a card punched with an asterisk in column 1. (For computer systems with the automatic end-of-file feature and the END= option in the READ, minor modifications can be made to the simulator to use these capabilities.) To run a program, the following card sequence is required:

1. The machine language program
2. An end-of-file record (asterisk in column 1)
3. The data deck
4. An end-of-file record (asterisk in column 1)

As an illustration, consider the following example program.

EXAMPLE

Each card in a data set contains two fields, A and B. Write a program to calculate

$$C = A + B$$

then print A, B, and C.

The program deck followed by the input data are shown in Figure III.1. Note that only the first card need be punched with a loading address (21 in this case); the storage assignment counter is automatically increased by one whenever an instruction card contains no address.

491

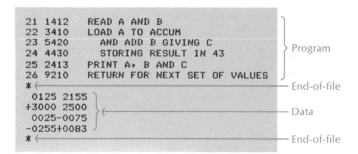

```
21 1412    READ A AND B
22 3410    LOAD A TO ACCUM
23 5420       AND ADD B GIVING C
24 4430        STORING RESULT IN 43
25 2413    PRINT A, B AND C
26 9210    RETURN FOR NEXT SET OF VALUES
 *
 0125 2155
+3000 2500
 0025-0075
-0255+0083
 *
```
Program
End-of-file
Data
End-of-file

Fig. III.1

Execution of the program always begins with the instruction address on the first card (21 in this case). Output from a run includes

1. A program listing
2. The program output computed results
3. A storage dump (refer to Figure 8.4)

```
C       ***********************************************       HYPO  10
C       **  HYPO SIMULATOR                        **          HYPO  20
C       **  PREPARED BY DONALD B. CASALEGGIO       **         HYPO  30
C       **  FOR W. PRICE       JANUARY, 1976       **         HYPO  40
C       ***********************************************       HYPO  50
C INTEGER VARIABLES USED IN THE PROGRAM ARE--                 HYPO  60
C    KARD   80 ELEMENT ARRAY FOR READING A CARD IN 80A1 FORMAT. HYPO 70
C    DATA   100 ELEMENT ARRAY - ELEMENTS 1-100 CORRESPONDING TO HYPO 80
C                         STORAGE LOCATIONS 00-99.             HYPO  90
C    LAC    LOCATION ASSIGNMENT COUNTER CONTAINS INSTRUCTION ADDRESS HYPO 100
C                         DURING LOADING. OBTAINED FROM CC 1-2 OF INSTR CARD. HYPO 110
C    IAR    INSTRUCTION ADDRESS REGISTER POINTS TO CURRENT INSTRUCTION HYPO 120
C                         DURING EXECUTION.                    HYPO 130
C    WORD   CONTAINS CONTENTS OF ADDRESSED WORD DURING EXECUTION OF HYPO 140
C                         MOST INSTRUCTIONS.                   HYPO 150
C    OP     OPERATION REGISTER   CONTAINS OP-CODE OF CURRENT INSTRUCTION HYPO 160
C    ADDR   ADDRESS REGISTER   CONTAINS ADDRESS PORTION OF CURRENT INSTR HYPO 170
C    MOD    MODIFIER REGISTER   CONTAINS MODIFIER OF CURRENT INSTR.  HYPO 180
C    ACCUM  THE ACCUMULATOR                                    HYPO 190
C    HP     HIGH/POSITIVE INDICATOR     VALUE OF               HYPO 200
C    EZ     EQUAL/ZERO INDICATOR         1 FOR ON              HYPO 210
C    LN     LOW/NEGATIVE INDICATOR       2 FOR OFF             HYPO 220
C    SW      DURING LOADING, CAUSES ADDRESS OF FIRST CARD TO BE SAVED HYPO 230
C                    AS BEGINNING EXECUTION ADDRESS            HYPO 240
C    SW2    IF ERROR OCCURS DURING LOAD, SW2 ABORTS A STORAGE DUMP -- HYPO 250
C                    EXECUTION ERROR AND END-OF-DATA TRIGGER A DUMP HYPO 260
      INTEGER DATA(100),DIGIT(10),KARD(80),WORK(4),JDATA(9)    HYPO 270
      INTEGER WORD,OP,ADDR,AST,HP,EZ,ACCUM,SW,BL,SW2           HYPO 280
      DATA DIGIT/1H0,1H1,1H2,1H3,1H4,1H5,1H6,1H7,1H8,1H9/      HYPO 290
      DATA AST/1H*/,MINUS/1H-/,BL/1H /                         HYPO 300
C******INITIALIZE ALL REGISTERS AND CONTROL VARIABLES         HYPO 310
      DO 500 I=1,100                                           HYPO 320
      DATA(I)=0                                                HYPO 330
  500 CONTINUE                                                 HYPO 340
      OP=0                                                     HYPO 350
      ADDR=0                                                   HYPO 360
      MOD=0                                                    HYPO 370
      IAR=0                                                    HYPO 380
      ACCUM=0                                                  HYPO 390
      HP = 2                                                   HYPO 400
      EZ = 2                                                   HYPO 410
      LN = 2                                                   HYPO 420
      RECNUM = 0                                               HYPO 430
      SW=1                                                     HYPO 440
      SW2=1                                                    HYPO 450
C*****************************************************************HYPO 460
C       PROGRAM LOADER                                         HYPO 470
C       LOADS ML PROGRAM AND PROVIDES 80-80 LIST               HYPO 480
```

Fig. III.2   Machine language program simulator.

```
C*******************************************************************************HYPO 490
              WRITE (3,3)                                                       HYPO 500
           3 FORMAT(1H1,15X,21H***PROGRAM LISTING*** //                         HYPO 510
           1        21H LOCATION OF ADDR MOD, 10X, 16HINSTRUCTION CARD /)        HYPO 520
C****** PROGRAM LOAD LOOP - WHEN COMPLETE, BEGIN EXECUTION                       HYPO 530
C****** SWITCH (SW) IS USED TO OBTAIN ADDRESS FROM FIRST INSTRUCTION             HYPO 540
C******    CARD TO BE USED AS START EXECUTION ADDRESS                            HYPO 550
         505 READ(1,4) KARD                                                      HYPO 560
           4 FORMAT(80A1)                                                        HYPO 570
C******    IF CC 1 CONTAINS *, THIS IS END OF FILE                              HYPO 580
              IF(KARD(1).EQ.AST) GO TO 600                                       HYPO 590
C****** IF CC 1 & 2 BLANK THEN INCREMENT LAC BY 1 EXCEPT FOR FIRST CARD          HYPO 600
              IF(KARD(1).EQ.BL .AND. KARD(2).EQ.BL) GO TO 508                    HYPO 610
              GO TO 509                                                          HYPO 620
         508 IF(SW.EQ.1) LAC=-1                                                  HYPO 630
              LAC = LAC+1                                                        HYPO 640
              GO TO 525                                                          HYPO 650
C******    CONVERT INSTR ADDRESS TO INTEGER                                      HYPO 660
         509 DO 520 J=1,2                                                        HYPO 670
              DO 510 I=1,10                                                      HYPO 680
              IF (KARD(J).EQ.DIGIT(I)) GO TO 520                                 HYPO 690
         510 CONTINUE                                                            HYPO 700
              GO TO 7200                                                         HYPO 710
         520 WORK(J)=I-1                                                         HYPO 720
              LAC = 10*WORK(1)+WORK(2)                                           HYPO 730
         525 GO TO (530,540), SW                                                 HYPO 740
C****      PLACE ADDRESS OF FIRST INSTR IN IAR FOR EXECUTION                     HYPO 750
         530 SW=2                                                                HYPO 760
              IAR=LAC                                                            HYPO 770
C****      CONVERT INSTR TO INTEGER THEN PLACE IN STORAGE (DATA)                 HYPO 780
         540 DO 560 J=1,4                                                        HYPO 790
              DO 550 I=1,10                                                      HYPO 800
              IF(KARD(J+3).EQ.DIGIT(I)) GO TO 560                                HYPO 810
         550 CONTINUE                                                            HYPO 820
              GO TO 7200                                                         HYPO 830
         560 WORK(J)=I-1                                                         HYPO 840
              DATA(LAC+1) = 1000*WORK(1)+100*WORK(2)+10*WORK(3)+WORK(4)          HYPO 850
              WRITE(3,5) LAC,KARD(4),KARD(5),KARD(6),KARD(7),KARD                HYPO 860
           5 FORMAT(4X,I2,4X,A1,3X,2A1,3X,A1,11X,80A1)                           HYPO 870
              IF(LAC.GT.99) GO TO 7300                                           HYPO 880
              GO TO 505                                                          HYPO 890
C******    PROGRAM LOADING COMPLETE                                             HYPO 900
         600 WRITE (3,6) IAR                                                     HYPO 910
           6 FORMAT(/47H PROGRAM LOADING COMPLETE. EXECUTION BEGINS AT ,I2)      HYPO 920

              WRITE(3,10)                                                        HYPO 930
          10 FORMAT(1H1)                                                         HYPO 940
              IAR=IAR-1                                                          HYPO 950
              SW2=2                                                              HYPO 960
C*******************************************************************************HYPO 970
C     INSTRUCTION ACCESS PHASE                                                   HYPO 980
C*******************************************************************************HYPO 990
         900 IAR = IAR + 1                                                       HYPO1000
         905 IF(IAR.GT.99) GO TO 7100                                            HYPO1010
         907 INST=DATA(IAR+1)                                                    HYPO1020
              IF(INST.LT.0) GO TO 7000                                           HYPO1030
              OP = INST/1000                                                     HYPO1040
              ADDR = (INST-OP*1000)/10                                           HYPO1050
              MOD = INST-ADDR*10-OP*1000                                         HYPO1060
              WORD = DATA(ADDR+1)                                                HYPO1070
              I = OP + 1                                                         HYPO1080
              GO TO(1000,1500,2000,3000,3500,4000,4500,5000,5500,6000),I        HYPO1090
C*******************************************************************************HYPO1100
C     INSTRUCTION SIMULATION ROUTINES FOLLOW                                     HYPO1110
C*******************************************************************************HYPO1120
C                                                                                HYPO1130
C****** HALT INSTRUCTION ****                                                    HYPO1140
        1000 WRITE(3,96)IAR                                                      HYPO1150
          96 FORMAT(///' EXECUTION TERMINATED BY HALT INSTR AT',I5)              HYPO1160
              GO TO 8100                                                         HYPO1170
C****** READ INSTRUCTION ****                                                    HYPO1180
        1500 IF(ADDR+MOD-1.GT.99) GO TO 7000                                     HYPO1190
              READ(1,7) JCOL1,JDATA                                              HYPO1200
           7 FORMAT(A1,I4,8I5)                                                   HYPO1210
              IF (JCOL1.EQ.AST) GO TO 9000                                       HYPO1220
              IF(JCOL1.EQ.MINUS) JDATA(1)=-JDATA(1)                              HYPO1230
              DO 1510 I=1,MOD                                                    HYPO1240
              I8=ADDR+I                                                          HYPO1250
        1510 DATA(I8)=JDATA(I)                                                   HYPO1260
              GO TO 900                                                          HYPO1270
```

Fig. III.2   (Cont.)

```
C****** WRITE INSTRUCTION ****                              HYPO1280
 2000 IF(MOD.NE.0)  GO TO 2010                              HYPO1290
      WRITE(3,8)                                            HYPO1300
      GO TO 900                                             HYPO1310
 2010 IF(ADDR+MOD-1.GT.99) GO TO 7000                       HYPO1320
      I8=ADDR+1                                             HYPO1330
      I9=ADDR+MOD                                           HYPO1340
      WRITE(3,8) (DATA(I),I=I8,I9)                          HYPO1350
    8 FORMAT(1X,9I7)                                        HYPO1360
      GO TO 900                                             HYPO1370
C****** LOAD ACCUMULATOR INSTRUCTION ****                   HYPO1380
 3000 ACCUM=WORD                                            HYPO1390
      GO TO 900                                             HYPO1400
C****** STORE ACCUMULATOR INSTRUCTION ****                  HYPO1410
 3500 DATA(ADDR+1)=ACCUM                                    HYPO1420
      GO TO 900                                             HYPO1430
C****** ADDITION INSTRUCTION ****                           HYPO1440
 4000 ACCUM = ACCUM + WORD                                  HYPO1450
      GO TO 4010                                            HYPO1460
C****** SUBTRACTION INSTRUCTION ****                        HYPO1470
 4500 ACCUM = ACCUM - WORD                                  HYPO1480
      GO TO 4010                                            HYPO1490
C****** MULTIPLY INSTRUCTION ****                           HYPO1500
 5000 ACCUM = ACCUM * WORD                                  HYPO1510
      GO TO 4010                                            HYPO1520
C****** COMPARE INSTRUCTION ****                            HYPO1530
 5500 IF(ACCUM - WORD)       4100,4200,4300                 HYPO1540
C****** SET INDICATORS FROM ARITH OPERATIONS ****           HYPO1550
 4010 IF(IABS(ACCUM).GT.9999)ACCUM=ACCUM-ACCUM/10000*10000  HYPO1560
      IF(ACCUM) 4100, 4200, 4300                            HYPO1570
 4100 HP = 2                                                HYPO1580
      EZ = 2                                                HYPO1590
      LN = 1                                                HYPO1600
      GO TO 900                                             HYPO1610
 4200 HP = 2                                                HYPO1620
      EZ = 1                                                HYPO1630
      LN = 2                                                HYPO1640
      GO TO 900                                             HYPO1650
 4300 HP = 1                                                HYPO1660
      EZ = 2                                                HYPO1670
      LN = 2                                                HYPO1680
      GO TO 900                                             HYPO1690
C******BRANCH INSTRUCTION****                               HYPO1700
 6000 I = MOD + 1                                           HYPO1710
      IF (I.GT.4) GO TO 7000                                HYPO1720
      GO TO (6080,6020,6040,6060),I                         HYPO1730
 6020 GO TO (6080,900),HP                                   HYPO1740
 6040 GO TO (6080,900),EZ                                   HYPO1750
 6060 GO TO (6080,900),LN                                   HYPO1760
 6080 IAR = ADDR                                            HYPO1770
      GO TO 905                                             HYPO1780
C     ********************************                      HYPO1790
C     *  E R R O R   R O U T I N E S  *                     HYPO1800
C     ********************************                      HYPO1810
C***      INVALID INSTRUCTION DURING EXECUTION              HYPO1820
 7000 WRITE(3,31) INST,IAR                                  HYPO1830
   31 FORMAT(/26H THE FOLLOWING INSTRUCTION,I7,13H  AT LOCATION,I5, HYPO1840
  1         14H  IS NOT VALID / 22H PROCESSING TERMINATED /) HYPO1850
      GO TO 8100                                            HYPO1860
C***      STORAGE EXCEEDED DURING EXECUTION                 HYPO1870
 7100 WRITE(3,32)                                           HYPO1880
   32 FORMAT(/49H YOU ARE LOOKING BEYOND THE END OF STORAGE FOR AN HYPO1890
  1        12H INSTRUCTION/ 33H THE ONLY INSTRUCTION YOU CAN PUT HYPO1900
  2        42H AT LOCATION 99 IS AN UNCONDITIONAL BRANCH /) HYPO1910
      GO TO 8100                                            HYPO1920
C***      INVALID INSTRUCTION CARD DURING PROGRAM LOADING   HYPO1930
 7200 WRITE(3,33) KARD                                      HYPO1940
   33 FORMAT(44H THE FOLLOWING INSTRUCTION CARD IS NOT VALID/1X,80A1/) HYPO1950
      GO TO 8000                                            HYPO1960
C***      STORAGE EXCEEDED DURING LOADING                   HYPO1970
 7300 WRITE (3,34)                                          HYPO1980
   34 FORMAT(/41H STORAGE HAS BEEN EXCEEDED DURING LOADING ) HYPO1990
C***      FLUSH ROUTINE -- FLUSHES REMAINING INSTRUCTION CARDS HYPO2000
 8000 WRITE(3,41)                                           HYPO2010
   41 FORMAT(50H1THE FOLLOWING INSTR CARDS HAVE NOT BEEN PROCESSED /) HYPO2020
 8010 READ(1,42) KARD                                       HYPO2030
   42 FORMAT(80A1)                                          HYPO2040
      IF(KARD(1).EQ.AST) GO TO 8100                         HYPO2050
      WRITE(3,43) KARD                                      HYPO2060
   43 FORMAT(1X,80A1)                                       HYPO2070
      GO TO 8010                                            HYPO2080
```

Fig. III.2   (Cont.)

```
C***        FLUSH ROUTINE -- FLUSHES REMAINING DATA CARDS                HYPO2090
 8100 WRITE(3,44)                                                        HYPO2100
   44 FORMAT(49H1THE FOLLOWING DATA CARDS HAVE NOT BEEN PROCESSED /)     HYPO2110
 8110 READ(1,42) KARD                                                    HYPO2120
      IF(KARD(1).EQ.AST) GO TO 9000                                      HYPO2130
      WRITE(3,43) KARD                                                   HYPO2140
      GO TO 8110                                                         HYPO2150
C     *******************************                                    HYPO2160
C     *   S T O R A G E   D U M P   *                                    HYPO2170
C     *******************************                                    HYPO2180
 9000 GO TO (9030,9010),SW2                                              HYPO2190
 9010 WRITE(3,18)                                                        HYPO2200
   18 FORMAT(13H1STORAGE DUMP//)                                         HYPO2210
      WRITE(3,19)                                                        HYPO2220
   19 FORMAT(9H REGISTER,8X,2HOP,6X,4HADDR,7X,3HMOD,8X,2HHP,8X,2HEZ,     HYPO2230
     1     8X,2HLN,5X,5HACCUM,8X,2HPC)                                   HYPO2240
      JHP=2-HP                                                           HYPO2250
      JEZ=2-EZ                                                           HYPO2260
      JLN=2-LN                                                           HYPO2270
      WRITE(3,20) OP,ADDR,MOD,JHP,JEZ,JLN,ACCUM,IAR                      HYPO2280
   20 FORMAT(9H CONTENTS,8I10 //)                                        HYPO2290



      WRITE(3,22)                                                        HYPO2300
   22 FORMAT(9H  STORAGE,14X,8HCONTENTS/9H LOCATION,4X,10H----------,    HYPO2310
     157H-------------------------------------------------------)       HYPO2320
      DO 9020  I=1,100,10                                                HYPO2330
      J = I + 9                                                          HYPO2340
      K = I - 1                                                          HYPO2350
      L = J - 1                                                          HYPO2360
 9020 WRITE(3,23)K,L,(DATA(N),N=I,J)                                     HYPO2370
   23 FORMAT(2X,I2,1H-,I2,3X,10I7)                                       HYPO2380
 9030 STOP                                                               HYPO2390
      END                                                                HYPO2400
```

Fig. III.2   (Cont.)

Index